CRITICAL AND MISCELLANEOUS

ESSAYS

COLLECTED & REPUBLISHED

BY

THOMAS CARLYLE

IN FOUR VOLUMES

VOL. II

BOSTON

M DCCC LX

CONTENTS OF VOLUME II.

APPENDIX.

MISCELLANIES.

VOLTAIRE.[1]

[1829.]

Could ambition always choose its own path, and were will in human undertakings synonymous with faculty, all truly ambitious men would be men of letters. Certainly, if we examine that love of power, which enters so largely into most practical calculations, nay which our Utilitarian friends have recognised as the sole end and origin, both motive and reward, of all earthly enterprises, animating alike the philanthropist, the conqueror, the money-changer and the missionary, we shall find that all other arenas of ambition, compared with this rich and boundless one of Literature, meaning thereby whatever respects the promulgation of Thought, are poor, limited and ineffectual. For dull, unreflective, merely instinctive as the ordinary man may seem, he has nevertheless, as a quite indispensable appendage, a head that in some degree considers and computes; a lamp or rushlight of understanding has been given him, which, through whatever dim, besmoked and strangely diffractive media it may shine, is the ultimate guiding light of his whole path: and here as

1 Foreign Review, No. 6. — *Mémoires sur Voltaire, et sur ses Ouvrages, par Longchamp et Wagnière, ses Secrétaires; suivis de divers Ecrits inédits de la Marquise du Châtelet, du Président Hénault, &c. tous relatifs à Voltaire.* (Memoirs concerning Voltaire and his Works, by Longchamp and Wagnière, his Secretaries; with various unpublished Pieces by the Marquis du Châtelet, &c. all relating to Voltaire.) 2 tomes. Paris, 1826.

well as there, now as at all times in man's history, Opinion rules the world.

Curious it is, moreover, to consider in this respect, how different appearance is from reality, and under what singular shape and circumstances the truly most important man of any given period might be found. Could some Asmodeus, by simply waving his arm, open asunder the meaning of the Present, even so far as the Future will disclose it, what a much more marvellous sight should we have, than that mere bodily one through the roofs of Madrid! For we know not what we are, any more than what we shall be. It is a high, solemn, almost awful thought for every individual man, that his earthly influence, which has had a commencement, will never through all ages, were he the very meanest of us, have an end! What is done is done; has already blended itself with the boundless, ever-living, ever-working Universe, and will also work there, for good or for evil, openly or secretly, throughout all time. But the life of every man is as the wellspring of a stream, whose small beginnings are indeed plain to all, but whose ulterior course and destination, as it winds through the expanses of infinite years, only the Omniscient can discern. Will it mingle with neighbouring rivulets, as a tributary; or receive them as their sovereign? Is it to be a nameless brook, and will its tiny waters, among millions of other brooks and rills, increase the current of some world-river? Or is it to be itself a Rhene or Danaw, whose goings-forth are to the uttermost lands, its flood an everlasting boundary-line on the globe itself, the bulwark and highway of whole kingdoms and continents? We know not; only in either case, we know, its path is to the great ocean; its waters, were they but a handful, are *here*, and cannot be annihilated or permanently held back.

As little can we prognosticate, with any certainty, the future influences from the present aspects of an individual. How many Demagogues, Crœsuses, Conquerors fill their own age with joy or terror, with a tumult that promises to be perennial; and in the next age die away into insignificance and oblivion! These are the forests of gourds, that overtop the infant cedars and aloe-trees, but, like the Prophet's gourd, wither on the third day. What was it to the Pharaohs of Egypt, in that old era, if Jethro the Midianitish priest and grazier accepted the Hebrew outlaw as his herdsman? Yet the Pharaohs, with all their chariots of war, are buried deep in the wrecks of time; and that Moses still lives, not among his own tribe only, but in the hearts and daily business of all civilised nations. Or figure Mahomet, in his youthful years, 'travelling to the horse-fairs of Syria.' Nay, to take an infinitely higher instance: who has ever forgotten those lines of Tacitus; inserted as a small, transitory, altogether trifling circumstance in the history of such a potentate as Nero? To us it is the most earnest, sad and sternly significant passage that we know to exist in writing: *Ergo abolendo rumori Nero subdidit reos, et quæsitissimis pœnis affecit, quos per flagitia invisos, vulgus* CHRISTIANOS *appellabat. Auctor nominis ejus* CHRISTUS, *qui, Tiberio imperitante, per Procuratorem Pontium Pilatum supplicio affectus erat. Repressaque in præsens exitiabilis superstitio rursus erumpebat, non modo per Judæam originem ejus mali, sed per urbem etiam, quo cuncta undique atrocia aut pudenda confluunt celebranturque.* 'So, for the quieting of this rumour,[1] Nero judi'cially charged with the crime, and punished with most 'studied severities, that class, hated for their general wicked'ness, whom the vulgar call *Christians*. The originator of 'that name was one *Christ*, who, in the reign of Tiberius, 'suffered death by sentence of the Procurator, Pontius Pi'late. The baneful superstition, thereby repressed for the 'time, again broke out, not only over Judea, the native soil 'of that mischief, but in the City also, where from every 'side all atrocious and abominable things collect and flour'ish.'[2] Tacitus was the wisest, most penetrating man of his generation; and to such depth, and no deeper, has he seen

1 Of his having set fire to Rome.

2 Tacit. *Annal.* xv. 44.

into this transaction, the most important that has occurred or can occur in the annals of mankind.

Nor is it only to those primitive ages, when religions took their rise, and a man of pure and high mind appeared not merely as a teacher and philosopher, but as a priest and prophet, that our observation applies. The same uncertainty, in estimating present things and men, holds more or less in all times; for in all times, even in those which seem most trivial, and open to research, human society rests on inscrutably deep foundations; which he is of all others the most mistaken, who fancies he has explored to the bottom. Neither is that sequence, which we love to speak of as 'a chain of causes,' properly to be figured as a 'chain,' or line, but rather as a tissue, or superficies of innumerable lines, extending in breadth as well as in length, and with a complexity, which will foil and utterly bewilder the most assiduous computation. In fact, the wisest of us must, for by far the most part, judge like the simplest; estimate importance by mere magnitude, and expect that what strongly affects our own generation, will strongly affect those that are to follow. In this way it is that Conquerors and political Revolutionists come to figure as so mighty in their influences; whereas truly there is no class of persons creating such an uproar in the world, who in the long-run produce so very slight an impression on its affairs. When Tamerlane had finished building his pyramid of seventy thousand human skulls, and was seen 'standing at the gate of Damascus, glittering in steel, with his battle-axe on his shoulder,' till his fierce hosts filed out to new victories and new carnage, the pale onlooker might have fancied that Nature was in her death-throes; for havoc and despair had taken possession of the earth, the sun of manhood seemed setting in seas of blood. Yet, it might be, on that very gala-day of Tamerlane, a little boy was playing nine-pins on the streets of Mentz, whose history was more important to men than that of twenty Tamerlanes. The Tartar Khan, with his shaggy demons of the wilderness, 'passed away like a whirlwind,' to be forgotten forever ; and that German artisan has wrought a benefit, which is yet immeasurably expanding itself, and will continue to expand itself through all countries and through all times. What are the conquests and expeditions of the whole corporation of captains, from Walter the Penniless to Napoleon Bonaparte, compared with these 'movable types' of Johannes Faust? Truly, it is a mortifying thing for your Conqueror to reflect, how perishable is the metal which he hammers with such violence: how the kind earth will soon shroud-up his bloody footprints ; and all that he achieved and skilfully piled together will be but like his own 'canvas city' of a camp, — this evening loud with life, to-morrow all struck and vanished, 'a few earth-pits and heaps of straw!' For here, as always, it continues true, that the deepest force is the stillest; that, as in the Fable, the mild shining of the sun shall silently accomplish what the fierce blustering of the tempest has in vain essayed. Above all, it is ever to be kept in mind, that not by material, but by moral power, are men and their actions governed. How noiseless is thought! No rolling of drums, no tramp of squadrons, or immeasurable tumult of baggage-wagons, attends its movements: in what obscure and sequestered places may the head be meditating, which is one day to be crowned with more than imperial authority ; for Kings and Emperors will be among its ministering servants; it will rule not over, but *in*, all heads, and with these its solitary combinations of ideas, as with magic formulas, bend the world to its will! The time may come, when Napoleon himself will be better known for his laws than for his battles; and the victory of Waterloo prove less momentous than the opening of the first Mechanics' Institute.

We have been led into such rather trite reflections, by these Volumes of *Memoirs on Voltaire ;* a man in whose history the relative importance of intellectual and physical power is again curiously evinced. This also was a private person, by birth nowise an elevated one; yet so far as present knowledge will enable us to judge, it may be said that to abstract Voltaire and his activity from the eighteenth century, were to produce a greater difference in the existing figure of things, than the want of any other individual, up to this day, could have occasioned. Nay, with the single exception of Luther, there is perhaps, in these modern ages, no other man of a merely intellectual character, whose influence and reputation have become so entirely European as that of Voltaire. Indeed, like the great German Reformer's, his doctrines too, almost from the first, have affected not only the belief of the thinking world, silently propagating themselves from mind to mind; but in a high degree also, the conduct of the active and political world; entering as a distinct element into some of the most fearful civil convulsions which European history has on record.

Doubtless, to his own contemporaries, to such of them at least as had any insight into the actual state of men's minds, Voltaire already appeared as a noteworthy and decidedly historical personage: yet, perhaps, not the wildest of his admirers ventured to assign him such a magnitude as he now figures in, even with his adversaries and detractors. He has grown in apparent importance, as we receded from him, as the nature of his endeavours became more and more visible in their results. For, unlike many great men, but like all great agitators, Voltaire everywhere shows himself emphatically as the man of his century: uniting in his own person whatever spiritual accomplishments were most valued by that age; at the same time, with no depth to discern its ulterior tendencies, still less with any magnanimity to attempt withstanding these, his greatness and his littleness alike fitted him to produce an immediate effect; for he leads whither the multitude was of itself dimly minded to run, and keeps the van not less by skill in commanding, than by cunning in obeying. Besides, now that we look on the matter from some distance, the efforts of a thousand coadjutors and disciples, nay a series of mighty political vicissitudes, in the production of which these efforts had but a subsidiary share, have all come, naturally in such a case, to appear as if exclusively his work; so that he rises before us as the paragon and epitome of a whole spiritual period, now almost passed away, yet remarkable in itself, and more than ever interesting to us, who seem to stand, as it were, on the confines of a new and better one.

Nay, had we forgotten that ours is the 'Age of the Press,' when he who runs may not only read, but furnish us with reading; and simply counted the books, and scattered leaves, thick as the autumnal in Vallombrosa, that have been written and printed concerning this man, we might almost fancy him the most important person, not of the eighteenth century, but of all the centuries from Noah's Flood downwards. We have *Lives* of Voltaire by friend and by foe: Condorcet, Duvernet, Lepan, have each given us a whole; portions, documents and all manner of authentic or spurious contributions have been supplied by innumerable hands; of which we mention only the labours of his various Secretaries: Collini's, published some twenty years ago, and now these Two massive Octavos from Longchamp and Wagnière. To say nothing of the Baron de Grimm's Collections, unparalleled in more than one respect; or of the six-and-thirty volumes of scurrilous eaves-dropping, long since printed under the title of *Mémoires de Bachaumont;* or of the daily and hourly attacks and defences that appeared separately in his lifetime, and all the judicial pieces, whether in the style of apotheosis or of excommunication, that have seen the light since then; a mass of fugitive writings, the very diamond edition of which might fill whole libraries. The peculiar talent of the French in all narrative, at least in all anecdotic, departments, rendering most of these works extremely readable, still farther favoured their circulation, both at home and abroad: so that now, in most countries, Voltaire has been read of and talked of, till his name and life have grown familiar like those of a village acquaintance. In England, at least, where for almost a century the study of foreign literature has, we may say, confined itself to that of the French, with a slight intermixture from the elder Italians, Voltaire's writings, and such writings as treated of him, were little likely to want readers. We suppose, there is no literary era, not even any domestic one, concerning which Englishmen in general have such information, at least have gathered so many anecdotes and opinions, as concerning this of Voltaire. Nor have native additions to the stock been wanting, and these of a due variety in purport and kind: maledictions, expostulations and dreadful death-scenes painted like Spanish *Sanbenitos*, by weak well-meaning persons of the hostile class; eulogies, generally of a gayer sort, by open or secret friends: all this has been long and extensively carried on among us. There is even an English *Life of Voltaire;*[1] nay, we remember to have seen portions of his writings cited *in terrorem*, and with criticisms, in some pamphlet, 'by a country gentleman,' either on the Education of the People, or else on the question of Preserving the Game.

With the 'Age of the Press,' and such manifestations of it on this subject, we are far from quarrelling. We have read great part of these thousand-and-first 'Memoirs on Voltaire,' by Longchamp and Wagnière, not without satisfaction; and can cheerfully look forward to still other 'Memoirs' following in their train. Nothing can be more in the course of Nature than the wish to satisfy oneself with knowledge of all sorts about any distinguished person, especially of our own era; the true study of his character, his spiritual individu-

[1] 'By Frank Hall Standish, Esq.' (London, 1821); a work, which we can recommend only to such as feel themselves in extreme want of information on this subject, and except in their own language unable to acquire any. It is written very badly, though with sincerity, and not without considerable indications of talent; to all appearance, by a minor; many of whose statements and opinions (for he seems an inquiring, honest-hearted, rather decisive character) must have begun to astonish even himself, several years ago.

ality and peculiar manner of existence, is full of instruction for all mankind: even that of his looks, sayings, habitudes and indifferent actions, were not the records of them generally lies, is rather to be commended; nay, are not such lies themselves, when they keep within bounds, and the subject of them has been dead for some time, equal to snipe-shooting, or Colburn-Novels, at least little inferior, in the great art of getting done with life, or, as it is technically called, killing time? For our own part, we say: Would that every Johnson in the world had his veridical Boswell, or leash of Boswells! We could then tolerate his Hawkins also, though not veridical. With regard to Voltaire, in particular, it seems to us not only innocent but profitable, that the whole truth regarding him should be well understood. Surely, the biography of such a man, who, to say no more of him, spent his best efforts, and as many still think, successfully, in assaulting the Christian religion, must be a matter of considerable import; what he did, and what he could not do; how he did it, or attempted it, that is, with what degree of strength, clearness, especially with what moral intents, what theories and feelings on man and man's life, are questions that will bear some discussing. To Voltaire individually, for the last fifty-one years, the discussion has been indifferent enough; and to us it is a discussion not on one remarkable person only, and chiefly for the curious or studious, but involving considerations of highest moment to all men, and inquiries which the utmost compass of our philosophy will be unable to embrace.

Here, accordingly, we are about to offer some farther observations on this *quæstio vexata;* not without hope that the reader may accept them in good part. Doubtless, when we look at the whole bearings of the matter, there seems little prospect of any unanimity respecting it, either now, or within a calculable period: it is probable that many will continue, for a long time, to speak of this 'universal genius,' this 'apostle of Reason,' and 'father of sound Philosophy;'

and many again, of this 'monster of impiety,' this 'sophist,' and 'atheist,' and 'ape-demon;' or, like the late Dr. Clarke of Cambridge, dismiss him more briefly with information that he is 'a driveller:' neither is it essential that these two parties should, on the spur of the instant, reconcile themselves herein. Nevertheless, truth is better than error, were it only 'on Hannibal's vinegar.' It may be expected that men's opinions concerning Voltaire, which is of some moment, and concerning Voltairism, which is of almost boundless moment, will, if they cannot meet, gradually at every new comparison approach towards meeting; and what is still more desirable, towards meeting somewhere nearer the truth than they actually stand.

With honest wishes to promote such approximation, there is one condition, which, above all others, in this inquiry, we must beg the reader to impose on himself: the duty of fairness towards Voltaire, of tolerance towards him, as towards all men. This, truly, is a duty, which we have the happiness to hear daily inculcated; yet which, it has been well said, no mortal is at bottom disposed to practise. Nevertheless, if we really desire to understand the truth on any subject, not merely, as is much more common, to confirm our already existing opinions, and gratify this and the other pitiful claim of vanity or malice in respect of it, tolerance may be regarded as the most indispensable of all pre-requisites; the condition, indeed, by which alone any real progress in the question becomes possible. In respect of our fellow-men, and all real insight into their characters, this is especially true. No character, we may affirm, was ever rightly understood, till it had first been regarded with a certain feeling, not of tolerance only, but of sympathy. For here, more than in any other case, it is verified that the heart sees farther than the head. Let us be sure, our enemy is *not* that hateful being we are too apt to paint him. His vices and basenesses lie combined in far other order before his own mind, than before ours; and under colours which palliate them, nay perhaps exhibit them as virtues. Were he the wretch of our imagining, his life would be a burden to himself: for it is not by bread alone that the basest mortal lives; a certain approval of conscience is equally essential even to physical existence; is the fine all-pervading cement by which that wondrous union, a Self, is held together. Since the man, therefore, is not in Bedlam, and has not shot or hanged himself, let us take comfort, and conclude that he is one of two things: either a vicious *dog*, in man's guise, to be muzzled and mourned over, and greatly marvelled at; or a real *man*, and consequently not without moral worth, which is to be enlightened, and so far approved of. But to judge rightly of his character, we must learn to look at it, not less with his eyes, than with our own; we must learn to pity him, to see him as a fellow-creature, in a word, to love him; or his real spiritual nature will ever be mistaken by us. In interpreting Voltaire, accordingly, it will be needful to bear some things carefully in mind, and to keep many other things as carefully in abeyance. Let us forget that *our* opinions were ever assailed by him, or ever defended; that *we* have to thank him, or upbraid him, for pain or for pleasure; let us forget that we are Deists or Millennarians, Bishops or Radical Reformers, and remember only that we are men. This is a European subject, or there never was one; and must, if we would in the least comprehend it, be looked at neither from the parish belfry, nor any Peterloo platform; but, if possible, from some natural and infinitely higher point of vision.

It is a remarkable fact, that throughout the last fifty years of his life, Voltaire was seldom or never named, even by his detractors, without the epithet 'great' being appended to him; so that, had the syllables suited such a junction, as they did in the happier case of *Charle-Magne*, we might almost have expected that, not *Voltaire*, but *Voltaire-ce-grand-homme* would be his designation with posterity. However, posterity is much more stinted in its allowances on that score; and a multitude of things remain to be adjusted, and questions of very dubious issue to be gone into, before such coronation-titles can be conceded with any permanence. The million, even the wiser part of them, are apt to lose their discretion, when 'tumultuously assembled;' for a small object, near at hand, may subtend a large angle; and often a Pennenden Heath has been mistaken for a Field of Runnymead; whereby the couplet on that immortal Dalhousie proves to be the emblem of many a man's real fortune with the public:

> And thou, Dalhousie, the great God of War,
> Lieutenant-Colonel to the Earl of Mar;

the latter end corresponding poorly with the beginning. To ascertain what was the true significance of Voltaire's history, both as respects himself and the world; what was his specific character and value as a man; what has been the character and value of his influence on society, of his appearance as an active agent in the culture of Europe: all this leads us into much deeper investigations; on the settlement of which, however, the whole business turns.

To our own view, we confess, on looking at Voltaire's life, the chief quality that shows itself is one for which *adroitness* seems the fitter name. Greatness implies several conditions, the existence of which in his case it might be difficult to demonstrate; but of his claim to this other praise there can be no disputing. Whatever be his aims, high or low, just or the contrary, he is, at all times and to the utmost degree, expert in pursuing them. It is to be observed, moreover, that his aims in general were not of a simple sort, and the attainment of them easy: few literary men have had a course so diversified with vicissitudes as Voltaire's. His life is not spent in a corner, like that of a studious recluse, but on the open theatre of the world; in an age full of commotion, when society is rending itself asunder, Superstition already armed for deadly battle against Unbelief; in which battle he himself plays a distinguished part. From his earliest years, we find him in perpetual communication with the higher personages of his time, often with the highest: it is in circles of authority, of reputation, at lowest of fashion and rank, that he lives and works. Ninon de l'Enclos leaves the boy a legacy to buy books; he is still young, when he can say of his supper companions, "We are all Princes or Poets." In after life, he exhibits himself in company or correspondence with all manner of principalities and powers, from Queen Caroline of England to the Empress Catherine of Russia, from Pope Benedict to Frederick the Great. Meanwhile, shifting from side to side of Europe, hiding in the country, or living sumptuously in capital cities, he quits not his pen; with which, as with some enchanter's rod, more potent than any king's sceptre, he turns and winds the mighty machine of European Opinion; approves himself, as his schoolmaster had predicted, the *Coryphée du Déisme;* and, not content with this elevation, strives, and nowise ineffectually, to unite with it a poetical, historical, philosophic and even scientific preëminence. Nay, we may add, a pecuniary one; for he speculates in the funds, diligently solicits pensions and promotions, trades to America, is long a regular victualling-contractor for armies; and thus, by one means and another, independently of literature which would never yield much money, raises his income from 800 francs a-year to more than centuple that sum.[1] And now, having, besides all this commercial and economical business, written some thirty quartos, the most popular that were ever written, he returns after long exile to his native city, to be welcomed there almost as a religious idol; and closes a life, prosperous alike in the building of country-seats, and the composition of *Henriades* and *Philosophical Dictionaries*, by the most appropriate demise, — by drowning, as it were, in an ocean of applause; so that as he lived for fame, he may be said to have died of it.

Such various, complete success, granted only to a small

[1] See Tome ii. p. 328 of these *Mémoires.*

portion of men in any age of the world, presupposes at least, with every allowance for good fortune, an almost unrivalled expertness of management. There must have been a great talent of some kind at work here; a cause proportionate to the effect. It is wonderful, truly, to observe with what perfect skill Voltaire steers his course through so many conflicting circumstances: how he weathers this Cape Horn, darts lightly through that Mahlstrom; always either sinks his enemy, or shuns him; here waters, and careens, and traffics with the rich savages; there lies land-locked till the hurricane is overblown; and so, in spite of all billows, and sea-monsters, and hostile fleets, finishes his long Manilla voyage, with streamers flying, and deck piled with ingots! To say nothing of his literary character, of which this same dexterous address will also be found to be a main feature, let us glance only at the general aspect of his conduct, as manifested both in his writings and actions. By turns, and ever at the right season, he is imperious and obsequious; now shoots abroad, from the mountain tops, Hyperion-like, his keen innumerable shafts; anon, when danger is advancing, flies to obscure nooks; or, if taken in the fact, swears it was but in sport, and that he is the peaceablest of men. He bends to occasion; can, to a certain extent, blow hot or blow cold; and never attempts force, where cunning will serve his turn. The beagles of the Hierarchy and of the Monarchy, proverbially quick of scent and sharp of tooth, are out in quest of him; but this is a lion-fox which cannot be captured. By wiles and a thousand doublings, he utterly distracts his pursuers; he can burrow in the earth, and all the trace of him is gone.[1] With a strange system of anonymity and publicity, of denial and assertion, of Mys-

[1] Of one such 'taking to cover' we have a curious and rather ridiculous account in this Work, by Longchamp. It was with the Duchess du Maine that he sought shelter, and on a very slight occasion: nevertheless he had to lie perdue, for two months, at the Castle of Sceaux; and, with closed windows, and burning candles in daylight, compose *Zadig*, *Babouc*, *Memnon*, *&c.* for his amusement.

tification in all senses, has Voltaire surrounded himself. He can raise no standing armies for his defence, yet he too is a 'European Power,' and not undefended; an invisible, impregnable, though hitherto unrecognised bulwark, that of Public Opinion, defends him. With great art, he maintains this stronghold; though ever and anon sallying out from it, far beyond the permitted limits. But he has his coat of darkness, and his shoes of swiftness, like that other Killer of Giants. We find Voltaire a supple courtier, or a sharp satirist; he can talk blasphemy, and build churches, according to the signs of the times. Frederick the Great is not too high for his diplomacy, nor the poor Printer of his *Zadig* too low;[1] he manages the Cardinal Fleuri, and the Curé of St. Sulpice; and laughs in his sleeve at all the world. We should pronounce him to be one of the best politicians on record; as we have said, the *adroitest* of all literary men.

At the same time, Voltaire's worst enemies, it seems to us, will not deny that he had naturally a keen sense for rectitude, indeed for all virtue: the utmost vivacity of temperament characterises him; his quick susceptibility for every form of beauty is moral as well as intellectual. Nor was his practice without indubitable and highly creditable proofs of this. To the help-needing he was at all times a ready benefactor: many were the hungry adventurers who profited of his bounty, and then bit the hand that had fed them. If we enumerate his generous acts, from the case of the Abbé Desfontaines down to that of the Widow Calas, and the Serfs of Saint Claude, we shall find that few private men have had so wide a circle of charity, and have watched over it so well. Should it be objected that love of reputation entered largely into these proceedings, Voltaire can afford a handsome deduction on that head: should the uncharitable even calculate that love of reputation was the sole motive, we can only remind them that love of *such* reputation is

[1] See in Longchamp (pp. 154–163) how, by natural legerdemain, a knave may be caught, and the *change rendu à des imprimeurs infidèles.*

itself the effect of a social, humane disposition; and wish, as an immense improvement, that all men were animated with it. Voltaire was not without his experience of human baseness; but he still had a fellow-feeling for human sufferings; and delighted, were it only as an honest luxury, to relieve them. His attachments seem remarkably constant and lasting: even such sots as Thiriot, whom nothing but habit could have endeared to him, he continues, and after repeated injuries, to treat and regard as friends. Of his equals we do not observe him envious, at least not palpably and despicably so; though this, we should add, might be in him, who was from the first so paramountly popular, no such hard attainment. Against Montesquieu, perhaps against him alone, he cannot help entertaining a small secret grudge; yet ever in public he does him the amplest justice; *l'Arlequin-Grotius* of the fireside becomes, on all grave occasions, the author of the *Esprit des Loix*. Neither to his enemies, and even betrayers, is Voltaire implacable or meanly vindictive: the instant of their submission is also the instant of his forgiveness; their hostility itself provokes only casual sallies from him; his heart is too kindly, indeed too light, to cherish any rancour, any continuation of revenge. If he has not the virtue to forgive, he is seldom without the prudence to forget: if, in his life-long contentions, he cannot treat his opponents with any magnanimity, he seldom, or perhaps never once, treats them quite basely; seldom or never with that absolute unfairness, which the law of retaliation might so often have seemed to justify. We would say that, if no heroic, he is at all times a perfectly civilised man; which, considering that his war was with exasperated theologians, and a 'war to the knife' on their part, may be looked upon as rather a surprising circumstance. He exhibits many minor virtues, a due appreciation of the highest; and fewer faults than, in his situation, might have been expected, and perhaps pardoned.

All this is well, and may fit out a highly expert and much

esteemed man of business, in the widest sense of that term; but is still far from constituting a 'great character.' In fact, there is one deficiency in Voltaire's original structure, which, it appears to us, must be quite fatal to such claims for him: we mean his inborn levity of nature, his entire want of Earnestness. Voltaire was by birth a Mocker, and light *Pococurante;* which natural disposition his way of life confirmed into a predominant, indeed all-pervading habit. Far be it from us to say, that solemnity is an essential of greatness; that no great man can have other than a rigid vinegar aspect of countenance, never to be thawed or warmed by billows of mirth! There are things in this world to be laughed at, as well as things to be admired; and his is no complete mind, that cannot give to each sort its due. Nevertheless, contempt is a dangerous element to sport in; a deadly one, if we habitually live in it. How, indeed, to take the lowest view of this matter, shall a man accomplish great enterprises; enduring all toil, resisting temptation, laying aside every weight, — unless he zealously love what he pursues? The faculty of love, of admiration, is to be regarded as the sign and the measure of high souls: unwisely directed, it leads to many evils; but without it, there cannot be any good. Ridicule, on the other hand, is indeed a faculty much prized by its possessors; yet, intrinsically, it is a small faculty; we may say, the smallest of all faculties that other men are at the pains to repay with any esteem. It is directly opposed to Thought, to Knowledge, properly so called; its nourishment and essence is Denial, which hovers only on the surface, while Knowledge dwells far below. Moreover, it is by nature selfish and morally trivial; it cherishes nothing but our Vanity, which may in general be left safely enough to shift for itself. Little 'discourse of reason,' in any sense, is implied in Ridicule: a scoffing man is in no lofty mood, for the time; shows more of the imp than of the angel. This too when his scoffing is what we call just, and has some foundation on truth; while again the laughter of fools, that vain sound said in Scripture to resemble the 'crackling of thorns under the pot' (which they cannot heat, but only soil and begrime), must be regarded, in these latter times, as a very serious addition to the sum of human wretchedness; nor perhaps will it always, when the Increase of Crime in the Metropolis comes to be debated, escape the vigilance of Parliament.

We have, oftener than once, endeavoured to attach some meaning to that aphorism, vulgarly imputed to Shaftesbury, which, however, we can find nowhere in his works, that *ridicule is the test of truth.* But of all chimeras that ever advanced themselves in the shape of philosophical doctrines, this is to us the most formless and purely inconceivable. Did or could the unassisted human faculties ever understand it, much more believe it? Surely, so far as the common mind can discern, laughter seems to depend not less on the laugher than on the laughee: and now, who gave laughers a patent to be always just, and always omniscient? If the philosophers of Nootka Sound were pleased to laugh at the manœuvres of Cook's seamen, did that render these manœuvres useless; and were the seamen to stand idle, or to take to leather canoes, till the laughter abated? Let a discerning public judge.

But, leaving these questions for the present, we may observe at least that all great men have been careful to subordinate this talent or habit of ridicule; nay, in the ages which we consider the greatest, most of the arts that contribute to it have been thought disgraceful for freemen, and confined to the exercise of slaves. With Voltaire, however, there is no such subordination visible: by nature, or by practice, mockery has grown to be the irresistible bias of his disposition; so that for him, in all matters, the first question is, not what is true, but what is false; not what is to be loved, and held fast, and earnestly laid to heart, but what is to be contemned, and derided, and sportfully cast out of doors. Here truly he earns abundant triumph as an image-breaker, but pockets little real wealth. Vanity, with its adjuncts, as we have said, finds rich solacement; but for aught better, there is not much. Reverence, the highest feeling that man's nature is capable of, the crown of his whole moral manhood, and precious, like fine gold, were it in the rudest forms, he seems not to understand, or have heard of even by credible tradition. The glory of knowing and believing is all but a stranger to him; only with that of questioning and qualifying is he familiar. Accordingly, he sees but a little way into Nature: the mighty All, in its beauty, and infinite mysterious grandeur, humbling the small *Me* into nothingness, has never even for moments been revealed to him; only this or that other atom of it, and the differences and discrepancies of these two, has he looked into and noted down. His theory of the world, his picture of man and man's life, is little; for a Poet and Philosopher, even pitiful. Examine it in its highest developments, you find it an altogether vulgar picture; simply a reflex, with more or fewer mirrors, of Self and the poor interests of Self. 'The Divine Idea, that which lies at the bottom of Appearance,' was never more invisible to any man. He reads History not with the eye of a devout seer, or even of a critic; but through a pair of mere anti-catholic spectacles. It is not a mighty drama, enacted on the theatre of Infinitude, with Suns for lamps, and Eternity as a background; whose author is God, and whose purport and thousandfold moral lead us up to the 'dark with excess of light' of the Throne of God; but a poor wearisome debating-club dispute, spun through ten centuries, between the *Encyclopédie* and the *Sorbonne*. Wisdom or folly, nobleness or baseness, are merely superstitious or unbelieving: God's Universe is a larger Patrimony of St. Peter, from which it were well and pleasant to hunt out the Pope.

In this way, Voltaire's nature, which was originally vehement rather than deep, came, in its maturity, in spite of all his wonderful gifts, to be positively shallow. We find no heroism of character in him, from first to last; nay there is not, that we know of, one great thought in all his six-and-thirty quartos. The high worth implanted in him by Nature, and still often manifested in his conduct, does not shine there like a light, but like a coruscation. The enthusiasm, proper to such a mind, visits him; but it has no abiding virtue in his thoughts, no local habitation and no name. There is in him a rapidity, but at the same time a pettiness; a certain violence, and fitful abruptness, which takes from him all dignity. Of his *emportemens*, and tragicomical explosions, a thousand anecdotes are on record; neither is he, in these cases, a terrific volcano, but a mere bundle of rockets. He is nigh shooting poor Dorn, the Frankfort constable; actually fires a pistol, into the lobby, at him; and this, three days after that melancholy business of the '*Œuvre de Poéshie du Roi mon Maître*' had been finally adjusted. A bookseller, who, with the natural instinct of fallen mankind, overcharges him, receives from this Philosopher, by way of payment at sight, a slap on the face. Poor Longchamp, with considerable tact, and a praiseworthy air of second-table respectability, details various scenes of this kind: how Voltaire dashed away his combs, and maltreated his wig, and otherwise fiercely comported himself, the very first morning: how once, having a keenness of appetite, sharpened by walking and a diet of weak tea, he became uncommonly anxious for supper; and Clairaut and Madame du Châtelet, sunk in algebraic calculations, twice promised to come down, but still kept the dishes cooling, and the Philosopher at last desperately battered open their locked door with his foot; exclaiming, "*Vous êtes donc de concert pour me faire mourir?*" — And yet Voltaire had a true kindness of heart; all his domestics and dependents loved him, and continued with him. He has many elements of goodness, but floating loosely; nothing is combined in stedfast union. It is true, he presents in general a surface of smoothness, of cultured regularity; yet, under it, there is not the silent rock-bound strength of a World, but the wild tumults of a Chaos are ever bursting through. He is a man of power, but not of beneficent authority; we fear, but cannot reverence him; we feel him to be stronger, not higher.

Much of this spiritual shortcoming and perversion might be due to natural defect; but much of it also is due to the age into which he was cast. It was an age of discord and division; the approach of a grand crisis in human affairs. Already we discern in it all the elements of the French Revolution; and wonder, so easily do we forget how entangled and hidden the meaning of the present generally is to us, that all men did not foresee the comings-on of that fearful convulsion. On the one hand, a high all-attempting activity of Intellect; the most peremptory spirit of inquiry abroad on every subject; things human and things divine alike cited without misgivings before the same boastful tribunal of so-called Reason, which means here a merely argumentative Logic; the strong in mind excluded from his regular influence in the state, and deeply conscious of that injury. On the other hand, a privileged few, strong in the subjection of the many, yet in itself weak; a piebald, and for most part altogether decrepit battalion of Clergy, of purblind Nobility, or rather of Courtiers, for as yet the Nobility is mostly on the other side: these cannot fight with Logic, and the day of Persecution is wellnigh done. The whole force of law, indeed, is still in their hands; but the far deeper force, which alone gives efficacy to law, is hourly passing from them. Hope animates one side, fear the other; and the battle will be fierce and desperate. For there is wit without wisdom on the part of the self-styled Philosophers; feebleness with exasperation on the part of their opponents; pride enough on all hands, but little magnanimity; perhaps nowhere any pure love of truth, only everywhere the purest, most ardent love of self. In such a state of things, there lay abundant principles of discord: these two influences hung like fast-gathering electric clouds, as yet on opposite sides of the horizon, but with a malignity of aspect, which boded, whenever they might meet, a sky of fire and blackness, thunderbolts to waste the earth; and the sun and stars, though but for a season, to be blotted out from the heavens. For there is no conducting medium to unite softly these hostile elements; there is no true virtue, no true wisdom, on the one side or on the other. Never perhaps was there an epoch, in the history of the world, when universal corruption called so loudly for reform; and they who undertook that task were men intrinsically so worthless. Not by Gracchi but by Catilines, not by Luthers but by Aretines, was Europe to be renovated. The task has been a long and bloody one; and is still far from done.

In this condition of affairs, what side such a man as Voltaire was to take could not be doubtful. Whether he ought to have taken either side; whether he should not rather have stationed himself in the middle; the partisan of neither, perhaps hated by both; acknowledging and forwarding, and striving to reconcile, what truth was in each; and preaching forth a far deeper truth, which, if his own century had neglected it, had persecuted it, future centuries would have recognised as priceless: all this was another question. Of no man, however gifted, can we require what he has not to give: but Voltaire called himself Philosopher, nay *the* Philosopher. And such has often, indeed generally, been the fate of great men, and Lovers of Wisdom: their own age and country have treated them as of no account; in the great Corn-Exchange of the world, their pearls have seemed but spoiled barley, and been ignominiously rejected. Weak in adherents, strong only in their faith, in their indestructible consciousness of worth and well-doing, they have silently, or in words, appealed to coming ages, when their own ear would indeed be shut to the voice of love and of hatred, but the Truth that had dwelt in them would speak with a voice audible to all. Bacon left his works to future generations, when some centuries should have elapsed. 'Is it much for me,' said Kepler, in his isolation, and extreme need, 'that men should 'accept my discovery? If the Almighty waited six thou-'sand years for one to see what He had made, I may surely 'wait two hundred for one to understand what I have seen!' All this, and more, is implied in love of wisdom, in genuine seeking of truth: the noblest function that can be appointed for a man, but requiring also the noblest man to fulfil it.

With Voltaire, however, there is no symptom, perhaps there was no conception, of such nobleness; the high call for which, indeed, in the existing state of things, his intellect may have had as little the force to discern, as his heart had the force to obey. He follows a simpler course. Heedless of remoter issues, he adopts the cause of his own party; of that class with whom he lived, and was most anxious to stand well: he enlists in their ranks, not without hopes that he may one day rise to be their general. A resolution perfectly accordant with his prior habits, and temper of mind; and from which his whole subsequent procedure, and moral aspect as a man, naturally enough evolves itself. Not that we would say, Voltaire was a mere prize-fighter; one of 'Heaven's Swiss,' contending for a cause which he only half, or not at all approved of. Far from it. Doubtless he loved truth, doubtless he partially felt himself to be advocating truth; nay we know not that he has ever yet, in a single instance, been convicted of wilfully perverting his belief; of uttering, in all his controversies, one deliberate falsehood. Nor should this negative praise seem an altogether slight one; for greatly were it to be wished that even the best of his better-intentioned opponents had always deserved the like. Nevertheless, his love of truth is not that deep infinite love, which beseems a Philosopher; which many ages have been fortunate enough to witness; nay, of which his own age had still some examples. It is a far inferior love, we should say, to that of poor Jean Jacques, half-sage, half-maniac as he was; it is more a prudent calculation than a passion. Voltaire loves Truth, but chiefly of the triumphant sort: we have no instance of his fighting for a quite discrowned and outcast Truth; it is chiefly when she walks abroad, in distress it may be, but still with queenlike insignia, and knighthoods and renown are to be earned in her battles, that he defends her, that he charges gallantly against the Cades and Tylers. Nay, at all times, belief itself seems, with him, to be less the product of Meditation than of Argument. His first question with regard to any doctrine, perhaps his final test of its worth and genuineness is: Can others be convinced of this? Can I truck it, in the market, for power? 'To such questioners,' it has been said, 'Truth, who buys not, and 'sells not, goes on her way, and makes no answer.'

In fact, if we inquire into Voltaire's ruling motive, we shall find that it was at bottom but a vulgar one: ambition, the desire of ruling, by such means as he had, over other men. He acknowledges no higher divinity than Public Opinion; for whatever he asserts or performs, the number of votes is the measure of strength and value. Yet let us be just to him; let us admit that he in some degree estimates his votes, as well as counts them. If love of fame, which, especially for such a man, we can only call another modification of Vanity, is always his ruling passion, he has a certain taste in gratifying it. His vanity, which cannot be extinguished, is ever skilfully concealed; even his just claims are never boisterously insisted on; throughout his whole life he shows no single feature of the quack. Nevertheless, even in the height of his glory, he has a strange sensitiveness to the judgment of the world: could he have contrived a Dionysius' Ear, in the Rue Traversière, we should have found him watching at it, night and day. Let but any little evil-disposed Abbé, any Fréron or Piron,

Pauvre Piron, qui ne fut jamais rien,
Pas même Académicien,

write a libel or epigram on him, what a fluster he is in! We grant he forbore much, in these cases; manfully consumed his own spleen, and sometimes long held his peace; but it was his part to have always done so. Why should such a man ruffle himself with the spite of exceeding small persons? Why not let these poor devils write; why should not they earn a dishonest penny, at his expense, if they had no readier way? But Voltaire cannot part with his 'voices,' his 'most sweet voices:' for they are his gods; take these, and what has he left? Accordingly, in literature and morals, in all his comings and goings, we find him striving, with a religious care, to sail strictly with the wind. In Art, the Parisian *Parterre* is his court of last appeal: he consults the *Café de Procope*, on his wisdom or his folly, as if it were a Delphic Oracle. The following adventure belongs to his fifty-fourth year, when his fame might long have seemed abundantly established. We translate from the Sieur Longchamp's thin, half-roguish, mildly obsequious, most lackey-like Narrative:

'Judges could appreciate the merits of *Sémiramis*, which has continued on the stage, and always been seen there with pleasure. Every one knows how the two principal parts in this piece contributed to the celebrity of two great tragedians, Mademoiselle Dumèsnil and M. le Kain. The enemies of M. de Voltaire renewed their attempts in the subsequent representations; but it only the better confirmed his triumph. Piron, to console himself for the defeat of his party, had recourse to his usual remedy; pelting the piece with some paltry epigrams, which did it no harm.

'Nevertheless, M. de Voltaire, who always loved to correct his works, and perfect them, became desirous to learn, more specially and at first hand, what good or ill the public were saying of his Tragedy; and it appeared to him that he could nowhere learn it better than in the *Café de Procope*, which was also called the *Antre* (Cavern) *de Procope*, because it was very dark even in full day, and ill-lighted in the evenings; and because you often saw there a set of lank, sallow poets, who had somewhat the air of apparitions. In this Café, which fronts the *Comédie Française*, had been held, for more than sixty years, the tribunal of those self-called *Aristarchs*, who fancied they could pass sentence without appeal, on plays, authors and actors. M. de Voltaire wished to compear there, but in disguise and altogether *incognito*. It was on coming out from the playhouse that the judges usually proceeded thither, to open what they called their great sessions. On the second night of *Sémiramis*, he borrowed a clergyman's clothes; dressed himself in cassock and long cloak: black stockings, girdle, bands, breviary itself; nothing was forgotten.

He clapt on a large peruke, unpowdered, very ill combed, which covered more than the half of his cheeks, and left nothing to be seen but the end of a long nose. The peruke was surmounted by a large three-cornered hat, corners half bruised-in. In this equipment, then, the author of *Sémiramis* proceeded on foot to the *Café de Procope*, where he squatted himself in a corner; and waiting for the end of the play, called for a *bavaroise*, a small roll of bread and the Gazette. It was not long till those familiars of the *Parterre* and tenants of the *Café* stept in. They instantly began discussing the new Tragedy. Its partisans and its adversaries pleaded their cause, with warmth; each giving his reasons. Impartial persons also spoke their sentiment; and repeated some fine verses of the piece. During all this time, M. de Voltaire, with spectacles on nose, head stooping over the Gazette which he pretended to be reading, was listening to the debate; profiting by reasonable observations, suffering much to hear very absurd ones, and not answer them, which irritated him. Thus during an hour and a half, had he the courage and patience to hear *Sémiramis* talked of and babbled of, without speaking a word. At last, all these pretended judges of the fame of authors having gone their ways, without converting one another, M. de Voltaire also went off; took a coach in the Rue Mazarine, and returned home about eleven o'clock. Though I knew of his disguise, I confess I was struck and almost frightened to see him accoutred so. I took him for a spectre, or shade of Ninus, that was appearing to me; or, at least, for one of those ancient Irish debaters, arrived at the end of their career, after wearing themselves out in school-syllogisms. I helped him to doff all that apparatus, which I carried next morning to its true owner, — a Doctor of the Sorbonne.'

This stroke of art, which cannot in anywise pass for sublime, might have its uses and rational purpose in one case, and only in one: if *Sémiramis* was meant to be a popular show, that was to live or die by its first impression on the idle multitude; which accordingly we must infer to have been its real, at least its chief destination. In any other case, we cannot but consider this Haroun-Alraschid visit to the *Café de Procope* as questionable, and altogether inadequate. If *Sémiramis* was a Poem, a living Creation, won from the empyrean by the silent power and long-continued Promethean toil of its author, what could the *Café de Procope* know of it, what could all Paris know of it, 'on the second night?'

Had it been a Milton's *Paradise Lost,* they might have despised it till after the fiftieth year! True, the object of the Poet is, and must be, to 'instruct by pleasing,' yet not by pleasing this man and that man; only by pleasing *man,* by speaking to the pure nature of man, can any real 'instruction,' in this sense, be conveyed. Vain does it seem to search for a judgment of this kind in the largest *Café,* in the largest Kingdom, 'on the second night.' The deep, clear consciousness of one mind comes infinitely nearer it, than the loud outcry of a million that have no such consciousness; whose 'talk,' or whose 'babble,' but distracts the listener; and to most genuine Poets has, from of old, been in a great measure indifferent. For the multitude of voices is no authority; a thousand voices may not, strictly examined, amount to one vote. Mankind in this world are divided into flocks, and follow their several bell-wethers. Now, it is well known, let the bell-wether rush through any gap, the rest rush after him, were it into bottomless quagmires. Nay, so conscientious are sheep in this particular, as a quaint naturalist and moralist has noted, 'if you hold a stick before the wether, 'so that he is forced to vault in his passage, the whole flock will 'do the like when the stick is withdrawn; and the thousandth 'sheep shall be seen vaulting impetuously over air, as the 'first did over an otherwise impassable barrier!' A farther peculiarity, which, in consulting Acts of Parliament, and other authentic records, not only as regards 'Catholic Disabilities,' but many other matters, you may find curiously verified in the human species also! — On the whole, we must consider this excursion to *Procope's* literary Cavern as illustrating Voltaire in rather pleasant style; but nowise much to his honour. Fame seems a far too high, if not the highest object with him; nay sometimes even popularity is clutched at: we see no heavenly polestar in this voyage of his; but only the guidance of a proverbially uncertain *wind.*

Voltaire reproachfully says of St. Louis, that 'he ought to have been above his age;' but in his own case we can find few symptoms of such heroic superiority. The same perpetual appeal to his contemporaries, the same intense regard to reputation, as he viewed it, prescribes for him both his enterprises and his manner of conducting them. His aim is to please the more enlightened, at least the politer part of the world; and he offers them simply what they most wish for, be it in theatrical shows for their pastime, or in sceptical doctrines for their edification. For this latter purpose, Ridicule is the weapon he selects, and it suits him well. This was not the age of deep thoughts; no Duc de Richelieu, no Prince Conti, no Frederick the Great would have listened to such: only sportful contempt, and a thin conversational logic will avail. There may be wool-quilts, which the lath-sword of Harlequin will pierce, when the club of Hercules has rebounded from them in vain. As little was this an age for high virtues; no heroism, in any form, is required, or even acknowledged; but only, in all forms, a certain *bienséance.* To this rule also Voltaire readily conforms; indeed, he finds no small advantage in it. For a lax public morality not only allows him the indulgence of many a little private vice, and brings him in this and the other windfall of *menus plaisirs,* but opens him the readiest resource in many enterprises of danger. Of all men, Voltaire has the least disposition to increase the Army of Martyrs. No testimony will he seal with his blood; scarcely any will he so much as sign with ink. His obnoxious doctrines, as we have remarked, he publishes under a thousand concealments; with underplots, and wheels within wheels; so that his whole track is in darkness, only his works see the light. No Proteus is so nimble, or assumes so many shapes: if, by rare chance, caught sleeping, he whisks through the smallest hole, and is out of sight, while the noose is getting ready. Let his judges take him to task, he will shuffle and evade; if directly questioned, he will even lie. In regard to this last point, the Marquis de Condorcet has set up a defence for him, which has at least the merit of being frank enough.

'The necessity of lying in order to disavow any work,' says he, 'is an extremity equally repugnant to conscience and nobleness of character: but the crime lies with those unjust men, who render such disavowal necessary to the safety of him whom they force to it. If you have made a crime of what is not one; if, by absurd or by arbitrary laws, you have infringed the natural right, which all men have, not only to form an opinion, but to render it public; then you deserve to lose the right which every man has of hearing the truth from the mouth of another; a right, which is the sole basis of that rigorous obligation, not to lie. If it is not permitted to deceive, the reason is, that to deceive any one, is to do him a wrong, or expose yourself to do him one; but a wrong supposes a right; and no one has the right of seeking to secure himself the means of committing an injustice.' [1]

It is strange, how scientific discoveries do maintain themselves: here, quite in other hands, and in an altogether different dialect, we have the old Catholic doctrine, if it ever was more than a Jesuitic one, 'that faith need not be kept with heretics.' Truth, it appears, is too precious an article for our enemies; is fit only for friends, for those who will pay us if we tell it them. It may be observed, however, that granting Condorcet's premises, this doctrine also must be granted, as indeed is usual with that sharp-sighted writer. If the doing of right depends on the receiving of it; if our fellow-men, in this world, are not persons, but mere things, that for services bestowed will return services, — steam-engines that will manufacture calico, if we put in coals and water, — then doubtless, the calico ceasing, our coals and water may also rationally cease; the questioner threatening to injure us for the truth, we may rationally tell him lies. But if, on the other hand, our fellow-man is no steam-engine, but a man; united with us, and with all men, and with the Maker of all men, in sacred, mysterious, indissoluble bonds, in an All-embracing Love, that encircles alike the seraph and the glow-worm; then will our duties to him rest on quite another basis than this very humble one of *quid pro quo;* and the

[1] Vie de Voltaire, p. 32.

Marquis de Condorcet's conclusion will be false; and might, in its practical extensions, be infinitely pernicious.

Such principles and habits, too lightly adopted by Voltaire, acted, as it seems to us, with hostile effect on his moral nature, not originally of the noblest sort, but which, under other influences, might have attained to far greater nobleness. As it is, we see in him simply a Man of the World, such as Paris and the eighteenth century produced and approved of: a polite, attractive, most cultivated, but essentially self-interested man; not without highly amiable qualities; indeed, with a general disposition which we could have accepted without disappointment in a mere Man of the World, but must find very defective, sometimes altogether out of place, in a Poet and Philosopher. Above this character of a Parisian 'honourable man,' he seldom or never rises; nay sometimes we find him hovering on the very lowest boundaries of it, or perhaps even fairly below it. We shall nowise accuse him of excessive regard for money, of any wish to shine by the influence of mere wealth: let those commercial speculations, including even the victualling-contracts, pass for laudable prudence, for love of independence, and of the power to do good. But what are we to make of that hunting after pensions, and even after mere titles? There is an assiduity displayed here, which sometimes almost verges towards sneaking. Well might it provoke the scorn of Alfieri; for there is nothing better than the spirit of 'a French plebeian' apparent in it. Much, we know, very much should be allowed for difference of national manners, which in general mainly determine the meaning of such things: nevertheless, to our insular feelings, that famous *Trajan est-il content?* especially when we consider who the Trajan was, will always remain an unfortunate saying. The more so, as Trajan himself turned his back on it, without answer; declining, indeed, through life, to listen to the voice of this charmer, or disturb his own '*âme paisible*,' for one moment, though with the best philosopher in Nature. Nay, Pompadour herself was applied to; and even some considerable progress made, by that underground passage, had not an envious hand too soon and fatally intervened. D'Alembert says, there are two things that can reach the top of a pyramid, the eagle and the reptile. Apparently, Voltaire wished to combine both methods; and he had, with one of them, but indifferent success.

The truth is, we are trying Voltaire by too high a standard; comparing him with an ideal, which he himself never strove after, perhaps never seriously aimed at. He is no great Man, but only a great *Persifleur;* a man for whom life, and all that pertains to it, has, at best, but a despicable meaning; who meets its difficulties not with earnest force, but with gay agility; and is found always at the top, less by power in swimming, than by lightness in floating. Take him in his character, forgetting that any other was ever ascribed to him, and we find that he enacted it almost to perfection. Never man better understood the whole secret of *Persiflage;* meaning thereby not only the external faculty of polite contempt, but that art of general inward contempt, by which a man of this sort endeavours to subject the circumstances of his Destiny to his Volition, and be, what is the instinctive effort of all men, though in the midst of material Necessity, morally Free. Voltaire's latent derision is as light, copious and all-pervading as the derision which he utters. Nor is this so simple an attainment as we might fancy; a certain kind and degree of Stoicism, or approach to Stoicism, is necessary for the completed *Persifleur;* as for moral, or even practical completion, in any other way. The most indifferent-minded man is not by nature indifferent to his own pain and pleasure: this is an indifference which he must by some method study to acquire, or acquire the show of; and which, it is fair to say, Voltaire manifests in a rather respectable degree. Without murmuring, he has reconciled himself to most things: the human lot, in this lower world, seems a strange business, yet, on the whole, with more of the farce in it than of the tragedy; to him it is nowise heart-rending, that this Planet of ours should be sent sailing through Space, like a miserable aimless Ship-of-Fools, and he himself be a fool among the rest, and only a very little wiser than they. He does not, like Bolingbroke, 'patronise Providence,' though such sayings as *Si Dieu n'existait pas, il faudrait l'inventer*, seem now and then to indicate a tendency of that sort: but, at all events, he never openly levies war against Heaven; well knowing that the time spent in frantic malediction, directed *thither*, might be spent otherwise with more profit. There is, truly, no *Werterism* in him, either in its bad or its good sense. If he sees no unspeakable majesty in heaven and earth, neither does he see any unsufferable horror there. His view of the world is a cool, gently scornful, altogether prosaic one: his sublimest Apocalypse of Nature lies in the microscope and telescope; the Earth is a place for producing corn; the Starry Heavens are admirable as a nautical time-keeper. Yet, like a prudent man, he has adjusted himself to his condition, such as it is: he does not chaunt any *Miserere* over human life, calculating that no charitable dole, but only laughter, would be the reward of such an enterprise; does not hang or drown himself, clearly understanding that death of itself will soon save him that trouble. Affliction, it is true, has not for him any precious jewel in its head; on the contrary, it is an unmixed nuisance; yet, happily, not one to be howled over, so much as one to be speedily removed out of sight: if he does not learn from it Humility, and the sublime lesson of Resignation, neither does it teach him hard-heartedness and sickly discontent; but he bounds lightly over it, leaving both the jewel and the toad at a safe distance behind him.

Nor was Voltaire's history without perplexities enough to keep this principle in exercise; to try whether in life, as in literature, the *ridiculum* were really better than the *acre*. We must own, that on no occasion does it altogether fail him; never does he seem perfectly at a nonplus; no adventure is so hideous, that he cannot, in the long-run, find some means to laugh at it, and forget it. Take, for instance, that last ill-omened visit of his to Frederick the Great. This was, probably, the most mortifying incident in Voltaire's whole life: an open experiment, in the sight of all Europe, to ascertain whether French Philosophy had virtue enough in it to found any friendly union, in such circumstances, even between its great master and his most illustrious disciple; and an experiment which answered in the negative. As was natural enough; for Vanity is of a divisive, not of a uniting nature; and between the King of Letters and the King of Armies there existed no other tie. They should have kept up an interchange of flattery, from afar: gravitating towards one another like celestial luminaries, if they reckoned themselves such; yet always with a due centrifugal force; for if either shot madly from his sphere, nothing but collision, and concussion, and mutual recoil, could be the consequence. On the whole, we must pity Frederick, environed with that cluster of Philosophers: doubtless he meant rather well; yet the French at Rosbach, with guns in their hands, were but a small matter, compared with these French in Sans-Souci. Maupertuis sits sullen, monosyllabic; gloomy like the bear of his own arctic zone: Voltaire is the mad piper that will make him dance to tunes and amuse the people. In this royal circle, with its parasites and bashaws, what heats and jealousies must there not have been; what secret heart-burnings, smooth-faced malice, plottings, counter-plottings, and laurel-water pharmacy, in all its branches, before the ring of etiquette fairly burst asunder, and the establishment, so to speak, exploded! Yet over all these distressing matters Voltaire has thrown a soft veil of gaiety; he remembers neither Dr. Akakia, nor Dr. Akakia's patron, with any animosity; but merely as actors in the grand farce of life along with him, a new scene of which has now commenced, quite displacing the other from the stage. The arrest at Frankfort, indeed, is a sour morsel; but this too he swallows, with an effort. Frederick, as we are given to understand, had these whims by kind; was, indeed, a wonderful scion from such a stock; for what could equal the avarice, malice and rabid snappishness of old Frederick William the father?

'He had a minister at the Hague, named Luicius,' says the wit: 'this Luicius was, of all royal ministers extant, the worst paid. The poor man, with a view to warm himself, had a few trees cut down, in the garden of Honslardik, then belonging to the House of Prussia; immediately thereafter he received despatches from the King his master, keeping back a year of his salary. Luicius, in despair, cut his throat with the only razor he had (*avec le seul rasoir qu'il eût*); an old lackey came to his assistance, and unfortunately saved his life. At an after period, I myself saw his Excellency at the Hague, and gave him an alms at the gate of that Palace called *La Vieille Cour*, which belongs to the King of Prussia, where this unhappy Ambassador had lived twelve years.'

With the *Roi-Philosophe* himself Voltaire, in a little while, recommences correspondence; and, to all appearance, proceeds quietly in his office of 'buckwasher,' that is, of verse-corrector to his Majesty, as if nothing whatever had happened.

Again, what human pen can describe the troubles this unfortunate philosopher had with his women? A gadding, feather-brained, capricious, old-coquettish, embittered and embittering set of wantons from the earliest to the last! Widow Denis, for example, that disobedient Niece, whom he rescued from furnished lodgings and spare diet, into pomp and plenty, how did she pester the last stage of his existence, for twenty-four years long! Blind to the peace and roses of Ferney; ever hankering and fretting after Parisian display; not without flirtation, though advanced in life; losing money at play, and purloining wherewith to make it good; scolding his servants, quarrelling with his secretaries, so that the too-indulgent uncle must turn off his beloved Collini, nay almost be run through the body by him, for her sake! The good Wagnière, who succeeded this fiery Italian in the secretaryship, and loved Voltaire with a most creditable affection, cannot, though a simple, humble and philanthropic man, speak of

Madame Denis without visible overflowings of gall. He openly accuses her of hastening her uncle's death by her importunate stratagems to keep him in Paris, where was her heaven. Indeed it is clear that, his goods and chattels once made sure of, her chief care was that so fiery a patient might die soon enough; or, at best, according to her own confession, 'how she was to get him buried.' We have known superannuated grooms, nay effete saddle-horses, regarded with more real sympathy in their home, than was the best of uncles by the worst of nieces. Had not this surprising old man retained the sharpest judgment, and the gayest, easiest temper, his last days and last years must have been a continued scene of violence and tribulation.

Little better, worse in several respects, though at a time when he could better endure it, was the far-famed Marquise du Châtelet. Many a tempestuous day and wakeful night had he with that scientific and too-fascinating shrew. She speculated in mathematics and metaphysics; but was an adept also in far, very far different acquirements. Setting aside its whole criminality, which, indeed, perhaps went for little there, this literary amour wears but a mixed aspect; short sun-gleams, with long tropical tornadoes; touches of guitar-music, soon followed by Lisbon earthquakes. Marmontel, we remember, speaks of *knives* being used, at least brandished, and for quite other purposes than carving. Madame la Marquise was no saint, in any sense; but rather a Socrates' spouse, who would keep patience, and the whole philosophy of gaiety, in constant practice. Like Queen Elizabeth, if she had the talents of a man, she had more than the caprices of a woman.

We shall take only one item, and that a small one, in this mountain of misery: her strange habits and methods of locomotion. She is perpetually travelling: a peaceful philosopher is lugged over the world, to Cirey, to Lunéville, to that *pied à terre* in Paris; resistance avails not; here, as in so many other cases, *il faut se ranger.* Sometimes, precisely on the eve of such a departure, her domestics, exasperated by hunger and ill usage, will strike work, in a body; and a new set has to be collected at an hour's warning. Then Madame has been known to keep the postilions cracking and *sacre*-ing at the gate from dawn till dewy eve, simply because she was playing cards, and the games went against her. But figure a lean and vivid-tempered philosopher starting from Paris at last; under cloud of night; during hard frost; in a huge lumbering coach, or rather wagon, compared with which, indeed, the generality of modern wagons were a luxurious conveyance. With four starved, and perhaps spavined hacks, he slowly sets forth, 'under a mountain of bandboxes:' at his side sits the wandering virago; in front of him, a serving-maid, with additional bandboxes '*et divers effets de sa maîtresse.*' At the next stage, the postilions have to be beat up; they come out swearing. Cloaks and fur-pelisses avail little against the January cold; 'time and hours' are, once more, the only hope; but, lo, at the tenth mile, this Tyburn-coach breaks down! One many-voiced discordant wail shrieks through the solitude, making night hideous, — but in vain; the axletree has given way, the vehicle has overset, and marchionesses, chambermaids, bandboxes and philosophers, are weltering in inextricable chaos.

'The carriage was in the stage next Nangis, about half-way to that town, when the hind axletree broke, and it tumbled on the road, to M. de Voltaire's side: Madame du Châtelet, and her maid, fell above him, with all their bundles and bandboxes, for these were not tied to the front, but only piled up on both hands of the maid; and so, observing the laws of equilibrium and gravitation of bodies, they rushed towards the corner where M. de Voltaire lay squeezed together. Under so many burdens, which half suffocated him, he kept shouting bitterly (*poussait des cris aigus*); but it was impossible to change place; all had to remain as it was, till the two lackeys, one of whom was hurt by the fall, could come up, with the postilions, to disencumber the vehicle; they first drew out all the luggage, next the women, then M. de Voltaire. Nothing could be got out except by the top, that is, by the coach-door, which now opened upwards:

one of the lackeys and a postilion clambering aloft, and fixing themselves on the body of the vehicle, drew them up, as from a well; seizing the first limb that came to hand, whether arm or leg; and then passed them down to the two stationed below, who set them finally on the ground.' [1]

What would Dr. Kitchiner, with his *Traveller's Oracle*, have said to all this? For there is snow on the ground: and four peasants must be roused from a village half a league off, before that accursed vehicle can so much as be lifted from its beam-ends! Vain it is for Longchamp, far in advance, sheltered in a hospitable though half-dismantled *château*, to pluck pigeons and be in haste to roast them: they will never, never be eaten to supper, scarcely to breakfast next morning! — Nor is it now only, but several times, that this unhappy axletree plays them foul; nay once, beggared by Madame's gambling, they have not cash to pay for mending it, and the smith, though they are in keenest flight, almost for their lives, will not trust them.

We imagine that these are trying things for any philosopher. Of the thousand other more private and perennial grievances; of certain discoveries and explanations, especially, which it still seems surprising that human philosophy could have tolerated, we make no mention; indeed, with regard to the latter, few earthly considerations could tempt a Reviewer of sensibility to mention them in this place.

The Marquise du Châtelet, and her husband, have been much wondered at in England: the calm magnanimity with which M. le Marquis conforms to the custom of the country, to the wishes of his helpmate, and leaves her, he himself meanwhile fighting, or at least drilling, for his King, to range over Space, in quest of loves and lovers; his friendly discretion, in this particular; no less so, his blithe benignant gullibility, the instant a *contretemps de famille* renders his countenance needful, — have had all justice done them among us. His lady too is a wonder; offers no mean

[1] Vol. ii. p. 166.

study to psychologists: she is a fair experiment to try how far that Delicacy, which we reckon innate in females, is only incidental and the product of fashion; how far a woman, not merely immodest, but without the slightest fig-leaf of common decency remaining, with the whole character, in short, of a *male* debauchee, may still have any moral worth as a woman. We ourselves have wondered a little over both these parties; and over the goal to which so strange a 'progress of society' might be tending. But still more wonderful, not without a shade of the sublime, has appeared to us the cheerful thraldom of this maltreated philosopher; and with what exhaustless patience, not being wedded, he endured all these forced-marches, whims, irascibilities, delinquencies and thousandfold unreasons; braving 'the battle and the breeze,' on that wild Bay of Biscay, for such a period. Fifteen long years, and was not mad, or a suicide at the end of them! But the like fate, it would seem, though worthy D'Israeli has omitted to enumerate it in his *Calamities of Authors*, is not unknown in literature. Pope also had his Mrs. Martha Blount; and, in the midst of that warfare with united Duncedom, his daily tale of Egyptian bricks to bake. Let us pity the lot of genius, in this sublunary sphere!

Every one knows the earthly termination of Madame la Marquise; and how, by a strange, almost satirical *Nemesis*, she was taken in her own nets, and her worst sin became her final punishment. To no purpose was the unparalleled credulity of M. le Marquis; to no purpose, the amplest toleration, and even helpful knavery of M. de Voltaire; '*les assiduités de M. de Saint-Lambert*,' and the unimaginable consultations to which they gave rise at Cirey, were frightfully parodied in the end. The last scene was at Lunéville, in the peaceable court of King Stanislaus.

'Seeing that the aromatic vinegar did no good, we tried to recover her from the sudden lethargy by rubbing her feet, and striking in the palms of her hands; but it was of no use: she had ceased to be. The maid was sent off to Madame de Boufflers' apartment, to inform the company that Madame du Châtelet was worse. Instantly they all rose from the supper-table: M. du Châtelet, M. de Voltaire, and the other guests, rushed into the room. So soon as they understood the truth, there was a deep consternation; to tears, to cries, succeeded a mournful silence. The husband was led away, the other individuals went out successively, expressing the keenest sorrow. M. de Voltaire and M. de Saint-Lambert remained the last by the bedside, from which they could not be drawn away. At length, the former, absorbed in deep grief, left the room, and with difficulty reached the main door of the Castle, not knowing whither he went. Arrived there, he fell down at the foot of the outer stairs, and near the box of a sentry, where his head came on the pavement. His lackey, who was following, seeing him fall and struggle on the ground, ran forward and tried to lift him. At this moment, M. de Saint-Lambert, retiring by the same way, also arrived; and observing M. de Voltaire in that situation, hastened to assist the lackey. No sooner was M. de Voltaire on his feet, than opening his eyes, dimmed with tears, and recognising M. de Saint-Lambert, he said to him, with sobs and the most pathetic accent: "Ah, my friend, it is you that have killed her!" Then, all on a sudden, as if he were starting from a deep sleep, he exclaimed in a tone of reproach and despair: "*Eh! mon Dieu! Monsieur, de quoi vous avisiez-vous de lui faire un enfant?*" They parted thereupon, without adding a single word; and retired to their several apartments, overwhelmed and almost annihilated by the excess of their sorrow.'[1]

Among all threnetical discourses on record, this last, between men overwhelmed and almost annihilated by the excess of their sorrow, has probably an unexampled character. Some days afterwards, the first paroxysm of 'reproach and despair' being somewhat assuaged, the sorrowing widower, not the glad legal one, composed this quatrain:

L'univers a perdu la sublime Emilie.
Elle aima les plaisirs, les arts, la vérité:
Les dieux, en lui donnant leur âme et leur génie,
N'avaient gardé pour eux que l'immortalité.

After which, reflecting, perhaps, that with this sublime Emilia, so meritoriously singular in loving pleasure, 'his happiness had been chiefly on paper,' he, like the bereaved Universe, consoled himself, and went on his way.

[1] Vol. ii. p. 250.

Woman, it has been sufficiently demonstrated, was given to man as a benefit, and for mutual support; a precious ornament and staff whereupon to lean in many trying situations: but to Voltaire she proved, so unlucky was he in this matter, little else than a broken reed, which only ran into his hand. We confess that, looking over the manifold trials of this poor philosopher with the softer, or as he may have reckoned it, the harder sex,—from that Dutchwoman who published his juvenile letters, to the Niece Denis who as good as killed him with racketing,—we see, in this one province, very great scope for almost all the cardinal virtues. And to these internal convulsions add an incessant series of controversies and persecutions, political, religious, literary, from without; and we have a life quite rent asunder, horrent with asperities and chasms, where even a stout traveller might have faltered. Over all which Chamouni-Needles and Staubbach-Falls the great *Persifleur* skims along in this his little poetical air-ship, more softly than if he travelled the smoothest of merely prosaic roads.

Leaving out of view the worth or worthlessness of such a temper of mind, we are bound, in all seriousness, to say, both that it seems to have been Voltaire's highest conception of moral excellence, and that he has pursued and realised it with no small success. One great praise therefore he deserves,—that of unity with himself; that of *having* an aim, and stedfastly endeavouring after it, nay, as we have found, of attaining it; for his ideal Voltaire seems, to an unusual degree, manifested, made practically apparent in the real one. There can be no doubt but this attainment of *Persifleur*, in the wide sense we here give it, was of all others the most admired and sought after in Voltaire's age and country; nay, in our own age and country we have still innumerable admirers of it, and unwearied seekers after it, on every hand of us: nevertheless, we cannot but believe that its acme is past; that the best sense of our generation has already weighed its significance, and found it wanting. Voltaire himself, it seems to us, were he alive at this day, would find other tasks than that of mockery, especially of mockery in that style: it is not by Derision and Denial, but by far deeper, more earnest, diviner means that aught truly great has been effected for mankind; that the fabric of man's life has been reared, through long centuries, to its present height. If we admit that this chief of *Persifleurs* had a steady conscious aim in life, the still higher praise of having had a right or noble aim cannot be conceded him without many limitations, and may, plausibly enough, be altogether denied.

At the same time, let it not be forgotten, that amid all these blighting influences, Voltaire maintains a certain indestructible humanity of nature; a soul never deaf to the cry of wretchedness; never utterly blind to the light of truth, beauty, goodness. It is even, in some measure, poetically interesting to observe this fine contradiction in him: the heart acting without directions from the head, or perhaps against its directions; the man virtuous, as it were, in spite of himself. For at all events, it will be granted that, as a private man, his existence was beneficial, not hurtful, to his fellow-men: the Calases, the Sirvens, and so many orphans and outcasts whom he cherished and protected, ought to cover a multitude of sins. It was his own sentiment, and to all appearance a sincere one:

J'ai fait un peu de bien; c'est mon meilleur ouvrage.

Perhaps there are few men, with such principles and such temptations as his were, that could have led such a life; few that could have done his work, and come through it with cleaner hands. If we call him the greatest of all *Persifleurs*, let us add that, morally speaking also, he is the best: if he excels all men in universality, sincerity, polished clearness of Mockery, he perhaps combines with it as much worth of heart as, in any man, that habit can admit of.

It is now wellnigh time that we should quit this part of our subject: nevertheless, in seeking to form some picture of Voltaire's practical life, and the character, outward as well as inward, of his appearance in society, our readers will not grudge us a few glances at the last and most striking scene he enacted there. To our view, that final visit to Paris has a strange half-frivolous, half-fateful aspect; there is, as it were, a sort of dramatic justice in this catastrophe, that he, who had all his life hungered and thirsted after public favour, should at length die by excess of it; should find the door of his Heaven-on-earth unexpectedly thrown wide open, and enter there, only to be, as he himself said, 'smothered under roses.' Had Paris any suitable theogony or theology, as Rome and Athens had, this might almost be reckoned, as those Ancients accounted of death by lightning, a sacred death, a death from the gods; from their many-headed god, POPULARITY. In the benignant quietude of Ferney, Voltaire had lived long, and as his friends calculated, might still have lived long; but a series of trifling causes lures him to Paris, and in three months he is no more. At all hours of his history, he might have said with Alexander: "O Athenians, what toil do I undergo to please you!" and the last pleasure his Athenians demand of him is, that he would die for them.

Considered with reference to the world at large, this journey is farther remarkable. It is the most splendid triumph of that nature recorded in these ages; the loudest and showiest homage ever paid to what we moderns call Literature; to a man that had merely thought, and published his thoughts. Much false tumult, no doubt, there was in it; yet also a certain deeper significance. It is interesting to see how universal and eternal in man is love of wisdom; how the highest and the lowest, how supercilious princes, and rude peasants, and all men must alike show honour to Wisdom, or the appearance of Wisdom; nay, properly speaking, can show honour to nothing else. For it is not in the power of all Xerxes' hosts to bend one thought of our proud heart: these 'may destroy the case of Anaxarchus;

himself they cannot reach:' only to spiritual worth can the spirit do reverence; only in a soul deeper and better than ours can we see any heavenly mystery, and in humbling ourselves feel ourselves exalted. That the so ebullient enthusiasm of the French was in this case perfectly well directed, we cannot undertake to say: yet we rejoice to see and know that such a principle exists perennially in man's inmost bosom; that there is no heart so sunk and stupefied, none so withered and pampered, but the felt presence of a nobler heart will inspire it and lead it captive.

Few royal progresses, few Roman triumphs, have equalled this long triumph of Voltaire. On his journey, at Bourg-en Bresse, 'he was recognised,' says Wagnière, 'while the 'horses were changing, and in a few moments the whole 'town crowded about the carriage; so that he was forced 'to lock himself for some time in a room of the inn.' The Maître-de-poste ordered his postilion to yoke better horses, and said to him with a broad oath: "*Va bon train, crève mes chevaux, je m'en f—; tu mènes M. de Voltaire.*" At Dijon, there were persons of distinction that wished even to dress themselves as waiters, that they might serve him at supper, and see him by this stratagem.

'At the barrier of Paris,' continues Wagnière, 'the officers asked if we had nothing with us contrary to the King's regulations: "On my word, gentlemen, *Ma foi, Messieurs,*" replied M. de Voltaire, "I believe there is nothing contraband here except myself." I alighted from the carriage, that the inspector might more readily examine it. One of the guards said to his comrade: *C'est, pardieu! M. de Voltaire.* He plucked at the coat of the person who was searching, and repeated the same words, looking fixedly at me. I could not help laughing; then all gazing with the greatest astonishment mingled with respect, begged M. de Voltaire to pass on whither he pleased.'[1]

Intelligence soon circulated over Paris; scarcely could the arrival of Kien-Long, or the Grand Lama of Thibet, have excited greater ferment. Poor Longchamp, demitted, or

[1] Vol. i. p. 121.

rather dismissed from Voltaire's service, eight-and-twenty years before, and now, as a retired map-dealer (having resigned in favour of his son), living quietly '*dans un petit logement à part*,' a fine smooth, garrulous old man, — heard the news next morning in his remote *logement*, in the Estrapade; and instantly huddled on his clothes, though he had not been out for two days, to go and see what truth was in it.

'Several persons of my acquaintance, whom I met, told me that they had heard the same. I went purposely to the *Café Procope*, where this news formed the subject of conversation among several politicians, or men of letters, who talked of it, with warmth. To assure myself still farther, I walked thence towards the *Quai des Theatins*, where he had alighted the night before, and, as was said, taken up his lodging in a mansion near the church. Coming out from the Rue de la Seine, I saw afar off a great number of people gathered on the Quai, not far from the Pont-Royal. Approaching nearer, I observed that this crowd was collected in front of the Marquis de Villette's Hôtel, at the corner of the Rue de Beaune. I inquired what the matter was. The people answered me, that M. de Voltaire was in that house; and they were waiting to see him when he came out. They were not sure, however, whether he would come out that day; for it was natural to think that an old man of eighty-four might need a day or two of rest. From that moment, I no longer doubted the arrival of M. de Voltaire in Paris.' [1]

By dint of address, Longchamp, in process of time, contrived to see his old master; had an interview of ten minutes; was for falling at his feet; and wept, with sad presentiments, at parting. Ten such minutes were a great matter; for Voltaire had his levees, and couchées, more crowded than those of any Emperor; princes and peers thronged his antechamber; and when he went abroad, his carriage was as the nucleus of a comet, whose train extended over whole districts of the city. He himself, says Wagnière, expressed dissatisfaction at much of this. Nevertheless, there were some plaudits which, as he confessed, went to his heart. Condorcet mentions that once a person in the crowd,

[1] Vol. ii. p. 353.

inquiring who this great man was, a poor woman answered, "*C'est le sauveur des Calas.*" Of a quite different sort was the tribute paid him by a quack, in the Place Louis Quinze, haranguing a mixed multitude on the art of juggling with cards: "*Here,* gentlemen," said he, "is a trick I learned at Ferney, from that great man who makes so much noise among you, that famous M. de Voltaire, the master of us all!" In fact, mere gaping curiosity, and even ridicule, was abroad, as well as real enthusiasm. The clergy too were recoiling into ominous groups; already some Jesuitic drums ecclesiastic had beat to arms.

Figuring the lean, tottering, lonely old man in the midst of all this, how he looks into it, clear and alert, though no longer strong and calm, we feel drawn towards him by some tie of affection, of kindly sympathy. Longchamp says, he appeared 'extremely worn, though still in the possession 'of all his senses, and with a very firm voice.' The following little sketch, by a hostile journalist of the day, has fixed itself deeply with us:

'M. de Voltaire appeared in full dress, on Tuesday, for the first time since his arrival in Paris. He had on a red coat lined with ermine; a large peruke, in the fashion of Louis XIV., black, unpowdered; and in which his withered visage was so buried that you saw only his two eyes shining like carbuncles. His head was surmounted by a square red cap in the form of a crown, which seemed only laid on. He had in his hand a small nibbed cane; and the public of Paris, not accustomed to see him in this accoutrement, laughed a good deal. This personage, singular in all, wishes doubtless to have nothing in common with ordinary men.' [1]

This head, — this wondrous microcosm in the *grande perruque à la Louis XIV.*, — was so soon to be distenanted of all its cunning gifts; these eyes, shining like carbuncles, were so soon to be closed in long night! — We must now give the coronation ceremony, of which the reader may have heard so much: borrowing from this same sceptical hand, which, however, is vouched for by Wagnière; as, indeed, La

[1] Vol. ii. p. 466.

Harpe's more heroical narrative of that occurrence is well known, and hardly differs from the following, except in style:

'On Monday, M. de Voltaire, resolving to enjoy the triumph which had been so long promised him, mounted his carriage, that azure-coloured vehicle, bespangled with gold stars, which a wag called the chariot of the empyrean; and so repaired to the Académie Française, which that day had a special meeting. Twenty-two members were present. None of the prelates, abbés or other ecclesiastics who belong to it, would attend, or take part in these singular deliberations. The sole exceptions were the Abbés de Boismont and Millot; the one a court rake-hell (*roué*), with nothing but the guise of his profession; the other a varlet (*cuistre*), having no favour to look for, either from the Court or the Church.

'The Académie went out to meet M. de Voltaire: he was led to the Director's seat, which that office-bearer and the meeting invited him to accept. His portrait had been hung up above it. The company, without drawing lots, as is the custom, proceeded to work, and named him, by acclamation, Director for the April quarter. The old man, once set a-going, was about to talk a great deal; but they told him, that they valued his health too much to hear him, — that they would reduce him to silence. M. d'Alembert accordingly occupied the session, by reading his *Eloge de Despréaux*, which had already been communiated on a public occasion, and where he had inserted various flattering things for the present visitor.

'M. de Voltaire then signified a wish to visit the Secretary of the Académie, whose apartments are above. With this gentleman he stayed some time; and at last set out for the Comédie Française. The court of the Louvre, vast as it is, was full of people waiting for him. So soon as his notable vehicle came in sight, the cry arose, *Le voilà!* The Savoyards, the apple-women, all the rabble of the quarter had assembled there; and the acclamations, *Vive Voltaire!* resounded as if they would never end. The Marquis de Villette, who had arrived before, came to hand him out of his carriage, where the Procureur Clos was seated beside him: both these gave him their arms, and could scarcely extricate him from the press. On his entering the playhouse, a crowd of more elegance, and seized with true enthusiasm for genius, surrounded him: the ladies, above all, threw themselves in his way, and stopped it, the better to look at him; some were seen squeezing forward to touch his clothes; some plucking hair from his fur. M. le Duc de Chartres,[1] not caring to advance too near, showed, though at a distance, no less curiosity than others.

[1] Afterwards Egalité.

'The saint, or rather the god, of the evening, was to occupy the box belonging to the Gentlemen of the Bedchamber,[1] opposite that of the Comte d'Artois. Madame Denis and Madame de Villette were already there; and the pit was in convulsions of joy, awaiting the moment when the poet should appear. There was no end till he placed himself on the front seat, beside the ladies. Then rose a cry: *La Couronne!* and Brizard, the actor, came and put the garland on his head. "Ah, Heaven! will you kill me then? (*Ah, Dieu! vous voulez donc me faire mourir?*)" cried M. de Voltaire, weeping with joy, and resisting this honour. He took the crown in his hand, and presented it to *Belle-et-Bonne:*[2] she withstood; and the Prince de Beauvau, seizing the laurel, replaced it on the head of our Sophocles, who could refuse no longer.

'The piece (*Irène*) was played, and with more applause than usual, though scarcely with enough to correspond to this triumph of its author. Meanwhile the players were in straits as to what they should do; and during their deliberations the tragedy ended; the curtain fell, and the tumult of the people was extreme, till it rose again, disclosing a show like that of the *Centênaire*. M. de Voltaire's bust, which had been placed shortly before in the *foyer* (greenroom) of the Comédie Française, had been brought upon the stage, and elevated on a pedestal; the whole body of comedians stood round it in a semicircle, with palms and garlands in their hands; there was a crown already on the bust. The pealing of musical flourishes, of drums, of trumpets, had announced the ceremony; and Madame Vestris held in her hand a paper, which was soon understood to contain verses, lately composed by the Marquis de Saint-Marc. She recited them with an emphasis proportioned to the extravagance of the scene. They ran as follows:

Aux yeux de Paris enchanté,
Reçois en ce jour un hommage,
Que confirmera d'âge en âge
La sévère postérité!

Non, tu n'as pas besoin d' atteindre au noir rivage
Pour jouir des honneurs de l' immortalité!

VOLTAIRE, *reçois la couronne*
Que l'on vient de te présenter;
Il est beau de la mériter,
Quand c'est la France qui la donne![3]

[1] He himself, as is perhaps too well known, was one.

[2] The Marquise de Villette, a foster-child of his.

[3] As Dryden said of Swift, so may we say: Our cousin Saint-Marc has no turn for poetry.

This was encored: the actress recited it again. Next, each of them went forward and laid his garland round the bust. Mademoiselle Fanier, in a fanatical ecstasy, kissed it, and all the others imitated her.

'This long ceremony, accompanied with infinite *vivats*, being over, the curtain again dropped; and when it rose for *Nanine*, one of M. de Voltaire's comedies, his bust was seen on the right-hand side of the stage, where it remained during the whole play.

'M. le Comte d'Artois did not choose to show himself too openly; but being informed, according to his orders, as soon as M. de Voltaire appeared in the theatre, he had gone thither incognito; and it is thought that the old man, once when he went out for a moment, had the honour of a short interview with his Royal Highness.

'*Nanine* finished, comes a new hurlyburly; a new trial for the modesty of our philosopher! He had got into his carriage, but the people would not let him go; they threw themselves on the horses, they kissed them: some young poets even cried to unyoke these animals, and draw the modern Apollo home with their own arms; unhappily, there were not enthusiasts enough to volunteer this service, and he at last got leave to depart, not without *vivats*, which he may have heard on the Pont-Royal, and even in his own house. . . .

'M. de Voltaire, on reaching home, wept anew; and modestly protested that if he had known the people were to play so many follies, he would not have gone.'

On all these wonderful proceedings we shall leave our readers to their own reflections; remarking only, that this happened on the 30th of March (1778), and that on the 30th of May, about the same hour, the object of such extraordinary adulation was in the article of death; the hearse already prepared to receive his remains, for which even a grave had to be stolen. 'He expired,' says Wagnière, 'about a quarter past eleven at night, with the most perfect 'tranquillity, after having suffered the cruellest pains, in 'consequence of those fatal drugs, which his own imprudence, and especially that of the persons who should have looked to it, made him swallow. Ten minutes before his last breath, he took the hand of Morand, his valet-de-chambre, who was watching by him; pressed it, and said: '"*Adieu, mon cher Morand, je me meurs*, Adieu, my dear

'Morand, I am gone." These are the last words uttered by 'M. de Voltaire.'[1]

We have still to consider this man in his specially intellectual capacity; which, as with every man of letters, is to be regarded as the clearest, and, to all practical intents, the most important aspect of him. Voltaire's intellectual endowment and acquirement, his talent or genius as a literary

[1] On this sickness of Voltaire, and his death-bed deportment, many foolish books have been written; concerning which it is not necessary to say anything. The conduct of the Parisian clergy, on that occasion, seems totally unworthy of their cloth; nor was their reward, so far as concerns these individuals, inappropriate: that of finding themselves once more bilked, once more *persiflés* by that strange old man, in his last decrepitude, who, in his strength, had wrought them and others so many griefs. Surely the parting agonies of a fellow mortal, when the spirit of our brother, rapt in the whirlwinds and thick ghastly vapours of death, clutches blindly for help, and no help is there, are not the scenes where a wise faith would seek to exult, when it can no longer hope to alleviate! For the rest, to touch farther on those their idle tales of dying horrors, remorse and the like; to write of such, to believe them, or disbelieve them, or in anywise discuss them, were but a continuation of the same ineptitude. He who, after the imperturbable exit of so many Cartouches and Thurtells, in every age of the world, can continue to regard the manner of a man's death as a test of his religious orthodoxy, may boast himself impregnable to merely terrestrial logic. Voltaire had enough of suffering, and of mean enough suffering, to encounter, without any addition from theological despair. His last interview with the clergy, who had been sent for by his friends, that the rites of burial might not be denied him, is thus described by Wagnière, as it has been by all other credible reporters of it:

'Two days before that mournful death, M. l'Abbé Mignot, his nephew, 'went to seek the Curé of Saint-Sulpice and the Abbé Guatier, and 'brought them into his uncle's sick-room; who, being informed that the 'Abbé Guatier was there, "Ah, well!" said he, "give him my compli'ments and my thanks." The Abbé spoke some words to him, exhorting 'him to patience. The Curé of Saint-Sulpice then came forward, having 'announced himself, and asked of M. de Voltaire, elevating his voice, if he 'acknowledged the divinity of our Lord Jesus Christ? The sick man 'pushed one of his hands against the Curé's *calotte* (coif), shoving him 'back, and cried, turning abruptly to the other side, "Let me die in 'peace (*Laissez-moi mourir en paix*)!" The Curé seemingly considered his person soiled, and his coif dishonoured, by the touch of a philosopher. He made the sicknurse give him a little brushing, and then went out with the Abbé Guatier.' Vol. i. p. 161.

man, lies opened to us in a series of Writings, unexampled, as we believe, in two respects, — their extent, and their diversity. Perhaps there is no writer, not a mere compiler, but writing from his own invention or elaboration, who has left so many volumes behind him; and if to the merely arithmetical, we add a critical estimate, the singularity is still greater; for these volumes are not written without an appearance of due care and preparation; perhaps there is not one altogether feeble and confused treatise, nay one feeble and confused sentence, to be found in them. As to variety, again, they range nearly over all human subjects; from Theology down to Domestic Economy; from the Familiar Letter to the Political History; from the Pasquinade to the Epic Poem. Some strange gift, or union of gifts, must have been at work here; for the result is, at least, in the highest degree uncommon, and to be wondered at, if not to be admired.

If, through all this many-coloured versatility, we try to decipher the essential, distinctive features of Voltaire's intellect, it seems to us that we find there a counterpart to our theory of his moral character; as, indeed, if that theory was accurate, we must do: for the thinking and the moral nature, distinguished by the necessities of speech, have no such distinction in themselves; but, rightly examined, exhibit in every case the strictest sympathy and correspondence, are, indeed, but different phases of the same indissoluble unity, — a living mind. In life, Voltaire was found to be without good claim to the title of philosopher; and now, in literature, and for similar reasons, we find in him the same deficiencies. Here too it is not greatness, but the very extreme of expertness, that we recognise; not strength, so much as agility, not depth, but superficial extent. That truly surprising ability seems rather the unparalleled combination of many common talents, than the exercise of any finer or higher one: for here too the want of earnestness, of intense continuance, is fatal to him. He has the eye of a lynx; sees deeper, at the first glance, than any other man; but no second glance is given. Thus Truth, which to the philosopher, has from of old been said to live in a well, remains for the most part hidden from him; we may say forever hidden, if we take the highest, and only philosophical species of Truth; for this does not reveal itself to any mortal, without quite another sort of meditation than Voltaire ever seems to have bestowed on it. In fact, his deductions are uniformly of a forensic, argumentative, immediately practical nature; often true, we will admit, so far as they go; but not the whole truth; and false, when taken for the whole. In regard to feeling, it is the same with him: he is, in general, humane, mildly affectionate, not without touches of nobleness; but light, fitful, discontinuous; 'a smart freethinker, all things in an hour.' He is no Poet and Philosopher, but a popular sweet Singer and Haranguer: in all senses, and in all styles, a *Concionator*, which, for the most part, will turn out to be an altogether different character. It is true, in this last province he stands unrivalled; for such an audience, the most fit and perfectly persuasive of all preachers: but in many far higher provinces, he is neither perfect nor unrivalled; has been often surpassed; was surpassed even in his own age and nation. For a decisive, thorough-going, in any measure gigantic force of thought, he is far inferior to Diderot: with all the liveliness he has not the soft elegance, with more than the wit he has but a small portion of the wisdom, that belonged to Fontenelle: as in real sensibility, so in the delineation of it, in pathos, loftiness and earnest eloquence, he cannot, making all fair abatements, and there are many, be compared with Rousseau.

Doubtless, an astonishing fertility, quickness, address; an openness also, and universal susceptibility of mind, must have belonged to him. As little can we deny that he manifests an assiduous perseverance, a capability of long-continued exertion, strange in so volatile a man; and consummate skill in husbanding and wisely directing his exertion.

The very knowledge he had amassed, granting, which is but partly true, that it was superficial remembered knowledge, might have distinguished him as a mere Dutch commentator. From Newton's *Principia* to the *Shaster* and *Vedam*, nothing has escaped him: he has glanced into all literatures and all sciences; nay studied in them, for he can speak a rational word on all. It is known, for instance, that he understood Newton when no other man in France understood him: indeed, his countrymen may call Voltaire their discoverer of intellectual England; — a discovery, it is true, rather of the Curtis than of the Columbus sort, yet one which in his day still remained to be made. Nay from all sides he brings new light into his country: now, for the first time, to the upturned wondering eyes of Frenchmen in general, does it become clear that Thought has actually a kind of existence in other kingdoms; that some glimmerings of civilisation had dawned here and there on the human species, prior to the *Siècle de Louis Quatorze*. Of Voltaire's acquaintance with History, at least with what he called History, be it civil, religious, or literary; of his innumerable, indescribable collection of facts, gathered from all sources, — from European Chronicles and State Papers, from eastern *Zends* and Jewish *Talmuds*, we need not remind any reader. It has been objected that his information was often borrowed at second-hand; that he had his plodders and pioneers, whom, as living dictionaries, he skilfully consulted in time of need. This also seems to be partly true, but deducts little from our estimate of him: for the skill *so* to borrow is even rarer than the power to lend. Voltaire's knowledge is not a mere show-room of curiosities, but truly a museum for purposes of teaching; every object is in its place, and there for its uses: nowhere do we find confusion or vain display; everywhere intention, instructiveness and the clearest order.

Perhaps it is this very power of Order, of rapid perspicuous Arrangement, that lies at the root of Voltaire's best gifts; or rather, we should say, it is that keen, accurate intellectual vision, from which, to a mind of any intensity, Order naturally arises. The clear quick vision, and the methodic arrangement which springs from it, are looked upon as peculiarly French qualities; and Voltaire, at all times, manifests them in a more than French degree. Let him but cast his eye over any subject, in a moment he sees, though indeed only to a short depth, yet with instinctive decision, where the main bearings of it for that short depth lie; what is, or appears to be, its logical coherence; how causes connect them selves with effects; how the whole is to be seized, and in lucid sequence represented to his own or to other minds. In this respect, moreover, it is happy for him that, below the short depth alluded to, his view does not properly grow dim, but altogether terminates: thus there is nothing farther to occasion him misgivings; has he not already sounded into that basis of bottomless Darkness on which all things firmly rest? What lies below is delusion, imagination, some form of Superstition or Folly; which he, nothing doubting, altogether casts away. Accordingly, he is the most intelligible of writers; everywhere transparent at a glance. There is no delineation or disquisition of his, that has not its whole purport written on its forehead; all is precise, all is rightly adjusted; that keen spirit of Order shows itself in the whole, and in every line of the whole.

If we say that this power of Arrangement, as applied both to the acquisition and to the communication of ideas, is Voltaire's most serviceable faculty in all his enterprises, we say nothing singular: for take the word in its largest acceptation, and it comprehends the whole office of Understanding, logically so called; is the means whereby man accomplishes whatever, in the way of outward force, has been made possible for him; conquers all practical obstacles, and rises to be the 'king of this lower world.' It is the organ of all that Knowledge which can properly be reckoned synonymous with Power; for hereby man strikes with wise aim, into the infinite agencies of Nature, and multiplies his own small strength to unlimited degrees. It has been said also that man may rise to be the 'god of this lower world;' but that is a far loftier height, not attainable by such power-knowledge, but by quite another sort, for which Voltaire in particular shows hardly any aptitude.

In truth, readily as we have recognised his spirit of Method, with its many uses, we are far from ascribing to him any perceptible portion of that greatest praise in thinking, or in writing, the praise of philosophic, still less of poetic Method; which, especially the latter, must be the fruit of deep feeling as well as of clear vision, — of genius as well as talent; and is much more likely to be found in the compositions of a Hooker or a Shakspeare than of a Voltaire. The Method discernible in Voltaire, and this on all subjects whatever, is a purely business Method. The order that arises from it is not Beauty, but, at best, Regularity. His objects do not lie round him in pictorial, not always in scientific grouping; but rather in commodious rows, where each may be seen and come at, like goods in a well-kept warehouse. We might say, there is not the deep natural symmetry of a forest oak, but the simple artificial symmetry of a parlour chandelier. Compare, for example, the plan of the *Henriade* to that of our so barbarous *Hamlet.* The plan of the former is a geometrical diagram by Fermat; that of the latter a cartoon by Raphael. The *Henriade*, as we see it completed, is a polished square-built Tuileries: *Hamlet* is a mysterious star-paved Valhalla and dwelling of the gods.

Nevertheless, Voltaire's style of Method is, as we have said, a business one; and for his purposes more available than any other. It carries him swiftly through his work, and carries his reader swiftly through it; there is a prompt intelligence between the two; the whole meaning is communicated clearly, and comprehended without effort. From this also it may follow, that Voltaire will please the young more than he does the old; that the first perusal of him will please better than the second, if indeed any second be thought necessary. But what merit (and it is considerable) the pleasure and profit of this first perusal presupposes, must be honestly allowed him. Herein, it seems to us, lies the grand quality in all his performances. These Histories of his, for instance, are felt, in spite of their sparkling rapidity, and knowing air of philosophic insight, to be among the shallowest of all histories; mere beadrolls of exterior occurrences, of battles, edifices, enactments, and other quite superficial phenomena; yet being clear beadrolls, well adapted for memory, and recited in a lively tone, we listen with satisfaction, and learn somewhat; learn much, if we began knowing nothing. Nay sometimes the summary, in its skilful though crowded arrangement, and brilliant well-defined outlines, has almost a poetical as well as a didactic merit. *Charles the Twelfth* may still pass for a model in that often-attempted species of Biography: the clearest details are given in the fewest words; we have sketches of strange men and strange countries, of wars, adventures, negotiations, in a style which, for graphic brevity, rivals that of Sallust. It is a line-engraving, on a reduced scale, of that Swede and his mad life; without colours, yet not without the fore-shortenings and perspective observances, nay not altogether without the deeper harmonies, which belong to a true Picture. In respect of composition, whatever may be said of its accuracy or worth otherwise, we cannot but reckon it greatly the best of Voltaire's Histories.

In his other prose works, in his Novels, and innumerable Essays and fugitive pieces, the same clearness of order, the same rapid precision of view, again forms a distinguishing merit. His *Zadigs* and *Baboucs* and *Candides*, which, considered as products of imagination, perhaps rank higher with foreigners than any of his professedly poetical performances, are instinct with this sort of intellectual life: the sharpest glances, though from an oblique point of sight, into at least the surface of human life, into the old familiar world of business; which truly, from his oblique station, looks oblique enough, and yields store of ridiculous combinations. The Wit, manifested chiefly in these and the like performances, but ever flowing, unless purposely restrained, in boundless abundance from Voltaire's mind, has been often and duly celebrated. It lay deep-rooted in his nature; the inevitable produce of such an understanding with such a character, and was from the first likely, as it actually proved in the latter period of his life, to become the main dialect in which he spoke and even thought. Doing all justice to the inexhaustible readiness, the quick force, the polished acuteness of Voltaire's Wit, we may remark, at the same time, that it was nowise the highest species of employment for such a mind as his; that, indeed, it ranks essentially among the lowest species even of Ridicule. It is at all times mere logical pleasantry; a gaiety of the head, not of the heart; there is scarcely a twinkling of Humour in the whole of his numberless sallies. Wit of this sort cannot maintain a demure sedateness; a grave yet infinitely kind aspect, warming the inmost soul with true loving mirth; it has not even the force to laugh outright, but can only sniff and titter. It grounds itself, not on fond sportful sympathy, but on contempt, or at best on indifference. It stands related to Humour as Prose does to Poetry; of which, in this department at least, Voltaire exhibits no symptom. The most determinedly ludicrous composition of his, the *Pucelle*, which cannot, on other grounds, be recommended to any reader, has no higher merit than that of an audacious caricature. True, he is not a buffoon; seldom or never violates the rules, we shall not say of propriety, yet of good breeding: to this negative praise he is entitled. But as for any high claim to positive praise, it cannot be made good. We look in vain, through his whole writings, for one lineament of a *Quixote* or a *Shandy;* even of a *Hudibras* or *Battle of the Books.* Indeed it has been more than once observed, that Humour is not a national gift with the French in late times; that since Montaigne's day it seems to have wellnigh vanished from among them.

Considered in his technical capacity of Poet, Voltaire need not, at present, detain us very long. Here too his excellence is chiefly intellectual, and shown in the way of business-like method. Everything is well calculated for a given end; there is the utmost logical fitness of sentiment, of incident, of general contrivance. Nor is he without an enthusiasm that sometimes resembles inspiration; a clear fellow-feeling for the personages of his scene he always has; with a chameleon susceptibility he takes some hue of every object; if he cannot *be* that object, he at least plausibly enacts it. Thus we have a result everywhere consistent with itself; a contrivance, not without nice adjustments and brilliant aspects, which pleases with that old pleasure of 'difficulties overcome,' and the visible correspondence of means to end. That the deeper portion of our soul sits silent, unmoved under all this; recognising no universal, everlasting Beauty, but only a modish Elegance, less the work of a poetical creation than a process of the toilette, need occasion no surprise. It signifies only that Voltaire was a French poet, and wrote as the French people of that day required and approved. We have long known that French poetry aimed at a different result from ours; that its splendour was what we should call a dead, artificial one; not the manifold soft summer glories of Nature, but a cold splendour, as of polished metal.

On the whole, in reading Voltaire's poetry, that adventure of the *Café de Procope* should ever be held in mind. He was not without an eye to have looked, had he seen others looking, into the deepest nature of poetry; nor has he failed here and there to cast a glance in that direction: but what preferment could such enterprises earn for him in the *Café de Procope?* What could it profit his all-precious 'fame' to pursue them farther? In the end, he seems to have heartily reconciled himself to use and wont, and striven only to do better what he saw all others doing. Yet his private poetical creed, which could not be a catholic one, was, nevertheless, scarcely so bigoted as might have been looked for. That censure of Shakspeare, which elicited a re-censure in England, perhaps rather deserved a 'recommendatory epistle,' all things being considered. He calls Shakspeare 'a genius 'full of force and fertility, of nature and sublimity,' though unhappily 'without the smallest spark of good taste, or the 'smallest acquaintance with the rules;' which, in Voltaire's dialect, is not so false; Shakspeare having really almost no Parisian *bon goût* whatever, and walking through '*the* rules,' so often as he sees good, with the most astonishing tranquillity. After a fair enough account of *Hamlet*, the best of those '*farces monstrueuses qu'on appelle tragédies*,' where, however, there are 'scenes so beautiful, passages so grand and so terrible,' Voltaire thus proceeds to resolve two great problems:

'The first, how so many wonders could accumulate in a single head; for it must be confessed that all the divine Shakspeare's plays are written in this taste: the second, how men's minds could have been elevated so as to look at these plays with transport; and how they are still followed after, in a century which has produced Addison's *Cato?*

'Our astonishment at the first wonder will cease, when we understand that Shakspeare took all his tragedies from histories or romances; and that in this case he only turned into verse the romance of *Claudius, Gertrude and Hamlet*, written in full by Saxo Grammaticus, to whom be the praise.

'The second part of the problem, that is to say, the pleasure men take in these tragedies, presents a little more difficulty; but here is (*en voici*) the solution, according to the deep reflections of certain philosophers.

'The English chairmen, the sailors, hackney-coachmen, shop-porters, butchers, clerks even, are passionately fond of shows; give them cock-fights, bull-baitings, fencing-matches, burials, duels, gibbets, witchcraft, apparitions, they run thither in crowds; nay there is more than one patrician as curious as the populace. The citizens of London found, in Shakspeare's tragedies, satisfaction enough for such a turn of mind. The courtiers were obliged to follow the torrent: how can you help admiring what the more sensible part of the town admires? There was nothing better for a hundred and fifty years: the admiration grew with age, and became an idolatry.

Some touches of genius, some happy verses full of force and nature, which you remember in spite of yourself, atoned for the remainder, and soon the whole piece succeeded by the help of some beauties of detail.' [1]

Here, truly, is a comfortable little theory, which throws light on more than one thing. However, it is couched in mild terms, comparatively speaking. Frederick the Great, for example, thus gives his verdict:

'To convince yourself of the wretched taste that up to this day prevails in Germany, you have only to visit the public theatres. You will there see, in action, the abominable plays of Shakspeare, translated into our language; and the whole audience fainting with rapture (*se pâmer d'aise*) in listening to those ridiculous farces, worthy of the savages of Canada. I call them such, because they sin against all the rules of the theatre. One may pardon those mad sallies in Shakspeare, for the birth of the arts is never the point of their maturity. But here, even now, we have a *Goetz de Berlichingen*, which has just made its appearance on the scene; a detestable imitation of those miserable English pieces; and the pit applauds, and demands with enthusiasm the repetition of these disgusting ineptitudes (*de ces dégoûtantes platitudes*).' [2]

We have not cited these criticisms with a view to impugn them; but simply to ascertain where the critics themselves are standing. This passage of Frederick's has even a touch of pathos in it; may be regarded as the expiring cry of '*Goût*' in that country, who sees himself suddenly beleaguered by strange, appalling Supernatural Influences, which he mistakes for Lapland witchcraft or Cagliostro jugglery; which nevertheless swell up round him, irrepressible, higher, ever higher; and so he drowns, grasping his opera-hat, in an ocean of '*dégoûtantes platitudes*.' On the whole, it would appear that Voltaire's view of poetry was radically different from ours; that, in fact, of what we should strictly call poetry, he had almost no view whatever. A Tragedy, a Poem, with him is not to be 'a manifestation of man's Reason

1 *Œuvres*, t. xlvii. p. 300.

2 *De la Littérature Allemande;* Berlin. 1780. We quote from the compilation, *Goethe in den Zeugnissen der Mitlebenden*, s. 124.

in forms suitable to his Sense;' but rather a highly complex egg-dance, to be danced before the King, to a given tune and without breaking a single egg. Nevertheless, let justice be shown to him, and to French poetry at large. This latter is a peculiar growth of our modern ages; has been laboriously cultivated, and is not without its own value. We have to remark also, as a curious fact, that it has been, at one time or other, transplanted into all countries, England, Germany, Spain; but though under the sunbeams of royal protection, it would strike root nowhere. Nay, now it seems falling into the sere and yellow leaf in its own natal soil: the axe has already been seen near its root; and perhaps, in no great lapse of years, this species of poetry may be to the French, what it is to all other nations, a pleasing reminiscence. Yet the elder French loved it with zeal; to them it must have had a true worth: indeed we can understand how, when Life itself consisted so much in Display, these representations of Life may have been the only suitable ones. And now, when the nation feels itself called to a more grave and nobler destiny among nations, the want of a new literature also begins to be felt. As yet, in looking at their too purblind, scrambling controversies of *Romanticists* and *Classicists*, we cannot find that our ingenious neighbours have done much more than make a commencement in this enterprise; however, a commencement seems to be made: they are in what may be called the eclectic state; trying all things, German, English, Italian, Spanish, with a candour and real love of improvement, which give the best omens of a still higher success. From the peculiar gifts of the French, and their peculiar spiritual position, we may expect, had they once more attained to an original style, many important benefits, and important accessions to the Literature of the World. Meanwhile, in considering and duly estimating what that people has, in past times, accomplished, Voltaire must always be reckoned among their most meritorious Poets. Inferior in what we may call general poetic temperament to Racine;

greatly inferior, in some points of it, to Corneille, he has an intellectual vivacity, a quickness both of sight and of invention, which belongs to neither of these two. We believe that, among foreign nations, his Tragedies, such works as *Zaire* and *Mahomet*, are considerably the most esteemed of this school.

However, it is nowise as a Poet, Historian or Novelist, that Voltaire stands so prominent in Europe; but chiefly as a religious Polemic, as a vehement opponent of the Christian Faith. Viewed in this last character, he may give rise to many grave reflections, only a small portion of which can here be so much as glanced at. We may say, in general, that his style of controversy is of a piece with himself; not a higher, and scarcely a lower style than might have been expected from him. As, in a moral point of view, Voltaire nowise wanted a love of truth, yet had withal a still deeper love of his own interest in truth; was, therefore, intrinsically no Philosopher, but a highly accomplished Trivialist; so likewise, in an intellectual point of view, he manifests himself ingenious and adroit, rather than noble or comprehensive; fights for truth or victory, not by patient meditation, but by light sarcasm, whereby victory may indeed, for a time, be gained; but little Truth, what can be named Truth, especially in such matters as this, is to be looked for.

No one, we suppose, ever arrogated for Voltaire any praise of originality in this discussion; we suppose there is not a single idea, of any moment, relating to the Christian Religion, in all his multifarious writings, that had not been set forth again and again before his enterprises commenced. The labours of a very mixed multitude, from Porphyry down to Shaftesbury, including Hobbeses, Tindals, Tolands, some of them sceptics of a much nobler class, had left little room for merit in this kind; nay, Bayle, his own countryman, had just finished a life spent in preaching scepticism precisely similar, and by methods precisely similar, when

Voltaire appeared on the arena. Indeed, scepticism, as we have before observed, was at this period universal among the higher ranks in France, with whom Voltaire chiefly associated. It is only in the merit and demerit of grinding down this grain into food for the people, and inducing so many to eat of it, that Voltaire can claim any singularity. However, we quarrel not with him on this head: there may be cases where the want of originality is even a moral merit. But it is a much more serious ground of offence that he intermeddled in Religion, without being himself, in any measure, religious; that he entered the Temple and continued there, with a levity, which, in any Temple where men worship, can beseem no brother man; that, in a word, he ardently, and with long-continued effort, warred against Christianity, without understanding beyond the mere superficies what Christianity was.

His polemical procedure in this matter, it appears to us, must now be admitted to have been, on the whole, a shallow one. Through all its manifold forms, and involutions, and repetitions, it turns, we believe exclusively, on one point: what Theologians have called the 'plenary Inspiration of the Scriptures.' This is the single wall, against which, through long years, and with innumerable battering-rams and catapults and pop-guns, he unweariedly batters. Concede him this, and his ram swings freely to and fro through space: there is nothing farther it can even aim at. That the Sacred Books could be aught else than a Bank-of-Faith Bill, for such and such quantities of Enjoyment, payable at sight in the other world, value received; which bill becomes waste paper, the stamp being questioned: — that the Christian Religion could have any deeper foundation than Books, could possibly be written in the purest nature of man, in mysterious, ineffaceable characters, to which Books, and all Revelations, and authentic traditions, were but a subsidiary matter, were but as the *light* whereby that divine *writing* was to be read; — nothing of this seems to have, even in the faintest manner, occurred to him. Yet herein, as we believe that the whole world has now begun to discover, lies the real essence of the question; by the negative or affirmative decision of which the Christian Religion, anything that is worth calling by that name, must fall or endure forever. We believe also, that the wiser minds of our age have already come to agreement on this question; or rather never were divided regarding it. Christianity, the 'Worship of Sorrow,' has been recognised as divine, on far other grounds than 'Essays on Miracles,' and by considerations infinitely deeper than would avail in any mere 'trial by jury.' He who argues against it, or for it, in this manner, may be regarded as mistaking its nature: the Ithuriel, though to our eyes he wears a body and the fashion of armour, cannot be wounded with material steel. Our fathers were wiser than we, when they said in deepest earnestness, what we often hear in shallow mockery, that Religion is 'not of Sense, but of Faith;' not of Understanding, but of Reason. He who finds himself without the latter, who by all his studying has failed to unfold it in himself, may have studied to great or to small purpose, we say not which; but of the Christian Religion, as of many other things, he has and can have no knowledge.

The Christian Doctrine we often hear likened to the Greek Philosophy, and found, on all hands, some measurable way superior to it: but this also seems a mistake. The Christian Doctrine, that Doctrine of Humility, in all senses godlike and the parent of all godlike virtues, is not superior, or inferior, or equal, to any doctrine of Socrates or Thales; being of a totally different nature; differing from these, as a perfect Ideal Poem does from a correct Computation in Arithmetic. He who compares it with such standards may lament that, beyond the mere letter, the purport of this divine Humility has never been disclosed to him; that the loftiest feeling hitherto vouchsafed to mankind is as yet hidden from his eyes.

For the rest, the question how Christianity originated is doubtless a high question; resolvable enough, if we view only its surface, which was all that Voltaire saw of it; involved in sacred, silent, unfathomable depths, if we investigate its interior meanings; which meanings, indeed, it may be, every new age will develop to itself in a new manner and with new degrees of light; for the whole truth may be called infinite, and to man's eye discernible only in parts; but the question itself is nowise the ultimate one in this matter.

We understand ourselves to be risking no new assertion, but simply reporting what is already the conviction of the greatest of our age, when we say, — that cheerfully recognising, gratefully appropriating whatever Voltaire has proved, or any other man has proved, or shall prove, the Christian Religion, once here, cannot again pass away; that in one or the other form, it will endure through all time; that as in Scripture, so also in the heart of man, is written, 'the Gates of Hell shall not prevail against it.' Were the memory of this Faith never so obscured, as, indeed, in all times, the coarse passions and perceptions of the world do all but obliterate it in the hearts of most; yet in every pure soul, in every Poet and Wise Man, it finds a new Missionary, a new Martyr, till the great volume of Universal History is finally closed, and man's destinies are fulfilled in this earth. 'It is a height to which the 'human species were fated and enabled to attain; and 'from which, having once attained it, they can never retro-'grade.'

These things, which it were far out of our place to attempt adequately elucidating here, must not be left out of sight, in appreciating Voltaire's polemical worth. We find no trace of these, or of any the like essential considerations having been present with him, in examining the Christian Religion; nor indeed was it consistent with his general habits that they should be so. Totally destitute of religious

Reverence, even of common practical seriousness; by nature or habit, undevout both in heart and head; not only without any Belief, in other than a material sense, but without the possibility of acquiring any, he can be no safe or permanently useful guide in this investigation. We may consider him as having opened the way to future inquirers of a truer spirit; but for his own part, as having engaged in an enterprise, the real nature of which was wellnigh unknown to him; and engaged in it with the issue to be anticipated in such a case; producing chiefly confusion, dislocation; destruction, on all hands; so that the good he achieved is still, in these times, found mixed with an alarming proportion of evil, from which, indeed, men rationally doubt whether much of it will in any time be separable.

We should err widely too, if, in estimating what quantity, altogether overlooking what quality, of intellect Voltaire may have manifested on this occasion, we took the result produced as any measure of the force applied. His task was not one of Affirmation, but of Denial; not a task of erecting and rearing up, which is slow and laborious; but of destroying and overturning, which in most cases is rapid and far easier. The force necessary for him was nowise a great and noble one; but a small, in some respects a mean one; to be nimbly and seasonably put in use. The Ephesian Temple, which it had employed many wise heads and strong arms for a lifetime to build, could be *un*built by one madman, in a single hour.

Of such errors, deficiencies and positive misdeeds, it appears to us a just criticism must accuse Voltaire: at the same time, we can nowise join in the condemnatory clamour which so many worthy persons, not without the best intentions, to this day keep up against him. His whole character seems to be plain enough, common enough, had not extraneous influences so perverted our views regarding it: nor, morally speaking, is it a worse character, but considerably a better one, than belongs to the mass of men. Voltaire's aims in opposing the Christian Religion were unhappily of a mixed nature; yet, after all, very nearly such aims as we have often seen directed against it, and often seen directed in its favour: a little love of finding Truth, with a great love of making Proselytes; which last is in itself a natural, universal feeling; and if honest, is, even in the worst cases, a subject for pity, rather than for hatred. As a light, careless, courteous Man of the World, he offers no hateful aspect; on the contrary, a kindly, gay, rather amiable one: hundreds of men, with half his worth of disposition, die daily, and their little world laments them. It is time that he too should be judged of by his intrinsic, not by his accidental qualities; that justice should be done to him also; for injustice can profit no man and no cause.

In fact, Voltaire's chief merits belong to Nature and himself; his chief faults are of his time and country. In that famous era of the Pompadours and *Encyclopédies*, he forms the main figure; and was such, we have seen, more by resembling the multitude, than by differing from them. It was a strange age that of Louis XV.; in several points a novel one in the history of mankind. In regard to its luxury and depravity, to the high culture of all merely practical and material faculties, and the entire torpor of all the purely contemplative and spiritual, this era considerably resembles that of the Roman Emperors. There too was external splendour and internal squalor; the highest completeness in all sensual arts, including among these not cookery and its adjuncts alone, but even 'effect-painting' and 'effect-writing;' only the art of virtuous living was a lost one. Instead of Love for Poetry, there was 'Taste' for it; refinement in manners, with utmost coarseness in morals: in a word, the strange spectacle of a Social System, embracing large, cultivated portions of the human species, and founded only on Atheism. With the Romans, things went what we should call their natural course: Liberty, public spirit quietly declined into *caput-mortuum;* Self-love, Materialism, Baseness even to the disbelief in all possibility of Virtue, stalked more and more imperiously abroad; till the body-politic, long since deprived of its vital circulating fluids, had now become a putrid carcass, and fell in pieces to be the prey of ravenous wolves. Then was there, under these Attilas and Alarics, a world-spectacle of destruction and despair, compared with which the often-commemorated 'horrors of the French Revolution,' and all Napoleon's wars, were but the gay jousting of a tournament to the sack of stormed cities. Our European community has escaped the like dire consummation; and by causes which, as may be hoped, will always secure it from such. Nay, were there no other cause, it may be asserted, that in a commonwealth where the Christian Religion exists, where it once has existed, public and private Virtue, the basis of all Strength, never can become extinct; but in every new age, and even from the deepest decline, there is a chance, and in the course of ages a certainty of renovation.

That the Christian Religion, or any Religion, continued to exist; that some martyr heroism still lived in the heart of Europe to rise against mailed Tyranny when it rode triumphant,— was indeed no merit in the age of Louis XV., but a happy accident which it could not altogether get rid of. For that age too is to be regarded as an experiment, on the great scale, to decide the question, not yet, it would appear, settled to universal satisfaction: With what degree of vigour a political system, grounded on pure Self-interest, never so enlightened, but without a God or any recognition of the godlike in man, can be expected to flourish; or whether, in such circumstances, a political system can be expected to flourish, or even to subsist at all? It is contended by many that our mere love of personal Pleasure, or Happiness as it is called, acting on every individual, with such clearness as he may easily have, will of itself lead him to respect the rights of others, and wisely employ his own; to fulfil, on a mere principle of economy, all the duties of a good patriot; so that, in what respects the State, or the mere social existence of mankind, Belief, beyond the testimony of the senses, and Virtue, beyond the very common Virtue of loving what is pleasant and hating what is painful, are to be considered as supererogatory qualifications, as ornamental, not essential. Many there are, on the other hand, who pause over this doctrine; cannot discover, in such a universe of conflicting atoms, any principle by which the whole shall cohere; for if every man's selfishness, infinitely expansive, is to be hemmed-in only by the infinitely-expansive selfishness of every other man, it seems as if we should have a world of mutually repulsive bodies with no centripetal force to bind them together; in which case, it is well known, they would, by and by, diffuse themselves over space, and constitute a remarkable Chaos, but no habitable Solar or Stellar System.

If the age of Louis XV. was not made an *experimentum crucis* in regard to this question, one reason may be, that such experiments are too expensive. Nature cannot afford, above once or twice in the thousand years, to destroy a whole world, for purposes of science; but must content herself with destroying one or two kingdoms. The age of Louis XV., so far as it went, seems a highly illustrative experiment. We are to remark also, that its operation was clogged by a very considerable disturbing force; by a large remnant, namely, of the old faith in Religion, in the invisible, celestial nature of Virtue, which our French Purifiers, by their utmost efforts of lavation, had not been able to wash away. The men did their best, but no man can do more. Their worst enemy, we imagine, will not accuse them of any undue regard to things unseen and spiritual: far from practising this invisible sort of Virtue, they cannot even believe in its possibility. The high exploits and endurances of old ages were no longer virtues, but 'passions;' these antique persons had a taste for being heroes, a certain fancy to die for the truth: the more fools they! With our *Philosophes*, the only virtue of any civilisation was what they call

'Honour,' the sanctioning deity of which is that wonderful 'Force of Public Opinion.' Concerning which virtue of Honour, we must be permitted to say, that she reveals herself too clearly as the daughter and heiress of our old acquaintance Vanity, who indeed has been known enough ever since the foundation of the world, at least since the date of that 'Lucifer, son of the Morning;' but known chiefly in her proper character of strolling actress, or cast-clothes Abigail; and never, till that new era, had seen her issue set up as Queen and all-sufficient Dictatress of man's whole soul, prescribing with nicest precision what, in all practical and all moral emergencies, he was to do and to forbear. Again, with regard to this same Force of Public Opinion, it is a force well known to all of us; respected, valued as of indispensable utility, but nowise recognised as a final or divine force. We might ask, What divine, what truly great thing had ever been effected by this force? Was it the Force of Public Opinion that drove Columbus to America; John Kepler, not to fare sumptuously among Rodolph's Astrologers and Fire-eaters, but to perish of want, discovering the true System of the Stars? Still more ineffectual do we find it as a basis of public or private Morals. Nay, taken by itself, it may be called a baseless basis: for without some ulterior sanction, common to all minds; without some belief in the necessary, eternal, or which is the same, in the supramundane, divine nature of Virtue, existing in each individual, what could the moral judgment of a thousand or a thousand-thousand individuals avail us? Without some celestial guidance, whencesoever derived, or howsoever named, it appears to us the Force of Public Opinion would, by and by, become an extremely unprofitable one. "Enlighten Self-interest!" cries the *Philosophe;* "do but sufficiently enlighten it!" We ourselves have seen enlightened Self-interests, ere now; and truly, for most part, their light was only as that of a horn-lantern, sufficient to guide the bearer himself out of various puddles; but to us and the world of comparatively small advantage. And figure the human species, like an endless host, seeking its way onwards through undiscovered Time, in black darkness, save that each had his horn-lantern, and the vanguard some few of glass!

However, we will not dwell on controversial niceties. What we had to remark was, that this era, called of Philosophy, was in itself but a poor era; that any little morality it had was chiefly borrowed, and from those very ages which it accounted so barbarous. For this 'Honour,' this 'Force of Public Opinion,' is not asserted, on any side, to have much renovating, but only a sustaining or preventive power; it cannot create new Virtue, but at best may preserve what is already there. Nay, of the age of Louis XV., we may say that its very Power, its material strength, its knowledge, all that it had, was borrowed. It boasted itself to be an age of illumination; and truly illumination there was of its kind: only, except the illuminated windows, almost nothing to be *seen* thereby. None of those great Doctrines or Institutions that have 'made man in all points a man;' none even of those Discoveries that have the most subjected external Nature to his purposes, were made in that age. What Plough or Printing-press, what Chivalry or Christianity, nay what Steam-engine, or Quakerism, or Trial by Jury, did these Encyclopedists invent for mankind? They invented simply nothing: not one of man's virtues, not one of man's powers, is due to them; in all these respects the age of Louis XV. is among the most barren of recorded ages. Indeed, the whole trade of our *Philosophes* was directly the opposite of invention: it was not to produce, that they stood there; but to criticise, to quarrel with, to rend in pieces, what had been already produced;—a quite inferior trade: sometimes a useful, but on the whole a mean trade; often the fruit, and always the parent, of meanness, in every mind that permanently follows it.

Considering the then position of affairs, it is not singular that the age of Louis XV. should have been what it was:

an age without nobleness, without high virtue, or high manifestations of talent; an age of shallow clearness, of polish, self-conceit, scepticism and all forms of *Persiflage*. As little does it seem surprising, or peculiarly blamable, that Voltaire, the leading man of that age, should have partaken largely of all its qualities. True his giddy activity took serious effect; the light firebrands, which he so carelessly scattered abroad, kindled fearful conflagrations: but in these there has been good as well as evil; nor is it just that, even for the latter, he, a limited mortal, should be charged with more than mortal's responsibility. After all, that parched, blighted period, and the period of earthquakes and tornadoes which followed it, have now wellnigh cleared away: they belong to the Past, and for us, and those that come after us, are not without their benefits, and calm historical meaning.

'The thinking heads of all nations,' says a deep observer, 'had in secret come to majority; and in a mistaken feeling of their vocation, rose the more fiercely against antiquated constraint. The Man of Letters is, by instinct, opposed to a Priesthood of old standing: the literary class and the clerical must wage a war of extermination, when they are divided; for both strive after one place. Such division became more and more perceptible, the nearer we approached the period of European manhood, the epoch of triumphant Learning; and Knowledge and Faith came into more decided contradiction. In the prevailing Faith, as was thought, lay the reason of the universal degradation; and by a more and more searching Knowledge men hoped to remove it. On all hands, the Religious feeling suffered, under manifold attacks against its actual manner of existence, against the forms in which hitherto it had embodied itself. The result of that modern way of thought was named Philosophy; and in this all was included that opposed itself to the ancient way of thought, especially, therefore, all that opposed itself to Religion. The original personal hatred against the Catholic Faith passed, by degrees, into hatred against the Bible, against the Christian Religion, and at last against Religion altogether. Nay more, this hatred of Religion naturally extended itself over all objects of enthusiasm in general; proscribed Fancy and Feeling, Morality and love of Art, the Future and the Antique; placed man, with an effort, foremost in the series of natural productions; and changed the infinite, creative music of the Universe into the monotonous clatter of a boundless

Mill, which, turned by the stream of Chance, and swimming thereon, was a Mill of itself, without Architect and Miller, properly a genuine *perpetuum mobile*, a real self-grinding Mill.

'One enthusiasm was generously left to poor mankind, and rendered indispensable as a touchstone of the highest culture, for all jobbers in the same: Enthusiasm for this magnanimous Philosophy, and above all, for these its priests and mystagogues. France was so happy as to be the birthplace and dwelling of this new Faith, which had thus, from patches of pure knowledge, been pasted together. Low as Poetry ranked in this new Church, there were some poets among them, who, for effect's sake, made use of the old ornaments and old lights; but in so doing, ran a risk of kindling the new world-system by ancient fire. More cunning brethren, however, were at hand to help; and always in season poured cold water on the warming audience. The members of this Church were restlessly employed in clearing Nature, the Earth, the Souls of men, the Sciences, from all Poetry; obliterating every vestige of the Holy; disturbing, by sarcasms, the memory of all lofty occurrences and lofty men; disrobing the world of all its variegated vesture. * * * Pity that Nature continued so wondrous and incomprehensible, so poetical and infinite, all efforts to modernise her notwithstanding! However, if anywhere an old superstition, of a higher world and the like, came to light, instantly, on all hands, was a springing of rattles; that, if possible, the dangerous spark might be extinguished, by appliances of philosophy and wit: yet Tolerance was the watchword of the cultivated; and in France, above all, synonymous with Philosophy. Highly remarkable is this history of modern Unbelief; the key to all the vast phenomena of recent times. Not till last century, till the latter half of it, does the novelty begin; and in a little while, it expands to an immeasurable bulk and variety: a second Reformation, a more comprehensive, and more specific, was unavoidable; and naturally it first visited that land which was the most modernised, and had the longest lain in an asthenic state, from want of freedom. * * *

'At the present epoch, however, we stand high enough to look back with a friendly smile on those bygone days; and even in those marvellous follies to discern curious crystallisations of historical matter. Thankfully will we stretch out our hands to those Men of Letters and *Philosophes:* for this delusion too required to be exhausted, and the scientific side of things to have full value given it. More beauteous and many-coloured stands Poesy, like a leafy India, when contrasted with the cold, dead Spitzbergen of that Closet-Logic. That in the middle of the globe, an India, so warm and lordly, might exist, must also a cold motionless sea, dead cliffs, mist instead of the starry sky, and a long night make both poles uninhabitable. The deep meaning of the laws of Mechanism lay heavy on those anchorites in the deserts of Understanding: the charm of the first glimpse into it overpowered them: the Old avenged itself on them; to the first feeling of self-consciousness, they sacrificed, with wondrous devotedness, what was holiest and fairest in the world; and were the first that, in practice, again recognised and preached forth the sacredness of Nature, the infinitude of Art, the independence of Knowledge, the worth of the Practical, and the all-presence of the Spirit of History; and so doing, put an end to a Spectre-dynasty, more potent, universal and terrific than perhaps they themselves were aware of.'[1]

How far our readers will accompany Novalis in such high-soaring speculation, is not for us to say. Meanwhile, that the better part of them have already, in their own dialect, united with him, and with us, in candid tolerance, in clear acknowledgment, towards French Philosophy, towards this Voltaire and the spiritual period which bears his name, we do not hesitate to believe. Intolerance, animosity can forward no cause; and least of all beseems the cause of moral and religious truth. A wise man has well reminded us, that 'in any controversy, the instant we feel 'angry, we have already ceased striving for Truth, and 'begun striving for Ourselves.' Let no man doubt but Voltaire and his disciples, like all men and all things that live and act in God's world, will one day be found to have 'worked together for good.' Nay that, with all his evil, he has already accomplished good, must be admitted in the soberest calculation. How much do we include in this little word: He gave the death-stab to modern Superstition! *That* horrid incubus, which dwelt in darkness, shunning the light, is passing away; with all its racks, and poison-chalices, and foul sleeping-draughts, is passing away without return. It was a most weighty service. Does not the cry of "No Popery," and some vague terror or sham-terror of 'Smithfield fires,' still act on certain minds in these very days?

[1] Novalis Schriften, i. s. 198.

He who sees even a little way into the signs of the times, sees well that both the Smithfield fires, and the Edinburgh thumb screws (for these too must be held in remembrance) are things which have long, very long, lain behind us; divided from us by a wall of Centuries, transparent indeed, but more impassable than adamant. For, as we said, Superstition is in its death-lair: the last agonies may endure for decades, or for centuries; but it carries the iron in its heart, and will not vex the earth any more.

That, with Superstition, Religion is also passing away, seems to us a still more ungrounded fear. Religion cannot pass away. The burning of a little straw may hide the stars of the sky; but the stars are there, and will re-appear. On the whole, we must repeat the often-repeated saying, that it is unworthy a religious man to view an irreligious one either with alarm or aversion; or with any other feeling than regret, and hope, and brotherly commiseration. If he seek Truth, is he not our brother, and to be pitied? If he do not seek Truth, is he not still our brother, and to be pitied still more? Old Ludovicus Vives has a story of a clown that killed his ass because it had drunk up the moon, and he thought the world could ill spare that luminary. So he killed his ass, *ut lunam redderet.* The clown was well-intentioned, but unwise. Let us not imitate him: let us not slay a faithful servant, who has carried us far. He has not drunk the moon; but only the *reflection* of the moon, in his own poor water-pail, where too, it may be, he was drinking with purposes the most harmless.

NOVALIS.[1]

[1829.]

A NUMBER of years ago, Jean Paul's copy of *Novalis* led him to infer that the German reading-world was of a quick disposition; inasmuch as, with respect to books that required more than one perusal, it declined perusing them at all. Paul's *Novalis*, we suppose, was of the first Edition, uncut, dusty, and lent him from the Public Library with willingness, nay with joy. But times, it would appear, must be considerably changed since then; indeed, were we to judge of German reading habits from these Volumes of ours, we should draw quite a different conclusion to Paul's; for they are of the fourth Edition, perhaps therefore the ten-thousandth copy, and that of a Book demanding, whether deserving or not, to be oftener read than almost any other it has ever been our lot to examine.

Without at all entering into the merits of Novalis, we may observe that we should reckon it a happy sign of Literature, were so solid a fashion of study here and there established in all countries: for directly in the teeth of most 'intellectual tea-circles,' it may be asserted that no good Book, or good thing of any sort, shows its best face at first; nay that the commonest quality in a true work of Art, if its excellence have any depth and compass, is that at first sight it occasions

[1] FOREIGN REVIEW, No. 7. — *Novalis Schriften. Herausgegeben von Ludwig Tieck und Friedrich Schlegel* (Novalis' Writings. Edited by Ludwig Tieck and Friedrich Schlegel). Fourth Edition. 2 vols. Berlin, 1826.

a certain disappointment; perhaps even, mingled with its undeniable beauty, a certain feeling of aversion. Not as if we meant, by this remark, to cast a stone at the old guild of literary Improvisators, or any of that diligent brotherhood, whose trade it is to blow soap-bubbles for their fellow-creatures; which bubbles, of course, if they are not seen and admired this moment, will be altogether lost to men's eyes the next. Considering the use of these blowers, in civilised communities, we rather wish them strong lungs, and all manner of prosperity: but simply we would contend that such soap-bubble guild should not become the sole one in Literature; that being indisputably the strongest, it should content itself with this preëminence, and not tyrannically annihilate its less prosperous neighbours. For it should be recollected that Literature positively has other aims than this of amusement from hour to hour; nay perhaps that this, glorious as it may be, is not its highest or true aim. We do say, therefore, that the Improvisator corporation should be kept within limits; and readers, at least a certain small class of readers, should understand that some few departments of human inquiry have still their depths and difficulties; that the abstruse is not precisely synonymous with the absurd; nay that light itself may be darkness, in a certain state of the eyesight; that, in short, cases may occur when a little patience and some attempt at thought would not be altogether superfluous in reading. Let the mob of gentlemen keep their own ground, and be happy and applauded there: if they overstep that ground, they indeed may flourish the better for it, but the reader will suffer damage. For in this way, a reader, accustomed to see through everything in one second of time, comes to forget that his wisdom and critical penetration are finite and not infinite; and so commits more than one mistake in his conclusions. The Reviewer too, who indeed is only a preparatory reader, as it were a sort of sieve and drainer for the use of more luxurious readers, soon follows his example: these two react still farther on the mob of gentlemen; and so among them all, with this action and reaction, matters grow worse and worse.

It rather seems to us as if, in this respect of faithfulness in reading, the Germans were somewhat ahead of us English; at least we have no such proof to show of it as that fourth Edition of *Novalis.* Our Coleridge's *Friend,* for example, and *Biographia Literaria* are but a slight business compared with these *Schriften;* little more than the Alphabet, and that in gilt letters, of such Philosophy and Art as is here taught in the form of Grammar and Rhetorical Compend: yet Coleridge's works were triumphantly condemned by the whole reviewing world, as clearly unintelligible; and among readers they have still but an unseen circulation; like living brooks, hidden for the present under mountains of froth and theatrical snow-paper, and which only at a distant day, when these mountains shall have decomposed themselves into gas and earthly residuum, may roll forth in their true limpid shape, to gladden the general eye with what beauty and everlasting freshness does reside in them. It is admitted too, on all hands, that Mr. Coleridge is a man of 'genius,' that is, a man having more intellectual insight than other men; and strangely enough, it is taken for granted, at the same time, that he has less intellectual insight than any other. For why else are his doctrines to be thrown out of doors, without examination, as false and worthless, simply because they are obscure? Or how is their so palpable falsehood to be accounted for to our minds, except on this extraordinary ground: that a man able to originate deep thoughts (such is the meaning of genius) is unable to *see* them when originated; that the creative intellect of a Philosopher is destitute of that mere faculty of logic which belongs to 'all Attorneys, and men educated in Edinburgh?' The Cambridge carrier, when asked whether his horse could "draw inferences," readily replied, "Yes, anything in reason;" but here, it seems, is a man of genius who has no similar gift.

We ourselves, we confess, are too young in the study of

human nature to have met with any such anomaly. Never yet has it been our fortune to fall in with any man of genius, whose conclusions did not correspond better with his premises, and not worse, than those of other men; whose genius, when it once came to be understood, did not manifest itself in a deeper, fuller, truer view of all things human and divine, than the clearest of your so laudable 'practical men' had claim to. Such, we say, has been our uniform experience; so uniform, that we now hardly ever expect to see it contradicted. True it is, the old Pythagorean argument of 'the master said it,' has long since ceased to be available: in these days, no man, except the Pope of Rome, is altogether exempt from error of judgment; doubtless a man of genius may chance to adopt false opinions; nay rather, like all other sons of Adam, except that same enviable Pope, *must* occasionally adopt such. Nevertheless, we reckon it a good maxim, That no error is fully confuted till we have seen not only *that* it is an error, but *how* it became one; till finding that it clashes with the principles of truth established in our own mind, we find also in what way it had seemed to harmonise with the principles of truth established in that other mind, perhaps so unspeakably superior to ours. Treated by this method, it still appears to us, according to the old saying, that the errors of a wise man are literally more instructive than the truths of a fool. For the wise man travels in lofty, far-seeing regions; the fool, in low-lying, high-fenced lanes: retracing the footsteps of the former, to discover where he deviated, whole provinces of the Universe are laid open to us; in the path of the latter, granting even that he have not deviated at all, little is laid open to us but two wheel-ruts and two hedges.

On these grounds we reckon it more profitable, in almost any case, to have to do with men of depth, than with men of shallowness: and were it possible, we would read no book that was not written by one of the former class; all members of which we would love and venerate, how perverse soever they might seem to us at first; nay though, after the fullest investigation, we still found many things to pardon in them. Such of our readers as at all participate in this predilection will not blame us for bringing them acquainted with Novalis, a man of the most indisputable talent, poetical and philosophical; whose opinions, extraordinary, nay altogether wild and baseless as they often appear, are not without a strict coherence in his own mind, and will lead any other mind, that examines them faithfully, into endless considerations; opening the strangest inquiries, new truths, or new possibilities of truth, a whole unexpected world of thought, where, whether for belief or denial, the deepest questions await us.

In what is called reviewing such a book as this, we are aware that to the judicious craftsman two methods present themselves. The first and most convenient is, for the Reviewer to perch himself resolutely, as it were, on the shoulder of his Author, and therefrom to show as if he commanded him and looked down on him by natural superiority of stature. Whatsoever the great man says or does, the little man shall treat with an air of knowingness and light condescending mockery; professing, with much covert sarcasm, that this and that other is beyond *his* comprehension, and cunningly asking his readers if they comprehend it! Herein it will help him mightily, if, besides description, he can quote a few passages, which, in their detached state, and taken most probably in quite a wrong acceptation of the words, shall sound strange, and, to certain hearers, even absurd; all which will be easy enough, if he have any handiness in the business, and address the right audience; truths, as this world goes, being true only for those that have *some* understanding of them; as, for instance, in the Yorkshire Wolds, and Thames Coal-ships, Christian men enough might be found, at this day, who, if you read them the Thirty-ninth of the *Principia*, would 'grin intelligence from ear to ear.' On the other hand, should our Reviewer meet with any passage, the wisdom of which, deep, plain and palpable to the simplest, might cause misgivings in the reader, as if here were a man of half-unknown endowment, whom perhaps it were better to wonder at than laugh at, our Reviewer either suppresses it, or citing it with an air of meritorious candour, calls upon his Author, in a tone of command and encouragement, to lay aside his transcendental crotchets, and write always thus, and *he* will admire him. Whereby the reader again feels comforted; proceeds swimmingly to the conclusion of the 'Article,' and shuts it with a victorious feeling, not only that he and the Reviewer understand this man, but also that, with some rays of fancy and the like, the man is little better than a living mass of darkness.

In this way does the small Reviewer triumph over great Authors; but it is the triumph of a fool. In this way too does he recommend himself to certain readers, but it is the recommendation of a parasite, and of no true servant. The servant would have spoken truth, in this case; truth, that it might have profited, however harsh: the parasite glozes his master with sweet speeches, that he may filch applause, and certain 'guineas per sheet,' from him; substituting for ignorance which was harmless, error which is not so. And yet to the vulgar reader, naturally enough, that flattering unction is full of solacement. In fact, to a reader of this sort few things can be more alarming than to find that his own little Parish, where he lived so snug and absolute, is, after all, *not* the whole Universe; that beyond the hill which screened his house from the west wind, and grew his kitchen-vegetables so sweetly, there are other hills and other hamlets, nay mountains and towered cities; with all which, if he would continue to pass for a geographer, he must forthwith make himself acquainted. Now this Reviewer, often his fellow Parishioner, is a safe man; leads him pleasantly to the hill-top; shows him that indeed there are, or seem to be, other expanses, these too of boundless extent: but with only cloud mountains, and *fata-morgana* cities; the true character of that region being Vacuity, or at best a stony desert tenanted by Gryphons and Chimeras.

Surely, if printing is not, like courtier speech, 'the art of *concealing* thought,' all this must be blamable enough. Is it the Reviewer's real trade to be a pander of laziness, self-conceit and all manner of contemptuous stupidity on the part of his reader; carefully ministering to these propensities; carefully fencing off whatever might invade that fool's-paradise with news of disturbance? Is he the priest of Literature and Philosophy, to interpret their mysteries to the common man; as a faithful preacher, teaching him to understand what is adapted for his understanding, to reverence what is adapted for higher understandings than his? Or merely the lackey of Dulness, striving for certain wages, of pudding or praise, by the month or quarter, to perpetuate the reign of presumption and triviality on earth? If the latter, will he not be counselled to pause for an instant, and reflect seriously, whether starvation were worse or were better than such a dog's-existence?

Our reader perceives that we are for adopting the second method with regard to Novalis; that we wish less to insult over this highly-gifted man, than to gain some insight into him; that we look upon his mode of being and thinking as very singular, but not therefore necessarily very contemptible; as a matter, in fact, worthy of examination, and difficult beyond most others to examine wisely and with profit. Let no man expect that, in this case, a Samson is to be led forth, blinded and manacled, to make him sport. Nay, might it not, in a spiritual sense, be death, as surely it would be damage, to the small man himself? For is not this habit of sneering at all greatness, of forcibly bringing down all greatness to his own height, one chief cause which keeps that height so very inconsiderable? Come of it what may, we have no refreshing dew for the small man's vanity in this place; nay rather, as charitable brethren, and fellow-sufferers from that same evil, we would gladly lay the sickle to that reed-grove of self-conceit, which has grown round him, and reap it altogether away, that so the true figure of the world, and his own true figure, might no longer be utterly hidden from him. Does this our brother, then, refuse to accompany us, without such allurements? He must even retain our best wishes, and abide by his own hearth.

Farther, to the honest few who still go along with us on this occasion, we are bound in justice to say that, far from looking down on Novalis, we cannot place either them or ourselves on a level with him. To explain so strange an individuality, to exhibit a mind of this depth and singularity before the minds of readers so foreign to him in every sense, would be a vain pretension in us. With the best will, and after repeated trials, we have gained but a feeble notion of Novalis for ourselves: his Volumes come before us with every disadvantage; they are the posthumous works of a man cut off in early life, while his opinions, far from being matured for the public eye, were still lying crude and disjointed before his own; for most part written down in the shape of detached aphorisms, 'none of them,' as he says himself, 'untrue or unimportant to his own mind,' but naturally requiring to be remodelled, expanded, compressed, as the matter cleared up more and more into logical unity; at best but fragments of a great scheme which he did not live to realise. If his Editors, Friedrich Schlegel and Ludwig Tieck, declined commenting on these Writings, we may well be excused for declining to do so. 'It cannot be our purpose here,' says Tieck, 'to recommend the following Works, 'or to judge them; probable as it must be that any judgment delivered at this stage of the matter would be a premature and unripe one: for a spirit of such originality 'must first be comprehended, his will understood, and his 'loving intention felt and replied to; so that not till his 'ideas have taken root in other minds, and brought forth 'new ideas, shall we see rightly, from the historical sequence, 'what place he himself occupied, and what relation to his 'country he truly bore.'

Meanwhile, Novalis is a figure of such importance in German Literature, that no student of it can pass him by without attention. If we must not attempt interpreting this Work for our readers, we are bound at least to point out its existence, and according to our best knowledge, direct such of them as take an interest in the matter how to investigate it farther for their own benefit. For this purpose, it may be well that we leave our Author to speak chiefly for himself; subjoining only such expositions as cannot be dispensed with for even verbal intelligibility, and as we can offer on our own surety with some degree of confidence. By way of basis to the whole inquiry, we prefix some particulars of his short life; a part of our task which Tieck's clear and graceful Narrative, given as 'Preface to the Third Edition,' renders easy for us.

Friedrich von Hardenberg, better known in Literature by the pseudonym 'Novalis,' was born on the 2d of May 1772, at a country residence of his family in the Grafschaft of Mansfeld, in Saxony. His father, who had been a soldier in youth, and still retained a liking for that profession, was at this time Director of the Saxon Salt-works; an office of some considerable trust and dignity. Tieck says, 'he was 'a vigorous, unweariedly active man, of open, resolute char'acter, a true German. His religious feelings made him a 'member of the Herrnhut Communion; yet his disposition 'continued gay, frank, rugged and downright.' The mother also was distinguished for her worth; 'a pattern of noble piety and Christian mildness;' virtues which her subsequent life gave opportunity enough for exercising.

On the young Friedrich, whom we may continue to call Novalis, the qualities of his parents must have exercised more than usual influence; for he was brought up in the most retired manner, with scarcely any associate but a sister one year older than himself, and the two brothers that were next to him in age. A decidedly religious temper seems to have infused itself, under many benignant aspects, over the whole family: in Novalis especially it continued the ruling principle through life; manifested no less in his scientific speculations, than in his feelings and conduct. In childhood he is said to have been remarkable chiefly for the entire, enthusiastic affection with which he loved his mother; and for a certain still, secluded disposition, such that he took no pleasure in boyish sports, and rather shunned the society of other children. Tieck mentions that, till his ninth year, he was reckoned nowise quick of apprehension; but at this period, strangely enough, some violent biliary disease, which had almost cut him off, seemed to awaken his faculties into proper life, and he became the readiest, eagerest learner in all branches of his scholarship.

In his eighteenth year, after a few months of preparation in some *Gymnasium*, the only instruction he appears to have received in any public school, he repaired to Jena; and continued there for three years; after which he spent one season in the Leipzig University, and another, 'to complete his studies,' in that of Wittenberg. It seems to have been at Jena that he became acquainted with Friedrich Schlegel; where also, we suppose, he studied under Fichte. For both of these men he conceived a high admiration and affection; and both of them had, clearly enough, 'a great and abiding effect on his whole life.' Fichte, in particular, whose lofty eloquence and clear calm enthusiasm are said to have made him irresistible as a teacher,[1] had quite gained Novalis to his doctrines; indeed the *Wissenschaftslehre*, which, as we are told of the latter, 'he studied with unwearied zeal,' appears to have been the groundwork of all his future spec-

[1] Schelling, we have been informed, gives account of Fichte and his *Wissenschaftslehre* to the following effect: 'The Philosophy of Fichte was 'like lightning; it appeared only for a moment, but it kindled a fire which 'will burn forever.'

ulations in Philosophy. Besides these metaphysical inquiries, and the usual attainments in classical literature, Novalis seems 'to have devoted himself with ardour to the Physical Sciences, and to Mathematics the basis of them:' at an early period of his life, he had read much of History 'with extraordinary eagerness;' Poems had from of old been 'the delight of his leisure;' particularly that species denominated *Mährchen* (Traditionary Tale), which continued a favourite with him to the last; as almost from infancy it had been a chosen amusement of his to read these compositions, and even to recite such, of his own invention. One remarkable piece of that sort he has himself left us, inserted in *Heinrich von Ofterdingen*, his chief literary performance.

But the time had now arrived, when study must become subordinate to action, and what is called a profession be fixed upon. At the breaking-out of the French War, Novalis had been seized with a strong and altogether unexpected taste for a military life: however, the arguments and pressing entreaties of his friends ultimately prevailed over this whim; it seems to have been settled that he should follow his father's line of occupation; and so, about the end of 1794, he removed to Arnstadt in Thuringia, 'to train himself in practical affairs under the Kreis-Amtmann Just.' In this *Kreis-Amtmann* (Manager of a Circle) he found a wise and kind friend; applied himself honestly to business; and in all his serious calculations may have looked forward to a life as smooth and commonplace as his past years had been. One incident, and that too of no unusual sort, appears, in Tieck's opinion, to have altered the whole form of his existence.

'It was not very long after his arrival at Arnstadt, when in a country mansion of the neighbourhood, he became acquainted with Sophie von K——. The first glance of this fair and wonderfully lovely form was decisive for his whole life; nay, we may say that the feeling, which now penetrated and inspired him, was the substance and essence of his whole life. Sometimes, in the look and figure of a child, there will stamp itself an expression, which, as it is too angelic and ethereally beautiful, we are forced to call unearthly or celestial; and commonly, at sight of such purified and almost transparent faces, there comes on us a fear that they are too tender and delicately fashioned for this life; that it is Death, or Immortality, which looks forth so expressively on us from these glancing eyes; and too often a quick decay converts our mournful foreboding into certainty. Still more affecting are such figures, when their first period is happily passed over, and they come before us blooming on the eve of maidhood. All persons that have known this wondrous loved one of our Friend, agree in testifying that no description can express in what grace and celestial harmony the fair being moved, what beauty shone in her, what softness and majesty encircled her. Novalis became a poet every time he chanced to speak of it. She had concluded her thirteenth year when he first saw her: the spring and summer of 1795 were the blooming time of his life; every hour that he could spare from business he spent in Grüningen: and in the fall of that same year he obtained the wished-for promise from Sophie's parents.'

Unhappily, however, these halcyon days were of too short continuance. Soon after this, Sophie fell dangerously sick 'of a fever, attended with pains in the side;' and her lover had the worst consequences to fear. By and by, indeed, the fever left her; but not the pain, 'which by its violence still spoiled for her many a fair hour,' and gave rise to various apprehensions, though the Physician asserted that it was of no importance. Partly satisfied with this favourable prognostication, Novalis had gone to Weissenfels, to his parents; and was full of business; being now appointed Auditor in the department of which his father was Director: through winter the news from Grüningen were of a favourable sort; in spring he visited the family himself, and found his Sophie to all appearance well. But suddenly, in summer, his hopes and occupations were interrupted by tidings that 'she was in Jena, and had undergone a surgical operation.' Her disease was an abscess in the liver: it had been her wish that he should not hear of her danger till the worst were over. The Jena Surgeon gave hopes of recovery though a slow one; but ere long the operation had to be repeated, and now it was feared that his patient's strength was too far exhausted. The young maiden bore all this with inflexible courage and the cheerfullest resignation: her Mother and Sister, Novalis, with his Parents and two of his Brothers, all deeply interested in the event, did their utmost to comfort her. In December, by her own wish, she returned home; but it was evident that she grew weaker and weaker. Novalis went and came between Grüningen and Weissenfels, where also he found a house of mourning; for Erasmus, one of these two Brothers, had long been sickly, and was now believed to be dying.

'The 17th of March,' says Tieck, 'was the fifteenth birthday of his Sophie; and on the 19th, about noon, she departed. No one durst tell Novalis these tidings; at last his Brother Carl undertook it. The poor youth shut himself up, and after three days and three nights of weeping, set out for Arnstadt, that there, with his true friend, he might be near the spot, which now hid the remains of what was dearest to him. On the 14th of April, his Brother Erasmus also left this world. Novalis wrote to inform his Brother Carl of the event, who had been obliged to make a journey into Lower Saxony: "Be of good courage," said he, "Erasmus has prevailed; the flowers of our fair garland are dropping off Here, one by one, that they may be united Yonder, lovelier and forever." '

Among the papers published in these Volumes are three letters written about this time, which mournfully indicate the author's mood. 'It has grown Evening around me,' says he, 'while I was looking into the red of Morning. My grief 'is boundless as my love. For three years she has been my 'hourly thought. She alone bound me to life, to the country, 'to my occupations. With her I am parted from all; for 'now I scarcely have *myself* any more. But it has grown 'Evening; and I feel as if I had to travel early; and so I 'would fain be at rest, and see nothing but kind faces about 'me; — all in her spirit would I live, be soft and mild-heart'ed as she was.' And again, some weeks later: 'I live over the old, bygone life here, in still meditation. Yesterday I 'was twenty-five years old. I was in Grüningen, and stood 'beside her grave. It is a friendly spot; enclosed with sim'ple white railing; lies apart and high. There is still room 'in it. The village, with its blooming gardens, leans up 'round the hill; and at this point and that, the eye loses 'itself in blue distances. I know you would have liked to 'stand by me, and stick the flowers, my birthday gifts, one 'by one into her hillock. This time two years, she made me 'a gay present, with a flag and national cockade on it. To-'day her parents gave me the little things which she, still 'joyfully, had received on her last birthday. Friend, — it 'continues Evening, and will soon be Night. If you go 'away, think of me kindly, and visit, when you return, the 'still house, where your Friend rests forever, with the ashes 'of his beloved. Fare you well!' — Nevertheless, a singular composure came over him; from the very depths of his grief arose a peace and pure joy, such as till then he had never known.

'In this season,' observes Tieck, 'Novalis lived only to his sorrow: it was natural for him to regard the visible and the invisible world as one; and to distinguish Life and Death only by his longing for the latter. At the same time too, Life became for him a glorified Life; and his whole being melted away as into a bright, conscious vision of a higher Existence. From the sacredness of Sorrow, from heart-felt love and the pious wish for death, his temper and all his conceptions are to be explained: and it seems possible that this time, with its deep griefs, planted in him the germ of death, if it was not, in any case, his appointed lot to be so soon snatched away from us.

'He remained many weeks in Thuringia; and came back comforted and truly purified, to his engagements; which he pursued more zealously than ever, though he now regarded himself as a stranger on the earth. In this period, some earlier, many later, especially in the Autumn of this year, occur most of those compositions, which, in the way of extract and selection, we have here given to the Public, under the title of *Fragments;* so likewise the *Hymns to the Night.*'

Such is our Biographer's account of this matter, and of the weighty inference it has led him to. We have detailed it the more minutely, and almost in the very words of the text, the better to put our readers in a condition for judging on what grounds Tieck rests his opinion, That herein lies the key to the whole spiritual history of Novalis, that 'the feeling which now penetrated and inspired him, may be said to have been the substance of his Life.' It would ill become us to contradict one so well qualified to judge of all subjects, and who enjoyed such peculiar opportunities for forming a right judgment of this: meanwhile we may say that, to our own minds, after all consideration, the certainty of this hypothesis will nowise become clear. Or rather, perhaps, it is to the expression, to the too determinate and exclusive language in which the hypothesis is worded, that we should object; for so plain does the truth of the case seem to us, we cannot but believe that Tieck himself would consent to modify his statement. That the whole philosophical and moral existence of such a man as Novalis should have been shaped and determined by the death of a young girl, almost a child, specially distinguished, so far as is shown, by nothing save her beauty, which at any rate must have been very short-lived, — will doubtless seem to every one a singular concatenation. We cannot but think that some result precisely similar in moral effect might have been attained by many different means; nay that by one means or another, it would not have failed to be attained. For spirits like Novalis, earthly fortune is in no instance so sweet and smooth, that it does not by and by teach the great doctrine of *Entsagen*, of 'Renunciation,' by which alone, as a wise man well known to Herr Tieck has observed, 'can the real entrance on Life be properly said to begin.' Experience, the grand Schoolmaster, seems to have taught Novalis this doctrine very early, by the wreck of his first passionate wish; and herein lies the real influence of Sophie von K. on his character; an influence which, as we imagine, many other things might and would have equally exerted: for it is less the severity of the Teacher than the aptness of the Pupil that secures the lesson; nor do the purifying effects of frustrated Hope, and Affection which in this world will ever be homeless, depend on the worth or loveliness of its objects, but on that of the heart which cherished it, and can draw mild wisdom from so stern a disappointment. We do not say that Novalis continued the same as if this young maiden had not been; causes and effects connecting every man and thing with every other extend through all Time and Space; but surely it appears unjust to represent him as so altogether pliant in the hands of Accident; a mere pipe for Fortune to play tunes on; and which sounded a mystic, deep, almost unearthly melody, simply because a young woman was beautiful and mortal.

We feel the more justified in these hard-hearted and so unromantic strictures, on reading the very next paragraph of Tieck's Narrative. Directly on the back of this occurrence, Novalis goes to Freyberg; and there in 1798, it may be therefore somewhat more or somewhat less than a year after the death of his first love, forms an acquaintance, and an engagement to marry, with a 'Julie von Ch——!' Indeed, ever afterwards, to the end, his life appears to have been more than usually cheerful and happy. Tieck knows not what well to say of this betrothment, which in the eyes of most Novel-readers will have so shocking an appearance: he admits that 'perhaps to any but his intimate friends it may seem singular;' asserts, notwithstanding, that 'Sophie, as 'may be seen also in his writings, continued the centre of his 'thoughts; nay, as one departed, she stood in higher rever- 'ence with him than when visible and near;' and hurrying on, almost as over an unsafe subject, declares that Novalis felt nevertheless 'as if loveliness of mind and person might, in some measure, replace his loss;' and so leaves us to our own reflections on the matter. We consider it as throwing light on the above criticism; and greatly restricting our acceptance of Tieck's theory. Yet perhaps, after all, it is only in a Minerva-Press Novel, or to the more tender Imagination, that such a proceeding would seem very blamable. Constancy, in its true sense, may be called the root of all excellence; especially excellent is constancy in active well-doing, in friendly helpfulness to those that love us, and to those that hate us: but constancy in passive suffering, again, in spite of the high value put upon it in Circulating Libraries, is a distinctly inferior virtue, rather an accident than a virtue, and at all events is of extreme rarity in this world. To Novalis, his Sophie might still be as a saintly presence, mournful and unspeakably mild, to be worshipped in the inmost shrine of his memory: but worship of this sort is not man's sole business; neither should we censure Novalis that he dries his tears, and once more looks abroad with hope on the earth, which is still, as it was before, the strangest complex of mystery and light, of joy as well as sorrow. 'Life belongs to the living; and he that lives must be prepared for vicissitudes.' The questionable circumstance with Novalis is his perhaps too great rapidity in that second courtship; a fault or misfortune the more to be regretted, as this marriage also was to remain a project, and only the anticipation of it to be enjoyed by him.

It was for the purpose of studying mineralogy, under the famous Werner, that Novalis had gone to Freyberg. For this science he had great fondness, as indeed for all the physical sciences; which, if we may judge from his writings, he seems to have prosecuted on a great and original principle, very different both from that of our idle theorisers and generalisers, and that of the still more melancholy class who merely 'collect facts,' and for the torpor or total extinction of the thinking faculty, strive to make up by the more assiduous use of the blowpipe and goniometer. The commencement of a work, entitled the *Disciples at Sais*, intended, as Tieck informs us, to be a 'Physical Romance,' was written in Freyberg, at this time: but it lay unfinished, unprosecuted; and now comes before us as a very mysterious fragment, disclosing scientific depths, which we have not light to see into, much less means to fathom and accurately measure. The various hypothetic views of 'Nature,' that is, of the visible Creation, which are here given out in the words of the several 'Pupils,' differ, almost all of them, more or less, from any that we have ever elsewhere met with. To this work we shall have occasion to refer more particularly in the sequel.

The acquaintance which Novalis formed, soon after this, with the elder Schlegel (August Wilhelm), and still more that of Tieck, whom also he first met in Jena, seems to have operated a considerable diversion in his line of study. Tieck and the Schlegels, with some less active associates, among whom are now mentioned Wackenroder and Novalis, were at this time engaged in their far-famed campaign against Duncedom, or what called itself the 'Old School' of Literature; which old and rather despicable 'School' they had already, both by regular and guerilla warfare, reduced to great straits; as ultimately, they are reckoned to have succeeded in utterly extirpating it, or at least driving it back to the very confines of its native Cimmeria.[1] It seems to have been in connexion with these men, that Novalis first came before the world as a writer: certain of his *Fragments* under the title of *Blüthenstaub* (Pollen of Flowers), his *Hymns to the Night* and various poetical compositions were sent forth in F. Schlegel's *Musen-Almanach* and other periodicals under the same or kindred management. Novalis himself seems to profess that it was Tieck's influence which chiefly 'reawakened Poetry in him.' As to what reception these pieces met with, we have no information: however, Novalis seems to have been ardent and diligent in his new pursuit, as in his old ones; and no less happy than diligent.

'In the summer of 1800,' says Tieck, 'I saw him for the first time while visiting my friend Wilhelm Schlegel; and our acquaintance soon became the most confidential friendship. They were bright days those, which we passed with Schlegel, Schelling and some other friends. On my return homewards, I visited him in his house, and made acquaintance with his family. Here he read me the *Disciples at Sais*, and many of his *Fragments*. He escorted me as far as Halle; and we enjoyed in Giebichenstein, in the Riech-

[1] See Appendix I. to Vol. I. § *Tieck*.

ardts' house, some other delightful hours. About this time, the first thought of his *Ofterdingen* had occurred. At an earlier period, certain of his *Spiritual Songs* had been composed: they were to form part of a Christian Hymn-book, which he meant to accompany with a collection of Sermons. For the rest, he was very diligent in his professional labours; whatever he did was done with the heart; the smallest concern was not insignificant to him.'

The professional labours here alluded to, seem to have left much leisure on his hands; room for frequent change of place, and even of residence. Not long afterwards, we find him 'living for a long while in a solitary spot of the 'Güldne Aue in Thuringia, at the foot of the Kyffhäuser 'Mountain;' his chief society two military men, subsequently Generals; 'in which solitude great part of his *Ofterdingen* was written.' The first volume of this *Heinrich von Ofterdingen*, a sort of Art-Romance, intended, as he himself said, to be an 'Apotheosis of Poetry,' was erelong published; under what circumstances, or with what result, we have, as before, no notice. Tieck had for some time been resident in Jena, and at intervals saw much of Novalis. On preparing to quit that abode, he went to pay him a farewell visit at Weissenfels; found him 'somewhat 'paler,' but full of gladness and hope; 'quite inspired with 'plans of his future happiness; his house was already fitted 'up; in a few months he was to be wedded: no less zeal'ously did he speak of the speedy conclusion of *Ofterdingen*, 'and other books; his life seemed expanding in the richest 'activity and love.' This was in 1800: four years ago Novalis had longed and looked for death, and it was not appointed him; now life is again rich and far-extending in his eyes, and its close is at hand. Tieck parted with him, and it proved to be forever.

In the month of August, Novalis, preparing for his journey to Freyberg on so joyful an occasion, was alarmed with an appearance of blood proceeding from the lungs. The Physician treated it as a slight matter; nevertheless, the marriage was postponed. He went to Dresden with his

Parents, for medical advice; abode there for some time in no improving state; on learning the accidental death of a young brother at home, he ruptured a blood-vessel; and the Doctor then declared his malady incurable. This, as usual in such maladies, was nowise the patient's own opinion; he wished to try a warmer climate, but was thought too weak for the journey. In January (1801) he returned home, visibly, to all but himself, in rapid decline. His bride had already been to see him, in Dresden. We may give the rest in Tieck's words:

'The nearer he approached his end, the more confidently did he expect a speedy recovery; for the cough diminished, and excepting languor, he had no feeling of sickness. With the hope and the longing for life, new talent and fresh strength seemed also to awaken in him; he thought, with renewed love, of all his projected labours; he determined on writing *Ofterdingen* over again from the very beginning; and shortly before his death, he said on one occasion, "Never till now did I know what Poetry was; innumerable Songs and Poems, and of quite different stamp from any of my former ones, have arisen in me." From the nineteenth of March, the death-day of his Sophie, he became visibly weaker; many of his friends visited him; and he felt great joy when, on the twenty-first, his true and oldest friend, Friedrich Schlegel, came to him from Jena. With him he conversed at great length; especially upon their several literary operations. During these days he was very lively; his nights too were quiet; and he enjoyed pretty sound sleep. On the twenty-fifth, about six in the morning, he made his brother hand him certain books, that he might look for something; then he ordered breakfast, and talked cheerfully till eight; towards nine he bade his brother play a little to him on the harpsichord, and in the course of the music fell asleep. Friedrich Schlegel soon afterwards came into the room, and found him quietly sleeping: this sleep lasted till near twelve, when without the smallest motion he passed away, and, unchanged in death, retained his common friendly look as if he yet lived.

'So died,' continues the affectionate Biographer, 'before he had completed his twenty-ninth year, this our Friend; in whom his extensive acquirements, his philosophical talent and his poetic genius must alike obtain our love and admiration. As he had so far outrun his time, our country might have expected extraordinary things from such gifts, had this early death not overtaken him: as it is, the unfinished Writings he left behind him have already had a wide influence; and many of his great thoughts will yet, in time coming, lend their inspiration, and noble minds and deep thinkers will be enlightened and enkindled by the sparks of his genius.

'Novalis was tall, slender and of noble proportions. He wore his light-brown hair in long clustering locks, which at that time was less unusual than it would be now; his hazel eye was clear and glancing; and the colour of his face, especially of the fine brow, almost transparent. Hand and foot were somewhat too large, and without fine character. His look was at all times cheerful and kind. For those who distinguish a man only in so far as he puts himself forward, or by studious breeding, by fashionable bearing, endeavours to shine or to be singular, Novalis was lost in the crowd: to the more practised eye, again, he presented a figure which might be called beautiful. In outline and expression, his face strikingly resembled that of the Evangelist John, as we see him in the large noble Painting by Albrecht Dürer, preserved at Nürnberg and München.

'In speaking, he was lively and loud, his gestures strong. I never saw him tired: though we had talked till far in the night, it was still only on purpose that he stopped, for the sake of rest, and even then he used to read before sleeping. Tedium he never felt, even in oppressive company, among mediocre men; for he was sure to find out one or other, who could give him yet some new piece of knowledge, such as he could turn to use, insignificant as it might seem. His kindliness, his frank bearing, made him a universal favourite: his skill in the art of social intercourse was so great, that smaller minds did not perceive how high he stood above them. Though in conversation he delighted most to unfold the deeps of the soul, and spoke as inspired of the regions of invisible worlds, yet was he mirthful as a child; would jest in free artless gaiety, and heartily give-in to the jestings of his company. Without vanity, without learned haughtiness, far from every affectation and hypocrisy, he was a genuine, true man, the purest and loveliest embodiment of a high immortal spirit.'

So much for the outward figure and history of Novalis. Respecting his inward structure and significance, which our readers are here principally interested to understand, we have already acknowledged that we had no complete insight to boast of. The slightest perusal of his Writings indicates to us a mind of wonderful depth and originality; but at the same time, of a nature or habit so abstruse, and altogether different from anything we ourselves have notice or experience of, that to penetrate fairly into its essential character, much more to picture it forth in visual distinctness, would be an extremely difficult task. Nay perhaps, if attempted by the means familiar to us, an impossible task: for Novalis belongs to that class of persons, who do not recognise the 'syllogistic method' as the chief organ for investigating truth, or feel themselves bound at all times to stop short where its light fails them. Many of his opinions he would despair of proving in the most patient Court of Law; and would remain well content that they should be disbelieved there. He much loved, and had assiduously studied, Jacob Böhme and other mystical writers; and was, openly enough, in good part a Mystic himself. Not indeed what we English, in common speech, call a Mystic; which means only a man whom we do not understand, and, in self-defence, reckon or would fain reckon a Dunce. Novalis was a Mystic, or had an affinity with Mysticism, in the primary and true meaning of that word, exemplified in some shape among our own Puritan Divines, and which at this day carries no opprobrium with it in Germany, or, except among certain more unimportant classes, in any other country. Nay, in this sense, great honours are recorded of Mysticism: Tasso, as may be seen in several of his prose writings, was professedly a Mystic; Dante is regarded as a chief man of that class.

Nevertheless, with all due tolerance or reverence for Novalis's Mysticism, the question still returns on us: How shall we understand it, and in any measure shadow it forth? How may that spiritual condition, which by its own account is like pure Light, colourless, formless, infinite, be represented by mere Logic-Painters, mere Engravers we might say, who, except copper and burin, producing the most finite black-on-white, have no means of representing anything? Novalis himself has a line or two, and no more, expressly on Mysticism: 'What is Mysticism?' asks he. 'What is it that 'should come to be treated mystically? Religion, Love, Na-'ture, Polity. — All select things (*alles Auserwählte*) have a 'reference to Mysticism. If all men were but one pair of 'lovers, the difference between Mysticism and Non-Mysticism 'were at an end.' In which little sentence, unhappily, our reader obtains no clearness; feels rather as if he were looking into darkness visible. We must entreat him, nevertheless, to keep up his spirits in this business; and above all, to assist us with his friendliest, cheerfullest endeavour: perhaps some faint far-off view of that same mysterious Mysticism may at length rise upon us.

To ourselves it somewhat illustrates the nature of Novalis's opinions, when we consider the then and present state of German metaphysical science generally; and the fact, stated above, that he gained his first notions on this subject from Fichte's *Wissenschaftslehre.* It is true, as Tieck remarks, 'he sought to open for himself a new path in Philosophy; to unite Philosophy with Religion:' and so diverged in some degree from his first instructor; or, as it more probably seemed to himself, prosecuted Fichte's scientific inquiry into its highest practical results. At all events, his metaphysical creed, so far as we can gather it from these Writings, appears everywhere in its essential lineaments synonymous with what little we understand of Fichte's, and might indeed, safely enough for our present purpose, be classed under the head of Kantism, or German metaphysics generally.

Now, without entering into the intricacies of German Philosophy, we need here only advert to the character of Idealism, on which it is everywhere founded, and which universally pervades it. In all German systems, since the time of Kant, it is the fundamental principle to deny the existence of Matter; or rather we should say, to believe it in a radically different sense from that in which the Scotch Philosopher strives to demonstrate it, and the English Unphilosopher believes it without demonstration. To any of our readers, who has dipped never so slightly into metaphysical reading, this Idealism will be no inconceivable thing. Indeed it is singular how widely diffused, and under what different aspects, we meet with it among the most dissimilar classes of mankind. Our Bishop Berkeley seems to have adopted it from religious inducements: Father Boscovich was led to a very cognate result, in his *Theoria Philosophiæ Naturalis*, from merely mathematical considerations. Of the ancient Pyrrho, or the modern Hume, we do not speak: but in the opposite end of the Earth, as Sir W. Jones informs us, a similar theory, of immemorial age, prevails among the theologians of Hindostan. Nay, Professor Stewart has declared his opinion, that whoever at some time of his life has not entertained this theory, may reckon that he has yet shown no talent for metaphysical research. Neither is it any argument against the Idealist to say that, since he denies the absolute existence of Matter, he ought in conscience to deny its relative existence; and plunge over precipices, and run himself through with swords, by way of recreation, since these, like all other material things, are only phantasms and spectra, and therefore of no consequence. If a man, corporeally taken, is but a phantasm and spectrum himself, all this will ultimately amount to much the same as it did before. Yet herein lies Dr. Reid's grand triumph over the Sceptics; which is as good as no triumph whatever. For as to the argument which he and his followers insist on, under all possible variety of figures, it amounts only to this very plain consideration, that 'men naturally, and without reasoning, *believe* in the existence of Matter;' and seems, philosophically speaking, not to have any value; nay, the introduction of it into Philosophy may be considered as an act of suicide on the part of that science, the life and business of which, that of '*interpreting* Appearances,' is hereby at an end. Curious it is, moreover, to observe how these Commonsense Philosophers, men who brag chiefly of their irrefragable logic, and keep watch and ward, as if this were their special trade, against 'Mysticism' and 'Visionary Theories,' are themselves obliged to base their whole system on Mysticism, and a Theory; on Faith, in short, and that of a very comprehensive kind; the Faith, namely, either that man's Senses are themselves Divine, or that they afford not only an honest, but a *literal* representation of the workings of some Divinity. So true is it that for these men also, all knowledge of the visible rests on belief of the invisible, and derives its first meaning and certainty therefrom!

The Idealist, again, boasts that his Philosophy is Transcendental, that is, 'ascending *beyond* the senses;' which, he asserts, *all* Philosophy, properly so called, by its nature is and must be: and in this way he is led to various unexpected conclusions. To a Transcendentalist, Matter has an existence, but only as a Phenomenon: were *we* not there, neither would it be there; it is a mere Relation, or rather the result of a Relation between our living Souls and the great First Cause; and depends for its apparent qualities on *our* bodily and mental organs; having itself *no* intrinsic qualities; being, in the common sense of that word, Nothing. The tree is green and hard, not of its own natural virtue, but simply because my eye and my hand are fashioned so as to discern such and such appearances under such and such conditions. Nay, as an Idealist might say, even on the most popular grounds, *must* it not be so? Bring a sentient Being, with eyes a little different, with fingers ten times harder than mine; and to him that Thing which I call Tree shall be yellow and soft, as truly as to me it is green and hard. Form his Nervous-structure in all points the *reverse* of mine, and this same Tree shall not be combustible or heat-producing, but dissoluble and cold-producing, not high and convex, but deep and concave; shall simply have *all* properties exactly the reverse of those I attribute to it. There is, in fact, says Fichte, no Tree there; but only a Manifestation of Power from something which is *not I.* The same is true of material Nature at large, of the whole visible Universe, with all its movements, figures, accidents and qualities; all are Impressions produced on *me* by something *different from me.* This, we suppose, may be the foundation of what Fichte means by his far-famed *Ich* and *Nicht-Ich* (I and Not-I); words which, taking lodging (to use the Hudibrastic phrase) in certain 'heads that were to be let unfurnished,' occasioned a hollow echo, as of Laughter, from the empty Apartments; though the words are in themselves quite harmless, and may represent the basis of a metaphysical Philosophy as fitly as any other words. But farther, and what is still stranger than such Idealism, according to these Kantean systems, the organs of the Mind too, what is called the Understanding, are of no less arbitrary, and, as it were, accidental character than those of the Body. Time and Space themselves are not external but internal entities: they have no outward existence, there is no Time and no Space *out* of the mind; they are mere *forms* of man's spiritual being, *laws* under which his thinking nature is constituted to act. This seems the hardest conclusion of all; but it is an important one with Kant; and is not given forth as a dogma; but carefully deduced in his *Critik der Reinen Vernunft* with great precision, and the strictest form of argument.

The reader would err widely who supposed that this Transcendental system of Metaphysics was a mere intellectual card-castle, or logical hocus-pocus, contrived from sheer idleness and for sheer idleness, being without any bearing on the practical interests of men. On the contrary, however false, or however true, it is the most serious in its purport of all Philosophies propounded in these latter centuries; has been taught chiefly by men of the loftiest and most earnest character; and does bear, with a direct and highly comprehensive influence, on the most vital interests of men. To say nothing of the views it opens in regard to the course and management of what is called Natural Science, we cannot but perceive that its effects, for such as adopt it, on Morals and Religion, must in these days be of almost boundless importance. To take only that last and seemingly strangest doctrine, for example, concerning Time and Space, we shall find that to the Kantist it yields, almost immediately, a remarkable result of this sort. If Time and Space have no absolute existence, no existence out of our minds, it removes a stumbling-block from the very threshold of our Theology. For on this ground, when we say that the Deity is omnipresent and eternal, that with Him it is a universal Here and Now, we say nothing wonderful; nothing but that He also created Time and Space, that Time and Space are not laws of His being, but only of ours. Nay to the Transcendentalist, clearly enough, the whole question of the origin and existence of Nature must be greatly simplified: the old hostility of Matter is at an end, for Matter is itself annihilated; and the black Spectre, Atheism, 'with all its sickly dews,' melts into nothingness forever. But farther, if it be, as Kant maintains, that the logical mechanism of the mind is arbitrary, so to speak, and might have been made different, it will follow, that all inductive conclusions, all conclusions of the Understanding, have only a relative truth, are true only for *us*, and *if* some other thing be true. Thus far Hume and Kant go together, in this branch of the inquiry: but here occurs the most total, diametrical divergence between them. We allude to the recognition, by these Transcendentalists, of a higher faculty in man than Understanding; of Reason (*Vernunft*), the pure, ultimate light of our nature; wherein, as they assert, lies the foundation of all Poetry, Virtue, Religion; things which are properly beyond the province of the Understanding, of which the Understanding *can* take no cognisance, except a false one. The elder Jacobi, who indeed is no Kantist, says once, we remember: 'It is the instinct of Understanding to *contradict* Reason.' Admitting this last distinction and subordination, supposing it scientifically demonstrated, what numberless and weightiest consequences would follow from it alone! These we must leave the considerate reader to deduce for himself; observing only farther, that the *Teologia Mistica*, so much venerated by Tasso in his philosophical writings; the 'Mysticism' alluded to by Novalis; and generally all true Christian Faith and Devotion, appear, so far as we can see, more or less included in this doctrine of the Transcendentalists; under their several shapes, the essence of them all being what is here designated by the name Reason, and set forth as the true sovereign of man's mind.

How deeply these and the like principles had impressed themselves on Novalis, we see more and more, the farther we study his Writings. Naturally a deep, religious, contemplative spirit; purified also, as we have seen, by harsh Affliction, and familiar in the 'Sanctuary of Sorrow,' he comes before us as the most ideal of all Idealists. For him the material Creation is but an Appearance, a typical shadow in which the Deity manifests himself to man. Not only has the unseen world a reality, but the only reality: the rest being not metaphorically, but literally and in scientific strictness, 'a show;' in the words of the Poet, '*Schall und Rauch umnebelnd Himmels Gluth*, Sound and Smoke overclouding the splendour of Heaven.' The Invisible World is near us: or rather it is here, in us and about us; were the fleshly coil removed from our Soul, the glories of the Unseen were even now around us; as the Ancients fabled of the Spheral Music. Thus, not in word only, but in truth and sober belief, he feels himself encompassed by the Godhead; feels in every thought, that 'in Him he lives, moves and has his being.'

On his Philosophic and Poetic procedure, all this has its natural influence. The aim of Novalis's whole Philosophy, we might say, is to preach and establish the Majesty of Reason, in that stricter sense; to conquer for it all provinces of human thought, and everywhere reduce its vassal, Understanding, into fealty, the right and only useful relation for it. Mighty tasks in this sort lay before himself; of which, in these Writings of his, we trace only scattered indications. In fact, all that he has left is in the shape of Fragment; detached expositions and combinations, deep, brief glimpses:

but such seems to be their general tendency. One character to be noted in many of these, often too obscure speculations, is his peculiar manner of viewing Nature: his habit, as it were, of considering Nature rather in the concrete, not analytically and as a divisible Aggregate, but as a self-subsistent universally connected Whole. This also is perhaps partly the fruit of his Idealism. 'He had formed the Plan,' we are informed, 'of a peculiar Encyclopedical 'Work, in which experiences and ideas from all the different sciences were mutually to elucidate, confirm and 'enforce each other.' In this work he had even made some progress. Many of the 'Thoughts,' and short Aphoristic observations, here published, were intended for it; of such, apparently, it was, for the most part, to have consisted.

As a Poet, Novalis is no less Idealistic than as a Philosopher. His poems are breathings of a high devout soul, feeling always that here he has no home, but looking, as in clear vision, to a 'city that hath foundations.' He loves external Nature with a singular depth; nay, we might say, he reverences her, and holds unspeakable communings with her: for Nature is no longer dead, hostile Matter, but the veil and mysterious Garment of the Unseen; as it were, the Voice with which the Deity proclaims himself to man. These two qualities, — his pure religious temper, and heartfelt love of Nature, — bring him into true poetic relation both with the spiritual and the material World, and perhaps constitute his chief worth as a Poet; for which art he seems to have originally a genuine, but no exclusive or even very decided endowment.

His moral persuasions, as evinced in his Writings and Life, derive themselves naturally enough from the same source. It is the morality of a man, to whom the Earth and all its glories are in truth a vapour and a Dream, and the Beauty of Goodness the *only* real possession. Poetry, Virtue, Religion, which for other men have but, as it were, a traditionary and imagined existence, are for him the everlasting basis of the Universe; and all earthly acquirements, all with which Ambition, Hope, Fear, can tempt us to toil and sin, are in very deed but a picture of the brain, some reflex shadowed on the mirror of the Infinite, but in themselves air and nothingness. Thus, to live in that Light of Reason, to have, even while here and encircled with this Vision of Existence, our abode in that Eternal City, is the highest and sole duty of man. These things Novalis figures to himself under various images: sometimes he seems to represent the Primeval essence of Being as Love; at other times, he speaks in emblems, of which it would be still more difficult to give a just account; which, therefore, at present, we shall not farther notice.

For now, with these far-off sketches of an exposition, the reader must hold himself ready to look into Novalis, for a little, with his own eyes. Whoever has honestly, and with attentive outlook, accompanied us along these wondrous outskirts of Idealism, may find himself as able to interpret Novalis as the majority of German readers would be; which, we think, is fair measure on our part. We shall not attempt any farther commentary; fearing that it might be too difficult and too unthankful a business. Our first extract is from the *Lehrlinge zu Sais* (Pupils at Sais), adverted to above. That 'Physical Romance,' which, for the rest, contains no story or indication of a story, but only poetised philosophical speeches, and the strangest shadowy allegorical allusions, and indeed is only carried the length of two Chapters, commences, without note of preparation, in this singular wise:

'I. The Pupil.—Men travel in manifold paths: whoso traces and compares these, will find strange Figures come to light; Figures which seem as if they belonged to that great Cipher-writing which one meets with everywhere, on wings of birds, shells of eggs, in clouds, in the snow, in crystals, in forms of rocks, in freezing waters, in the interior and exterior of mountains, of plants, animals, men, in the lights of the sky, in plates of glass and pitch when touched and struck on, in the filings round the magnet, and the singular conjunctures of Chance. In such Figures one anticipates the key to that wondrous Writing, the grammar of it; but this Anticipation will not fix itself into shape, and appears as if, after all, it would not become such a key for us. An *Alcahest* seems poured out over the senses of men. Only for a moment will their wishes, their thoughts thicken into form. Thus do their Anticipations arise; but after short whiles, all is again swimming vaguely before them, even as it did.

'From afar I heard say, that Unintelligibility was but the result of Unintelligence; that this sought what itself had, and so could find nowhere else; also that we did not understand Speech, because Speech did not, would not, understand itself; that the genuine Sanscrit spoke for the sake of speaking, because speaking was its pleasure and its nature.

'Not long thereafter, said one: No explanation is required for Holy Writing. Whoso speaks truly is full of eternal life, and wonderfully related to genuine mysteries does his Writing appea to us, for it is a Concord from the Symphony of the Universe.

'Surely this voice meant our Teacher; for it is he that can collect the indications which lie scattered on all sides. A singular light kindles in his looks, when at length the high Rune lies before us, and he watches in our eyes whether the star has yet risen upon us, which is to make the Figure visible and intelligible. Does he see us sad, that the darkness will not withdraw? He consoles us, and promises the faithful assiduous seer better fortune in time. Often has he told us how, when he was a child, the impulse to employ his senses, to busy to fill them, left him no rest. He looked at the stars, and imitated their courses and positions in the sand. Into the ocean of air he gazed incessantly; and never wearied contemplating its clearness, its movements, its clouds, its lights. He gathered stones, flowers, insects, of all sorts, and spread them out in manifold wise, in rows before him. To men and animals he paid heed; on the shore of the sea he sat, collected muscles. Over his own heart and his own thoughts he watched attentively. He knew not whither his longing was carrying him. As he grew up he wandered far and wide; viewed other lands, other seas, new atmospheres, new rocks, unknown plants, animals, men; descended into caverns, saw how in courses and varying strata the edifice of the Earth was completed, and fashioned clay into strange figures of rocks. By and by, he came to find everywhere objects already known, but wonderfully mingled, united; and thus often extraordinary things came to shape in him. He soon became aware of combinations in all, of conjunctures, concurrences. Erelong, he no more saw anything alone.—In great variegated images, the perceptions of his senses crowded round him; he heard, saw, touched and thought at once. He rejoiced to bring strangers together. Now the stars were men, now men were stars, the stones animals, the clouds plants; he sported with powers and appearances; he knew where and how this and that was to be found, to be brought into action; and so himself struck over the strings, for tones and touches of his own.

'What has passed with him since then he does not disclose to us. He tells us that we ourselves, led on by him and our own desire, will discover what has passed with him. Many of us have withdrawn from him. They returned to their parents, and learned trades. Some have been sent out by him, we know not whither; he selected them. Of these, some have been but a short time there, others longer. One was still a child; scarcely was he come, when our Teacher was for passing him any more instruction. This Child had large dark eyes with azure ground, his skin shone like lilies, and his locks like light little clouds when it is growing evening. His voice pierced through all our hearts; willingly would we have given him our flowers, stones, pens, all we had. He smiled with an infinite earnestness; and we had a strange delight beside him. One day he will come again, said our Teacher, and then our lessons end.—Along with him he sent one, for whom we had often been sorry. Always sad he looked; he had been long years here; nothing would succeed with him; when we sought crystals or flowers, he seldom found. He saw dimly at a distance; to lay down variegated rows skilfully he had no power. He was so apt to break everything. Yet none had such eagerness, such pleasure in hearing and listening. At last,—it was before that Child came into our circle,—he all at once grew cheerful and expert. One day he had gone out sad; he did not return, and the night came on. We were very anxious for him; suddenly, as the morning dawned, we heard his voice in a neighbouring grove. He was singing a high, joyful song; we were all surprised; the Teacher looked to the East, such a look as I shall never see in him again. The singer soon came forth to us, and brought, with unspeakable blessedness on his face, a simple-looking little stone, of singular shape. The Teacher took it in his hand, and kissed him long; then looked at us with wet eyes, and laid this little stone on an empty space, which lay in the midst of other stones, just where, like radii, many rows of them met together.

'I shall in no time forget that moment. We felt as if we had had in our souls a clear passing glimpse into this wondrous World.'

In these strange Oriental delineations the judicious reader will suspect that more may be meant than meets the ear.

But who this teacher at Sais is, whether the personified Intellect of Mankind; and who this bright-faced golden-locked Child (Reason, Religious Faith?), that was 'to come again,' to conclude these lessons; and that awkward unwearied Man (Understanding?), that 'was so apt to break everything,' we have no data for determining, and would not undertake to conjecture with any certainty. We subjoin a passage from the second chapter, or section, entitled '*Nature*,' which, if possible, is of a still more surprising character than the first. After speaking at some length on the primeval views Man seems to have formed with regard to the external Universe, or 'the manifold Objects of his Senses;' and how in those times his mind had a peculiar unity, and only by Practice divided itself into separate faculties, as by Practice it may yet farther do, 'our Pupil' proceeds to describe the conditions requisite in an inquirer into Nature, observing, in conclusion, with regard to this,—

'No one, of a surety, wanders farther from the mark, than he who fancies to himself that he already understands this marvellous Kingdom, and can, in few words, fathom its constitution, and everywhere find the right path. To no one, who has broken off, and made himself an Island, will insight rise of itself, nor even without toilsome effort. Only to children, or childlike men, who know not what they do, can this happen. Long, unwearied intercourse, free and wise Contemplation, attention to faint tokens and indications; an inward poet-life, practised senses, a simple and devout spirit: these are the essential requisites of a true Friend of Nature; without these no one can attain his wish. Not wise does it seem to attempt comprehending and understanding a Human World without full perfected Humanity. No talent must sleep; and if all are not alike active, all must be alert, and not oppressed and enervated. As we see a future Painter in the boy who fills every wall with sketches and variedly adds colour to figure; so we see a future Philosopher in him who restlessly traces and questions all natural things, pays heed to all, brings together whatever is remarkable, and rejoices when he has become master and possessor of a new phenomenon, of a new power and piece of knowledge.

'Now to Some it appears not at all worth while to follow out the endless divisions of Nature; and moreover a dangerous undertaking, without fruit and issue. As we can never reach, say they, the absolutely smallest grain of material bodies, never find their simplest compartments, since all magnitude loses itself, forwards and backwards, in infinitude; so likewise is it with the species of bodies and powers; here too one comes on new species, new combinations, new appearances, even to infinitude. These seem only to stop, continue they, when our diligence tires; and so it is spending precious time with idle contemplations and tedious enumerations; and this becomes at last a true delirium, a real vertigo over the horrid Deep. For Nature too remains, so far as we have yet come, ever a frightful Machine of Death: everywhere monstrous revolution, inexplicable vortices of movement; a kingdom of Devouring, of the maddest tyranny; a baleful Immense: the few light-points disclose but a so much the more appalling Night, and terrors of all sorts must palsy every observer. Like a saviour does Death stand by the hapless race of mankind; for without Death, the maddest were the happiest. And precisely this striving to fathom that gigantic Mechanism is already a draught towards the Deep, a commencing giddiness; for every excitement is an increasing whirl, which soon gains full mastery over its victim, and hurls him forward with it into the fearful Night. Here, say those lamenters, lies the crafty snare for Man's understanding, which Nature everywhere seeks to annihilate as her greatest foe. Hail to that childlike ignorance and innocence of men, which kept them blind to the horrible perils that everywhere, like grim thunder-clouds, lay round their peaceful dwelling, and each moment were ready to rush down on them. Only inward disunion among the powers of Nature has preserved men hitherto; nevertheless, that great epoch cannot fail to arrive, when the whole family of mankind, by a grand universal Resolve, will snatch themselves from this sorrowful condition, from this frightful imprisonment; and by a voluntary Abdication of their terrestrial abode, redeem their race from this anguish, and seek refuge in a happier world, with their ancient Father. Thus might they end worthily; and prevent a necessary, violent destruction; or a still more horrible degenerating into Beasts, by gradual dissolution of their thinking organs, through Insanity. Intercourse with the powers of Nature, with animals, plants, rocks, storms and waves, must necessarily assimilate men to these objects; and this Assimilation, this Metamorphosis, and dissolution of the Divine and the Human, into ungovernable Forces, is even the Spirit of Nature, that frightfully voracious Power: and is not all that we see even now a prey from Heaven, a great Ruin of former Glories, the Remains of a terrific Repast?

'Be it so, cry a more courageous Class; let our species maintain a stubborn, well-planned war of destruction with this same Nature, then. By slow poisons must we endeavour to subdue her. The Inquirer into Nature is a noble hero, who rushes into the open abyss for the deliverance of his fellow-citizens. Artists have already played her many a trick: do but continue in this course; get hold of the secret threads, and bring them to act against each other. Profit by these discords, that so in the end you may lead her, like that fire-breathing Bull, according to your pleasure. To you she must become obedient. Patience and Faith beseem the children of men. Distant Brothers are united with us for one object; the wheel of the Stars must become the cistern-wheel of our life, and then, by our slaves, we can build us a new Fairyland. With heartfelt triumph let us look at her devastations, her tumults; she is selling herself to us, and every violence she will pay by a heavy penalty. In the inspiring feeling of our Freedom, let us live and die; here gushes forth the stream, which will one day overflow and subdue her; in it let us bathe, and refresh ourselves for new exploits. Hither the rage of the Monster does not reach; one drop of Freedom is sufficient to cripple her forever, and forever set limits to her havoc.

'They are right, say Several: here, or nowhere, lies the talisman. By the well of Freedom we sit and look; it is the grand magic Mirror, where the whole Creation images itself, pure and clear; in it do the tender Spirits and Forms of all Natures bathe; all chambers we here behold unlocked. What need have we toilsomely to wander over the troublous World of visible things? The purer World lies even in us, in this Well. Here discloses itself the true meaning of the great, many-coloured, complected Scene; and if full of these sights we return into Nature, all is well known to us, with certainty we distinguish every shape. We need not to inquire long; a light Comparison, a few strokes in the sand, are enough to inform us. Thus, for us, is the whole a great Writing, to which we have the key; and nothing comes to us unexpected, for the course of the great Horologe is known to us beforehand. It is only we that enjoy Nature with full senses, because she does not frighten us from our senses; because no fever-dreams oppress us, and serene consciousness makes us calm and confiding.

'They are *not* right, says an earnest Man to these latter. Can they not recognise in Nature the true impress of their own Selves? It is even they that consume themselves in wild hostility to Thought. They know not that this so-called Nature of theirs is a Sport of the Mind, a waste Fantasy of their Dream. Of a surety, it is for them a horrible Monster, a strange grotesque Shadow of their own Passions. The waking man looks without fear at this offspring of his lawless Imagination; for he knows that they are but vain Spectres of his weakness. He feels himself lord of the world: his *Me* hovers victorious over the Abyss; and will through Eternities hover aloft above that endless Vicissitude. Harmony is what his spirit strives to promulgate, to extend. He will even to infinitude grow more and more harmonious with himself and with his Creation; and at every step behold the all-efficiency of a high moral Order in the Universe, and what is purest of his *Me* come forth into brighter and brighter clearness. The significance of the World is Reason; for her sake is the World here; and when it is grown to be the arena of a childlike, expanding Reason, it will one day become the divine Image of her Activity, the scene of a genuine Church. Till then let man honour Nature as the Emblem of his own Spirit; the Emblem ennobling itself, along with him, to unlimited degrees. Let him, therefore, who would arrive at knowledge of Nature, train his moral sense, let him act and conceive in accordance with the noble Essence of his Soul; and as if of herself, Nature will become open to him. Moral Action is that great and only Experiment, in which all riddles of the most manifold appearances explain themselves. Whoso understands it, and in rigid sequence of Thought can lay it open, is forever Master of Nature.'[1]

'The Pupil,' it is added, 'listens with alarm to these conflicting voices.' If such was the case in half-supernatural Sais, it may well be much more so in mere sublunary London. Here again, however, in regard to these vaporous lucubrations, we can only imitate Jean Paul's Quintus Fixlein, who, it is said, in his elaborate *Catalogue of German Errors of the Press*, 'states that important inferences are to 'be drawn from it, and advises the reader to draw them.' Perhaps these wonderful paragraphs, which look, at this distance, so like chasms filled with mere sluggish mist, might prove valleys, with a clear stream and soft pastures, were we near at hand. For one thing, either Novalis, with Tieck and Schlegel at his back, are men in a state of derangement; or there is more in Heaven and Earth than has been dreamt of in our Philosophy. We may add that, in our view, this last Speaker, the 'earnest Man,' seems evidently to be Fichte; the first two Classes look like some sceptical or atheistic brood, unacquainted with Bacon's *Novum Organum*, or having, the First class at least, almost no faith in it. That

[1] Bd. ii. s. 43–57.

theory of the human species ending by a universal simultaneous act of Suicide, will, to the more simple sort of readers, be new.

As farther and more directly illustrating Novalis's scientific views, we may here subjoin two short sketches, taken from another department of this Volume. To all who prosecute Philosophy, and take interest in its history and present aspects, they will not be without interest. The obscure parts of them are not perhaps unintelligible, but only obscure; which unluckily cannot, at all times, be helped in such cases:

'Common Logic is the Grammar of the higher Speech, that is of Thought; it examines merely the *relations* of ideas to one another, the *Mechanics* of Thought, the pure Physiology of ideas. Now logical ideas stand related to one another, like words without thoughts. Logic occupies itself with the mere dead Body of the Science of Thinking. — Metaphysics, again, is the *Dynamics* of Thought; treats of the primary *Powers* of Thought; occupies itself with the mere Soul of the Science of Thinking. Metaphysical ideas stand related to one another, like thoughts without words. Men often wondered at the stubborn Incompletibility of these two Sciences; each followed its own business by itself; there was a want everywhere, nothing would suit rightly with either. From the very first, attempts were made to unite them, as everything about them indicated relationship; but every attempt failed; the one or the other Science still suffered in these attempts, and lost its essential character. We had to abide by metaphysical Logic, and logical Metaphysic, but neither of them was as it should be. With Physiology and Psychology with Mechanics and Chemistry, it fared no better. In the latter half of this Century there arose, with us Germans, a more violent commotion than ever; the hostile masses towered themselves up against each other more fiercely than heretofore; the fermentation was extreme; there followed powerful explosions. And now some assert that a real Compenetration has somewhere or other taken place; that the germ of a union has arisen, which will grow by degrees, and assimilate all to one indivisible form: that this principle of Peace is pressing out irresistibly, on all sides, and that erelong there will be but one Science and one Spirit, as one Prophet and one God.' —

'The rude, discursive Thinker is the Scholastic (Schoolman Logician). The true Scholastic is a mystical Subtlist; out of logical

Atoms he builds his Universe; he annihilates all living Nature, to put an Artifice of Thoughts (*Gedankenkunststück*, literally Conjuror's-trick of Thoughts) in its room. His aim is an infinite Automaton. Opposite to him is the rude, intuitive Poet: this is a mystical Macrologist: he hates rules and fixed form; a wild, violent life reigns instead of it in Nature; all is animate, no law; wilfulness and wonder everywhere. He is merely dynamical. Thus does the Philosophic Spirit arise at first, in altogether separate masses. In the *second* stage of culture these masses begin to come in contact, multifariously enough; and, as in the union of infinite Extremes, the Finite, the Limited arises, so here also arise "Eclectic Philosophers" without number; the time of misunderstanding begins. The most limited is, in this stage, the most important, the purest Philosopher of the second stage. This class occupies itself wholly with the actual, present world, in the strictest sense. The Philosophers of the first class look down with contempt on those of the second; say, they are a little of everything, and so nothing; hold their views as the results of weakness, as Inconsequentism. On the contrary, the second class, in their turn, pity the first; lay the blame on their visionary enthusiasm, which they say is absurd, even to insanity. If, on the one hand, the Scholastics and Alchemists seem to be utterly at variance, and the Eclectics on the other hand quite at one, yet, strictly examined, it is altogether the reverse. The former, in essentials, are indirectly of one opinion; namely, as regards the non-dependence and infinite character of Meditation, they both set out from the Absolute: whilst the Eclectic and limited sort are essentially at variance; and agree only in what is deduced. The former are infinite but uniform, the latter bounded but multiform; the former have genius, the latter talent; those have Ideas, these have knacks (*Handgriffe*); those are heads without hands, these are hands without heads. The *third* stage is for the Artist, who can be at once implement and genius. He finds that that primitive Separation in the absolute Philosophical Activities' (between the Scholastic, and the "rude, intuitive Poet") 'is a deeper-lying Separation in his own Nature; which Separation indicates, by its existence as such, the possibility of being adjusted, of being joined: he finds that, heterogeneous as these Activities are, there is yet a faculty in him of passing from the one to the other, of changing his *polarity* at will. He discovers in them, therefore, necessary members of his spirit; he observes that both must be united in some common Principle. He infers that Eclecticism is nothing but the imperfect defective employment of this Principle. It becomes ——'

— But we need not struggle farther, wringing a significance

out of these mysterious words: in delineating the genuine Transcendentalist, or 'Philosopher of the third stage,' properly speaking *the* Philosopher, Novalis ascends into regions whither few readers would follow him. It may be observed here, that British Philosophy, tracing it from Duns Scotus to Dugald Stewart, has now gone through the first and second of these 'stages,' the Scholastic and the Eclectic, and in considerable honour. With our amiable Professor Stewart, than whom no man, not Cicero himself, was ever more entirely Eclectic, that second or Eclectic class may be considered as having terminated; and now Philosophy is at a stand among us, or rather there is now no Philosophy visible in these Islands. It remains to be seen, whether we also are to have our 'third stage;' and how that new and highest 'class' will demean itself here. The French Philosophers seem busy studying Kant, and writing of him: but we rather imagine Novalis would pronounce them still only in the Eclectic stage. He says afterwards, that 'all Eclectics are essentially and at bottom sceptics; the more comprehensive, the more sceptical.'

These two passages have been extracted from a large series of *Fragments*, which, under the three divisions of Philosophical, Critical, Moral, occupy the greatest part of Volume Second. They are fractions, as we hinted above, of that grand 'encyclopedical work' which Novalis had planned. Friedrich Schlegel is said to be the selector of those published here. They come before us without note or comment; worded for the most part in very unusual phraseology; and without repeated and most patient investigation, seldom yield any significance, or rather we should say, often yield a false one. A few of the clearest we have selected for insertion: whether the reader will think them 'Pollen of Flowers,' or a baser kind of dust, we shall not predict. We give them in a miscellaneous shape; overlooking those classifications which, even in the text, are not and could not be very rigidly adhered to.

'Philosophy can bake no bread; but she can procure for us God, Freedom, Immortality. Which then is more practical, Philosophy or Economy? —

'Philosophy is properly Home-sickness; the wish to be everywhere at home. —

'We are near awakening when we dream that we dream. —

'The true philosophical Act is annihilation of self (*Selbsttödtung*); this is the real beginning of all Philosophy; all requisites for being a Disciple of Philosophy point hither. This Act alone corresponds to all the conditions and characteristics of transcendental conduct. —

'To become properly acquainted with a truth, we must first have disbelieved it, and disputed against it. —

'Man is the higher Sense of our Planet; the star which connects it with the upper world; the eye which it turns towards Heaven. —

'Life is a disease of the spirit; a working incited by Passion. Rest is peculiar to the spirit. —

'Our life is no Dream, but it may and will perhaps become one. —

'What is Nature? An encyclopedical, systematic Index or Plan of our Spirit. Why will we content us with the mere Catalogue of our Treasures? Let us contemplate them ourselves, and in all ways elaborate and use them. —

'If our Bodily Life is a burning, our Spiritual Life is a being burnt, a Combustion (or, is precisely the inverse the case?); Death, therefore, perhaps a Change of Capacity. —

'Sleep is for the inhabitants of Planets only. In another time. Man will sleep and wake continually at once. The greater part of our Body, of our Humanity itself, yet sleeps a deep sleep. —

'There is but one Temple in the World; and that is the Body of Man. Nothing is holier than this high form. Bending before men is a reverence done to this Revelation in the Flesh. We touch Heaven, when we lay our hand on a human body. —

'Man is a Sun; his Senses are the Planets. —

'Man has ever expressed some symbolical Philosophy of his Being in his Works and Conduct; he announces himself and his Gospel of Nature; he is the Messiah of Nature. —

'Plants are Children of the Earth; we are Children of the Æther. Our Lungs are properly our Root; we live, when we breathe; we begin our life with breathing. —

'Nature is an Æolian Harp, a musical instrument; whose tones again are keys to higher strings in us. —

'Every beloved object is the centre of a Paradise. —

'The first Man is the first Spirit-seer; all appears to him as Spirit. What are children, but first men? The fresh gaze of the Child is richer in significance than the forecasting of the most indubitable Seer. —

'It depends only on the weakness of our organs and of our self-excitement (*Selbstberührung*), that we do not see ourselves in a Fairy-world. All Fabulous Tales (*Mährchen*) are merely dreams of that home-world, which is everywhere and nowhere. The higher powers in us, which one day as Genies, shall fulfil our will,[1] are, for the present, Muses, which refresh us on our toilsome course with sweet remembrances. —

'Man consists in Truth. If he exposes Truth, he exposes himself. If he betrays Truth, he betrays himself. We speak not here of Lies, but of acting against Conviction. —

'A character is a completely fashioned will (*vollkommen gebildeter Wille*). —

'There is, properly speaking, no Misfortune in the world. Happiness and Misfortune stand in continual balance. Every Misfortune is, as it were, the obstruction of a stream, which, after overcoming this obstruction, but bursts through with the greater force. —

'The ideal of Morality has no more dangerous rival than the ideal of highest Strength, of most powerful life; which also has been named (very falsely as it was there meant) the ideal of poetic greatness. It is the maximum of the savage; and has, in these times, gained, precisely among the greatest weaklings, very many proselytes. By this ideal, man becomes a Beast-Spirit, a Mixture; whose brutal wit has, for weaklings, a brutal power of attraction. —

'The spirit of Poesy is the morning light, which makes the Statue of Memnon sound. —

'The division of Philosopher and Poet is only apparent, and to the disadvantage of both. It is a sign of disease, and of a sickly constitution. —

'The true Poet is all-knowing; he is an actual world in miniature. —

'Klopstock's works appear, for the most part, free Translations of an unknown Poet, by a very talented but unpoetical Philologist. —

'Goethe is an altogether practical Poet. He is in his works what the English are in their wares: highly simple, neat, convenient and

[1] Novalis's ideas, on what has been called the 'perfectibility of man,' ground themselves on his peculiar views of the constitution of material and spiritual Nature, and are of the most original and extraordinary character. With our utmost effort, we should despair of communicating other than a quite false notion of them. He asks, for instance, with scientific gravity: Whether any one, that recollects the first kind glance of her he loved, can doubt the possibility of *Magic?*

durable. He has done in German Literature what Wedgwood did in English Manufacture. He has, like the English, a natural turn for Economy, and a noble Taste acquired by Understanding. Both these are very compatible, and have a near affinity in the chemical sense. * *— *Wilhelm Meister's Apprenticeship* may be called throughout prosaic and modern. The Romantic sinks to ruin, the Poesy of Nature, the Wonderful. The Book treats merely of common worldly things: Nature and Mysticism are altogether forgotten. It is a poetised civic and household History; the Marvellous is expressly treated therein as imagination and enthusiasm. Artistic Atheism is the spirit of the Book. * * * It is properly a *Candide,* directed against Poetry: the Book is highly unpoetical in respect of spirit, poetical as the dress and body of it is. * * * The introduction of Shakspeare has almost a tragic effect. The hero retards the triumph of the Gospel of Economy; and economical Nature is finally the true and only remaining one. —

'When we speak of the aim and Art observable in Shakspeare's works, we must not forget that Art belongs to Nature; that it is, so to speak, self-viewing, self-imitating, self-fashioning Nature. The Art of a well-developed genius is far different from the Artfulness of the Understanding, of the merely reasoning mind. Shakspeare was no calculator, no learned thinker; he was a mighty, many-gifted soul, whose feelings and works, like products of Nature, bear the stamp of the same spirit; and in which the last and deepest of observers will still find new harmonies with the infinite structure of the Universe; concurrences with later ideas, affinities with the higher powers and senses of man. They are emblematic, have many meanings, are simple and inexhaustible, like products of Nature; and nothing more unsuitable could be said of them than that they are works of Art, in that narrow mechanical acceptation of the word.'

The reader understands that we offer these specimens not as the best to be found in Novalis's *Fragments,* but simply as the most intelligible. Far stranger and deeper things there are, could we hope to make them in the smallest degree understood. But in examining and re-examining many of his *Fragments,* we find ourselves carried into more complex, more subtle regions of thought than any we are elsewhere acquainted with: here we cannot always find our own latitude and longitude, sometimes not even approximate to finding them; much less teach others such a secret.

What has been already quoted may afford some knowledge

of Novalis, in the characters of Philosopher and Critic: there is one other aspect under which it would be still more curious to view and exhibit him, but still more difficult, — we mean that of his Religion. Novalis nowhere specially records his creed, in these Writings: he many times expresses, or implies, a zealous, heartfelt belief in the Christian system; yet with such adjuncts and coexisting persuasions, as to us might seem rather surprising. One or two more of these his Aphorisms, relative to this subject, we shall cite, as likely to be better than any description of ours. The whole Essay at the end of Volume First, entitled *Die Christenheit oder Europa* (Christianity or Europe) is also well worthy of study, in this as in many other points of view.

'Religion contains infinite sadness. If we are to love God, he must be in distress (*hülfsbedürftig*, help-needing). In how far is this condition answered in Christianity? —

'Spinoza is a God-intoxicated man (*Gott-trunkener Mensch*). —

'Is the Devil, as Father of Lies, himself but a necessary illusion? —

'The Catholic Religion is to a certain extent applied Christianity. Fichte's Philosophy too is perhaps applied Christianity. —

'Can Miracles work Conviction? Or is not real Conviction, this highest function of our soul and personality, the only true God-announcing Miracle?

'The Christian Religion is especially remarkable, moreover, as it so decidedly lays claim to mere good-will in Man, to his essential Temper, and values this independently of all Culture and Manifestation. It stands in opposition to Science and to Art, and *properly to Enjoyment.*[1]

'Its origin is with the common people. It inspires the great majority of the *limited* in this Earth.

'It is the Light that begins to shine in the Darkness.

'It is the root of *all Democracy*, the highest Fact in the Rights of Man (*die höchste Thatsache der Popularität*).

'Its unpoetical exterior, its resemblance to a modern family-picture, *seems only to be lent it.*[1]

'Martyrs are spiritual heroes. Christ was the greatest martyr of our species; through him has martyrdom become infinitely significant and holy. —

[1] Italics also in the text.

'The Bible begins nobly, with Paradise, the symbol of youth; and concludes with the Eternal Kingdom, the Holy City. Its two main divisions, also, are genuine grand-historical divisions (*ächt gross-historisch*). For in every grand-historical compartment (*Glied*), the grand history must lie, as it were, symbolically re-created (*verjüngt*, made young again). The beginning of the New Testament is the second higher Fall (the Atonement of the Fall), and the commencement of the new Period. The history of every individual man should be a Bible. Christ is the new Adam. A Bible is the highest problem of Authorship. —

'As yet there is no Religion. You must first make a Seminary (*Bildungs-schule*) of genuine Religion. Think ye that there is Religion? Religion has to be made and produced (*gemacht und hervorgebracht*) by the union of a number of persons.'

Hitherto our readers have seen nothing of Novalis in his character of Poet, properly so called; the *Pupils at Sais* being fully more of a scientific than poetic nature. As hinted above, we do not account his gifts in this latter province as of the first, or even of a high order; unless, indeed, it be true, as he himself maintains, that 'the distinction of Poet and Philosopher is apparent only, and to the injury of both.' In his professedly poetical compositions there is an indubitable prolixity, a degree of languor, not weakness but sluggishness; the meaning is too much diluted; and diluted, we might say, not in a rich, lively, varying music, as we find in Tieck, for example; but rather in a low-voiced, not unmelodious monotony, the deep hum of which is broken only at rare intervals, though sometimes by tones of purest and almost spiritual softness. We here allude chiefly to his unmetrical pieces, his prose fictions: indeed the metrical are few in number; for the most part, on religious subjects; and in spite of a decided truthfulness both in feeling and word, seem to bespeak no great skill or practice in that form of composition. In his prose style he may be accounted happier; he aims in general at simplicity, and a certain familiar expressiveness; here and there in his more elaborate passages, especially in his *Hymns to the Night*, he has reminded us of Herder.

These *Hymns to the Night*, it will be remembered, were written shortly after the death of his mistress: in that period of deep sorrow, or rather of holy deliverance from sorrow. Novalis himself regarded them as his most finished productions. They are of a strange, veiled, almost enigmatical character; nevertheless, more deeply examined, they appear nowise without true poetic worth; there is a vastness, an immensity of idea; a still solemnity reigns in them, a solitude almost as of extinct worlds. Here and there too some light-beam visits us in the void deep; and we cast a glance, clear and wondrous, into the secrets of that mysterious soul. A full commentary on the *Hymns to the Night* would be an exposition of Novalis's whole theological and moral creed; for it lies recorded there, though symbolically, and in lyric, not in didactic language. We have translated the Third, as the shortest and simplest; imitating its light, half-measured style, above all deciphering its vague deep-laid sense, as accurately as we could. By the word 'Night,' it will be seen, Novalis means much more than the common opposite of Day. 'Light, seems, in these poems, to shadow forth our terrestrial life; Night the primeval and celestial life:

'Once when I was shedding bitter tears, when dissolved in pain my Hope had melted away, and I stood solitary by the grave that in its dark narrow space concealed the Form of my life; solitary as no other had been; chased by unutterable anguish; powerless; one thought and that of misery; — here now as I looked round for help; forward could not go, nor backward, but clung to a transient extinguished Life with unutterable longing; — lo, from the azure distance, down from the heights of my old Blessedness, came a chill breath of Dusk, and suddenly the band of Birth, the fetter of Light was snapped asunder. Vanishes the Glory of Earth, and with it my Lamenting; rushes together the infinite Sadness into a new unfathomable World: thou Night's-inspiration, Slumber of Heaven, camest over me; the scene rose gently aloft; over the scene hovered my enfranchised new-born spirit; to a cloud of dust that grave changed itself; through the cloud I beheld the transfigured features of my Beloved. In her eyes lay Eternity; I clasped her hand, and my tears became a glittering indissoluble chain. Centuries of Ages moved away into the distance, like thunder-clouds. On her neck I wept, for this new life, enrapturing tears. — It was my first, only Dream; and ever since then do I feel this changeless everlasting faith in the Heaven of Night, and its Sun my Beloved.'

What degree of critical satisfaction, what insight into the grand crisis of Novalis's spiritual history, which seems to be here shadowed forth, our readers may derive from this Third *Hymn to the Night*, we shall not pretend to conjecture. Meanwhile, it were giving them a false impression of the Poet, did we leave him here; exhibited only under his more mystic aspects: as if his Poetry were exclusively a thing of Allegory, dwelling amid Darkness and Vacuity, far from all paths of ordinary mortals and their thoughts. Novalis can write in the most common style, as well as in this most uncommon one; and there too not without originality. By far the greater part of his First Volume is occupied with a Romance, *Heinrich von Ofterdingen*, written, so far as it goes, much in the every-day manner; we have adverted the less to it, because we nowise reckoned it among his most remarkable compositions. Like many of the others, it has been left as a Fragment; nay, from the account Tieck gives of its ulterior plan, and how from the solid prose world of the First part, this 'Apotheosis of Poetry' was to pass, in the Second, into a mythical, fairy and quite fantastic world, critics have doubted whether, strictly speaking, it *could* have been completed. From this work we select two passages, as specimens of Novalis's manner in the more common style of composition; premising, which in this one instance we are entitled to do, that whatever excellence they may have will be universally appreciable. The first is the introduction to the whole Narrative, as it were the text of the whole; the 'Blue Flower' there spoken of being Poetry, the real object, passion and vocation of young Heinrich, which, through manifold adventures, exertions and sufferings, he is to seek and find. His history commences thus:

'The old people were already asleep; the clock was beating its monotonous tick on the wall; the wind blustered over the rattling windows; by turns, the chamber was lighted by the sheen of the moon. The young man lay restless in his bed; and thought of the stranger and his stories. "Not the treasures is it," said he to himself, "that have awakened in me so unspeakable a desire; far from me is all covetousness; but the Blue Flower is what I long to behold. It lies incessantly in my heart, and I can think and fancy of nothing else. Never did I feel so before: it is as if, till now, I had been dreaming, or as if sleep had carried me into another world; for in the world I used to live in, who troubled himself about flowers? Such wild passion for a Flower was never heard of there. But whence could that stranger have come? None of us ever saw such a man; yet I know not how I alone was so caught with his discourse: the rest heard the very same, yet none seems to mind it. And then that I cannot even speak of my strange condition! I feel such rapturous contentment; and only then when I have not the Flower rightly before my eyes, does so deep heartfelt an eagerness come over me: these things no one will or can believe. I could fancy I were mad, if I did not see, did not think with such perfect clearness; since that day, all is far better known to me. I have heard tell of ancient times; how animals and trees and rocks used to speak with men. This is even my feeling; as if they were on the point of breaking out, and I could see in them, what they wished to say to me. There must be many a word which I know not; did I know more, I could better comprehend these matters. Once I liked dancing; now I had rather think to the music." — The young man lost himself, by degrees, in sweet fancies, and fell asleep. He dreamed first of immeasurable distances, and wild unknown regions. He wandered over seas with incredible speed; strange animals he saw; he lived with many varieties of men, now in war, in wild tumult, now in peaceful huts. He was taken captive, and fell into the lowest wretchedness. All emotions rose to a height as yet unknown to him. He lived through an infinitely variegated life; died and came back; loved to the highest passion, and then again was forever parted from his loved one. At length towards morning, as the dawn broke up without, his spirit also grew stiller, the images grew clearer and more permanent. It seemed to him he was walking alone in a dark wood. Only here and there did day glimmer through the green net. Erelong he came to a rocky chasm, which mounted upwards. He had to climb over many crags, which some former stream had rolled down. The higher he came, the lighter grew the wood. At last he arrived at a little meadow, which lay on the declivity of the mountain. Beyond the meadow rose a high cliff, at the foot of which he observed an opening, that seemed to be the entrance of a passage hewn in the rock. The passage led him easily on, for some time, to a great subterranean expanse, out of which from afar a bright gleam was visible. On entering, he perceived a strong beam of light, which sprang as if from a fountain to the roof of the cave, and sprayed itself into innumerable sparks, which collected below in a great basin: the beam glanced like kindled gold; not the faintest noise was to be heard, a sacred silence encircled the glorious sight. He approached the basin, which waved and quivered with infinite hues. The walls of the cave were coated with this fluid, which was not hot but cool, and on the walls threw out a faint bluish light. He dipt his hand in the basin, and wetted his lips. It was as if the breath of a spirit went through him; and he felt himself in his inmost heart strengthened and refreshed. An irresistible desire seized him to bathe; he undressed himself and stept into the basin. He felt as if a sunset cloud were floating round him; a heavenly emotion streamed over his soul; in deep pleasure innumerable thoughts strove to blend within him; new, unseen images arose, which also melted together, and became visible beings around him; and every wave of that lovely element pressed itself on him like a soft bosom. The flood seemed a Spirit of Beauty, which from moment to moment was taking form round the youth.

'Intoxicated with rapture, and yet conscious of every impression, he floated softly down that glittering stream, which flowed out from the basin into the rocks. A sort of sweet slumber fell upon him, in which he dreamed indescribable adventures, and out of which a new light awoke him. He found himself on a soft sward at the margin of a spring, which welled out into the air, and seemed to dissipate itself there. Dark-blue rocks, with many-coloured veins, rose at some distance; the daylight which encircled him was clearer and milder than the common; the sky was black-blue, and altogether pure. But what attracted him infinitely most was a high, light-blue Flower, which stood close by the spring, touching it with its broad glittering leaves. Round it stood innumerable flowers of all colours, and the sweetest perfume filled the air. He saw nothing but the Blue Flower; and gazed on it long with nameless tenderness. At last he was for approaching, when all at once it began to move and change; the leaves grew more resplendent, and clasped themselves round the waxing stem; the Flower bent itself towards him; and the petals showed like a blue spreading ruff, in which hovered a lovely face. His sweet astonishment at this transformation was increasing, — when suddenly his mother's voice awoke him, and he found himself in the house of his parents, which the morning sun was already gilding.'

Our next and last extract is likewise of a dream. Young Heinrich with his mother travels a long journey to see his grandfather at Augsburg; converses, on the way, with merchants, miners, and red-cross warriors (for it is in the time of the Crusades); and soon after his arrival falls immeasurably in love with Matilda, the Poet Klingsohr's daughter, whose face was that fairest one he had seen in his old vision of the Blue Flower. Matilda, it would appear, is to be taken from him by death (as Sophie was from Novalis): meanwhile, dreading no such event, Heinrich abandons himself with full heart to his new emotions:

'He went to the window. The choir of the Stars stood in the deep heaven; and in the east, a white gleam announced the coming day.

'Full of rapture, Heinrich exclaimed: "You, ye everlasting Stars, ye silent wanderers, I call you to witness my sacred oath. For Matilda will I live, and eternal faith shall unite my heart and hers. For me too, the morn of an everlasting day is dawning. The night is by: to the rising Sun, I kindle myself as a sacrifice that will never be extinguished."

'Heinrich was heated; and not till late, towards morning, did he fall asleep. In strange dreams, the thoughts of his soul embodied themselves. A deep-blue river gleamed from the plain. On its smooth surface floated a bark; Matilda was sitting there, and steering. She was adorned with garlands; was singing a simple Song, and looking over to him with fond sadness. His bosom was full of anxiety. He knew not why. The sky was clear, the stream calm. Her heavenly countenance was mirrored in the waves. All at once the bark began to whirl. He called earnestly to her. She smiled, and laid down her oar in the boat, which continued whirling. An unspeakable terror took hold of him. He dashed into the stream; but he could not get forward; the water carried him. She beckoned, she seemed as if she wished to say something to him; the bark was filling with water; yet she smiled with unspeakable affection, and looked cheerfully into the vortex. All at once it drew her in. A faint breath rippled over the stream, which flowed on as calm and glittering as before. His horrid agony robbed him of consciousness.

His heart ceased beating. On returning to himself, he was again on dry land. It seemed as if he had floated far. It was a strange region. He knew not what had passed with him. His heart was gone. Unthinking he walked deeper into the country. He felt inexpressibly weary. A little well gushed from a hill; it sounded like perfect bells. With his hand he lifted some drops, and wetted his parched lips. Like a sick dream, lay the frightful event behind him. Farther and farther he walked; flowers and trees spoke to him. He felt so well, so at home in the scene. Then he heard that simple Song again. He ran after the sounds. Suddenly some one held him by the clothes. "Dear Henry," cried a well-known voice. He looked round, and Matilda clasped him in her arms. "Why didst thou run from me, dear heart?" said she, breathing deep: "I could scarcely overtake thee." Heinrich wept. He pressed her to him. "Where is the river?" cried he in tears. — "Seest thou not its blue waves above us?" He looked up, and the blue river was flowing softly over their heads. "Where are we, dear Matilda?" — "With our Fathers." — "Shall we stay together?" — "Forever," answered she, pressing her lips to his, and so clasping him that she could not again quit hold. She put a wondrous, secret Word in his mouth, and it pierced through all his being. He was about to repeat it, when his Grandfather called, and he awoke. He would have given his life to remember that Word.'

This image of Death, and of the River being the Sky in that other and eternal country, seems to us a fine and touching one: there is in it a trace of that simple sublimity, that soft still pathos, which are characteristics of Novalis, and doubtless the highest of his specially poetic gifts.

But on these, and what other gifts and deficiencies pertain to him, we can no farther insist: for now, after such multifarious quotations, and more or less stinted commentaries, we must consider our little enterprise in respect of Novalis to have reached its limits; to be, if not completed, concluded. Our reader has heard him largely; on a great variety of topics, selected and exhibited here in such manner as seemed the fittest for our object, and with a true wish on our part, that what little judgment was in the mean while to be formed of such a man, might be a fair and honest one. Some of the passages we have translated will appear obscure; others, we hope, are not without symptoms of a wise and deep meaning; the rest may excite wonder, which wonder again it will depend on each reader for himself, whether he turn to right account or to wrong account, whether he entertain as the parent of Knowledge, or as the daughter of Ignorance. For the great body of readers, we are aware, there can be little profit in Novalis, who rather employs our time than helps us to kill it; for such any farther study of him would be unadvisable. To others again, who prize Truth as the end of all reading, especially to that class who cultivate moral science as the development of purest and highest Truth, we can recommend the perusal and reperusal of Novalis with almost perfect confidence. If they feel, with us, that the most profitable employment any book can give them, is to study honestly some earnest, deep-minded, truth-loving Man, to work their way into his manner of thought, till they see the world with his eyes, feel as he felt and judge as he judged, neither believing nor denying, till they can in some measure so feel and judge, — then we may assert, that few books known to us are more worthy of their attention than this. They will find it, if we mistake not, an unfathomed mine of philosophical ideas, where the keenest intellect may have occupation enough; and in such occupation, without looking farther, reward enough. All this, if the reader proceed on candid principles; if not, it will be all otherwise. To no man, so much as to Novalis is that famous motto applicable:

Leser, wie gefall' ich Dir?
Leser, wie gefällst Du mir?

Reader, how likest thou me?
Reader, how like I thee?

For the rest, it were but a false proceeding did we attempt any formal character of Novalis in this place; did we pretend with such means as ours to reduce that extraordinary nature under common formularies; and in few words sum up the net total of his worth and worthlessness. We have repeatedly expressed our own imperfect knowledge of the matter, and our entire despair of bringing even an approximate picture of it before readers so foreign to him. The kind words, 'amiable enthusiast,' 'poetic dreamer;' or the unkind ones, 'German mystic,' 'crackbrained rhapsodist,' are easily spoken and written; but would avail little in this instance. If we are not altogether mistaken, Novalis cannot be ranged under any one of these noted categories; but belongs to a higher and much less known one, the significance of which is perhaps also worth studying, at all events will not till after long study become clear to us.

Meanwhile let the reader accept some vague impressions of ours on this subject, since we have no fixed judgment to offer him. We might say, that the chief excellence we have remarked in Novalis is his to us truly wonderful subtlety of intellect; his power of intense abstraction, of pursuing the deepest and most evanescent ideas through their thousand complexities, as it were, with lynx vision, and to the very limits of human Thought. He was well skilled in mathematics, and, as we can easily believe, fond of that science; but his is a far finer species of endowment than any required in mathematics, where the mind, from the very beginning of *Euclid* to the end of *Laplace*, is assisted with visible symbols, with safe *implements* for thinking; nay, at least in what is called the higher mathematics, has often little more than a mechanical superintendence to exercise over these. This power of abstract meditation, when it is so sure and clear as we sometimes find it with Novalis, is a much higher and rarer one; its element is not mathematics, but that *Mathesis*, of which it has been said many a Great Calculist has not even a notion. In this power, truly, so far as logical and not moral power is concerned, lies the summary of all Philosophic talent: which talent, accordingly, we imagine Novalis to have possessed in a very high degree; in a higher degree than almost any other modern writer we have met with.

His chief fault, again, figures itself to us as a certain undue softness, a want of rapid energy ; something which we might term *passiveness* extending both over his mind and his character. There is a tenderness in Novalis, a purity, a clearness, almost as of a woman ; but he has not, at least not at all in that degree, the emphasis and resolute force of a man. Thus, in his poetical delineations, as we complained above, he is too diluted and diffuse ; not verbose properly ; not so much abounding in superfluous words as in superfluous circumstances, which indeed is but a degree better. In his philosophical speculations, we feel as if, under a different form, the same fault were now and then manifested. Here again, he seems to us, in one sense, too languid, too passive. He *sits*, we might say, among the rich, fine, thousandfold combinations, which his mind almost of itself presents him ; but, perhaps, he shows too little activity in the process, is too lax in separating the true from the doubtful, is not even at the trouble to express his truth with any laborious accuracy. With his stillness, with his deep love of Nature, his mild, lofty, spiritual tone of contemplation, he comes before us in a sort of Asiatic character, almost like our ideal of some antique Gymnosophist, and with the weakness as well as the strength of an Oriental. However, it should be remembered that his works both poetical and philosophical, as we now see them, appear under many disadvantages ; altogether immature, and not as doctrines and delineations, but as the rude draught of such ; in which, had they been completed, much was to have changed its shape, and this fault, with many others, might have disappeared. It may be, therefore, that this is only a superficial fault, or even only the appearance of a fault, and has its origin in these circumstances, and in our imperfect understanding of him. In personal and bodily habits, at least, Novalis appears to have been the opposite of inert ; we hear expressly of his quickness and vehemence of movement.

In regard to the character of his genius, or rather perhaps of his literary significance, and the form under which he displayed his genius, Tieck thinks he may be likened to Dante. 'For him,' says he, 'it had become the most natural disposi- 'tion to regard the commonest and nearest as a wonder, and 'the strange, the supernatural as something common; men's 'every-day life itself lay round him like a wondrous fable, 'and those regions which the most dream of or doubt of as 'of a thing distant, incomprehensible, were for him a beloved 'home. Thus did he, uncorrupted by examples, find out for 'himself a new method of delineation; and in his multipli- 'city of meaning; in his view of Love, and his belief in 'Love, as at once his Instructor, his Wisdom, his Religion; 'in this too that a single grand incident of life, and one deep 'sorrow and bereavement grew to be the essence of his Po- 'etry and Contemplation, — he, alone among the moderns, 'resembles the lofty Dante; and sings us, like him, an un- 'fathomable, mystic song, far different from that of many 'imitators, who think to put on mysticism and put it off, like 'a piece of dress.' Considering the tendency of his poetic endeavours, as well as the general spirit of his philosophy, this flattering comparison may turn out to be better founded than at first sight it seems to be. Nevertheless, were we required to illustrate Novalis in this way, which at all times must be a very loose one, we should incline rather to call him the German Pascal than the German Dante. Between Pascal and Novalis, a lover of such analogies might trace not a few points of resemblance. Both are of the purest, most affectionate moral nature; both of a high, fine, discursive intellect; both are mathematicians and naturalists, yet occupy themselves chiefly with Religion; nay, the best writings of both are left in the shape of 'Thoughts,' materials of a grand scheme, which each of them, with the views peculiar to his age, had planned, we may say, for the furtherance of Religion, and which neither of them lived to execute. Nor in all this would it fail to be carefully remarked, that Novalis was not the French but the *German* Pascal; and from the intellectual habits of the one and the other, many national contrasts and conclusions might be drawn; which we leave to those that have a taste for such parallels.

We have thus endeavoured to communicate some views not of what is vulgarly called, but of what *is* a German Mystic; to afford English readers a few glimpses into his actual household establishment, and show them by their own inspection how he lives and works. We have done it, moreover, not in the style of derision, which would have been so easy, but in that of serious inquiry, which seemed so much more profitable. For this we anticipate not censure, but thanks from our readers. Mysticism, whatever it may be, should, like other actually existing things, be understood in well-informed minds. We have observed, indeed, that the old-established laugh on this subject has been getting rather hollow of late; and seems as if, erelong, it would in a great measure die away. It appears to us that, in England, there is a distinct spirit of tolerant and sober investigation abroad, in regard to this and other kindred matters; a persuasion, fast spreading wider and wider, that the plummet of French or Scotch Logic, excellent, nay indispensable as it is for surveying all coasts and harbours, will absolutely not sound the deep-seas of human Inquiry; and that many a Voltaire and Hume, well-gifted and highly meritorious men, were far wrong in reckoning that when their six-hundred fathoms were out, they had reached the bottom, which, as in the Atlantic, may lie unknown miles lower. Six-hundred fathoms is the longest, and a most valuable nautical line: but many men sound with six and fewer fathoms, and arrive at precisely the same conclusion.

'The day will come,' said Lichtenberg, in bitter irony, 'when the belief in God will be like that in nursery Spectres;' or, as Jean Paul has it, 'Of the World will be made a World-Machine, of the Æther a Gas, of God a Force, and of the Second World — a Coffin.' We rather think, such a day will *not* come. At all events, while the battle is still waging, and that Coffin-and-Gas Philosophy has not yet secured itself with tithes and penal statutes, let there be free scope for Mysticism, or whatever else honestly opposes it. A fair field and no favour, and the right *will* prosper! 'Our 'present time,' says Jean Paul elsewhere, 'is indeed a criti-'cising and critical time, hovering betwixt the wish and the 'inability to believe; a chaos of conflicting times: but even 'a chaotic world must have its centre, and revolution round 'that centre; there *is* no pure entire Confusion, but all such 'presupposes its opposite, before it can begin.'

SIGNS OF THE TIMES.[1]

[1829.]

It is no very good symptom either of nations or individuals, that they deal much in vaticination. Happy men are full of the present, for its bounty suffices them; and wise men also, for its duties engage them. Our grand business undoubtedly is, not to *see* what lies dimly at a distance, but to *do* what lies clearly at hand.

Know'st thou *Yesterday*, its aim and reason;
Work'st thou well *To-day*, for worthy things?
Calmly wait the *Morrow's* hidden season,
Need'st not fear what hap soe'er it brings.

But man's 'large discourse of reason' *will* look 'before and after;' and, impatient of the 'ignorant present time,' will indulge in anticipation far more than profits him. Seldom can the unhappy be persuaded that the evil of the day is sufficient for it; and the ambitious will not be content with present splendour, but paints yet more glorious triumphs, on the cloud-curtain of the future.

The case, however, is still worse with nations. For here the prophets are not one, but many; and each incites and confirms the other; so that the fatidical fury spreads wider and wider, till at last even Saul must join in it. For there is still a real magic in the action and reaction of minds on one another. The casual deliration of a few becomes, by this mysterious reverberation, the frenzy of many; men lose the use, not only of their understandings, but of their bodily

[1] Edinburgh Review, No. 98.

senses; while the most obdurate unbelieving hearts melt, like the rest, in the furnace where all are cast as victims and as fuel. It is grievous to think, that this noble omnipotence of Sympathy has been so rarely the Aaron's-rod of Truth and Virtue, and so often the Enchanter's-rod of Wickedness and Folly! No solitary miscreant, scarcely any solitary maniac, would venture on such actions and imaginations, as large communities of sane men have, in such circumstances, entertained as sound wisdom. Witness long scenes of the French Revolution, in these late times! Levity is no protection against such visitations, nor the utmost earnestness of character. The New-England Puritan burns witches, wrestles for months with the horrors of Satan's invisible world, and all ghastly phantasms, the daily and hourly precursors of the Last Day; then suddenly bethinks him that he is frantic, weeps bitterly, prays contritely, and the history of that gloomy season lies behind him like a frightful dream.

Old England too has had her share of such frenzies and panics; though happily, like other old maladies, they have grown milder of late: and since the days of Titus Oates have mostly passed without loss of men's lives; or indeed without much other loss than that of reason, for the time, in the sufferers. In this mitigated form, however, the distemper is of pretty regular recurrence; and may be reckoned on at intervals, like other natural visitations; so that reasonable men deal with it, as the Londoners do with their fogs, — go cautiously out into the groping crowd, and patiently carry lanterns at noon; knowing, by a well-grounded faith, that the sun is still in existence, and will one day reappear. How often have we heard, for the last fifty years, that the country was wrecked, and fast sinking; whereas, up to this date, the country is entire and afloat! The 'State in Danger' is a condition of things, which we have witnessed a hundred times; and as for the Church, it has seldom been out of 'danger' since we can remember it.

All men are aware that the present is a crisis of this sort;

and why it has become so. The repeal of the Test Acts, and then of the Catholic disabilities, has struck many of their admirers with an indescribable astonishment. Those things seemed fixed and immovable; deep as the foundations of the world; and lo, in a moment they have vanished, and their place knows them no more! Our worthy friends mistook the slumbering Leviathan for an island; often as they had been assured, that Intolerance was, and could be nothing but a Monster; and so, mooring under the lee, they had anchored comfortably in his scaly rind, thinking to take good cheer; as for some space they did. But now their Leviathan has suddenly dived under; and they can no longer be fastened in the stream of time; but must drift forward on it, even like the rest of the world: no very appalling fate, we think, could they but understand it; which, however, they will not yet, for a season. Their little island is gone; sunk deep amid confused eddies; and what is left worth caring for in the universe? What is it to them, that the great continents of the earth are still standing; and the polestar and all our loadstars, in the heavens, still shining and eternal? Their cherished little haven is gone, and they will not be comforted! And therefore, day after day, in all manner of periodical or perennial publications, the most lugubrious predictions are sent forth. The King has virtually abdicated; the Church is a widow, without jointure; public principle is gone; private honesty is going; society, in short, is fast falling in pieces; and a time of unmixed evil is come on us. At such a period, it was to be expected that the rage of prophecy should be more than usually excited. Accordingly, the Millenarians have come forth on the right hand, and the Millites on the left. The Fifth-monarchy men prophesy from the Bible, and the Utilitarians from Bentham. The one announces that the last of the seals is to be opened, positively, in the year 1860; and the other assures us, that 'the greatest-happiness principle' is to make a heaven of earth, in a still shorter time. We know these symptoms too well, to think it necessary or safe to interfere with them. Time and the hours will bring relief to all parties. The grand encourager of Delphic or other noises is — the Echo. Left to themselves, they will the sooner dissipate, and die away in space.

Meanwhile, we too admit that the present is an important time; as all present time necessarily is. The poorest Day that passes over us is the conflux of two Eternities; it is made up of currents that issue from the remotest Past, and flow onwards into the remotest Future. We were wise indeed, could we discern truly the signs of our own time; and by knowledge of its wants and advantages, wisely adjust our own position in it. Let us, instead of gazing idly into the obscure distance, look calmly around us, for a little, on the perplexed scene where we stand. Perhaps, on a more serious inspection, something of its perplexity will disappear, some of its distinctive characters and deeper tendencies more clearly reveal themselves; whereby our own relations to it, our own true aims and endeavours in it, may also become clearer.

Were we required to characterise this age of ours by any single epithet, we should be tempted to call it, not an Heroical, Devotional, Philosophical, or Moral Age, but, above all others, the Mechanical Age. It is the Age of Machinery, in every outward and inward sense of that word; the age which, with its whole undivided might, forwards, teaches and practises the great art of adapting means to ends. Nothing is now done directly, or by hand; all is by rule and calculated contrivance. For the simplest operation, some helps and accompaniments, some cunning abbreviating process is in readiness. Our old modes of exertion are all discredited, and thrown aside. On every hand, the living artisan is driven from his workshop, to make room for a speedier, inanimate one. The shuttle drops from the fingers of the weaver, and falls into iron fingers that ply it faster. The sailor furls his sail, and lays down his oar; and bids a strong, unwearied servant, on vaporous wings, bear him through the waters. Men have crossed oceans by steam; the Birmingham Fire-king has visited the fabulous East; and the genius of the Cape, were there any Camoens now to sing it, has again been alarmed, and with far stranger thunders than Gama's. There is no end to machinery. Even the horse is stripped of his harness, and finds a fleet fire-horse yoked in his stead. Nay, we have an artist that hatches chickens by steam; the very brood-hen is to be superseded! For all earthly, and for some unearthly purposes, we have machines and mechanic furtherances; for mincing our cabbages; for casting us into magnetic sleep. We remove mountains, and make seas our smooth highway; nothing can resist us. We war with rude Nature; and, by our resistless engines, come off always victorious, and loaded with spoils.

What wonderful accessions have thus been made, and are still making, to the physical power of mankind; how much better fed, clothed, lodged and, in all outward respects, accommodated, men now are, or might be, by a given quantity of labour, is a grateful reflection which forces itself on every one. What changes, too, this addition of power is introducing into the Social System; how wealth has more and more increased, and at the same time gathered itself more and more into masses, strangely altering the old relations, and increasing the distance between the rich and the poor, will be a question for Political Economists, and a much more complex and important one than any they have yet engaged with. But leaving these matters for the present, let us observe how the mechanical genius of our time has diffused itself into quite other provinces. Not the external and physical alone is now managed by machinery, but the internal and spiritual also. Here too nothing follows its spontaneous course, nothing is left to be accomplished by old, natural methods. Everything has its cunningly devised implements, its preëstablished apparatus; it is not done by hand, but by machinery. Thus we have machines for Education: Lancastrian machines; Hamiltonian machines; monitors, maps and emblems. Instruction, that mysterious communing of Wisdom with Ignorance, is no longer an indefinable tentative process, requiring a study of individual aptitudes, and a perpetual variation of means and methods, to attain the same end; but a secure, universal, straightforward business, to be conducted in the gross, by proper mechanism, with such intellect as comes to hand. Then, we have Religious machines, of all imaginable varieties; the Bible-Society, professing a far higher and heavenly structure, is found, on inquiry, to be altogether an earthly contrivance; supported by collection of moneys, by fomenting of vanities, by puffing, intrigue and chicane; a machine for converting the Heathen. It is the same in all other departments. Has any man, or any society of men, a truth to speak, a piece of spiritual work to do; they can nowise proceed at once and with the mere natural organs, but must first call a public meeting, appoint committees, issue prospectuses, eat a public dinner; in a word, construct or borrow machinery, wherewith to speak it and do it. Without machinery they were hopeless, helpless; a colony of Hindoo weavers squatting in the heart of Lancashire. Mark, too, how every machine must have its moving power, in some of the great currents of society; every little sect among us, Unitarians, Utilitarians, Anabaptists, Phrenologists, must have its Periodical, its monthly or quarterly Magazine; — hanging out, like its windmill, into the *popularis aura*, to grind meal for the society.

With individuals, in like manner, natural strength avails little. No individual now hopes to accomplish the poorest enterprise single-handed, and without mechanical aids; he must make interest with some existing corporation, and till his field with their oxen. In these days, more emphatically than ever, 'to live, signifies to unite with a party, or to make one.' Philosophy, Science, Art, Literature, all depend on machinery. No Newton, by silent meditation, now discovers the system of the world from the falling of an apple; but some quite other than Newton stands in his Museum, his Scientific Institution, and behind whole batteries of retorts, digesters and galvanic piles imperatively 'interrogates Nature,' — who, however, shows no haste to answer. In defect of Raphaels, and Angelos, and Mozarts, we have Royal Academies of Painting, Sculpture, Music; whereby the languishing spirit of Art may be strengthened, as by the more generous diet of Public Kitchen. Literature, too, has its Paternoster-row mechanism, its Trade-dinners, its Editorial conclaves, and huge subterranean, puffing bellows; so that books are not only printed, but, in a great measure, written and sold, by machinery. National culture, spiritual benefit of all sorts, is under the same management. No Queen Christina, in these times, needs to send for her Descartes; no King Frederick for his Voltaire, and painfully nourish him with pensions and flattery: any sovereign of taste, who wishes to enlighten his people, has only to impose a new tax, and with the proceeds establish Philosophic Institutes. Hence the Royal and Imperial Societies, the Bibliothèques, Glyptothèques, Technothèques, which front us in all capital cities; like so many well-finished hives, to which it is expected the stray agencies of Wisdom will swarm of their own accord, and hive and make honey. In like manner, among ourselves, when it is thought that religion is declining, we have only to vote half-a-million's worth of bricks and mortar, and build new churches. In Ireland, it seems they have gone still farther; having actually established a 'Penny-a-week Purgatory-Society!' Thus does the Genius of Mechanism stand by to help us in all difficulties and emergencies; and, with his iron back, bears all our burdens.

These things, which we state lightly enough here, are yet of deep import, and indicate a mighty change in our whole manner of existence. For the same habit regulates not our modes of action alone, but our modes of thought and feeling. Men are grown mechanical in head and in heart, as well as in hand. They have lost faith in individual endeavour, and in natural force, of any kind. Not for internal perfection, but for external combinations and arrangements, for institutions, constitutions, — for Mechanism of one sort or other, do they hope and struggle. Their whole efforts, attachments, opinions, turn on mechanism, and are of a mechanical character.

We may trace this tendency in all the great manifestations of our time; in its intellectual aspect, the studies it most favours and its manner of conducting them; in its practical aspects, its politics, arts, religion, morals; in the whole sources, and throughout the whole currents, of its spiritual, no less than its material activity.

Consider, for example, the state of Science generally, in Europe, at this period. It is admitted, on all sides, that the Metaphysical and Moral Sciences are falling into decay, while the Physical are engrossing, every day, more respect and attention. In most of the European nations, there is now no such thing as a Science of Mind; only more or less advancement in the general science, or the special sciences, of matter. The French were the first to desert Metaphysics; and though they have lately affected to revive their school, it has yet no signs of vitality. The land of Malebranche, Pascal, Descartes and Fenelon, has now only its Cousins and Villemains; while, in the department of Physics, it reckons far other names. Among ourselves, the Philosophy of Mind, after a rickety infancy, which never reached the vigour of manhood, fell suddenly into decay, languished and finally died out, with its last amiable cultivator, Professor Stewart. In no nation but Germany has any decisive effort been made in psychological science; not to speak of any decisive result. The science of the age, in short, is physical, chemical, physiological; in all shapes mechanical. Our favorite Mathematics, the highly prized exponent of all these other sciences, has also become more and more mechanical. Excellence in what is called its higher departments depends less on natural genius, than on acquired expertness in wielding its machinery. Without undervaluing the wonderful results which a Lagrange or Laplace educes by means of it, we may remark, that their calculus, differential and integral, is little else than a more cunningly-constructed arithmetical mill; where the factors being put in, are, as it were, ground into the true product, under cover, and without other effort on our part than steady turning of the handle. We have more Mathematics than ever; but less Mathesis. Archimedes and Plato could not have read the *Mécanique Céleste;* but neither would the whole French Institute see aught in that saying, 'God geometrises!' but a sentimental rodomontade.

Nay, our whole Metaphysics itself, from Locke's time downwards, has been physical; not a spiritual philosophy, but a material one. The singular estimation in which his Essay was so long held as a scientific work (an estimation grounded, indeed, on the estimable character of the man) will one day be thought a curious indication of the spirit of these times. His whole doctrine is mechanical, in its aim and origin, in its method and its results. It is not a philosophy of the mind: it is a mere discussion concerning the origin of our consciousness, or ideas, or whatever else they are called; a genetic history of what we see *in* the mind. The grand secrets of Necessity and Freewill, of the Mind's vital or non-vital dependence on Matter, of our mysterious relations to Time and Space, to God, to the Universe, are not, in the faintest degree, touched on in these inquiries; and seem not to have the smallest connexion with them.

The last class of our Scotch Metaphysicians had a dim notion that much of this was wrong; but they knew not how to right it. The school of Reid had also from the first taken a mechanical course, not seeing any other. The singular conclusions at which Hume, setting out from their admitted premises, was arriving, brought this school into being; they let loose Instinct, as an undiscriminating bandog, to guard them against these conclusions; — they tugged lustily at the logical chain by which Hume was so coldly towing them and the world into bottomless abysses of Atheism and Fatalism. But the chain somehow snapped between them; and the issue has been that nobody now cares about either, — any more than about Hartley's, Darwin's, or Priestley's contemporaneous doings in England. Hartley's vibrations and vibratiuncles, one would think, were material and mechanical enough; but our Continental neighbours have gone still farther. One of their philosophers has lately discovered, that 'as the liver secretes bile, so does the brain secrete thought;' which astonishing discovery, Dr. Cabanis, more lately still, in his *Rapports du Physique et du Morale de l'Homme*, has pushed into its minutest developments. The metaphysical philosophy of this last inquirer is certainly no shadowy or unsubstantial one. He fairly lays open our moral structure with his dissecting-knives and real metal probes; and exhibits it to the inspection of mankind, by Leuwenhoek microscopes, and inflation with the anatomical blowpipe. Thought, he is inclined to hold, is still secreted by the brain; but then Poetry and Religion (and it is really worth knowing) are 'a product of the smaller intestines!' We have the greatest admiration for this learned doctor: with what scientific stoicism he walks through the land of wonders, unwondering; like a wise man through some huge, gaudy, imposing Vauxhall, whose fire-works, cascades and symphonies, the vulgar may enjoy and believe in, — but where he finds nothing real but the saltpetre, pasteboard and catgut. His book may be regarded as the ultimatum of mechanical metaphysics in our time; a remarkable realisation of what in Martinus Scriblerus was still only an idea, that 'as the jack had a meat-roasting quality, so had the body a thinking quality,' — upon the strength of which the Nurembergers were to build a wood-and-leather man, 'who should reason as well as most country parsons.' Vaucanson did indeed make a wooden duck, that seemed to eat and digest;

but that bold scheme of the Nurembergers remained for a more modern virtuoso.

This condition of the two great departments of knowledge, — the outward, cultivated exclusively on mechanical principles; the inward, finally abandoned, because, cultivated on such principles, it is found to yield no result, — sufficiently indicates the intellectual bias of our time, its all-pervading disposition towards that line of inquiry. In fact, an inward persuasion has long been diffusing itself, and now and then even comes to utterance, That, except the external, there are no true sciences; that to the inward world (if there be any) our only conceivable road is through the outward; that, in short, what cannot be investigated and understood mechanically, cannot be investigated and understood at all. We advert the more particularly to these intellectual propensities, as to prominent symptoms of our age, because Opinion is at all times doubly related to Action, first as cause, then as effect; and the speculative tendency of any age will therefore give us, on the whole, the best indications of its practical tendency.

Nowhere, for example, is the deep, almost exclusive faith we have in Mechanism more visible than in the Politics of this time. Civil government does, by its nature, include much that is mechanical, and must be treated accordingly. We term it indeed, in ordinary language, the Machine of Society, and talk of it as the grand working wheel from which all private machines must derive, or to which they must adapt, their movements. Considered merely as a metaphor, all this is well enough; but here, as in so many other cases, the 'foam hardens itself into a shell,' and the shadow we have wantonly evoked stands terrible before us, and will not depart at our bidding. Government includes much also that is not mechanical, and cannot be treated mechanically; of which latter truth, as appears to us, the political speculations and exertions of our time are taking less and less cognisance.

Nay, in the very outset, we might note the mighty interest taken in *mere political arrangements*, as itself the sign of a mechanical age. The whole discontent of Europe takes this direction. The deep, strong cry of all civilised nations, — a cry which, every one now sees, must and will be answered, is: Give us a reform of Government! A good structure of legislation, a proper check upon the executive, a wise arrangement of the judiciary, is *all* that is wanting for human happiness. The Philosopher of this age is not a Socrates, a Plato, a Hooker, or Taylor, who inculcates on men the necessity and infinite worth of moral goodness, the great truth that our happiness depends on the mind which is within us, and not on the circumstances which are without us; but a Smith, a De Lolme, a Bentham, who chiefly inculcates the reverse of this, — that our happiness depends entirely on external circumstances; nay, that the strength and dignity of the mind within us is itself the creature and consequence of these. Were the laws, the government, in good order, all were well with us; the rest would care for itself! Dissentients from this opinion, expressed or implied, are now rarely to be met with; widely and angrily as men differ in its application, the principle is admitted by all.

Equally mechanical, and of equal simplicity, are the methods proposed by both parties for completing or securing this all-sufficient perfection of arrangement. It is no longer the moral, religious, spiritual condition of the people that is our concern, but their physical, practical, economical condition, as regulated by public laws. Thus is the Body-politic more than ever worshipped and tendered; but the Soul-politic less than ever. Love of country, in any high or generous sense, in any other than an almost animal sense, or mere habit, has little importance attached to it in such reforms, or in the opposition shown them. Men are to be guided only by their self-interests. Good government is a good balancing of these; and, except a keen eye and appetite for self-interest, requires no virtue in any quarter. To both parties it is emphatically a machine: to the discontented, a 'taxing-machine;' to the contented, a 'machine for securing property.' Its duties and its faults are not those of a father, but of an active parish-constable.

Thus it is by the mere condition of the machine; by preserving it untouched, or else by reconstructing it, and oiling it anew, that man's salvation as a social being is to be insured and indefinitely promoted. Contrive the fabric of law aright, and without farther effort on your part, that divine spirit of Freedom which all hearts venerate and long for, will of herself come to inhabit it; and under her healing wings every noxious influence will wither, every good and salutary one more and more expand. Nay, so devoted are we to this principle, and at the same time so curiously mechanical, that a new trade, specially grounded on it, has arisen among us, under the name of 'Codification,' or code-making in the abstract; whereby any people, for a reasonable consideration, may be accommodated with a patent code; — more easily than curious individuals with patent breeches, for the people does *not* need to be measured first.

To us who live in the midst of all this, and see continually the faith, hope and practice of every one founded on Mechanism of one kind or other, it is apt to seem quite natural, and as if it could never have been otherwise. Nevertheless, if we recollect or reflect a little, we shall find both that it has been, and might again be otherwise. The domain of Mechanism, — meaning thereby political, ecclesiastical or other outward establishments, — was once considered as embracing, and we are persuaded can at any time embrace, but a limited portion of man's interests, and by no means the highest portion.

To speak a little pedantically, there is a science of *Dynamics* in man's fortunes and nature, as well as of *Mechanics*. There is a science which treats of, and practically addresses, the primary, unmodified forces and energies of man, the mysterious springs of Love, and Fear, and Wonder, of Enthusiasm, Poetry, Religion, all which have a truly vital and *infinite* character; as well as a science which practically addresses the finite, modified developments of these, when they take the shape of immediate 'motives,' as hope of reward, or as fear of punishment.

Now it is certain, that in former times the wise men, the enlightened lovers of their kind, who appeared generally as Moralists, Poets or Priests, did, without neglecting the Mechanical province, deal chiefly with the Dynamical; applying themselves chiefly to regulate, increase and purify the inward primary powers of man; and fancying that herein lay the main difficulty, and the best service they could undertake. But a wide difference is manifest in our age. For the wise men, who now appear as Political Philosophers, deal exclusively with the Mechanical province; and occupying themselves in counting up and estimating men's motives, strive by curious checking and balancing, and other adjustments of Profit and Loss, to guide them to their true advantage: while, unfortunately, those same 'motives' are so innumerable, and so variable in every individual, that no really useful conclusion can ever be drawn from their enumeration. But though Mechanism, wisely contrived, has done much for man in a social and moral point of view, we cannot be persuaded that it has ever been the chief source of his worth or happiness. Consider the great elements of human enjoyment, the attainments and possessions that exalt man's life to its present height, and see what part of these he owes to institutions, to Mechanism of any kind; and what to the instinctive, unbounded force, which Nature herself lent him, and still continues to him. Shall we say, for example, that Science and Art are indebted principally to the founders of Schools and Universities? Did not Science originate rather, and gain advancement, in the obscure closets of the Roger Bacons, Keplers, Newtons; in the workshops of the Fausts and the Watts; wherever, and in what guise soever Nature, from the first times downwards, had sent a gifted spirit upon the earth? Again, were Homer and Shakspeare members of any beneficed guild, or made Poets by means of it? Were Painting and Sculpture created by forethought, brought into the world by institutions for that end? No; Science and Art have, from first to last, been the free gift of Nature; an unsolicited, unexpected gift; often even a fatal one. These things rose up, as it were, by spontaneous growth, in the free soil and sunshine of Nature. They were not planted or grafted, nor even greatly multiplied or improved by the culture or manuring of institutions. Generally speaking, they have derived only partial help from these; often enough have suffered damage. They made constitutions for themselves. They originated in the Dynamical nature of man, not in his Mechanical nature.

Or, to take an infinitely higher instance, that of the Christian Religion, which, under every theory of it, in the believing or unbelieving mind, must ever be regarded as the crowning glory, or rather the life and soul, of our whole modern culture: How did Christianity arise and spread abroad among men? Was it by institutions, and establishments, and well-arranged systems of mechanism? Not so; on the contrary, in all past and existing institutions for those ends, its divine spirit has invariably been found to languish and decay. It arose in the mystic deeps of man's soul; and was spread abroad by the 'preaching of the word,' by simple, altogether natural and individual efforts; and flew, like hallowed fire, from heart to heart, till all were purified and illuminated by it; and its heavenly light shone, as it still shines, and (as sun or star) will ever shine, through the whole dark destinies of man. Here again was no Mechanism; man's highest attainment was accomplished Dynamically, not Mechanically. Nay, we will venture to say, that no high attainment, not even any far-extending movement among men, was ever accomplished otherwise. Strange as it may seem, if we read History with any degree of thoughtfulness, we shall find, that the checks and balances of Profit and Loss have never been the grand agents with men; that they have never been roused into deep, thorough, all-pervading efforts by any computable prospect of Profit and Loss, for any visible, finite object; but always for some invisible and infinite one. The Crusades took their rise in Religion; their visible object was, commercially speaking, worth nothing. It was the boundless Invisible world that was laid bare in the imaginations of those men; and in its burning light, the visible shrunk as a scroll. Not mechanical, nor produced by mechanical means, was this vast movement. No dining at Freemasons' Tavern, with the other long train of modern machinery; no cunning reconciliation of 'vested interests,' was required here: only the passionate voice of one man, the rapt soul looking through the eyes of one man; and rugged, steel-clad Europe trembled beneath his words, and followed him whither he listed. In later ages it was still the same. The Reformation had an invisible, mystic and ideal aim; the result was indeed to be embodied in external things; but its spirit, its worth, was internal, invisible, infinite. Our English Revolution too originated in Religion. Men did battle, in those old days, not for Purse-sake, but for Conscience-sake. Nay, in our own days it is no way different. The French Revolution itself had something higher in it than cheap bread and a Habeas-corpus act. Here too was an Idea; a Dynamic, not a Mechanic force. It was a struggle, though a blind and at last an insane one, for the infinite, divine nature of Right of Freedom, of Country.

Thus does man, in every age, vindicate, consciously or unconsciously, his celestial birthright. Thus does Nature hold on her wondrous, unquestionable course; and all our systems and theories are but so many froth-eddies or sand-banks, which from time to time she casts up, and washes away. When we can drain the Ocean into mill-ponds, and bottle up the Force of Gravity, to be sold by retail, in gas-jars; then may we hope to comprehend the infinitudes of man's soul under formulas of Profit and Loss; and rule over this too, as over a patent engine, by checks, and valves, and balances.

Nay, even with regard to Government itself, can it be necessary to remind any one that Freedom, without which indeed all spiritual life is impossible, depends on infinitely more complex influences than either the extension or the curtailment of the 'democratic interest?' Who is there that, 'taking the high *priori* road,' shall point out what these influences are; what deep, subtle, inextricably entangled influences they have been and may be? For man is not the creature and product of Mechanism; but, in a far truer sense, its creator and producer: it is the noble People that makes the noble Government; rather than conversely. On the whole, Institutions are much; but they are not all. The freest and highest spirits of the world have often been found under strange outward circumstances: Saint Paul and his brother Apostles were politically slaves; Epictetus was personally one. Again, forget the influences of Chivalry and Religion, and ask: What countries produced Columbus and Las Casas? Or, descending from virtue and heroism, to mere energy and spiritual talent: Cortes, Pizarro, Alba, Ximenes? The Spaniards of the sixteenth century were indisputably the noblest nation of Europe; yet they had the Inquisition and Philip II. They have the same government at this day; and are the lowest nation. The Dutch too have retained their old constitution; but no Siege of Leyden, no William the Silent, not even an Egmont or De Witt any longer appears among them. With ourselves also, where much has changed, effect has nowise followed cause as it should have done: two centuries ago, the Commons Speaker addressed Queen Elizabeth on bended knees, happy that the virago's foot did not even smite him; yet the people were then governed, not by a Castlereagh, but by a Burghley; they had their Shakspeare and Philip Sidney, where we have our Sheridan Knowles and Beau Brummel.

These and the like facts are so familiar, the truths which

they preach so obvious, and have in all past times been so universally believed and acted on, that we should almost feel ashamed for repeating them; were it not that, on every hand, the memory of them seems to have passed away, or at best died into a faint tradition of no value as a practical principle. To judge by the loud clamour of our Constitution-builders, Statists, Economists, directors, creators, reformers of Public Societies; in a word, all manner of Mechanists, from the Cartwright up to the Code-maker; and by the nearly total silence of all Preachers and Teachers who should give a voice to Poetry, Religion and Morality, we might fancy either that man's Dynamical nature was, to all spiritual intents, extinct, or else so perfected that nothing more was to be made of it by the old means; and henceforth, only in his Mechanical contrivances did any hope exist for him.

To define the limits of these two departments of man's activity, which work into one another, and by means of one another, so intricately and inseparably, were by its nature an impossible attempt. Their relative importance, even to the wisest mind, will vary in different times, according to the special wants and dispositions of these times. Meanwhile, it seems clear enough that only in the right coördination of the two, and the vigorous forwarding of *both*, does our true line of action lie. Undue cultivation of the inward or Dynamical province leads to idle, visionary, impracticable courses, and, especially in rude eras, to Superstition and Fanaticism, with their long train of baleful and well-known evils. Undue cultivation of the outward, again, though less immediately prejudicial, and even for the time productive of many palpable benefits, must, in the long-run, by destroying Moral Force, which is the parent of all other Force, prove not less certainly, and perhaps still more hopelessly, pernicious. This, we take it, is the grand characteristic of our age. By our skill in Mechanism, it has come to pass, that in the management of external things we excel all other ages; while in whatever respects the pure moral nature, in true dignity of soul and character, we are perhaps inferior to most civilised ages.

In fact, if we look deeper, we shall find that this faith in Mechanism has now struck its roots down into man's most intimate, primary sources of conviction; and is thence sending up, over his whole life and activity, innumerable stems, — fruit-bearing and poison-bearing. The truth is, men have lost their belief in the Invisible, and believe, and hope, and work only in the Visible; or, to speak it in other words: This is not a Religious age. Only the material, the immediately practical, not the divine and spiritual, is important to us. The infinite, absolute character of Virtue has passed into a finite, conditional one; it is no longer a worship of the Beautiful and Good; but a calculation of the Profitable. Worship, indeed, in any sense, is not recognised among us, or is mechanically explained into Fear of pain, or Hope of pleasure. Our true Deity is Mechanism. It has subdued external Nature for us, and we think it will do all other things. We are Giants in physical power: in a deeper than metaphorical sense, we are Titans, that strive, by heaping mountain on mountain, to conquer Heaven also.

The strong Mechanical character, so visible in the spiritual pursuits and methods of this age, may be traced much farther into the condition and prevailing disposition of our spiritual nature itself. Consider, for example, the general fashion of Intellect in this era. Intellect, the power man has of knowing and believing, is now nearly synonymous with Logic, or the mere power of arranging and communicating. Its implement is not Meditation, but Argument. 'Cause and effect' is almost the only category under which we look at, and work with, all Nature. Our first question with regard to any object is not, What is it? but, How is it? We are no longer instinctively driven to apprehend, and lay to heart, what is Good and Lovely, but rather to inquire, as onlookers, how it is produced, whence it comes, whither it goes. Our favourite Philosophers have no love and no hatred; they stand among us not to do, nor to create anything, but as a sort of Logic-mills to grind out the true causes and effects of all that is done and created. To the eye of a Smith, a Hume or a Constant, all is well that works quietly. An Order of Ignatius Loyola, a Presbyterianism of John Knox, a Wickliffe or a Henry the Eighth, are simply so many mechanical phenomena, caused or causing.

The *Euphuist* of our day differs much from his pleasant predecessors. An intellectual dapperling of these times boasts chiefly of his irresistible perspicacity, his 'dwelling in the daylight of truth,' and so forth; which, on examination, turns out to be a dwelling in the *rush*-light of 'closet-logic,' and a deep unconsciousness that there is any other light to dwell in or any other objects to survey with it. Wonder, indeed, is, on all hands, dying out: it is the sign of uncultivation to wonder. Speak to any small man of a high, majestic Reformation, of a high, majestic Luther; and forthwith he sets about 'accounting' for it; how the 'circumstances of the time' called for such a character, and found him, we suppose, standing girt and road-ready, to do its errand; how the 'circumstances of the time' created, fashioned, floated him quietly along into the result; how, in short, this small man, had he been there, could have performed the like himself! For it is the 'force of circumstances' that does everything; the force of one man can do nothing. Now all this is grounded on little more than a metaphor. We figure Society as a 'Machine,' and that mind is opposed to mind, as body is to body; whereby two, or at most ten, little minds must be stronger than one great mind. Notable absurdity! For the plain truth, very plain, we think, is, that minds are opposed to minds in quite a different way; and *one* man that has a higher Wisdom, a hitherto unknown spiritual Truth in him, is stronger, not than ten men that have it not, or than ten thousand, but than *all* men that have it not; and stands among them with a quite ethereal, angelic power, as with a sword out of Heaven's own armory, sky-tempered, which no buckler, and no tower of brass, will finally withstand.

But to us, in these times, such considerations rarely occur. We enjoy, we see nothing by direct vision; but only by reflection, and in anatomical dismemberment. Like Sir Hudibras, for every Why we must have a Wherefore. We have our little *theory* on all human and divine things. Poetry, the workings of genius itself, which in all times, with one or another meaning, has been called Inspiration, and held to be mysterious and inscrutable, is no longer without its scientific exposition. The building of the lofty rhyme is like any other masonry or bricklaying: we have theories of its rise, height, decline and fall, — which latter, it would seem, is now near, among all people. Of our 'Theories of Taste,' as they are called, wherein the deep, infinite, unspeakable Love of Wisdom and Beauty, which dwells in all men, is 'explained,' made mechanically visible, from 'Association' and the like, why should we say anything? Hume has written us a 'Natural History of Religion;' in which one Natural History all the rest are included. Strangely too does the general feeling coincide with Hume's in this wonderful problem; for whether his 'Natural History' be the right one or not, that Religion must have a Natural History, all of us, cleric and laic, seem to be agreed. He indeed regards it as a Disease, we again as Health; so far there is a difference; but in our first principle we are at one.

To what extent theological Unbelief, we mean intellectual dissent from the Church, in its view of Holy Writ, prevails at this day, would be a highly important, were it not, under any circumstances, an almost impossible inquiry. But the Unbelief, which is of a still more fundamental character, every man may see prevailing, with scarcely any but the faintest contradiction, all around him; even in the Pulpit itself. Religion in most countries, more or less in every country, is no longer what it was, and should be, — a thousand-voiced psalm from the heart of Man to his invisible

Father, the fountain of all Goodness, Beauty, Truth, and revealed in every revelation of these; but for the most part, a wise prudential feeling grounded on mere calculation; a matter, as all others now are, of Expediency and Utility; whereby some smaller quantum of earthly enjoyment may be exchanged for a far larger quantum of celestial enjoyment. Thus Religion too is Profit, a working for wages; not Reverence, but vulgar Hope or Fear. Many, we know, very many, we hope, are still religious in a far different sense; were it not so, our case were too desperate: but to witness that such is the temper of the times, we take any calm observant man, who agrees or disagrees in our feeling on the matter, and ask him whether our *view* of it is not in general well-founded.

Literature too, if we consider it, gives similar testimony. At no former era has Literature, the printed communication of Thought, been of such importance as it is now. We often hear that the Church is in danger; and truly so it is, — in a danger it seems not to know of: for, with its tithes in the most perfect safety, its functions are becoming more and more superseded. The true Church of England, at this moment, lies in the Editors of its Newspapers. These preach to the people daily, weekly; admonishing kings themselves; advising peace or war, with an authority which only the first Reformers, and a long-past class of Popes, were possessed of; inflicting moral censure; imparting moral encouragement, consolation, edification; in all ways diligently 'administering the Discipline of the Church.' It may be said too, that in private disposition the new Preachers somewhat resemble the Mendicant Friars of old times: outwardly full of holy zeal; inwardly not without stratagem, and hunger for terrestrial things. But omitting this class, and the boundless host of watery personages who pipe, as they are able, on so many scrannel straws, let us look at the higher regions of Literature, where, if anywhere, the pure melodies of Poesy and Wisdom should be heard. Of natural talent there is no deficiency: one or two richly-endowed individuals even give us a superiority in this respect. But what is the song they sing? Is it a tone of the Memnon Statue, breathing music as the *light* first touches it? A 'liquid wisdom,' disclosing to our sense the deep, infinite harmonies of Nature and man's soul? Alas, no! It is not a matin or vesper hymn to the Spirit of Beauty, but a fierce clashing of cymbals, and shouting of multitudes, as children pass through the fire to Moloch! Poetry itself has no eye for the Invisible. Beauty is no longer the god it worships, but some brute image of Strength; which we may well call an idol, for true Strength is one and the same with Beauty, and its worship also is a hymn. The meek, silent Light can mould, create and purify all Nature; but the loud Whirlwind, the sign and product of Disunion, of Weakness, passes on, and is forgotten. How widely this veneration for the physically Strongest has spread itself through Literature, any one may judge, who reads either criticism or poem. We praise a work, not as 'true,' but as 'strong;' our highest praise is that it has 'affected' us, has 'terrified' us. All this, it has been well observed, is the 'maximum of the Barbarous,' the symptom, not of vigorous refinement, but of luxurious corruption. It speaks much, too, for men's indestructible love of truth, that nothing of this kind will abide with them; that even the talent of a Byron cannot permanently seduce us into idol-worship; that he too, with all his wild siren charming, already begins to be disregarded and forgotten.

Again, with respect to our Moral condition: here also, he who runs may read that the same physical, mechanical influences are everywhere busy. For the 'superior morality,' of which we hear so much, we too would desire to be thankful: at the same time, it were but blindness to deny that this 'superior morality' is properly rather an 'inferior criminality,' produced not by greater love of Virtue, but by greater perfection of Police; and of that far subtler and stronger Police, called Public Opinion. This last watches over us with its Argus eyes more keenly than ever; but the 'inward eye' seems heavy with sleep. Of any belief in invisible, divine things, we find as few traces in our Morality as elsewhere. It is by tangible, material considerations that we are guided, not by inward and spiritual. Self-denial, the parent of all virtue, in any true sense of that word, has perhaps seldom been rarer: so rare is it, that the most, even in their abstract speculations, regard its existence as a chimera. Virtue is Pleasure, is Profit; no celestial, but an earthly thing. Virtuous men, Philanthropists, Martyrs are happy accidents; their 'taste' lies the right way! In all senses, we worship and follow after Power; which may be called a physical pursuit. No man now loves Truth, as Truth must be loved, with an infinite love; but only with a finite love, and as it were *par amours.* Nay, properly speaking, he does not *believe* and know it, but only '*thinks*' it, and that 'there is every probability!' He preaches it aloud, and rushes courageously forth with it, — if there is a multitude huzzaing at his back; yet ever keeps looking over his shoulder, and the instant the huzzaing languishes, he too stops short. In fact, what morality we have takes the shape of Ambition, of Honour: beyond money and money's worth, our only rational blessedness is Popularity. It were but a fool's trick to die for conscience. Only for 'character,' by duel, or, in case of extremity, by suicide, is the wise man bound to die. By arguing on the 'force of circumstances,' we have argued away all force from ourselves; and stand leashed together, uniform in dress and movement, like the rowers of some boundless galley. This and that may be right and true; *but* we must not do it. Wonderful 'Force of Public Opinion!' We must act and walk in all points as it prescribes; follow the traffic it bids us, realise the sum of money, the degree of 'influence' it expects of us, *or* we shall be lightly esteemed; certain mouthfuls of articulate wind will be blown at us, and this what mortal courage can front? Thus, while civil liberty is more and more secured to us, our moral liberty is all but lost. Practically considered, our creed is Fatalism; and, free in hand and foot, we are shackled in heart and soul with far straiter than feudal chains. Truly may we say, with the Philosopher, 'the deep meaning of the Laws of Mechanism lies heavy on us;' and in the closet, in the market-place, in the temple, by the social hearth, encumbers the whole movements of our mind, and over our noblest faculties is spreading a nightmare sleep.

These dark features, we are aware, belong more or less to other ages, as well as to ours. This faith in Mechanism, in the all-importance of physical things, is in every age the common refuge of Weakness and blind Discontent; of all who believe, as many will ever do, that man's true good lies without him, not within. We are aware also, that, as applied to ourselves in all their aggravation, they form but half a picture; that in the whole picture there are bright lights as well as gloomy shadows. If we here dwell chiefly on the latter, let us not be blamed: it is in general more profitable to reckon up our defects than to boast of our attainments.

Neither, with all these evils more or less clearly before us, have we at any time despaired of the fortunes of society. Despair, or even despondency, in that respect, appears to us, in all cases, a groundless feeling. We have a faith in the imperishable dignity of man; in the high vocation to which, throughout this his earthly history, he has been appointed. However it may be with individual nations, whatever melancholic speculators may assert, it seems a well-ascertained fact, that in all times, reckoning even from those of the Heraclides and Pelasgi, the happiness and greatness of mankind at large have been continually progressive. Doubtless this age also is advancing. Its very unrest, its ceaseless activity, its discontent contains matter of promise. Knowledge, education are opening the eyes of the humblest; are increasing the number of thinking minds without limit. This is as it should be; for not in turning back, not in resisting, but only in resolutely struggling forward, does our life consist. Nay, after all, our spiritual maladies are but of Opinion; we are but fettered by chains of our own forging, and which ourselves also can rend asunder. This deep, paralysed subjection to physical objects comes not from Nature, but from our own unwise mode of *viewing* Nature. Neither can we understand that man wants, at this hour, any faculty of heart, soul or body, that ever belonged to him. 'He, who has been born, has been a First Man;' has had lying before his young eyes, and as yet unhardened into scientific shapes, a world as plastic, infinite, divine, as lay before the eyes of Adam himself. If Mechanism, like some glass bell, encircles and imprisons us; if the soul looks forth on a fair heavenly country which it cannot reach, and pines, and in its scanty atmosphere is ready to perish, — yet the bell is but of glass; 'one bold stroke to break the bell in pieces, and thou art delivered!' Not the invisible world is wanting, for it dwells in man's soul, and this last is still here. Are the solemn temples, in which the Divinity was once visibly revealed among us, crumbling away? We can repair them, we can rebuild them. The wisdom, the heroic worth of our forefathers, which we have lost, we can recover. That admiration of old nobleness, which now so often shows itself as a faint *dilettanteism*, will one day become a generous emulation, and man may again be all that he has been, and more than he has been. Nor are these the mere daydreams of fancy; they are clear possibilities; nay, in this time they are even assuming the character of hopes. Indications we do see, in other countries and in our own, signs infinitely cheering to us, that Mechanism is not always to be our hard taskmaster, but one day to be our pliant, all-ministering servant; that a new and brighter spiritual era is slowly evolving itself for all men. But on these things our present course forbids us to enter.

Meanwhile, that great outward changes are in progress, can be doubtful to no one. The time is sick and out of joint. Many things have reached their height; and it is a wise adage that tells us, 'the darkest hour is nearest the dawn.' Wherever we can gather indication of the public thought, whether from printed books, as in France or Germany, or from Carbonari rebellions and other political tumults, as in Spain, Portugal, Italy and Greece, the voice it utters is the same. The thinking minds of all nations call for change. There is a deep-lying struggle in the whole fabric of society; a boundless grinding collision of the New with the Old. The French Revolution, as is now visible enough, was not the parent of this mighty movement, but its offspring. Those two hostile influences, which always exist in human things, and on the constant intercommunion of which depends their health and safety, had lain in separate masses, accumulating through generations, and France was the scene of their fiercest explosion; but the final issue was not unfolded in that country: nay it is not yet anywhere unfolded. Political freedom is hitherto the object of these efforts; but they will not and cannot stop there. It is towards a higher freedom than mere freedom from oppression from his fellow-mortal, that man dimly aims. Of this higher, heavenly freedom, which is 'man's reasonable service,' all his noble institutions, his faithful endeavours and loftiest attainments, are but the body, and more and more approximated emblem.

On the whole, as this wondrous planet, Earth, is journeying with its fellows through infinite Space, so are the wondrous destinies embarked on it journeying through infinite Time, under a higher guidance than ours. For the present, as our astronomy informs us, its path lies towards *Hercules*, the constellation of *Physical Power*: but that is not our most pressing concern. Go where it will, the deep HEAVEN will be around it. Therein let us have hope and sure faith. To reform a world, to reform a nation, no wise man will undertake; and all but foolish men know, that the only solid, though a far slower reformation, is what each begins and perfects on *himself*.

JEAN PAUL FRIEDRICH RICHTER AGAIN.[1]

[1830.]

It is some six years since the name 'Jean Paul Friedrich Richter' was first printed with English types; and some six-and-forty since it has stood emblazoned and illuminated on all true literary Indicators among the Germans; a fact which, if we consider the history of many a Kotzebue and Chateaubriand, within that period, may confirm the old doctrine, that the best celebrity does not always spread the fastest; but rather, quite contrariwise, that as blown bladders are far more easily carried than metallic masses, though gold ones, of equal bulk, so the Playwright, Poetaster, Philosophe, will often pass triumphantly beyond seas, while the Poet and Philosopher abide quietly at home. Such is the order of Nature: a Spurzheim flies from Vienna to Paris and London within the year; a Kant, slowly advancing, may perhaps reach us from Königsberg within the century: Newton, merely to cross the narrow Channel, required fifty years; Shakspeare, again, three times as many. It is true, there are examples of an opposite sort; now and then, by some rare chance, a Goethe, a Cervantes, will occur in literature, and Kings may laugh over *Don Quixote* while it is yet unfinished, and scenes from *Werter* be painted on Chinese teacups while the author is still a stripling. These, however, are not the rule, but the exceptions; nay, rightly interpreted, the exceptions which confirm it. In general, that

[1] Foreign Review, No. 9. — *Wahrheit aus Jean Pauls Leben* (Biography of Jean Paul). 1stes, 2tes, 3tes Bändchen. Breslau, 1826, '27, '28.

sudden tumultuous popularity comes more from partial delirium on both sides, than from clear insight; and is of evil omen to all concerned with it. How many loud Bacchus-festivals of this sort have we seen prove to be pseudo-Bacchanalia, and end in directly the inverse of Orgies! Drawn by his team of lions, the jolly god advances as a real god, with all his thyrsi, cymbals, phallophori and Mænadic women; the air, the earth is giddy with their clangour, their Evohes: but, alas, in a little while, the lion-team shows long ears, and becomes too clearly an ass-team in lion-skins; the Mænads wheel round in amazement; and then the jolly god, dragged from his chariot, is trodden into the kennels as a drunk mortal.

That no such apotheosis was appointed for Richter in his own country, or is now to be anticipated in any other, we cannot but regard as a natural and nowise unfortunate circumstance. What divinity lies in him requires a calmer worship, and from quite another class of worshippers. Neither, in spite of that forty-years abeyance, shall we accuse England of any uncommon blindness towards him: nay, taking all things into account, we should rather consider his actual footing among us as evincing not only an increased rapidity in literary intercourse, but an intrinsic improvement in the manner and objects of it. Our feeling of foreign excellence, we hope, must be becoming truer; our Insular taste must be opening more and more into a European one. For Richter is by no means a man whose merits, like his singularities, force themselves on the general eye; indeed, without great patience, and some considerable catholicism of disposition, no reader is likely to prosper much with him. He has a fine, high, altogether unusual talent; and a manner of expressing it perhaps still more unusual. He is a Humorist heartily and throughout; not only in low provinces of thought, where this is more common, but in the loftiest provinces, where it is wellnigh unexampled; and thus, in wild sport, 'playing bowls with the sun and moon,' he fashions the strangest ideal world, which at first glance looks no better than a chaos. The Germans themselves find much to bear with in him; and for readers of any other nation, he is involved in almost boundless complexity; a mighty maze, indeed, but in which the plan, or traces of a plan, are nowhere visible. Far from appreciating and appropriating the spirit of his writings, foreigners find it in the highest degree difficult to seize their grammatical meaning. Probably there is not, in any modern language, so intricate a writer; abounding, without measure, in obscure allusions, in the most twisted phraseology; perplexed into endless entanglements and dislocations, parenthesis within parenthesis; not forgetting elisions, sudden whirls, quips, conceits and all manner of inexplicable crotchets: the whole moving on in the gayest manner, yet nowise in what seem military lines, but rather in huge parti-coloured mob-masses. How foreigners must find themselves bested in this case, our readers may best judge from the fact, that a work with the following title was undertaken some twenty years ago, for the benefit of Richter's own countrymen: '*K. Reinhold's Lexicon for Jean Paul's* '*Works, or explanation of all the foreign words and unusual* '*modes of speech which occur in his writings; with short* '*notices of the historical persons and facts therein alluded to;* '*and plain German versions of the more difficult passages in* '*the context: — a necessary assistance for all who would read* '*those works with profit!*' So much for the dress or vehicle of Richter's thoughts: now let it only be remembered farther, that the thoughts themselves are often of the most abstruse description, so that not till after laborious meditation, can much, either of truth or of falsehood, be discerned in them; and we have a man, from whom readers with weak nerves, and a taste in any degree sickly, will not fail to recoil, perhaps with a sentiment approaching to horror. And yet, as we said, notwithstanding all these drawbacks, Richter already meets with a certain recognition in England; he has his readers and admirers; various translations from his works have been published among us; criticisms also, not without clear discernment, and nowise wanting in applause; and to all this, so far as we can see, even the Un-German part of the public has listened with some curiosity and hopeful anticipation. From which symptoms we should infer two things, both very comfortable to us in our present capacity: First, that the old strait-laced, microscopic sect of *Belles-lettres* men, whose divinity was 'Elegance,' a creed of French growth, and more admirable for men-milliners than for critics and philosophers, must be rapidly declining in these Islands; and, secondly, which is a much more personal consideration, that, in still farther investigating and exhibiting this wonderful Jean Paul, we have attempted what will be, for many of our readers, no unwelcome service.

Our inquiry naturally divides itself into two departments, the Biographical and the Critical; concerning both of which, in their order, we have some observations to make; and what, in regard to the latter department at least, we reckon more profitable, some rather curious documents to present.

It does not appear that Richter's life, externally considered, differed much in general character from other literary lives, which, for most part, are so barren of incident: the earlier portion of it was straitened enough, but not otherwise distinguished; the latter and busiest portion of it was, in like manner, altogether private; spent chiefly in provincial towns, and apart from high scenes or persons; its principal occurrences the new books he wrote, its whole course a spiritual and silent one. He became an author in his nineteenth year; and with a conscientious assiduity adhered to that employment; not seeking, indeed carefully avoiding, any interruption or disturbance therein, were it only for a day or an hour. Nevertheless, in looking over those Sixty Volumes of his, we feel as if Richter's history must have another, much deeper interest and worth, than outward incidents could impart to it. For the spirit which shines more or less completely through his writings is one of perennial excellence; rare in all times and situations, and perhaps nowhere and in no time more rare than in literary Europe at this era. We see in this man a high, self-subsistent, original and, in many respects, even great character. He shows himself a man of wonderful gifts, and with, perhaps, a still happier combination and adjustment of these: in whom Philosophy and Poetry are not only reconciled, but blended together into a purer essence, into Religion; who, with the softest, most universal sympathy for outward things, is inwardly calm, impregnable; holds on his way through all temptations and afflictions, so quietly, yet so inflexibly; the true literary man among a thousand false ones, the Apollo among neatherds; in one word, a man understanding the nineteenth century, and living in the midst of it, yet whose life is, in some measure, a heroic and devout one. No character of this kind, we are aware, is to be formed without manifold and victorious struggling with the world; and the narrative of such struggling, what little of it can be narrated and interpreted, will belong to the highest species of history. The acted life of such a man, it has been said, 'is itself a Bible;' it is a 'Gospel of Freedom,' preached abroad to all men; whereby, among mean unbelieving souls, we may know that nobleness has not yet become impossible; and, languishing amid boundless triviality and despicability, still understand that man's nature is indefeasibly divine, and so hold fast what is the most important of all faiths, the faith in ourselves.

But if the acted life of a *pius Vates* is so high a matter, the written life, which, if properly written, would be a translation and interpretation thereof, must also have great value. It has been said that no Poet is equal to his Poem, which saying is partially true; but, in a deeper sense, it may also be asserted, and with still greater truth, that no Poem is equal to its Poet. Now, it is Biography that first gives us both Poet and Poem; by the significance of the one elucidating and completing that of the other. That ideal outline of himself, which a man unconsciously shadows forth in his writings, and which, rightly deciphered, will be truer than any other representation of him, it is the task of the Biographer to fill-up into an actual coherent figure, and bring home to our experience, or at least our clear undoubting admiration, thereby to instruct and edify us in many ways. Conducted on such principles, the Biography of great men, especially of great Poets, that is, of men in the highest degree noble-minded and wise, might become one of the most dignified and valuable species of composition. As matters stand, indeed, there are few Biographies that accomplish anything of this kind: the most are mere Indexes of a Biography, which each reader is to write out for himself, as he peruses them; not the living body, but the dry bones of a body, which should have been alive. To expect any such Promethean virtue in a common Life-writer were unreasonable enough. How shall that unhappy Biographic brotherhood, instead of writing like Index-makers and Government-clerks, suddenly become enkindled with some sparks of intellect, or even of genial fire; and not only collecting dates and facts, but making use of them, look beyond the surface and economical form of a man's life, into its substance and spirit? The truth is, Biographies are in a similar case with Sermons and Songs: they have their scientific rules, their ideal of perfection and of imperfection, as all things have; but hitherto their rules are only, as it were, unseen Laws of Nature, not critical Acts of Parliament, and threaten us with no immediate penalty: besides, unlike Tragedies and Epics, such works may be something without being all: their simplicity of form, moreover, is apt to seem easiness of execution; and thus, for one artist in those departments, we have a thousand bunglers.

With regard to Richter, in particular, to say that his biographic treatment has been worse than usual, were saying much; yet worse than we expected, it has certainly been. Various 'Lives of Jean Paul,' anxiously endeavouring to profit by the public excitement while it lasted, and communicating in a given space almost a minimum of information, have been read by us, within the last four years, with no great disappointment. We strove to take thankfully what little they had to give ; and looked forward, in hope, to that promised 'Autobiography,' wherein all deficiencies were to be supplied. Several years before his death, it would seem, Richter had determined on writing some account of his own life ; and with his customary honesty, had set about a thorough preparation for this task. After revolving many plans, some of them singular enough, he at last determined on the form of composition ; and with a half-sportful allusion to Goethe's *Dichtung und Wahrheit aus meinem Leben*, had prefixed to his work the title *Wahrheit aus meinem Leben* (Truth from my Life) ; having relinquished, as impracticable, the strange idea of 'writing, parallel to it, a *Dichtung* (Fiction) also, under cover of Nicolaus Margraf,' — a certain Apothecary, existing only as hero of one of his last Novels ! In this work, which weightier avocations had indeed retarded or suspended, considerable progress was said to have been made ; and on Richter's decease, Herr Otto, a man of talents, who had been his intimate friend for half a lifetime, undertook the editing and completing of it ; not without sufficient proclamation and assertion, which in the mean while was credible enough, that to him only could the post of Richter's Biographer belong.

Three little Volumes of that *Wahrheit aus Jean Pauls Leben*, published in the course of as many years, are at length before us. The First volume, which came out in 1826, occasioned some surprise, if not disappointment ; yet still left room for hope. It was the commencement of a real Autobiography, and written with much heartiness and even dignity of manner ; though taken up under a quite unexpected point of view ; in that spirit of genial humour, of gay earnestness, which, with all its strange fantastic accompaniments, often sat on Jean Paul so gracefully, and to which, at any rate, no reader of his works could be a stranger. By virtue of an autocratic ukase, Paul had appointed himself 'Professor of his own History,' and delivered to the Universe three beautiful 'Lectures' on that subject; boasting, justly enough, that, in his special department, he was better informed than any other man whatever. He was not without his oratorical secrets and professorial habits: thus, as Mr. Wortley, in writing his parliamentary speech to be read within his hat, had marked, in various passages, 'Here cough,' so Paul, with greater brevity, had an arbitrary hieroglyph introduced here and there, among his papers, and purporting, as he tells us, "*Meine Herren, niemand scharre, niemand gähne*, Gentlemen, no scraping, no yawning!" — a hieroglyph, we must say, which many public speakers might stand more in need of than he.

Unfortunately, in the Second volume, no other Lectures came to light, but only a string of disconnected, indeed quite heterogeneous Notes, intended to have been fashioned into such; the full free stream of oratory dissipated itself into unsatisfactory drops. With the Third volume, which is by much the longest, Herr Otto appears more decidedly in his own person, though still rather with the scissors than with the pen; and, behind a multitude of circumvallations and outposts, endeavours to advance his history a little; the Lectures having left it still almost at the very commencement. His peculiar plan, and the too manifest purpose to continue speaking in Jean Paul's manner, greatly obstruct his progress; which, indeed, is so inconsiderable, that at the end of this third volume, that is, after some seven hundred small octavo pages, we find the hero, as yet, scarcely beyond his twentieth year, and the history proper still only, as it were, beginning. We cannot but regret that Herr Otto, whose talent and good purpose, to say nothing of his relation to Richter, demand regard from us, had not adopted some straightforward method, and spoken out in plain prose, which seems a more natural dialect for him, what he had to say on this matter. Instead of a multifarious combination, tending so slowly, if at all, towards unity, he might, without omitting those 'Lectures,' or any 'Note' that had value, have given us a direct Narrative, which, if it had wanted the line of Beauty, might have had the still more indispensable line of Regularity, and been, at all events, far shorter. Till Herr Otto's work is completed, we cannot speak positively; but, in the mean while, we must say that it wears an unprosperous aspect, and leaves room to fear that, after all, Richter's Biography may still long continue a problem. As for ourselves, in this state of matters, what help, towards characterising Jean Paul's practical Life, we can afford, is but a few slight facts gleaned from Herr Otto's and other meaner works; and which, even in our own eyes, are extremely insufficient.

Richter was born at Wonsiedel in Bayreuth, in the year 1763; and as his birthday fell on the 21st of March, it was sometimes wittily said that he and the Spring were born together. He himself mentions this, and with a laudable intention: 'this epigrammatic fact,' says he, 'that I the 'Professor and the Spring came into the world together, I 'have indeed brought out a hundred times in conversation, 'before now; but I fire it off here purposely, like a cannon-'salute, for the hundred and first time, that so by printing I 'may ever henceforth be unable to offer it again as *bon-mot-'bonbon*, when, through the Printer's Devil, it has already 'been presented to all the world.' Destiny, he seems to think, made another witticism on him; the word *Richter* being appellative as well as proper, in the German tongue, where it signifies *Judge*. His Christian name, Jean Paul, which long passed for some freak of his own, and a pseudonym, he seems to have derived honestly enough from his maternal grandfather, Johann Paul Kuhn, a substantial cloth-maker in Hof; only translating the German *Johann* into the French *Jean*. The Richters, for at least two generations, had been schoolmasters, or very subaltern churchmen, distinguished for their poverty and their piety: the grandfather, it appears, is still remembered in his little circle, as a man of quite remarkable innocence and holiness; 'in Neustadt,' says his descendant, 'they will show 'you a bench behind the organ, where he knelt on Sundays, 'and a cave he had made for himself in what is called the 'Little Culm, where he was wont to pray.' Holding, and laboriously discharging, three school or church offices, his yearly income scarcely amounted to fifteen pounds: 'and at 'this Hunger-fountain, common enough for Bayreuth school-'people, the man stood thirty-five years long, and cheerfully 'drew.' Preferment had been slow in visiting him: but at length 'it came to pass,' says Paul, 'just in my birth-year, 'that, on the 6th of August, probably through special con-'nexions with the *Higher Powers*, he did obtain one of the 'most important places; in comparison with which, truly, 'Rectorate, and Town, and cave in the Culmberg, were 'well worth exchanging; a place, namely, in the Neustadt 'Churchyard.[1] — His good wife had been promoted thither 'twenty years before him. My parents had taken me, an 'infant, along with them to his death-bed. He was in the 'act of departing, when a clergyman (as my father has often 'told me) said to them: Now, let the old Jacob lay his hand 'on the child, and bless him. I was held into the bed of 'death, and he laid his hand on my head. — Thou good old 'grandfather! Often have I thought of thy hand, blessing 'as it grew cold, — when Fate led me out of dark hours into 'clearer, — and already I can believe in thy blessing, in 'this material world, whose life, foundation and essence is 'Spirit!'

The father, who at this time occupied the humble post of *Tertius* (Under-schoolmaster) and Organist at Wonsiedel, was shortly afterwards appointed Clergyman in the hamlet of Jodiz; and thence, in the course of years, transferred to

[1] *Gottesacker* (God's-field), not *Kirchhof*, the more common term and exactly corresponding to ours, is the word Richter uses here, — and almost always elsewhere, which in his writings he has often occasion to do.

Schwarzenbach on the Saale. He too was of a truly devout disposition, though combining with it more energy of character, and apparently more general talent; being noted in his neighbourhood as a bold, zealous preacher; and still partially known to the world, we believe, for some meritorious compositions in Church-music. In poverty he cannot be said to have altogether equalled his predecessor, who through life ate nothing but bread and beer; yet poor enough he was; and no less cheerful than poor. The thriving burgher's daughter, whom he took to wife, had, as we guess, brought no money with her, but only habits little advantageous for a schoolmaster or parson; at all events, the worthy man, frugal as his household was, had continual difficulties, and even died in debt. Paul, who in those days was called Fritz, narrates gaily, how his mother used to despatch him to Hof, her native town, with a provender-bag strapped over his shoulders, under pretext of purchasing at a cheaper rate there; but in reality to get his groceries and dainties furnished gratis by his grandmother. He was wont to kiss his grandfather's hand behind the loom, and speak with him; while the good old lady, parsimonious to all the world, but lavish to her own, privily filled his bag with the good things of this life, and even gave him almonds for himself, which, however, he kept for a friend. One other little trait, quite new in ecclesiastical annals, we must here communicate. Paul, in summing up the joys of existence at Jodiz, mentions this among the number:

'In Autumn evenings (and though the weather were bad) the Father used to go in his night-gown, with Paul and Adam into a potato-field lying over the Saale. The one younker carried a mattock, the other a hand-basket. Arrived on the ground, the Father set to digging new potatoes, so many as were wanted for supper; Paul gathered them from the bed into the basket, whilst Adam, clambering in the hazel thickets, looked out for the best nuts. After a time, Adam had to come down from his boughs into the bed, and Paul in his turn ascended. And thus, with potatoes and nuts, they returned contentedly home; and the pleasure of having run abroad, some mile in space, some hour in time, and then of celebrating the harvest-home, by candlelight, when they came back, — let every one paint to himself as brilliantly as the receiver thereof.'

To such persons as argue that the respectability of the cloth depends on its price at the clothier's, it must appear surprising that a Protestant clergyman, who not only was in no case to keep fox-hounds, but even saw it convenient to dig his own potatoes, should not have fallen under universal odium, and felt his usefulness very considerably diminished. Nothing of this kind, however, becomes visible in the history of the Jodiz Parson: we find him a man powerful in his vocation; loved and venerated by his flock; nay, associating at will, and ever as an honoured guest, with the gentry of Voigtland, not indeed in the character of a gentleman, yet in that of priest, which he reckoned far higher. Like an old Lutheran, says his son, he believed in the great, as he did in ghosts; but without any shade of fear. The truth is, the man had a cheerful, pure, religious heart; was diligent in business, and fervent in spirit: and, in all the relations of his life, found this wellnigh sufficient for him.

To our Professor, as to Poets in general, the recollections of childhood had always something of an ideal, almost celestial character. Often, in his fictions, he describes such scenes with a fond minuteness; nor is poverty any deadly, or even unwelcome ingredient in them. On the whole, it is not by money, or money's worth, that man lives and has his being. Is not God's Universe *within* our head, whether there be a torn skull-cap or a king's diadem *without?* Let no one imagine that Paul's young years were unhappy; still less that he looks back on them in a lachrymose, sentimental manner, with the smallest symptom either of boasting or whining. Poverty of a far sterner sort than this would have been a light matter to him; for a kind mother, Nature herself, had already provided against it; and, like the mother of Achilles, rendered him invulnerable to outward things. There was a bold, deep, joyful spirit looking through those young eyes; and to such a spirit the world *has* nothing poor, but all is rich, and full of loveliness and wonder. That our readers may glance with us into this foreign Parsonage, we shall translate some paragraphs from Paul's second Lecture, and thereby furnish, at the same time, a specimen of his professorial style and temper:

'To represent the Jodiz life of our Hans Paul, — for by this name we shall for a time distinguish him, yet ever changing it with others, — our best course, I believe, will be to conduct him through a whole Idyl-year; dividing the normal year into four seasons, as so many quarterly Idyls; four Idyls exhaust his happiness.

'For the rest, let no one marvel at finding an Idyl-kingdom and pastoral-world in a little hamlet and parsonage. In the smallest bed you can raise a tulip-tree, which shall extend its flowery boughs over all the garden; and the life-breath of joy can be inhaled as well through a window, as in the open wood and sky. Nay, is not Man's Spirit (with all its infinite celestial-spaces) walled-in within a six-feet Body, with integuments, and Malpighian mucuses, and capillary tubes; and has only five strait world-windows, of Senses, to open for the boundless, round-eyed, round-sunned All; — and yet it discerns and reproduces an All!

'Scarcely do I know with which of the four quarterly Idyls to begin; for each is a little heavenly forecourt to the next: however, the climax of joys, if we start with Winter and January, will perhaps be most apparent. In the cold, our Father had commonly, like an Alpine herdsman, come down from the upper altitude of his study; and, to the joy of the children, was dwelling on the plain of the general family-room. In the morning, he sat by a window, committing his Sunday's sermon to memory; and the three sons, Fritz (who I myself am), and Adam, and Gottlieb carried, by turns, the full coffee-cup to him, and still more gladly carried back the empty one, because the carrier was then entitled to pick the unmelted remains of the sugar-candy (taken against cough) from the bottom thereof. Out of doors, truly, the sky covered all things with silence; the brook with ice, the village with snow: but in our room there was life; under the stove a pigeon-establishment; on the windows finch-cages; on the floor the invincible bull brach, our *Bonne,* the night-guardian of the court-yard; and a poodle, and the pretty *Scharmantel* (Poll), a present from the Lady von Plotho; — and close by, the kitchen, with two maids; and farther off, against the other end of the house, our stable, with all sorts of bovine, swinish and feathered cattle, and their noises: the threshers, with their flails, also at work within the court-yard, I might reckon as another item. In this way, with nothing but society on all hands, the whole male portion of the household easily spent their forenoon in tasks of memory, not far from the female portion, as busily employed in cooking.

'Holidays occur in every occupation; thus I too had my airing holidays, — analogous to watering holidays, — so that I could travel out in the snow of the court-yard, and to the barn with its threshing. Nay, was there a delicate embassy to be transacted in the village, — for example, to the schoolmaster, to the tailor, — I was sure to be despatched thither in the middle of my lessons; and thus I still got forth into the open air and the cold, and measured myself with the new snow. At noon, before our own dinner, we children might also, in the kitchen, have the hungry satisfaction to see the threshers fall-to and consume their victuals.

'The afternoon, again, was still more important, and richer in joys. Winter shortened and sweetened our lessons. In the long dusk, our Father walked to and fro; and the children, according to ability, trotted under his night-gown, holding by his hands. At sound of the Vesper-bell, we placed ourselves in a circle, and in concert devotionally chaunted the hymn, *Die finstre Nacht bricht stark herein* (The gloomy Night is gathering round). Only in villages, not in towns, where probably there is more night than day labour, have the evening chimes a meaning and beauty, and are the swan-song of the day; the evening-bell is as it were the muffle of the over-loud heart, and, like a *rance des vaches* of the plains, calls men from their running and toiling, into the land of silence and dreams. After a pleasant watching about the kitchen-door for the moonrise of candlelight, we saw our wide room at once illuminated and barricaded; to wit, the window-shutters were closed and bolted; and behind these window bastions and breast-works the child felt himself snugly nestled, and well secured against Knecht Ruprecht,[1] who on the outside could not get in, but only in vain keep growling and humming.

'About this period too it was that we children might undress, and in long train-shirts skip up and down. Idyllic joys of various sorts alternated: our Father either had his quarto Bible, interleaved with blank folio sheets, before him, and was marking, at each verse, the book wherein he had read anything concerning it; — or more commonly he had his ruled music-paper; and, undisturbed by this racketing of children, was composing whole concerts of church-music, with all their divisions; constructing his internal melody without any help of external tones (as Reichard too advises), or rather in spite

[1] The *Rawhead* (with bloody bones) of Germany.

of all external mistones. In both cases, in the last with the more pleasure, I looked on as he wrote; and rejoiced specially, when, by pauses of various instruments, whole pages were at once filled up. The children all sat sporting *on* that long writing and eating table, or even *under* it. * * *

'Then, at length, how did the winter evening, once a week, mount in worth, when the old errand-woman, coated in snow, with her fruit, flesh and general-ware basket, entered the kitchen from Hof; and we all, in this case, had the distant town in miniature before our eyes, nay before our noses, for there were pastry-cakes in it!'

Thus, in dull winter imprisonment, among all manner of bovine, swinish and feathered cattle, with their noises, may Idyllic joys be found, if there is an eye to see them, and a heart to taste them. Truly happiness is cheap, did we apply to the right merchant for it. Paul warns us elsewhere not to believe, for these Idyls, that there were no sour days, no chidings and the like, at Jodiz: yet, on the whole, he had good reason to rejoice in his parents. They loved him well; his Father, he says, would 'shed tears' over any mark of quickness or talent in little Fritz: they were virtuous also, and devout, which, after all, is better than being rich. 'Ever 'and anon,' says he, 'I was hearing some narrative from my 'Father, how he and other clergymen had taken parts of 'their dress and given them to the poor; he related these 'things with joy, not as an admonition, but merely as a 'necessary occurrence. O God! I thank thee for my 'Father!'

Richter's education was not of a more sumptuous sort than his board and lodging. Some disagreement with the Schoolmaster at Jodiz had induced the Parson to take his sons from school, and determine to teach them himself. This determination he executed faithfully indeed, yet in the most limited style; his method being no Pestalozzian one, but simply the old scheme of task-work and force-work, operating on a Latin grammar and a Latin vocabulary: and the two boys sat all day, and all year, at home, without other preceptorial nourishment than getting by heart long lists of words. Fritz learned honestly nevertheless, and in spite of his brother Adam's bad example. For the rest, he was totally destitute of books, except such of his Father's theological ones as he could come at by stealth: these, for want of better, he eagerly devoured; understanding, as he says, nothing whatever of their contents. With no less impetuosity, and no less profit, he perused the antiquated sets of Newspapers, which a kind patroness, the Lady von Plotho, already mentioned, was in the habit of furnishing to his Father, not in separate sheets, but in sheaves monthly. This was the extent of his reading. Jodiz, too, was the most sequestered of all hamlets; had neither natural nor artificial beauty; no memorable thing could be seen there in a lifetime. Nevertheless, under an immeasurable Sky, and in a quite wondrous World it did stand; and glimpses into the infinite spaces of the Universe, and even into the infinite spaces of Man's Soul, could be had there as well as elsewhere. Fritz had his own thoughts, in spite of schoolmasters: a little heavenly seed of Knowledge, nay of Wisdom, had been laid in him, and with no gardener but Nature herself, it was silently growing. To some of our readers, the following circumstance may seem unparalleled, if not unintelligible; to others nowise so:

'In the future Literary History of our hero, it will become doubtful whether he was not born more for Philosophy than for Poetry. In earliest times, the word *Weltweisheit* (Philosophy, *World-wisdom*), — yet also another word, *Morgenland* (East, *Morning-land*), — was to me an open Heaven's-gate, through which I looked-in over long, long gardens of joy. — Never shall I forget that inward occurrence, till now narrated to no mortal, wherein I witnessed the birth of my Self-consciousness, of which I can still give the place and time. One forenoon, I was standing, a very young child, in the outer door, and looking leftward at the stack of the fuel-wood, — when, all at once, the internal vision, "I am a Me (*ich bin ein Ich*)," came like a flash from heaven before me, and in gleaming light ever afterwards continued: then had my Me, for the first time, seen itself, and forever. Deceptions of memory are scarcely conceivable here; for, in regard to an event occurring altogether in the veiled Holy-of-Holies of man, and whose novelty alone has given permanence to such every-day recollections accompanying it, no posterior description from another party would have mingled itself with accompanying circumstances at all.'

It was in his thirteenth year that the family removed to that better church-living at Schwarzenbach; with which change, so far as school-education was concerned, prospects considerably brightened for him. The public Teacher there was no deep scholar or thinker, yet a lively, genial man, and warmly interested in his pupils; among whom he soon learned to distinguish Fritz, as a boy of altogether superior gifts. What was of still more importance, Fritz now got access to books; entered into a course of highly miscellaneous, self-selected reading; and what with Romances, what with Belles-Lettres works, and Hutchesonian Philosophy, and controversial Divinity, saw an astonishing scene opening round him on all hands. His Latin and Greek were now better taught; he even began learning Hebrew. Two clergymen of the neighbourhood took pleasure in his company, young as he was; and were of great service now and afterwards: it was under their auspices that he commenced composition, and also speculating on Theology, wherein he 'inclined strongly to the heterodox side.'

In the 'family-room,' however, things were not nearly so flourishing. The Professor's three Lectures terminate before this date; but we gather from his Notes that surly clouds hung over Schwarzenbach, that 'his evil days began there.' The Father was engaged in more complex duties than formerly, went often from home, was encumbered with debt, and lost his former cheerfulness of humour. For his sons he saw no outlet except the hereditary craft of School-keeping; and let the matter rest there, taking little farther charge of them. In some three years, the poor man, worn down with manifold anxieties, departed this life; leaving his pecuniary affairs, which he had long calculated on rectifying by the better income of Schwarzenbach, sadly deranged.

Meanwhile, Friedrich had been sent to the Hof *Gymna-*

sium (Town-school), where, notwithstanding this event, he continued some time; two years in all; apparently the most profitable period of his whole tuition; indeed, the only period when, properly speaking, he had any tutor but himself. The good old cloth-making grandfather and grandmother took charge of him, under their roof; and he had a body of teachers, all notable in their way. Herr Otto represents him as a fine, trustful, kindly yet resolute youth, who went through his persecutions, preferments, studies, friendships and other school-destinies in a highly creditable manner; and demonstrates this, at great length, by various details of facts, far too minute for insertion here. As a trait of Paul's intellectual habitudes, it may be mentioned that, at this time, he scarcely made any progress in History or Geography, much as he profited in all other branches; nor was the dull teacher entirely to blame, but also the indisposed pupil: indeed, it was not till long afterwards, that he overcame or suppressed his contempt for those studies, and with an effort of his own acquired some skill in them.[1] The like we have heard of other Poets and Philosophers, especially when their teachers chanced to be prosaists and unphilosophical. Richter boasts that he was never punished at school; yet between him and the Historico-geographical *Conrector* (Second Master) no good understanding could subsist. On one tragi-comical occasion, of another sort, they came into still more decided collision. The zealous Conrector, a most solid painstaking man, desirous to render his Gymnasium as like a University as possible, had imagined that a series of 'Disputations,' some foreshadow of those held at College, might be a useful,

[1] 'All History,' thus he writes in his thirty-second year, 'in so far as it 'is an affair of memory, can only be reckoned a sapless heartless thistle 'for pedantic chaffinches; — but, on the other hand, like Nature, it has 'highest value, in as far as we, by means of it, as by means of Nature, 'can divine and read the Infinite Spirit, who, with Nature and History, as 'with letters, legibly writes to us. He who finds a God in the physical 'world, will also find one in the moral, which is History. Nature forces on 'our heart a Creator; History a Providence.'

as certainly enough it would be an ornamental thing. By ill-luck, the worthy President had selected some church-article for the theme of such a Disputation: one boy was to defend, and it fell to Paul's lot to impugn the dogma; a task which, as hinted above, he was very specially qualified to undertake. Now, honest Paul knew nothing of the limits of this game; never dreamt but he might argue with his whole strength, to whatever results it might lead. In a very few rounds, accordingly, his antagonist was borne out of the ring, as good as lifeless; and the Conrector himself, seeing the danger, had, as it were, to descend from his presiding chair, and clap the gauntlets on his own more experienced hands. But Paul, nothing daunted, gave him also a Rowland for an Oliver; nay, as it became more and more manifest to all eyes, was fast reducing him also to the frightfullest extremity. The Conrector's tongue threatened cleaving to the roof of his mouth; for his brain was at a stand, or whirling in eddies; only his gall was in active play. Nothing remained for him but to close the debate by a "Silence, Sirrah!" — and leave the room, with a face (like that of the much more famous Subrector Hans von Füchslein[1]) 'of a mingled colour, like 'red bole, green chalk, tinsel-yellow, and *vomissement de la 'reine.*'

With his studies in the Leipzig University, whither he proceeded in 1781, begins a far more important era for Paul; properly, the era of his manhood, and first entire dependence on himself. In regard to literary or scientific culture, it is not clear that he derived much furtherance from Leipzig; much more, at least, than the mere neighbourhood of libraries and fellow-learners might anywhere else have afforded him. Certain professorial courses he did attend, and with diligence; but too much in the character of critic, as well as of pupil: he was in the habit of 'measuring minds' with men so much older and more honourable than he; and erelong his respect for many of them had not a little abated. What his original

[1] See *Quintus Fixlein*, c. 7.

plan of studies was, or whether he had any fixed plan, we do not learn; at Hof, without election or rejection on his own part, he had been trained with some view to Theology; but this and every other professional view soon faded away in Leipzig, owing to a variety of causes; and Richter, now still more decidedly a self-teacher, broke loose from all corporate guilds whatsoever, and in intellectual culture, as in other respects, endeavoured to seek out a basis of his own. He read multitudes of books, and wrote down whole volumes of excerpts, and private speculations; labouring in all directions with insatiable eagerness; but from the University he derived little guidance, and soon came to expect little. Ernesti, the only truly eminent man of the place, had died shortly after Paul's arrival there.

Nay, it was necessity as well as choice that detached him from professions; he had not the means to enter any. Quite another and far more pressing set of cares lay round him; not how he could live easily in future years, but how he could live at all in the present, was the grand question with him. Whatever it might be in regard to intellectual matters, certainly, in regard to moral matters, Leipzig was his true seminary, where, with many stripes, Experience taught him the wisest lessons. It was here that he first saw Poverty, not in the shape of Parsimony, but in the far sterner one of actual Want; and, unseen and single-handed, wrestling with Fortune for life or death, first proved what a rugged, deep-rooted, indomitable strength, under such genial softness, dwelt in him; and from a buoyant cloud-capt Youth, perfected himself into a clear, free, benignant and lofty-minded Man.

Meanwhile the steps towards such a consummation were painful enough. His old Schoolmaster at Schwarzenbach, himself a Leipziger, had been wont to assure him that he might live for nothing in Leipzig, so easily were 'free-tables,' '*stipendia*,' private teaching and the like, to be procured there, by youths of merit. That Richter was of this latter species, the Rector of the Hof Gymnasium bore honourable witness; inviting the Leipzig dignitaries, in his *Testimonium*, to try the candidate themselves; and even introducing him in person (for the two had travelled together) to various influential men: but all these things availed him nothing. The Professors he found beleaguered by a crowd of needy sycophants, diligent in season and out of season, whose whole tactics were too loathsome to him; on all hands, he heard the sad saying: *Lipsia vult expectari*, Leipzig preferments must be waited for. Now, waiting was of all things the most inconvenient for poor Richter. In his pocket he had little; friends, except one fellow-student, he had none; and at home the finance-department had fallen into a state of total perplexity, fast verging towards final ruin. The worthy old Cloth-manufacturer was now dead; his Wife soon followed him; and the Widow Richter, her favourite daughter, who had removed to Hof, though against the advice of all friends, that she might be near her, now stood alone there, with a young family, and in the most forlorn situation. She was appointed chief heir, indeed; but former benefactions had left far less to inherit than had been expected; nay, the other relatives contested the whole arrangement, and she had to waste her remaining substance in lawsuits, scarcely realising from it, in the shape of borrowed pittances and by forced sales, enough to supply her with daily bread. Nor was it poverty alone that she had to suffer, but contumely no less; the Hof public openly finding her guilty of Unthrift, and, instead of assistance, repeating to her dispraise, over their coffee, the old proverb, 'Hard got, soon gone;' for all which evils she had no remedy, but loud complaining to Heaven and Earth. The good woman, with the most honest dispositions, seems in fact to have had but a small share of wisdom; far too small for her present trying situation. Herr Otto says that Richter's portraiture of Lenette, in the *Blumen-Frucht-und Dornen-Stücke* (Flower, Fruit and Thorn Pieces) contains many features of his mother: Lenette is of 'an upright, but common and limited nature;' assiduous, even to excess, in sweeping and scouring; true-hearted, religious in her way, yet full of discontents, suspicion and headstrong whims; a spouse forever plagued and plaguing; as the brave Stanislaus Siebenkäs, that true Diogenes of impoverished Poors'-Advocates, often felt, to his cost, beside her. Widow Richter's family, as well as her fortune, was under bad government, and sinking into lower and lower degradation: Adam, the brother, mentioned above, as Paul's yokefellow in Latin and potato-digging, had now fallen away even from the humble pretension of being a Schoolmaster, or indeed of being anything; for, after various acts of vagrancy, he had enlisted in a marching regiment; with which, or in other devious courses, he marched on, and only the grand billet-master, Death, found him fixed quarters. The Richter establishment had parted from its old moorings, and was now, with wind and tide, fast drifting towards fatal whirlpools.

In this state of matters, the scarcity of Leipzig could nowise be supplied from the fulness of Hof; but rather the two households stood like concave mirrors reflecting one another's keen hunger into a still keener for both. What outlook was there for the poor Philosopher of nineteen? Even his meagre 'bread and milk' could not be had for nothing; it became a serious consideration for him that the shoemaker, who was to sole his boots, 'did not trust.' Far from affording him any sufficient moneys, his straitened mother would willingly have made him borrow for her own wants; and was incessantly persuading him to get places for his brothers. Richter felt too, that except himself, desolate, helpless as he was, those brothers, that old mother, had no stay on earth. There are men with whom it is as with Schiller's Friedland: 'Night must it be ere Friedland's star will beam.' On this forsaken youth Fortune seemed to have let loose her bandogs, and hungry Ruin had him in the wind; without was no help, no counsel: but there lay a giant force within; and so from the depths of that sorrow and abasement, his better soul rose purified and invincible, like Hercules from his long Labours. A high, cheerful Stoicism grew up in the man. Poverty, Pain and all Evil, he learned to regard, not as what they seemed, but as what they were; he learned to despise them, nay in kind mockery to sport with them, as with bright-spotted wild-beasts which he had tamed and harnessed. 'What is Pov-'erty,' said he; 'who is the man that whines under it? The 'pain is but as that of piercing the ears is to a maiden, and 'you hang jewels in the wound.' Dark thoughts he had, but they settled into no abiding gloom: 'sometimes,' says Otto, 'he would wave his finger across his brow, as if driving back some hostile series of ideas;' and farther complaint he did not utter.[1] During this sad period, he wrote out for himself a little manual of practical philosophy, naming it *Andachtsbuch* (Book of Devotion), which contains such maxims as these:

'Every unpleasant feeling is a sign that I have become untrue to my resolutions. — Epictetus was not unhappy. —

'Not chance, but I am to blame for my sufferings.

'It were an impossible miracle if none befell thee: look for their coming, therefore; each day make thyself sure of many.

'Say not, were my sorrows other than these, I should bear them better.

'Think of the host of Worlds, and of the plagues on this World-mote. — Death puts an end to the whole. —

'For virtue's sake I am here: but if a man, for his task, forgets and sacrifices all, why shouldst not thou? —

'Expect injuries, for men are weak, and thou thyself doest such too often.

'Mollify thy heart by painting out the sufferings of thy enemy; think of him as of one spiritually sick, who deserves sympathy. —

'Most men judge so badly; why wouldst thou be praised by a child? — No one would respect thee in a beggar's coat: what is a respect that is paid to woollen cloth, not to thee?'

[1] In bodily pain, he was wont to show the like endurance and indifference. At one period of his life, he had violent headaches, which forced him, for the sake of a slight alleviation, to keep his head perfectly erect; you might see him talking with a calm face and all his old gaiety, and only know by this posture that he was suffering.

These are wise maxims for so young a man; but what was wiser still, he did not rest satisfied with mere maxims, which, how true soever, are only a dead letter, till Action first gives them life and worth. Besides devout prayer to the gods, he set his own shoulder to the wheel. 'Evil,' says he, 'is like a nightmare; the instant you begin to strive 'with it, to bestir yourself, it has already ended.' Without farther parleying, there as he stood, Richter grappled with his Fate, and resolutely determined on self-help. His means, it is true, were of the most unpromising sort, yet the only means he had: the writing of Books! He forthwith commenced writing them. The *Grönländische Prozesse* (Greenland Lawsuits), a collection of satirical sketches, full of wild gay wit and keen insight, was composed in that base environment of his, with unpaid milkscores and unsoled boots; and even still survives, though the Author, besides all other disadvantages, was then only in his nineteenth year. But the heaviest part of the business yet remained; that of finding a purchaser and publisher. Richter tried all Leipzig with his manuscript, in vain; to a man, with that total contempt of Grammar which Jedediah Cleishbotham also complains of, they 'declined the *article*.' Paul had to stand by, as so many have done, and see his sunbeams weighed on hay-scales, and the hay-balance give no symptoms of moving. But Paul's heart moved as little as the balance. Leipzig being now exhausted, the World was all before him where to try; he had nothing for it, but to search till he found, or till he died searching. One Voss of Berlin at length bestirred himself; accepted, printed the Book, and even gave him sixteen *louis d'or* for it. What a Potosi was here! Paul determined to be an author henceforth, and nothing but an author; now that his soul might even be kept in his body by that trade. His mother, hearing that he had written a book, thought that perhaps he could even write a sermon, and was for his coming down to preach in the High Church of Hof. 'What is a sermon,' said Paul, 'which 'every miserable student can spout forth? Or, think you, 'there is a parson in Hof that, not to speak of writing my 'Book, can, in the smallest degree, understand it?'

But unfortunately his Potosi was like other mines; the metalliferous vein did not last; what miners call a *shift* or *trouble* occurred in it, and now there was nothing but hard rock to hew on. The *Grönländische Prozesse*, though printed, did not sell; the public was in quest of pap and treacle, not of fierce curry like this. The Reviewing world mostly passed it by without notice; one poor dog in Leipzig even lifted up his leg over it. 'For anything we know,' saith he, 'much, if not all of what the Author here, in bitter tone, sets forth on bookmaking, theologians, women and 'so on, may be true; but throughout the whole work, the 'determination to be witty acts on him so strongly, that we 'cannot doubt but his book will excite in all rational readers 'so much disgust, that they will see themselves constrained to 'close it again without delay.' And herewith the ill-starred quadruped passes on, as if nothing special had happened. 'Singular!' adds Herr Otto, 'this review, which at the 'time pretended to some ephemeral attention, and likely 'enough obtained it, would have fallen into everlasting oblivion, had not its connexion with that very work, which 'every rational reader was to close again, or rather never 'to open, raised it up for moments!' One moment, say we, is enough: let it drop again into that murky pool, and sink there to endless depths; for all flesh, and reviewer-flesh too, is fallible and pardonable.

Richter's next Book was soon ready; but, in this position of affairs, no man would buy it. The *Selection from the Papers of the Devil*, such was its wonderful title, lay by him, on quite another principle than the Horatian one, for seven long years. It was in vain that he exhibited, and corresponded, and left no stone unturned, ransacking the world for a publisher; there was none anywhere to be met with. The unwearied Richter tried other plans. He presented Magazine Editors with Essays, some one in ten of which might be accepted; he made joint-stock with certain provincial literati of the Hof district, who had cash, and published for themselves; he sometimes borrowed, but was in hot haste to repay; he lived as the young ravens; he was often in danger of starving. 'The prisoner's allowance,' says he, 'is bread and water; but I had only the latter.'

'Nowhere,' observes Richter on another occasion, 'can 'you collect the stress-memorials and siege-medals of Pov- 'erty more pleasantly and philosophically than at College: 'the Academic Burschen exhibit to us how many Humorists 'and Diogeneses Germany has in it.'[1] Travelling through this parched Sahara, with nothing round him but stern sandy solitude, and no landmark on Earth, but only loadstars in the Heaven, Richter does not anywhere appear to have faltered in his progress; for a moment to have lost heart, or even to have lost good humour. 'The man who fears not death,' says the Greek Poet, 'will start at no shadows.' Paul had looked Desperation full in the face, and found that for him she was not desperate. Sorely pressed on from without, his inward energy, his strength both of thought and resolve did but increase, and establish itself on a surer and surer foundation; he stood like a rock amid the beating of continual tempests; nay, a rock crowned with foliage; and

[1] By certain speculators on German affairs, much has been written and talked about what is, after all, a very slender item in German affairs, the *Burschenleben*, or manners of the young men at Universities. We must regret that in discussing this matter, since it was thought worth discussing, the true significance and soul of it should not have been, by some faint indication, pointed out to us. Apart from its duelling punctilios, and beer-songs, and tobacco-smoking, and other fopperies of the system, which are to the German student merely what coach-driving and horse-dealing, and other kindred fopperies, are to the English, Burschenism is not without its meaning more than Oxfordism or Cambridgeism. The Bursch strives to say in the strongest language he can: "See! I am an unmoneyed scholar, and a free *man;*" the Oxonian and Cantab, again, endeavour to say: "See! I am a moneyed scholar, and a spirited *gentleman.*" We rather think the Bursch's assertion, were it rightly worded, would be the more profitable of the two.

in its clefts nourishing flowers of sweetest perfume. For there was a passionate fire in him, as well as a stoical calmness; tenderest Love was there, and Devout Reverence; and a deep genial Humour lay, like warm sunshine, softening the whole, blending the whole into light sportful harmony. In these its hard trials, whatever was noblest in his nature came out in still purer clearness. It was here that he learned to distinguish what is perennial and imperishable in man, from what is transient and earthly; and to prize the latter, were it king's crowns and conqueror's triumphal chariots, but as the wrappage of the jewel; we might say, but as the finer or coarser Paper on which the Heroic Poem of Life is to be written. A lofty indestructible faith in the dignity of man took possession of him, and a disbelief in all other dignities; and the vulgar world, and what it could give him, or withhold from him, was, in his eyes, but a small matter. Nay, had he not found a voice for these things; which, though no man would listen to it, he felt to be a true one, and that if true no tone of it could be altogether lost. Preaching forth the Wisdom, which in the dark deep wells of Adversity he had drawn up, he felt himself strong, courageous, even gay. He had 'an internal world wherewith to fence himself against the frosts and heats of the external.' Studying, writing, in this mood, though grim Scarcity looked-in on him through the windows, he ever looked out again on that fiend with a quiet, half-satirical eye. Surely, we should find it hard to wish any generous nature such fortune: yet is one such man, nursed into manhood amid these stern, truth-telling influences, worth a thousand popular ballad-mongers, and sleek literary gentlemen, kept in perpetual boyhood by influences that always lie.

'In my Historical Lectures,' says Paul, 'the business of Hungering will in truth more and more make its appearance, — with the hero it rises to a great height, — about as often as Feasting in *Thummel's Travels*, and Tea-drinking in Richardson's *Clarissa;* nevertheless, I cannot help saying to Poverty: Welcome! so thou come not at quite too late a time! Wealth bears heavier on talent than Poverty; under gold-mountains and thrones, who knows how many a spiritual giant may lie crushed down and buried! When among the flames of youth, and above all of hotter powers as well, the oil of Riches is also poured in, — little will remain of the Phœnix but his ashes; and only a Goethe has force to keep, even at the sun of good fortune, his phœnix-wings unsinged. The poor Historical Professor, in this place, would not, for much money, have had much money in his youth. Fate manages Poets, as men do singing-birds; you overhang the cage of the singer and make it dark, till at length he has caught the tunes you play to him, and can sing them rightly.'

There have been many Johnsons, Heynes and other meaner natures, in every country, that have passed through as hard a probation as Richter's was, and borne permanent traces of its good and its evil influences; some, with their modesty and quiet endurance, combining a sickly dispiritment, others a hardened dulness or even deadness of heart; nay, there are some whom Misery itself cannot teach, but only exasperate; who far from parting with the mirror of their Vanity, when it is trodden in pieces, rather collect the hundred fragments of it, and with more fondness and more bitterness than ever, behold not one but a hundred images of Self therein: to these men Pain is a pure evil, and as school-dunces their hard Pedagogue will only whip them to the end. But in modern days, and even among the better instances, there is scarcely one that we remember who has drawn, from poverty and suffering, such unmixed advantage as Jean Paul; acquiring under it not only Herculean strength, but the softest tenderness of soul; a view of man and man's life not less cheerful, even sportful, than it is deep and calm. To Fear he is a stranger; not only the rage of men, 'the ruins of Nature would strike him fearless;' yet he has a heart vibrating to all the finest thrills of Mercy, a deep loving sympathy with all created things. There is, we must say, something Old-Grecian in this form of mind; yet Old-Grecian under the new conditions of our own time; not an Ethnic, but a Christian greatness. Richter might have stood beside Socrates, as a faithful though rather tumultuous disciple; or better still, he might have bandied repartees with Diogenes, who, if he could nowhere find Men, must at least have admitted that this too was a Spartan Boy. Diogenes and he, much as they differed, mostly to the disadvantage of the former, would have found much in common: above all, that resolute self-dependence, and quite settled indifference to the 'force of public opinion.' Of this latter quality, as well as of various other qualities in Richter, we have a curious proof in the Episode, which Herr Otto here for the first time details with accuracy, and at large, 'concerning the Costume controversies.' There is something great as well as ridiculous in this whole story of the Costume, which we must not pass unnoticed. It was in the second year of his residence at Leipzig, and when, as we have seen, his necessities were pressing enough, that Richter, finding himself unpatronised by the World, thought it might be reasonable if he paid a little attention, as far as convenient, to the wishes, rational orders and even whims of his only other Patron, namely, of Himself. Now the long visits of the hair-dresser, with his powders, puffs and pomatums, were decidedly irksome to him, and even too expensive; besides, his love of Swift and Sterne made him love the English and their modes; which things being considered, Paul made free to cut off his cue altogether, and with certain other alterations in his dress, to walk abroad in what was called the English fashion. We rather conjecture that, in some points, it was, after all, but Pseudo-English; at least, we can find no tradition of any such mode having then or ever been prevalent here in its other details. For besides the docked cue, he had shirts *à la Hamlet;* wore his breast open, without neckcloth: in such guise did he appear openly. Astonishment took hold of the minds of men. German students have more license than most people in selecting fantastic garbs; but the bare neck and want of cue seemed graces beyond the reach of true art. We can figure the massive, portly cynic, with what humour twinkling in his eye he came forth among the elegant gentlemen; feeling, like that juggler-divinity Ramdass, well known to Baptist Missionaries, that 'he had fire enough in his stomach to burn away all the sins of the world.' It was a species of pride, even of foppery, we will admit; but a tough, strong-limbed species, like that which in ragged gown 'trampled on the pride of Plato.'

Nowise in so respectable a light, however, did a certain *Magister*, or pedagogue dignitary, of Richter's neighbourhood, regard the matter. Poor Richter, poor in purse, rich otherwise, had, at this time, hired for himself a small mean garden-house, that he might have a little fresh air, through summer, in his studies: the Magister, who had hired a large sumptuous one in the same garden, naturally met him in his walks, bare-necked, cueless; and perhaps not liking the cast of his countenance, strangely twisted into Sardonic wrinkles, with all its broad honest benignity,—took it in deep dudgeon that such an unauthorized character should venture to enjoy Nature beside him. But what was to be done? Supercilious looks, even frowning, would accomplish nothing; the Sardonic visage was not to be frowned into the smallest terror. The Magister wrote to the landlord, demanding that this nuisance should be abated. Richter, with a praiseworthy love of peace, wrote to the Magister, promising to do what he could: he would not approach his (the Magister's) house so near as last night; would walk only in the evenings and mornings, and thereby for most part keep out of sight the apparel 'which convenience, health and poverty had prescribed for him.' These were fair conditions of a boundary-treaty; but the Magister interpreted them in too literal a sense, and soon found reason to complain that they had been infringed. He again took pen and ink, and in peremptory language represented that Paul had actually come past a certain Statue, which, without doubt, stood within the debatable land; threatening him, therefore, with Herr Körner, the landlord's vengeance, and withal openly testifying his own contempt and just rage against him. Paul answered, also in writing, That he had nowise infringed his promise, this Statue, or any other Statue, having nothing to do with it; but that now he did altogether revoke said promise, and would henceforth walk whensoever and wheresoever seemed good to him, seeing he too paid for the privilege. 'To me,' observed he, 'Herr Körner is not dreadful (*fürchterlich*);' and for the Magister himself he put down these remarkable words: 'You despise my mean name; *nevertheless take note* '*of it; for you will not have done the latter long, till the former* '*will not be in your power to do:* I speak ambiguously, that I 'may not speak arrogantly.' Be it noted, at the same time, that with a noble spirit of accommodation, Richter proposed yet new terms of treaty; which being accepted, he, pursuant thereto, with bag and baggage forthwith evacuated the garden, and returned to his 'town-room at the Three Roses, in Peterstrasse;' glorious in retreat, and 'leaving his Paradise,' as Herr Otto with some conceit remarks, 'no less guiltlessly 'than voluntarily, for a certain bareness of breast and neck; 'whereas our First Parents were only allowed to retain theirs 'so long as they felt themselves innocent in total nudity.' What the Magister thought of the 'mean name' some years afterwards, we do not learn.

But if such tragical things went on in Leipzig, how much more when he went down to Hof in the holidays, where, at any rate, the Richters stood in slight esteem! It will surprise our readers to learn that Paul, with the mildest-tempered pertinacity, resisted all expostulations of friends, and persecutions of foes, in this great cause; and went about *à la Hamlet*, for the space of no less than seven years! He himself seemed partly sensible that it was affectation; but the man would have his humour out. 'On the whole,' says he, '*I hold the constant regard we pay, in all our actions, to the* '*judgments of others, as the poison of our peace, our reason* '*and our virtue.* At this slave-chain I have long filed, and I 'scarcely ever hope to break it entirely asunder. I wish to 'accustom myself to the censure of others, and *appear* a fool, 'that I may learn to endure fools.' So speaks the young Diogenes, embracing his frozen pillar, by way of 'exercitation;' as if the world did not give us frozen pillars enough in this kind, without our wilfully stepping aside to seek them! Better is that other maxim: 'He who differs from the world 'in important matters, should the more carefully conform to 'it in indifferent ones.' Nay, by degrees, Richter himself saw into this; and having now proved satisfactorily enough that he could take his own way when he so pleased, — leaving, as is fair, the 'most sweet voices' to take theirs also, — he addressed to his friends (chiefly the Voigtland Literati above alluded to) the following circular:

'ADVERTISEMENT.

'The Undersigned begs to give notice, that whereas cropt hair has as many enemies as red hair, and said enemies of the hair are enemies likewise of the person it grows on; whereas farther, such a fashion is in no respect Christian, since otherwise Christian persons would have adopted it; and whereas, especially, the Undersigned has suffered no less from his hair than Absalom did from his, though on contrary grounds; and whereas it has been notified that the public purposed to send him into his grave, since the hair grew there without scissors: he hereby gives notice that he will not push matters to such extremity. Be it known, therefore, to the nobility, gentry and a discerning public in general, that the Undersigned proposes, on Sunday next, to appear in various important streets (of Hof) with a short false cue; and with this cue as with a magnet, and cord-of-love, and magic-rod, to possess himself forcibly of the affections of all and sundry, be who they may.'

And thus ended 'gloriously,' as Herr Otto thinks, the long 'clothes-martyrdom;' from the course of which, besides its intrinsic comicality, we may learn two things: first, that Paul nowise wanted a due indifference to the popular wind, but, on fit or unfit occasion, could stand on his own basis stoutly enough, wrapping his cloak as himself listed; and secondly, that he had such a buoyant, elastic humour of spirit, that besides counter-pressure against Poverty, and Famine itself, there was still a clear overplus left to play fantastic tricks with, at which the angels could not indeed weep, but might well shake their heads and smile. We return to our history.

Several years before the date of this 'Advertisement,' namely in 1784, Paul, who had now determined on writing, with or without readers, to the end of the chapter, finding no furtherance in Leipzig but only hunger and hardship, bethought him that he might as well write in Hof beside his mother as there. His publishers, when he had any, were in other cities; and the two households, like two dying embers, might perhaps show some feeble point of red-heat between them, if cunningly laid together. He quitted Leipzig, after a three-years' residence there; and fairly commenced housekeeping on his own score. Probably there is not in the whole history of Literature any record of a literary establishment like that at Hof; so ruggedly independent, so simple, not to say altogether unfurnished. Lawsuits had now done their work, and the Widow Richter, with her family, was living in a 'house containing one apartment.' Paul had no books, except 'twelve manuscript volumes of excerpts,' and the considerable library which he carried in his head; with which small resources, the public, especially as he had still no cue, could not well see what was to become of him. Two great furtherances, however, he had, of which the public took no sufficient note: a real Head on his shoulders, not, as is more common, a mere hat-wearing empty *effigies* of a head; and the strangest, stoutest, indeed a quite noble Heart within him. Here, then, he could, as is the duty of man, 'prize his existence more than his manner of existence,' which latter was, indeed, easily enough disesteemed. Come of it what might, he determined, on his own strength, to try issues to the uttermost with Fortune; nay, while fighting like a very Ajax against her, to 'keep laughing in her face till she too burst into laughter, and ceased frowning at him.' He would nowise slacken in his Authorship, therefore, but continued stubbornly toiling, as at his right work, let the weather be sunny or snowy. For the rest, Poverty was written on the posts of his door, and within on every equipment of his existence; he that ran might read in large characters: "Good Christian people, you perceive that I have little money; what inference do you draw from it?" So hung the struggle, and as yet were no signs of victory for Paul. It was not till 1788 that he could find a publisher for his *Teufels Papieren;* and even then few readers. But no disheartenment availed with him; Authorship was once for all felt to be his true vocation; and by it he was minded to continue at all hazards. For a short while, he had been tutor in some family, and had again a much more tempting offer of the like sort, but he refused it, purposing henceforth to 'bring up no children but his own, — his books,' let Famine say to it what she pleased.

'With his mother,' says Otto, 'and at times also with several of his brothers, but always with one, he lived in a mean house, which had only a single apartment; and this went on even when, — after the appearance of the *Mümien,* — his star began to rise, ascending higher and higher, and never again declining. * * *

'As Paul, in the characters of Walt and Vult[1] (it is his direct statement in these Notes), meant to depict himself; so it may be remarked, that in the delineation of Lenette, his Mother stood before his mind, at the period when this down-pressed and humiliated woman began to gather heart, and raise herself up again;[2] seeing she could no longer doubt the truth of his predictions, that Authorship must and would prosper with him. She now the more busily, in one and the same room where Paul was writing and studying, managed the household operations; cooking, washing, scouring, handling the broom, and these being finished, spinning cotton. Of the painful income earned by this latter employment, she kept a

[1] *Gottwalt* and *Quoddeusvult,* two Brothers (see Paul's *Flegeljahre*) of the most opposite temperaments: the former a still, soft-hearted, tearful enthusiast; the other a madcap humorist, honest at bottom, but bursting out on all hands with the strangest explosions, speculative and practical.

[2] 'Quite up, indeed, she could never more rise; and in silent humility, 'avoiding any loud expression of satisfaction, she lived to enjoy with 'timorous gladness, the delight of seeing her son's worth publicly rec'ognised, and his acquaintance sought by the most influential men, and 'herself too honoured on this account, as she had never before been.'

written account. One such revenue-book, under the title, *Was ich ersponnen* (Earned by spinning), which extends from March 1793 to September 1794, is still in existence. The produce of March, the first year, stands entered there as 2 florins, 51 kreutzers, 3 pfennigs' (somewhere about four shillings!); 'that of April,' &c.; 'at last, that of September 1794, 2 fl. 1 kr.; and on the last page of the little book, stands marked, that Samuel (the youngest son) had, on the 9th of this same September, got new boots, which cost 3 thalers,'—almost a whole quarter's revenue!

Considering these things, how mournful would it have seemed to Paul that Bishop Dogbolt could not get translated, because of Politics; and the too high-souled Viscount Plumcake, thwarted in courtship, was seized with a perceptible dyspepsia!

We have dwelt the longer on this portion of Paul's history, because we reckon it interesting in itself; and that if the spectacle of a great man struggling with adversity be a fit one for the gods to look down on, much more must it be so for mean fellow-mortals to look up to. For us in Literary England, above all, such conduct as Richter's has a peculiar interest in these times; the interest of entire novelty. Of all literary phenomena, that of a literary man daring to believe that he is *poor*, may be regarded as the rarest. Can a man without capital actually open his lips and speak to mankind? Had he no landed property, then; no connexion with the higher classes; did he not even keep a gig? By these documents it would appear so. This was not a nobleman, nor gentleman, nor gigman;[1] but simply a man!

On the whole, what a wondrous spirit of gentility does animate our British Literature at this era! We have no Men of Letters now, but only Literary Gentlemen. Samuel

[1] In Thurtell's trial (says the *Quarterly Review*) occurred the following colloquy: '*Q.* What sort of person was Mr. Weare? *A.* He was always a respectable person. *Q.* What do you mean by respectable? *A.* He kept a gig.'—Since then we have seen a '*Defensio Gigmanica*, or Apology for the Gigmen of Great Britain,' composed not without eloquence, and which we hope one day to prevail on our friend, a man of some whims, to give to the public.

Johnson was the last that ventured to appear in that former character, and support himself, on his own legs, without any crutches, purchased or stolen: rough old Samuel, the last of all the Romans! Time was, when in English Literature, as in English Life, the comedy of 'Every Man in his Humour' was daily enacted among us; but now the poor French word, French in every sense, '*Qu'en dira-t-on?*' spellbinds us all, and we have nothing for it but to drill and cane each other into one uniform, regimental 'nation of gentlemen.' 'Let him who would write heroic poems,' said Milton, 'make his life a heroic poem.' Let him who would write heroic poems, say we, put money in his purse; or if he have no gold-money, let him put in copper-money, or pebbles, and chink with it as with true metal, in the ears of mankind, that they may listen to him. Herein does the secret of good writing now consist, as that of good living has always done. When we first visited Grub-street, and with bared head did reverence to the genius of the place, with a "*Salve, magna parens!*" we were astonished to learn, on inquiry, that the Authors did not dwell there now, but had all removed, years ago, to a sort of 'High Life below Stairs,' far in the West. For why, what remedy was there; did not the wants of the age require it? How can men write without High Life; and how, except below Stairs, as Shoulder-knot, or as talking Katerfelto, or by secondhand communication with these two, can the great body of men acquire any knowledge thereof? Nay, has not the Atlantis, or true Blissful Island of Poesy, been, in all times, understood to lie Westward, though never rightly discovered till now? Our great fault with writers used to be, not that they were intrinsically more or less completed Dolts, with no eye or ear for the 'open secret' of the world, or for anything save the 'open display' of the world, — for its gilt ceilings, marketable pleasures, war-chariots, and all manner, to the highest manner, of Lord-Mayor shows, and Guildhall dinners, and their own small part and lot therein; but the head and front of their offence lay in this, that they had not 'frequented the society of the upper classes.' And now, with our improved age, and this so universal extension of 'High Life below Stairs,' what a blessed change has been introduced; what benign consequences will follow therefrom! One consequence has already been a degree of Dapperism and Dilettanteism, and rickety Debility, unexampled in the history of Literature, and enough of itself to make us 'the envy of surrounding nations;' for hereby the literary man, once so dangerous to the quiescence of society, has now become perfectly innoxious, so that a look will quail him, and he can be tied hand and foot by a spinster's thread. Hope there is, that henceforth neither Church nor State will be put in jeopardy by Literature. The old literary man, as we have said, stood on his own legs; had a whole heart within him, and might be provoked into many things. But the new literary man, on the other hand, cannot stand at all, save in stays; he must first gird up his weak sides with the whalebone of a certain fashionable, knowing, half-squirarchal air, — be it inherited, bought, or, as is more likely, borrowed or stolen, whalebone; and herewith he stands a little without collapsing. If the man now twang his jew's-harp to please the children, what is to be feared from him; what more is to be required of him?

Seriously speaking, we must hold it a remarkable thing that every Englishman should be a 'gentleman;' that in so democratic a country, our common title of honour, which all men assert for themselves, should be one which professedly depends on station, on accidents rather than on qualities; or at best, as Coleridge interprets it, 'on a certain indifference to money matters,' which certain indifference again must be wise or mad, you would think, exactly as one possesses much money, or possesses little! We suppose it must be the commercial genius of the nation, counteracting and suppressing its political genius; for the Americans are said to be still more notable in this respect than we. Now, what a hollow, windy vacuity of internal character this indicates; how, in place of a rightly ordered heart, we strive only to exhibit a full purse; and all pushing, rushing, elbowing on towards a false aim, the courtier's kibes are more and more galled by the toe of the peasant: and on every side, instead of Faith, Hope and Charity, we have Neediness, Greediness and Vainglory; all this is palpable enough. Fools that we are! Why should we wear our knees to horn, and sorrowfully beat our breasts, praying day and night to Mammon, who, if he would even hear us, has almost nothing to give? For, granting that the deaf brute-god were to relent for our sacrificings; to change our gilt brass into solid gold, and instead of hungry actors of rich gentility, make us all in very deed Rothschild-Howards to-morrow, what good were it? Are we not already denizens of this wondrous England, with its high Shakspeares and Hampdens; nay, of this wondrous Universe, with its Galaxies and Eternities, and unspeakable Splendours, that we should so worry and scramble, and tear one another in pieces, for some acres (nay, still oftener, for the *show* of some acres), more or less, of clay property, the largest of which properties, the Sutherland itself, is invisible even from the Moon? Fools that we are! To dig and bore like ground-worms in those acres of ours, even if we have acres; and far from beholding and enjoying the heavenly Lights, not to know of them except by unheeded and unbelieved report! Shall certain pounds sterling that we may have in the Bank of England, or the ghosts of certain pounds that we would fain seem to have, hide from us the treasures we are all born to in this the 'City of God?'

> My inheritance how wide and fair;
> TIME is my estate, to TIME I'm heir!

But leaving the money-changers, and honour-hunters, and gigmen of every degree, to their own wise ways, which they will not alter, we must again remark as a singular circumstance, that the same spirit should, to such an extent, have taken possession of Literature also. This is the eye of the world; enlightening all, and instead of the shows of things unfolding to us things themselves: has the eye too gone blind; has the Poet and Thinker adopted the philosophy of the Grocer and Valet in Livery? Nay, let us hear Lord Byron himself on the subject. Some years ago, there appeared in the Magazines, and to the admiration of most editorial gentlemen, certain extracts from Letters of Lord Byron's, which carried this philosophy to rather a high pitch. His Lordship, we recollect, mentioned, that 'all rules for Poetry were not worth a d—n' (saving and excepting, doubtless, the ancient Rule-of-Thumb, which must still have place here); after which aphorism, his Lordship proceeded to state that the great ruin of all British Poets sprang from a simple source; their exclusion from High Life in London, excepting only some shape of that High Life below Stairs, which, however, was nowise adequate: he himself and Thomas Moore were perfectly familiar in such upper life; he by birth, Moore by happy accident, and so they could both write Poetry; the others were not familiar, and so could not write it. — Surely it is fast growing time that all this should be drummed out of our Planet, and forbidden to return.

Richter, for his part, was quite excluded from the West-end of Hof: for Hof too has its West-end; 'every mortal 'longs for his parade-place; would still wish, at banquets, to 'be master of some seat or other, wherein to overtop this or 'that plucked goose of the neighbourhood.' So poor Richter could only be admitted to the West-end of the Universe, where truly he had a very superior establishment. The legal, clerical and other conscript fathers of Hof might, had they so inclined, have lent him a few books, told or believed some fewer lies of him, and thus positively and negatively shown the young adventurer many a little service; but they inclined to none of these things, and happily he was enabled to do without them. Gay, gentle, frolicsome as a lamb, yet strong, forbearant and royally courageous as a lion, he worked along, amid the scouring of kettles, the hissing of frying-pans, the hum of his mother's wheel; — and it is not without a proud feeling that our reader (for he too is a man) hears of victory being at last gained, and of Works, which the most reflective nation in Europe regards as classical, being written under such accompaniments.

However, it is at this lowest point of the Narrative that Herr Otto for the present stops short; leaving us only the assurance that better days are coming: so that concerning the whole ascendant and dominant portion of Richter's history, we are left to our own resources; and from these we have only gathered some scanty indications, which may be summed up with a very disproportionate brevity. It appears that the *Unsichtbare Loge* (Invisible Lodge), sent forth from the Hof spinning-establishment in 1793, was the first of his works that obtained any decisive favour. A long trial of faith; for the man had now been besieging the literary citadel upwards of ten years, and still no breach visible! With the appearance of *Hesperus*, another wondrous Novel, which proceeded from the same 'single apartment,' in 1796, the siege may be said to have terminated by storm; and Jean Paul, whom the most knew not what in the world to think of, whom here and there a man of weak judgment had not even scrupled to declare half-mad, made it universally indubitable, that though encircled with dusky vapours, and shining out only in strange many-hued irregular bursts of flame, he was and would be one of the celestial Luminaries of his day and generation. The keen intellectual energy displayed in *Hesperus*, still more the nobleness of mind, the sympathy with Nature, the warm, impetuous, yet pure and lofty delineations of Friendship and Love; in a less degree perhaps, the wild boisterous humour that everywhere prevails in it, secured Richter not only admirers, but personal well-wishers in all quarters of his country. Gleim, for example, though then eighty years of age, and among the last survivors of a quite different school, could not contain himself with rapture. 'What a divine genius (*Gottgenius*),' thus wrote he some time afterwards, 'is our Friedrich Richter! I am reading 'his *Blumenstücke* for the second time: here is more than 'Shakspeare, said I, at fifty passages I have marked. What 'a divine genius! I wonder over the human head, out of 'which these streams, these brooks, these Rhine-falls, these 'Blandusian fountains pour forth over human nature to make 'human nature humane; and if to-day I object to the plan, 'object to phrases, to words, I am contented with all to-mor-'row.' The kind lively old man, it appears, had sent him a gay letter, signed 'Septimus Fixlein,' with a present of money in it; to which Richter, with great heartiness, and some curiosity to penetrate the secret, made answer in this very *Blumenstücke;* and so erelong a joyful acquaintance and friendship was formed; Paul had visited Halberstadt, with warmest welcome, and sat for his picture there (an oil painting by Pfenninger), which is still to be seen in Gleim's *Ehrentempel* (Temple of Honour). About this epoch too, the Reviewing world, after a long conscientious silence, again opened its thick lips; and in quite another dialect; screeching out a rusty *Nunc Domine dimittas,* with considerable force of pipe, instead of its last monosyllabic and very unhandsome *grunt.* For the credit of our own guild, we could have wished that the Reviewing world had struck up its *Dimittas* a little sooner.

In 1797, the Widow Richter was taken away from the strange variable climate of this world, — we shall hope, into a sunnier one; her kettles hung unscoured on the wall; and the spool, so often filled with her cotton-thread and wetted with her tears, revolved no more. Poor old weather-beaten, heavy-laden soul! And yet a light-beam from on high was in her also; and the 'twelve shillings for Samuel's new boots' were more bounteous and more blessed than many a king's ransom. Nay, she saw before departing, that she, even she, had born a mighty man; and her early sunshine, long drowned in deluges, again looked out at evening with sweet farewell.

The Hof household being thus broken up, Richter for some years led a wandering life. In the course of this same 1797, we find him once more in Leipzig; and truly under far other circumstances than of old. For instead of silk-stockinged, shovel-hatted, but too imperious Magisters, that would not let him occupy his own hired dog-hutch in peace, 'he here,' says Heinrich Döring,[1] 'became acquainted with 'the three Princesses, adorned with every charm of person 'and of mind, the daughters of the Duchess of Hildburg-'hausen! The Duke, who also did justice to his extraordi-'nary merits, conferred on him, some years afterwards, the 'title of *Legationsrath* (Councillor of Legation).' To Princes and Princesses, indeed, Jean Paul seems, ever henceforth, to have had what we should reckon a surprising access. For example: — 'the social circles where the Duchess Ame-'lia (of Weimar) was wont to assemble the most talented 'men, first, in Ettersburg, afterwards in Tiefurt;' — then the 'Duke of Meinungen at Coburg, who had with pressing 'kindness invited him;' — the Prince Primate Dalberg, who did much more than invite him; — late in life, 'the gifted 'Duchess Dorothea, in Lobichau, of which visit he has him-'self commemorated the festive days,' &c. &c.; — all which small matters, it appears to us, should be taken into consideration by that class of British philosophers, troublesome in many an intellectual tea-circle, who deduce the 'German bad taste' from our own old everlasting 'want of intercourse;' whereby, if it so seemed good to them, their tea, till some less self-evident proposition were started, might be 'consumed with a certain stately silence.'

But next year (1798) there came on Paul a far grander piece of good fortune than any of these; namely, a good wife; which, as Solomon has long recorded, is a 'good thing.' He had gone from Leipzig to Berlin, still busily writing; 'and 'during a longer residence in this latter city,' says Döring,

[1] *Leben Jean Pauls.* Gotha, 1826.

'Caroline Mayer, daughter of the Royal Prussian Privy 'Councillor and Professor of Medicine, Dr. John Andrew 'Mayer' (these are all his titles), 'gave him her hand; nay 'even,' continues the microscopic Döring, 'as is said in a 'public paper, bestowed on him (*aufdrückte*) the bride-kiss 'of her own accord.' What is still more astonishing, she is recorded to have been a 'chosen one of her sex,' one that, 'like a gentle, guardian, care-dispelling genius, went by his 'side through all his pilgrimage.'

Shortly after this great event, Paul removed with his new wife to Weimar, where he seems to have resided some years, in high favour with whatever was most illustrious in that city. His first impression on Schiller is characteristic enough. 'Of 'Hesperus,' thus writes Schiller, 'I have yet made no mention 'to you. I found him pretty much what I expected; foreign 'like a man fallen from the Moon; full of good-will, and 'heartily inclined to see things about him, but without the 'organ for seeing them. However, I have only spoken to 'him once, and so I can say little of him.'[1] In answer to which, Goethe also expresses his love for Richter, but 'doubts whether in literary practice he will ever fall-in with them two, much as his theoretical creed inclined that way.' Hesperus proved to have more 'organ' than Schiller gave him credit for; nevertheless Goethe's doubt had not been unfounded. It was to Herder that Paul chiefly attached himself here; esteeming the others as high-gifted, friendly men, but only Herder as a teacher and spiritual father; of which latter relation, and the warm love and gratitude accompanying it on Paul's side, his writings give frequent proof. 'If Herder was not a Poet,' says he once, 'he was something more, — a Poem!' With Wieland too he stood on the friendliest footing, often walking out to visit him at Osmanstädt, whither the old man had now retired. Perhaps these years spent at Weimar, in close intercourse with so

[1] *Briefwechsel zwischen Schiller und Goethe* (Correspondence between Schiller and Goethe), b. ii. 77.

many distinguished persons, were, in regard to outward matters, among the most instructive of Richter's life: in regard to inward matters, he had already served, and with credit, a hard apprenticeship elsewhere. We must not forget to mention that *Titan*, one of his chief romances (published at Berlin in 1800), was written during his abode at Weimar; so likewise the *Flegeljahre* (Wild Oats); and the eulogy of *Charlotte Corday*, which last, though originally but a Magazine Essay, deserves notice for its bold eloquence, and the antique republican spirit manifested in it. With respect to *Titan*, which, together with its *Comic Appendix*, forms six very extraordinary volumes, Richter was accustomed, on all occasions, to declare it his masterpiece, and even the best he could ever hope to do; though there are not wanting readers who continue to regard *Hesperus* with preference. For ourselves, we have read *Titan* with a certain disappointment, after hearing so much of it; yet on the whole must incline to the Author's opinion. One day we hope to afford the British public some sketch of both these works, concerning which, it has been said, 'there is solid metal enough in them 'to fit out whole circulating libraries, were it beaten into the 'usual filigree; and much which, attenuate it as we might, no 'Quarterly Subscriber could well carry with him.' Richter's other Novels published prior to this period are, the *Invisible Lodge;* the *Siebenkäs* (or Flower, Fruit and Thorn Pieces); the *Life of Quintus Fixlein;* the *Jubelsenior* (Parson in Jubilee): *Jean Paul's Letters and Future History*, the *Dejeuner in Kuhschnappel*, the *Biographical Recreations under the Cranium of a Giantess*, scarcely belonging to this species. The Novels published afterwards, which we may as well catalogue here, are, the *Leben Fibels* (Life of Fibel); *Katzenbergers Badereise* (Katzenberger's Journey to the Bath); *Schmelzles Reise nach Flätz* (Schmelzle's Journey to Flätz); the *Comet*, named also *Nicholaus Margraf.*

It seems to have been about the year 1802, that Paul had a pension bestowed upon him by the *Fürst Primas* (Prince

Primate) von Dalberg, a prelate famed for his munificence, whom we have mentioned above. What the amount was, we do not find specified, but only that it 'secured him the means of a comfortable life,' and was 'subsequently,' we suppose after the Prince Primate's decease, 'paid him by the King of Bavaria.' On the strength of which fixed revenue, Paul now established for himself a fixed household; selecting for this purpose, after various intermediate wanderings, the city of Bayreuth, 'with its kind picturesque environment;' where, with only brief occasional excursions, he continued to live and write. We have heard that he was a man universally loved, as well as honoured there: a friendly, true and high-minded man; copious in speech, which was full of grave genuine humour; contented with simple people and simple pleasures; and himself of the simplest habits and wishes. He had three children; and a guardian angel, doubtless not without her flaws, yet a reasonable angel notwithstanding. For a man with such obdured Stoicism, like triple steel, round his breast; and of such gentle, deep-lying, ever-living springs of Love within it, — all this may well have made a happy life. Besides, Paul was of exemplary, unwearied diligence in his vocation; and so had, at all times, 'perennial, fire-proof Joys, namely Employments.' In addition to the latter part of the Novels named above, which, with the others, as all of them are more or less genuine poetical productions, we feel reluctant to designate even transiently by so despicable an English word, — his philosophical and critical performances, especially the *Vorschule der Aesthetik* (Introduction to Æsthetics), and the *Levana* (Doctrine of Education), belong wholly to Bayreuth; not to enumerate a multitude of miscellaneous writings (on moral, literary, scientific subjects, but always in a humorous, fantastic, poetic dress), which of themselves might have made the fortune of no mean man. His heart and conscience, as well as his head and hand, were in the work; from which no temptation could withdraw him. 'I hold my duty,' says he in these Biographical Notes, 'not to lie in enjoying or acquir- 'ing, but in writing, — whatever time it may cost, whatever 'money may be forborne, — nay whatever pleasure; for ex- 'ample, that of seeing Switzerland, which nothing but the 'sacrifice of time forbids.' — 'I deny myself my evening 'meal (*Vesperessen*) in my eagerness to work; but the in- 'terruptions by my children I cannot deny myself.' And again: 'A Poet, who presumes to give poetic delight, should 'contemn and willingly forbear all enjoyments, the sacrifice 'of which affects not his creative powers; that so he may 'perhaps delight a century and a whole people.' In Richter's advanced years, it was happy for him that he could say: 'When I look at what has been made out of me, I must 'thank God that I paid no heed to external matters, neither 'to time nor toil, nor profit nor loss; the thing is there, and 'the instruments that did it I have forgotten, and none else 'knows them. In this wise has the unimportant series of 'moments been changed into something higher that remains.' — 'I have described so much,' says he elsewhere, 'and I die 'without ever having seen Switzerland, and the Ocean, and 'so many other sights. But the Ocean of Eternity I shall in 'no case fail to see.'

A heavy stroke fell on him in the year 1821, when his only son, a young man of great promise, died at the University. Paul lost not his composure; but was deeply, incurably wounded. 'Epistolary lamentations on my misfor- 'tune,' says he, 'I read unmoved, for the bitterest is to be 'heard within myself, and I must shut the ears of my soul to 'it; but a single new trait of Max's fair nature opens the 'whole lacerated heart asunder again, and it can only drive 'its blood into the eyes.' New personal sufferings awaited him: a decay of health, and what to so indefatigable a reader and writer was still worse, a decay of eyesight, increasing at last to almost total blindness. This too he bore with his old stedfastness, cheerfully seeking what help was to be had; and when no hope of help remained, still cheerfully labouring at his vocation, though in sickness and in blindness.[1] Dark without, he was inwardly full of light; busied on his favourite theme, the *Immortality of the Soul;* when (on the 14th of November 1825) Death came, and Paul's work was all accomplished, and that great question settled for him on far higher and indisputable evidence. The unfinished Volume (which under the title of *Selina* we now have) was carried on his bier to the grave; for his funeral was public, and in Bayreuth, and elsewhere, all possible honour was done to his memory.

In regard to Paul's character as a man we have little to say, beyond what the facts of this Narrative have already said more plainly than in words. We learn from all quarters, in one or the other dialect, that the pure high morality which adorns his writings, stamped itself also on his life and actions. 'He was a tender husband and father,' says Döring, 'and 'goodness itself towards his friends and all that was near 'him.' The significance of such a spirit as Richter's, practically manifested in such a life, is deep and manifold, and at this era will merit careful study. For the present, however, we must leave it, in this degree of clearness, to the reader's own consideration; another and still more immediately needful department of our task still remains for us.

Richter's intellectual and Literary character is, perhaps, in a singular degree the counterpart and image of his practical and moral character: his Works seem to us a more than usually faithful transcript of his mind; written with great warmth direct from the heart, and like himself, wild, strong, original, sincere. Viewed under any aspect, whether as

[1] He begins a letter applying for spectacles (August 1824) in these terms:—'Since last winter, my eyes (the left had already, without cata-'ract, been long half-blind, and, like Reviewers and *Littérateurs,* read 'nothing but title-pages) have been seized by a daily increasing Night-'Ultra and Enemy-to-Light, who, did I not withstand him, would shortly 'drive me into the Orcus of Amaurosis. Then, *Addio, opera omnia!*'—*Döring*, 32.

Thinker, Moralist, Satirist, Poet, he is a phenomenon; a vast, many-sided, tumultuous, yet noble nature; for faults as for merits, 'Jean Paul the Unique.' In all departments, we find in him a subduing force; but a lawless, untutored, as it were half-savage force. Thus, for example, few understandings known to us are of a more irresistible character than Richter's; but its strength is a natural, unarmed, Orson-like strength: he does not cunningly undermine his subject, and lay it open, by syllogistic implements or any rule of art; but he crushes it to pieces in his arms, he treads it asunder, not without gay triumph, under his feet; and so in almost monstrous fashion, yet with piercing clearness, lays bare the inmost heart and core of it to all eyes. In passion again, there is the same wild vehemence: it is a voice of softest pity, of endless boundless wailing, a voice as of Rachel weeping for her children; — or the fierce bellowing of lions amid savage forests. Thus too, he not only loves Nature, but he revels in her; plunges into her infinite bosom, and fills his whole heart to intoxication with her charms. He tells us that he was wont to study, to write, almost to live, in the open air; and no skyey aspect was so dismal that it altogether wanted beauty for him. We know of no Poet with so deep and passionate and universal a feeling towards Nature: 'from 'the solemn phases of the starry heaven to the simple 'floweret of the meadow, his eye and his heart are open for 'her charms and her mystic meanings.' But what most of all shadows forth the inborn, essential temper of Paul's mind, is the sportfulness, the wild heartfelt Humour, which, in his highest as in his lowest moods, ever exhibits itself as a quite inseparable ingredient. His Humour, with all its wildness, is of the gravest and kindliest, a genuine Humour; 'consistent with utmost earnestness, or rather, inconsistent with the want of it.' But on the whole, it is impossible for him to write in other than a humorous manner, be his subject what it may. His Philosophical Treatises, nay, as we have seen, his Autobiography itself, everything that comes from him, is encased in some quaint fantastic framing; and roguish eyes (yet with a strange sympathy in the matter, for his Humour, as we said, is heartfelt and true) look out on us through many a grave delineation. In his Novels, above all, this is ever an indispensable quality, and, indeed, announces itself in the very entrance of the business, often even on the title-page. Think, for instance, of that *Selection from the Papers of the Devil; Hesperus,* OR *the Dog-post-days; Siebenkäs's Wedded-life, Death* AND *Nuptials!*

'The first aspect of these peculiarities,' says one of Richter's English critics, 'cannot prepossess us in his favour; we are too forcibly reminded of theatrical clap-traps and literary quackery: nor on opening one of the works themselves is the case much mended. Piercing gleams of thought do not escape us; singular truths, conveyed in a form as singular; grotesque, and often truly ludicrous delineations; pathetic, magnificent, far-sounding passages; effusions full of wit, knowledge and imagination, but difficult to bring under any rubric whatever; all the elements, in short, of a glorious intellect, but dashed together in such wild arrangement, that their order seems the very ideal of confusion. The style and structure of the book appear alike incomprehensible. The narrative is every now and then suspended, to make way for some "Extra-leaf," some wild digression upon any subject but the one in hand; the language groans with indescribable metaphors, and allusions to all things human and divine; flowing onward, not like a river, but like an inundation; circling in complex eddies, chafing and gurgling, now this way, now that, till the proper current sinks out of view amid the boundless uproar. We close the work with a mingled feeling of astonishment, oppression and perplexity; and Richter stands before us in brilliant cloudy vagueness, a giant mass of intellect, but without form, beauty or intelligible purpose.

'To readers who believe that intrinsic is inseparable from superficial excellence, and that nothing can be good or beautiful which is not to be seen through in a moment, Richter can occasion little difficulty. They admit him to be a man of vast natural endowments, but he is utterly uncultivated, and without command of them; full of monstrous affectation, the very high-priest of Bad Taste; knows not the art of writing, scarcely that there is such an art; an insane visionary, floating forever among baseless dreams that hide the firm earth from his view; an intellectual Polyphemus, in short, a *monstrum horrendum, informe, ingens,* (carefully adding) *cui lumen ademptum;*

and they close their verdict reflectively with his own praiseworthy maxim: "Providence has given to the English the empire of the sea, to the French that of the land, to the Germans that of—the air."

'In this way the matter is adjusted; briefly, comfortably and wrong. The casket was difficult to open: did we know, by its very shape, that there was nothing in it, that so we should cast it into the sea? Affectation is often singularity, but singularity is not always affectation. If the nature and condition of a man be really and truly, not conceitedly and untruly, singular, so also will his manner be, so also ought it to be. Affectation is the product of Falsehood, a heavy sin, and the parent of numerous heavy sins; let it be severely punished, but not too lightly imputed. Scarcely any mortal is absolutely free from it. neither most probably is Richter; but it is in minds of another substance than his that it grows to be the ruling product. Moreover, he is actually not a visionary; but, with all his visions, will be found to see the firm Earth, in its whole figures and relations, much more clearly than thousands of such critics, who too probably can see nothing else. Far from being untrained or uncultivated, it will surprise these persons to discover that few men have studied the art of writing, and many other arts besides, more carefully than he; that his *Vorschule der Aesthetik* abounds with deep and sound maxims of criticism; in the course of which, many complex works, his own among others, are rigidly and justly tried, and even the graces and minutest qualities of style are by no means overlooked or unwisely handled.

'Withal, there is something in Richter that incites us to a second, to a third perusal. His works are hard to understand, but they always *have* a meaning. often a true and deep one. In our closer, more comprehensive glance, their truth steps forth with new distinctness, their error dissipates and recedes, passes into veniality, often even into beauty; and at last the thick haze which encircled the form of the writer melts away, and he stands revealed to us in his own stedfast features, a colossal spirit, a lofty and original thinker, a genuine poet, a high-minded, true and most amiable man.

'I have called him a colossal spirit, for this impression continues with us: to the last we figure him as something gigantic: for all the elements of his structure are vast, and combined together in living and life-giving, rather than in beautiful or symmetrical order. His Intellect is keen, impetuous, far-grasping. fit to rend in pieces the stubbornest materials, and extort from them their most hidden and refractory truth. In his Humour he sports with the highest and the lowest, he can play at bowls with the Sun and Moon. His Imagination opens for us the Land of Dreams; we sail with him through the boundless Abyss; and the secrets of Space, and Time, and Life, and Annihilation, hover round us in dim, cloudy forms; and darkness, and immensity, and dread encompass and overshadow us. Nay, in handling the smallest matter, he works it with the tools of a giant. A common truth is wrenched from its old combinations, and presented to us in new, impassable, abysmal contrast with its opposite error. A trifle, some slender character, some jest, or quip, or spiritual toy, is shaped into most quaint, yet often truly living form; but shaped somehow as with the hammer of Vulcan, with three strokes that might have helped to forge an Ægis. The treasures of his mind are of a similar description with the mind itself; his knowledge is gathered from all the kingdoms of Art, and Science, and Nature, and lies round him in huge unwieldy heaps. His very language is Titanian; deep, strong, tumultuous; shining with a thousand hues, fused from a thousand elements, and winding in labyrinthic mazes.

'Among Richter's gifts,' continues this critic, 'the first that strikes us as truly great is his Imagination; for he loves to dwell in the loftiest and most solemn provinces of thought: his works abound with mysterious allegories, visions and typical adumbrations; his Dreams, in particular, have a gloomy vastness, broken here and there by wild far-darting splendour; and shadowy forms of meaning rise dimly from the bosom of the void Infinite. Yet, if I mistake not, Humour is his ruling quality, the quality which lives most deeply in his inward nature, and most strongly influences his manner of being. In this rare gift, for none is rarer than true Humour, he stands unrivalled in his own country, and among late writers in every other. To describe Humour is difficult at all times, and would perhaps be more than usually difficult in Richter's case. Like all his other qualities, it is vast, rude, irregular; often perhaps overstrained and extravagant; yet, fundamentally, it is genuine Humour, the Humour of Cervantes and Sterne; the product not of Contempt, but of Love, not of superficial distortion of natural forms, but of deep though playful sympathy with all forms of Nature. * *

'So long as Humour will avail him, his management even of higher and stronger characters may still be pronounced successful; but wherever Humour ceases to be applicable, his success is more or less imperfect. In the treatment of heroes proper he is seldom completely happy. They shoot into rugged exaggeration in his hands; their sensibility becomes too copious and tearful, their magnanimity too fierce, abrupt and thorough-going. In some few instances, they verge towards absolute failure: compared with their less ambitious brethren, they are almost of a vulgar cast; with all their brilliancy and vigour, too like that positive, determinate, volcanic class of personages whom we meet with so frequently in Novels; they call themselves Men, and do their utmost to prove the assertion, but they cannot make us believe it; for, after all their vapouring and storming, we see well enough that they are but Engines, with no more life than the Freethinkers' model in *Martinus Scriblerus*, the Nuremberg Man, who operated by a combination of pipes and levers, and though he could breathe and digest perfectly, and even reason as well as most country parsons, was made of wood and leather. In the general conduct of such histories and delineations, Richter seldom appears to advantage: the incidents are often startling and extravagant; the whole structure of the story has a rugged, broken, huge, artificial aspect, and will not assume the air of truth. Yet its chasms are strangely filled up with the costliest materials; a world, a universe of wit, and knowledge, and fancy, and imagination has sent its fairest products to adorn the edifice; the rude and rent Cyclopean walls are resplendent with jewels and beaten gold; rich stately foliage screens it, the balmiest odours encircle it; we stand astonished if not captivated, delighted if not charmed, by the artist and his art.'

With these views, so far as they go, we see little reason to disagree. There is doubtless a deeper meaning in the matter, but perhaps this is not the season for evolving it. To depict, with true scientific accuracy, the essential purport and character of Richter's genius and literary endeavour; how it originated, whither it tends, how it stands related to the general tendencies of the world in this age; above all, what is its worth and want of worth to ourselves, — may one day be a necessary problem; but, as matters actually stand, would be a difficult and no very profitable one. The English public has not yet seen Richter; and must know him before it can judge him. For us, in the present circumstances, we hold it a more promising plan to exhibit some specimens of his workmanship itself, than to attempt describing it anew or better. The general outline of his intellectual aspect, as sketched in few words by the writer already quoted, may stand here by way of preface to these Extracts: as was the case above, whatever it may want, it contains nothing that we dissent from.

'To characterise Jean Paul's Works,' says he, 'would be difficult after the fullest inspection: to describe them to English readers would be next to impossible. Whether poetical, philosophical, didactic, fantastic, they seem all to be emblems, more or less complete, of the singular mind where they originated. As a whole, the first perusal of them, more particularly to a foreigner, is almost infallibly offensive; and neither their meaning nor their no-meaning is to be discerned without long and sedulous study. They are a tropical wilderness, full of endless tortuosities; but with the fairest flowers and the coolest fountains; now overarching us with high umbrageous gloom, now opening in long gorgeous vistas. We wander through them, enjoying their wild grandeur; and, by degrees, our half-contemptuous wonder at the Author passes into reverence and love. His face was long hid from us; but we see him, at length, in the firm shape of spiritual manhood; a vast and most singular nature, but vindicating his singular nature by the force, the beauty and benignity which pervade it. In fine, we joyfully accept him for what he is and was meant to be. The graces, the polish, the sprightly elegancies, which belong to men of lighter make, we cannot look for or demand from him. His movement is essentially slow and cumbrous, for he advances not with one faculty, but with a whole mind; with intellect, and pathos, and wit, and humour, and imagination, moving onward like a mighty host, motley, ponderous, irregular, irresistible. He is not airy, sparkling and precise; but deep, billowy and vast. The melody of his nature is not expressed in common note-marks, or written down by the critical gamut: for it is wild and manifold; its voice is like the voice of cataracts, and the sounding of primeval forests. To feeble ears it is discord; but to ears that understand it, deep majestic music.'[1]

As our first specimen, which also may serve for proof that Richter, in adopting his own extraordinary style, did it with clear knowledge of what excellence in style, and the various kinds and degrees of excellence therein, properly signified, we select, from his *Vorschule der Aesthetik* (above mentioned and recommended), the following miniature sketches: the reader acquainted with the persons, will find these sentences, as we believe, strikingly descriptive and exact.

'Visit Herder's creations, where Greek life-freshness, and Hindoo life-weariness are wonderfully blended: you walk, as it were, amid

1 *German Romance*, iii. 6, 18. *Suprà*, Appendix, § *Richter*.

moonshine, into which the red dawn is already falling; but one hidden sun is the painter of both.'

'Similar, but more compacted into periods, is Friedrich Heinrich Jacobi's vigorous, German-hearted prose; musical in every sense, for even his images are often derived from tones. The rare union between cutting force of intellectual utterance, and infinitude of sentiment, gives us the tense metallic chord with its soft tones.'

'In Goethe's prose, on the other hand, his fixedness of form gives us the Memnon's-tone. A plastic rounding, a pictorial determinateness, which even betrays the manual artist, make his works a fixed still gallery of figures and bronze statues.'

'Luther's prose is a half-battle; few deeds are equal to his words.'

'Klopstock's prose frequently evinces a sharpness of diction bordering on poverty of matter; a quality peculiar to Grammarians, who most of all know *distinctly*, but least of all know *much*. From want of matter, one is apt to think too much of language. New views of the world, like these other poets, Klopstock scarcely gave. Hence the naked winter-boughs, in his prose; the multitude of circumscribed propositions; the brevity; the return of the same small sharp-cut figures, for instance, of the Resurrection, as of a Harvest-field.'

'The perfection of pomp-prose we find in Schiller: what the utmost splendour of reflection in images, in fulness and antithesis can give, he gives. Nay, often he plays on the poetic strings with so rich and jewel-loaded a hand, that the sparkling mass disturbs, if not the playing, yet our hearing of it.'[1]

That Richter's own playing and painting differed widely from all of these, the reader has already heard, and may now convince himself. Take, for example, the following of a fair-weather scene, selected from a thousand such that may be found in his writings; nowise as the best, but simply as the briefest. It is in the May season, the last evening of Spring:

'Such a May as the present (of 1794) Nature has not in the memory of man — begun; for this is but the fifteenth of it. People of reflection have long been vexed once every year, that our German singers should indite May-songs, since several other months deserve such a poetical Night-music better; and I myself have often gone so far as to adopt the idiom of our market-women, and instead of May butter to say June butter, as also June, March, April songs. But

[1] *Vorschule*, s. 545.

thou, kind May of this year, thou deservest to thyself all the songs which were ever made on thy rude namesakes! — By Heaven! when I now issue from the wavering chequered acacia-grove of the Castle, in which I am writing this Chapter, and come forth into the broad living light, and look up to the warming Heaven, and over its Earth budding out beneath it, — the Spring rises before me like a vast full cloud, with a splendour of blue and green. I see the Sun standing amid roses in the western sky, into which he has *thrown his ray-brush wherewith he has to-day been painting the Earth;* — and when I look round a little in our picture-exhibition, — his enamelling is still hot on the mountains; on the moist chalk of the moist earth, the flowers, full of sap-colours, are laid out to dry, and the forget-me-not, with miniature colours; under the varnish of the streams the skyey Painter has pencilled his own eye; and the clouds, like a decoration-painter, he has touched-off with wild outlines and single tints; and so he stands at the border of the Earth, and looks back on his stately Spring, whose robe-folds are valleys, whose breast-bouquet is gardens, and whose blush is a vernal evening, and who, when she arises, will be — Summer!'[1]

Or the following, in which, moreover, are two happy living figures, a bridegroom and a bride on their marriage-day:

'He led her from the crowded dancing-room into the cool evening. Why does the evening, does the night, put warmer love in our hearts? Is it the nightly pressure of helplessness; or is it the exalting separation from the turmoils of life, that veiling of the world, in which for the soul nothing then remains but souls: — is it therefore that the letters in which the loved name stands written on our spirit, appear, like phosphorus writing, by night, *on fire*, while by day in their *cloudy* traces they but smoke?

'He walked with his bride into the Castle-garden: she hastened quickly through the Castle, and past its servants'-hall, where the fair flowers of her young life had been crushed broad and dry, under a long dreary pressure; and her soul expanded, and breathed in the free open garden, on whose flowery soil Destiny had cast forth the first seeds of the blossoms which to-day were gladdening her existence. Still Eden! Green, flower-chequered *chiaroscuro!* — The moon is sleeping under ground, like a dead one; but beyond the garden, the sun's red evening-clouds have fallen down like rose-leaves; and the evening-star, the brideman of the sun, hovers like a glancing butterfly above the rosy red, and, modest as a bride, deprives no single starlet of its light.'

[1] *Fixlein*, z. 11.

'The wandering pair arrived at the old gardener's-hut; now standing locked and dumb, with dark windows in the light garden, like a fragment of the Past surviving in the Present. Bared twigs of trees were folding, with clammy half-formed leaves, over the thick intertwisted tangles of the bushes. The Spring was standing, like a conqueror, with Winter at his feet. In the blue pond, now bloodless, a dusky evening-sky lay hollowed out; and the gushing waters were moistening the flower-beds. The silver sparks of stars were rising on the altar of the East, and falling down extinguished in the red-sea of the West.'

'The wind whirred, like a night-bird, louder through the trees; and gave tones to the acacia-grove, and the tones called to the pair who had first become happy within it: "Enter, new mortal pair, and think of what is past, and of my withering and your own; and be holy as Eternity, and weep, not for joy only, but for gratitude also!" * * *

'They reached the blazing, rustling marriage-house, but their softened hearts sought stillness; and a foreign touch, as in the blossoming vine, would have disturbed the flower-nuptials of their souls. They turned rather, and winded up into the churchyard, to preserve their mood. Majestic on the groves and mountains stood the Night before man's heart, and made it also great. Over the white steeple-obelisk the sky rested bluer and darker; and behind it wavered the withered summit of the Maypole with faded flag. The son noticed his father's grave, on which the wind was opening and shutting, with harsh noise, the small lid on the metal cross, to let the year of his death be read on the brass plate within. An overpowering grief seized his heart with violent streams of tears, and drove him to the sunk hillock; and he led his bride to the grave, and said: "Here sleeps he, my good father; in his thirty-second year he was carried hither to his long rest. O thou good dear father, couldst thou to-day but see the happiness of thy son, like my mother! But thy eyes are empty, and thy breast is full of ashes, and thou seest us not." — He was silent. The bride wept aloud; she saw the mouldering coffins of her parents open, and the two dead arise, and look round for their daughter, who had stayed so long behind them, forsaken on the earth. She fell on his neck and faltered: "O beloved, I have neither father nor mother, do not forsake me!"

'O thou who hast still a father and a mother, thank God for it on the day when thy soul is full of glad tears, and needs a bosom wherein to shed them. . . . . . .

'And with this embracing at a father's grave, let this day of joy be holily concluded.' [1]

[1] *Fixlein*, z. 9.

In such passages, slight as they are, we fancy an experienced eye will trace some features of originality, as well as of uncommonness: an open sense for Nature, a soft heart, a warm rich fancy, and here and there some under-current of Humour are distinctly enough discernible. Of this latter quality, which, as has been often said, forms Richter's grand characteristic, we would fain give our readers some correct notion; but see not well how it is to be done. Being genuine poetic humour, not drollery or vulgar caricature, it is like a fine essence, like a soul; we discover it only in whole works and delineations; as the soul is only to be seen in the living body, not in detached limbs and fragments. Richter's Humour takes a great variety of forms, some of them sufficiently grotesque and piebald; ranging from the light kindly-comic vein of Sterne in his *Trim* and *Uncle Toby*, over all intermediate degrees, to the rugged grim farce-tragedy often manifested in Hogarth's pictures; nay, to still darker and wilder moods than this. Of the former sort are his characters of Fixlein, Schmelzle, Fibel; of the latter, his Vult, Giannozzo, Leibgeber, Schoppe, which last two are indeed one and the same. Of these, of the spirit that reigns in them, we should despair of giving other than the most inadequate and even incorrect idea, by any extracts or expositions that could possibly be furnished here. Not without reluctance we have accordingly renounced that enterprise; and must content ourselves with some 'Extra-leaf,' or other separable passage; which, if it afford no emblem of Richter's Humour, may be, in these circumstances, our best approximation to such. Of the 'Extra-leaves' in *Hesperus* itself, a considerable volume might be formed, and truly one of the strangest. Most of them, however, are national; could not be apprehended without a commentary; and even then much to their disadvantage, for Humour must be seen, not through a glass, but face to face. The following is nowise one of the best; but it turns on what we believe is a quite European subject, at all events is certainly an English one.

'*Extra-leaf on Daughter-full Houses.*

'The Minister's house was an open bookshop, the books in which (the daughters) you might read there, but could not take home with you. Though five other daughters were already standing in five private libraries, as wives, and one under the ground at Maienthal was sleeping off the child's-play of life, yet still in this daughter-warehouse there remained three gratis copies to be disposed of to good friends. The Minister was always prepared, in drawings from the office-lottery, to give his daughters as premiums to winners, and holders of the lucky ticket. Whom God gives an office, he also gives, if not sense for it, at least a wife. In a daughter-full house, there must, as in the Church of St. Peter's, be *confessionals* for all nations, for all characters, for all faults; that the daughters may sit as confessoresses therein, and absolve from all, bachelorship only excepted. As a Natural-Philosopher, I have many times admired the wise methods of Nature for distributing daughters and plants: Is it not a fine arrangement, said I to the Natural-Historian Goeze, that Nature should have bestowed specially on young women, who for their growth require a rich mineralogical soil, some sort of hooking apparatus, whereby to stick themselves on miserable marriage-cattle, that they may carry them to fat places? Thus Linnæus,[1] as you know, observes that such seeds as can flourish only in fat earth are furnished with barbs, and so fasten themselves the better on grazing quadrupeds, which transport them to stalls and dunghills. Strangely does Nature, by the wind, — which father and mother must raise, — scatter daughters and fir-seeds into the arable spots of the forest. Who does not remark the final cause here, and how Nature has equipped many a daughter with such and such charms, simply that some Peer, some mitred Abbot, Cardinal-deacon, appanaged Prince, or mere country Baron, may lay hold of said charmer, and in the character of Father or Brideman, hand her over ready-made to some gawk of the like sort, as a wife acquired by purchase? And do we find in bilberries a slighter attention on the part of Nature? Does not the same Linnæus notice, in the same treatise, that they too are cased in a nutritive juice to incite the Fox to eat them; after which, the villain, — digest them he cannot, — in such sort as he may, becomes their sower? —

'Oh, my heart is more in earnest than you think; the parents anger me, who are soul-brokers; the daughters sadden me, who are made slave-negresses. — Ah, is it wonderful that these, who, in their West-Indian market-place, must dance, laugh, speak, sing, till some

[1] 'His *Amœn. Acad.* — The Treatise on the Habitable Globe.'

lord of a plantation take them home with him, — that these, I say, should be as slavishly treated, as they are sold and bought? Ye poor lambs! — And yet ye too are as bad as your sale-mothers and sale-fathers: — what is one to do with his enthusiasm for your sex, when one travels through German towns, where every heaviest-pursed, every longest-titled individual, were he second cousin to the Devil himself, can point with his finger to thirty houses, and say: "I know not, shall it be from the pearl-coloured, or the nut-brown, or the steel-green house, that I wed; open to customers are they all!" — How, my girls! Is your heart so little worth that you cut it, like old clothes, after any fashion, to fit any breast; and does it wax or shrink, then, like a Chinese ball, to fit itself into the ball-mould and marriage ring-case of any male heart whatever? "Well, it must; unless we would sit at home, and grow Old Maids," answer they; whom I will not answer, but turn scornfully away from them, to address that same Old Maid in these words:

'"Forsaken, but patient one! misknown and mistreated! Think not of the times when thou hadst hope of better than the present are, and repent the noble pride of thy heart never! It is not always our duty to marry, but it is always our duty to abide by right, not to purchase happiness by loss of honour, not to avoid unweddedness by untruthfulness. Lonely, unadmired heroine! in thy last hour, when all Life and the bygone possessions and scaffoldings of Life shall crumble to pieces, ready to fall down; in that hour thou wilt look back on thy untenanted life; no children, no husband, no wet eyes will be there; but in the empty dusk, one high, pure, angelic, smiling, beaming Figure, godlike and mounting to the Godlike, will hover, and beckon thee to mount with her; — mount thou with her, the Figure is thy Virtue."'

We have spoken above, and warmly, of Jean Paul's Imagination, of his high devout feeling, which it were now a still more grateful part of our task to exhibit. But in this also our readers must content themselves with some imperfect glimpses. What religious opinions and aspirations he specially entertained, how that noblest portion of man's interest represented itself in such a mind, were long to describe, did we even know it with certainty. He hints somewhere that 'the soul, which by nature looks Heavenward, is without a Temple in this age;' in which little sentence, the careful reader will decipher much.

'But there will come another era,' says Paul, 'when it shall be light, and man will awaken from his lofty dreams, and find — his dreams still there, and that nothing is gone save his sleep.

'The stones and rocks, which two veiled Figures (Necessity and Vice), like Deucalion and Pyrrha, are casting behind them, at Goodness, will themselves become men.

'And on the Western-gate (*Abendthor*, evening-gate) of this century stands written: Here is the way to Virtue and Wisdom; as on the Western-gate at Cherson stands the proud Inscription: Here is the way to Byzance.

'Infinite Providence, Thou wilt cause the day to dawn.

'But as yet, struggles the twelfth-hour of the Night: the nocturnal birds of prey are on the wing, spectres uproar, the dead walk, the living dream.' [1]

Connected with this, there is one other piece, which also, for its singular poetic qualities, we shall translate here. The reader has heard much of Richter's Dreams, with what strange prophetic power he rules over that chaos of spiritual Nature, bodying forth a whole world of Darkness, broken by pallid gleams or wild sparkles of light, and peopled with huge, shadowy, bewildered shapes, full of grandeur and meaning. No Poet known to us, not Milton himself, shows such a vastness of Imagination; such a rapt, deep, Old-Hebrew spirit as Richter in these scenes. He mentions, in his Biographical Notes, the impression which these lines of the *Tempest* had on him, as recited by one of his companions:

> 'We are such stuff
> As Dreams are made of, and our little Life
> Is rounded with a sleep.

'The passage of Shakspeare,' says he, '*rounded with a sleep* '(*mit Schlaf umgeben*), in Plattner's mouth, created whole 'books in me.' — The following Dream is perhaps his grandest, as undoubtedly it is among his most celebrated. We shall give it entire, long as it is, and therewith finish our quotations. What value he himself put on it, may be gathered from the following Note: 'If ever my heart,' says he, 'were to grow so wretched and so dead that all feelings

[1] *Hesperus:* Preface.

'in it which announce the being of a God were extinct 'there, I would terrify myself with this sketch of mine; it 'would heal me, and give me my feelings back.' We translate from *Siebenkäs*, where it forms the first Chapter, or *Blumenstück* (Flower-Piece).

'The purpose of this Fiction is the excuse of its boldness. Men deny the Divine Existence with as little feeling as the most assert it. Even in our true systems we go on collecting mere words, playmarks and medals, as misers do coins; and not till late do we transform the words into feelings, the coins into enjoyments. A man may, for twenty years, believe the Immortality of the Soul; — in the one-and-twentieth, in some great moment, he for the first time discovers with amazement the rich meaning of this belief, the warmth of this Naphtha-well.

'Of such sort, too, was my terror, at the poisonous stifling vapour which floats out round the heart of him who, for the first time, enters the school of Atheism. I could with less pain deny Immortality than Deity: there I should lose but a world covered with mists, here I should lose the present world, namely, the Sun thereof: the whole spiritual Universe is dashed asunder by the hand of Atheism into numberless quicksilver-points of *Me's*, which glitter, run, waver, fly together or asunder, without unity or continuance. No one in Creation is so alone, as the denier of God; he mourns, with an orphaned heart that has lost its great Father, by the Corpse of Nature, which no World-spirit moves and holds together, and which grows in its grave; and he mourns by that Corpse till he himself crumble off from it. The whole world lies before him, like the Egyptian Sphinx of stone, half-buried in the sand; and the All is the cold iron mask of a formless Eternity. * * *

'I merely remark farther, that with the belief of Atheism, the belief of Immortality is quite compatible; for the same Necessity, which in this Life threw my light dewdrop of a *Me* into a flower-bell and — under a Sun, can repeat that process in a second life; nay, more easily embody me the second time than the first.

'If we hear, in childhood, that the Dead, about midnight, when our *sleep reaches near the soul*, and darkens even our dreams, awake out of theirs, and in the church mimic the worship of the living, we shudder at Death by reason of the dead, and in the night-solitude turn away our eyes from the long silent windows of the church, and fear to search in their gleaming, whether it proceed from the moon.

'Childhood, and rather its terrors than its raptures, take wings and radiance again in dreams, and sport like fire-flies in the little night of the soul. Crush not these flickering sparks! — Leave us even our dark painful dreams as higher half-shadows of reality! — And wherewith will you replace to us *those* dreams, which bear us away from under the tumult of the waterfall into the still heights of childhood, where the stream of life yet ran silent in its little plain, and flowed towards its abysses, a mirror of the Heaven? —

'I was lying once, on a summer evening, in the sunshine; and I fell asleep. Methought I awoke in the Churchyard. The down-rolling wheels of the steeple-clock, which was striking eleven, had awakened me. In the emptied night-heaven I looked for the Sun; for I thought an eclipse was veiling him with the Moon. All the Graves were open, and the iron doors of the charnel-house were swinging to and fro by invisible hands. On the walls flitted shadows, which proceeded from no one, and other shadows stretched upwards in the pale air. In the open coffins none now lay sleeping, but the children. Over the whole heaven hung, in large folds, a gray sultry mist; which a giant shadow, like vapour, was drawing down, nearer, closer and hotter. Above me I heard the distant fall of avalanches; under me the first step of a boundless earthquake. The Church wavered up and down with two interminable Dissonances, which struggled with each other in it; endeavouring in vain to mingle in unison. At times, a gray glimmer hovered along the windows, and under it the lead and iron fell down molten. The net of the mist, and the tottering Earth brought me into that hideous Temple; at the door of which, in two poison-bushes, two glittering Basilisks lay brooding. I passed through unknown Shadows, on whom ancient centuries were impressed. — All the Shadows were standing round the empty Altar; and in all, not the heart, but the breast quivered and pulsed. One dead man only, who had just been buried there, still lay on his coffin without quivering breast; and on his smiling countenance stood a happy dream. But at the entrance of one Living, he awoke, and smiled no longer; he lifted his heavy eyelids, but within was no eye; and in his beating breast there lay, instead of a heart, a wound. He held up his hands, and folded them to pray; but the arms lengthened out and dissolved; and the hands, still folded together, fell away. Above, on the Church-dome, stood the dial-plate of *Eternity*, whereon no number appeared, and which was its own index: but a black finger pointed thereon, and the Dead sought to see the time by it.

'Now sank from aloft a noble, high Form, with a look of unefffaceable sorrow, down to the Altar, and all the Dead cried out, "Christ! is there no God?" He answered, "There is none!" The whole Shadow of each then shuddered, not the breast alone; and one after the other, all, in this shuddering, shook into pieces.

'Christ continued: "I went through the Worlds, I mounted into the Suns, and flew with the Galaxies through the wastes of Heaven; but there is no God! I descended as far as Being casts its shadow, and looked down into the Abyss and cried, Father, where art thou? But I heard only the everlasting storm which no one guides, and the gleaming Rainbow of Creation hung without a Sun that made it, over the Abyss, and trickled down. And when I looked up to the immeasurable world for the Divine *Eye*, it glared on me with an empty, black, bottomless *Eye-socket*; and Eternity lay upon Chaos, eating it and ruminating it. Cry on, ye Dissonances; cry away the Shadows, for He is not!"

'The pale-grown Shadows flitted away, as white vapour which frost has formed with the warm breath disappears; and all was void. O, then came, fearful for the heart, the dead Children who had been awakened in the Churchyard, into the Temple, and cast themselves before the high Form on the Altar, and said, "Jesus, have we no Father?" And he answered, with streaming tears, "We are all orphans, I and you: we are without Father!"

'Then shrieked the Dissonances still louder, — the quivering walls of the Temple parted asunder; and the Temple and the Children sank down, and the whole Earth and the Sun sank after it, and the whole Universe sank with its immensity before us; and above, on the summit of immeasurable Nature, stood Christ, and gazed down into the Universe chequered with its thousand Suns, as into the Mine bored out of the Eternal Night, in which the Suns run like mine-lamps, and the Galaxies like silver veins.

'And as he saw the grinding press of Worlds, the torch-dance of celestial wildfires, and the coral-banks of beating hearts; and as he saw how world after world shook off its glimmering souls upon the Sea of Death, as a water-bubble scatters swimming lights on the waves, then majestic as the Highest of the Finite, he raised his eyes towards the Nothingness, and towards the void Immensity, and said: "Dead, dumb Nothingness! Cold, everlasting Necessity! Frantic Chance! Know ye what this is that lies beneath you? When will ye crush the Universe in pieces, and me? Chance, knowest thou what thou doest, when with thy hurricanes thou walkest through that snow-powder of Stars, and extinguishest Sun after Sun, and that sparkling dew of heavenly lights goes out, as thou passest over it? How is each so solitary in this wide grave of the All! I am alone with myself! O Father, O Father! where is thy infinite bosom, that I might rest on it? Ah, if each soul is its own father and creator, why can it not be its own destroyer too?

'"Is this beside me yet a Man? Unhappy one! Your little life is the sigh of Nature, or only its echo; a convex-mirror throws its rays into that dust-cloud of dead men's ashes, down on the Earth; and thus you, cloud-formed wavering phantasms, arise. — Look down into the Abyss, over which clouds of ashes are moving; mists full of Worlds reek up from the Sea of Death; the *Future* is a mounting mist, and the *Present* is a falling one. — Knowest thou thy Earth again?"

'Here Christ looked down, and his eye filled with tears, and he said: "Ah, I was once there; I was still happy then; I had still my Infinite Father, and looked up cheerfully from the mountains, into the immeasurable Heaven, and pressed my mangled breast on his healing form, and said even in the bitterness of death: Father, take thy son from this bleeding hull, and lift him to thy heart! — Ah, ye too happy inhabitants of Earth, ye still believe in *Him*. Perhaps even now your Sun is going down, and ye kneel amid blossoms, and brightness, and tears, and lift trustful hands, and cry with joy-streaming eyes, to the opened Heaven: "Me too thou knowest, Omnipotent, and all my wounds; and at death thou receivest me, and closest them all!" Unhappy creatures, at death they will not be closed! Ah, when the sorrow-laden lays himself, with galled back, into the Earth, to sleep till a fairer Morning full of Truth, full of Virtue and Joy, — he awakens in a stormy Chaos, in the everlasting Midnight, — and there comes no Morning, and no soft healing hand, and no Infinite Father! — Mortal, beside me! if thou still livest, pray to *Him;* else hast thou lost him forever!"

'And as I fell down, and looked into the sparkling Universe, I saw the upborne Rings of the Giant-Serpent, the Serpent of Eternity, which had coiled itself round the All of Worlds, — and the Rings sank down, and encircled the All doubly; and then it wound itself, innumerable ways, round Nature, and swept the Worlds from their places, and crashing, squeezed the Temple of Immensity together, into the Church of a Burying-ground, — and all grew strait, dark, fearful, — and an immeasurably extended Hammer was to strike the last hour of Time, and shiver the Universe asunder, . . . WHEN I AWOKE.

'My soul wept for joy that I could still pray to God; and the joy, and the weeping, and the faith on him were my prayer. And as I arose, the Sun was glowing deep behind the full purpled corn-ears, and casting meekly the gleam of its twilight-red on the little Moon, which was rising in the East without an Aurora; and between the sky and the earth, a gay transient air-people was stretching out its short wings and living, as I did, before the Infinite Father; and from all Nature around me flowed peaceful tones as from distant evening-bells.'

Without commenting on this singular piece, we must here for the present close our lucubrations on Jean Paul. To delineate, with any correctness, the specific features of such a genius, and of its operations and results in the great variety of provinces where it dwelt and worked, were a long task; for which, perhaps, some groundwork may have been laid here, and which, as occasion serves, it will be pleasant for us to resume.

Probably enough, our readers, in considering these strange matters, will too often bethink them of that 'Episode concerning Paul's Costume;' and conclude that, as in living, so in writing, he was a Mannerist, and man of continual Affectations. We will not quarrel with them on this point; we must not venture among the intricacies it would lead us into. At the same time, we hope many will agree with us in honouring Richter, such as he was; and 'in spite of his hundred real, and his ten thousand seeming faults,' discern under this wondrous guise the spirit of a true Poet and Philosopher. A Poet, and among the highest of his time, we must reckon him, though he wrote no verses; a Philosopher, though he promulgated no systems: for, on the whole, that 'Divine Idea of the World' stood in clear ethereal light before his mind; he recognised the Invisible, even under the mean forms of these days, and with a high, strong, not uninspired heart, strove to represent it in the Visible, and publish tidings of it to his fellow-men. This one virtue, the foundation of all the other virtues, and which a long study more and more clearly reveals to us in Jean Paul, will cover far greater sins than his were. It raises him into quite another sphere than that of the thousand elegant Sweet-singers, and cause-and-effect *Philosophes*, in his own country, or in this; the million Novel-manufacturers, Sketchers, practical Discoursers and so forth, not once reckoned in. Such a man we can safely recommend to universal study; and for those who, in the actual state of matters, may the most blame him, repeat the old maxim: 'What is extraordinary try to look at with your own eyes.'

ON HISTORY.[1]

[1830.]

Clio was figured by the ancients as the eldest daughter of Memory, and chief of the Muses; which dignity, whether we regard the essential qualities of her art, or its practice and acceptance among men, we shall still find to have been fitly bestowed. History, as it lies at the root of all science, is also the first distinct product of man's spiritual nature; his earliest expression of what can be called Thought. It is a looking both before and after; as, indeed, the coming Time already waits, unseen, yet definitely shaped, predetermined and inevitable, in the Time come; and only by the combination of both is the meaning of either completed. The Sibylline Books, though old, are not the oldest. Some nations have prophecy, some have not: but of all mankind, there is no tribe so rude that it has not attempted History, though several have not arithmetic enough to count Five. History has been written with quipo-threads, with feather-pictures, with wampum-belts; still oftener with earth-mounds and monumental stone-heaps, whether as pyramid or cairn; for the Celt and the Copt, the Red man as well as the White, lives between two eternities, and warring against Oblivion, he would fain unite himself in clear conscious relation, as in dim unconscious relation he is already united, with the whole Future and the whole Past.

A talent for History may be said to be born with us, as our chief inheritance. In a certain sense all men are his-

[1] Fraser's Magazine, No. 10.

torians. Is not every memory written quite full with Annals, wherein joy and mourning, conquest and loss manifoldly alternate; and, with or without philosophy, the whole fortunes of one little inward Kingdom, and all its politics, foreign and domestic, stand ineffaceably recorded? Our very speech is curiously historical. Most men, you may observe, speak only to narrate; not in imparting what they have thought, which indeed were often a very small matter, but in exhibiting what they have undergone or seen, which is a quite unlimited one, do talkers dilate. Cut us off from Narrative, how would the stream of conversation, even among the wisest, languish into detached handfuls, and among the foolish utterly evaporate! Thus, as we do nothing but enact History, we say little but recite it: nay rather, in that widest sense, our whole spiritual life is built thereon. For, strictly considered, what is all Knowledge too but recorded Experience, and a product of History; of which, therefore, Reasoning and Belief, no less than Action and Passion, are essential materials?

Under a limited, and the only practicable shape, History proper, that part of History which treats of remarkable action, has, in all modern as well as ancient times, ranked among the highest arts, and perhaps never stood higher than in these times of ours. For whereas, of old, the charm of History lay chiefly in gratifying our common appetite for the wonderful, for the unknown; and her office was but as that of a Minstrel and Story-teller, she has now farther become a Schoolmistress, and professes to instruct in gratifying. Whether, with the stateliness of that venerable character, she may not have taken up something of its austerity and frigidity; whether, in the logical terseness of a Hume or Robertson, the graceful ease and gay pictorial heartiness of a Herodotus or Froissart may not be wanting, is not the question for us here. Enough that all learners, all inquiring minds of every order, are gathered round her footstool, and reverently pondering her lessons, as the true basis of Wisdom. Poetry, Divinity, Politics, Physics, have each their adherents and adversaries; each little guild supporting a defensive and offensive war for its own special domain; while the domain of History is as a Free Emporium, where all these belligerents peaceably meet and furnish themselves; and Sentimentalist and Utilitarian, Sceptic and Theologian, with one voice advise us: Examine History, for it is 'Philosophy teaching by Experience.'

Far be it from us to disparage such teaching, the very attempt at which must be precious. Neither shall we too rigidly inquire: How much it has hitherto profited? Whether most of what little practical wisdom men have, has come from study of professed History, or from other less boasted sources, whereby, as matters now stand, a Marlborough may become great in the world's business, with no History save what he derives from Shakspeare's Plays? Nay, whether in that same teaching by Experience, historical Philosophy has yet properly deciphered the first element of all science in this kind? What the aim and significance of that wondrous changeful Life it investigates and paints may be? Whence the course of man's destinies in this Earth originated, and whither they are tending? Or, indeed, if they have any course and tendency, are really guided forward by an unseen mysterious Wisdom, or only circle in blind mazes, without recognisable guidance? Which questions, altogether fundamental, one might think, in any Philosophy of History, have, since the era when Monkish Annalists were wont to answer them by the long-ago extinguished light of their Missal and Breviary, been by most philosophical Historians only glanced at dubiously and from afar; by many, not so much as glanced at.

The truth is, two difficulties, never wholly surmountable, lie in the way. Before Philosophy can teach by Experience, the Philosophy has to be in readiness, the Experience must be gathered and intelligibly recorded. Now, overlooking the former consideration, and with regard only to the latter, let any one who has examined the current of human affairs, and how intricate, perplexed, unfathomable, even when seen into with our own eyes, are their thousandfold blending movements, say whether the true representing of it is easy or impossible. Social Life is the aggregate of all the individual men's Lives who constitute society; History is the essence of innumerable Biographies. But if one Biography, nay our own Biography, study and recapitulate it as we may, remains in so many points unintelligible to us; how much more must these million, the very facts of which, to say nothing of the purport of them, we know not, and cannot know!

Neither will it adequately avail us to assert that the general inward condition of Life is the same in all ages; and that only the remarkable deviations from the common endowment and common lot, and the more important variations which the outward figure of Life has from time to time undergone, deserve memory and record. The inward condition of Life, it may rather be affirmed, the conscious or half-conscious aim of mankind, so far as men are not mere digesting-machines, is the same in no two ages; neither are the more important outward variations easy to fix on, or always well capable of representation. Which was the greatest innovator, which was the more important personage in man's history, he who first led armies over the Alps, and gained the victories of Cannæ and Thrasymene; or the nameless boor who first hammered out for himself an iron spade? When the oak-tree is felled, the whole forest echoes with it; but a hundred acorns are planted silently by some unnoticed breeze. Battles and war-tumults, which for the time din every ear, and with joy or terror intoxicate every heart, pass away like tavern-brawls; and except some few Marathons and Morgartens, are remembered by accident, not by desert. Laws themselves, political Constitutions, are not our Life, but only the house wherein our Life is led: nay, they are but the bare walls of the house; all whose essential furniture, the inventions and traditions, and daily habits that regulate and support our existence, are the work not of Dracos and Hampdens, but of Phœnician mariners, of Italian masons and Saxon metallurgists, of philosophers, alchymists, prophets, and all the long forgotten train of artists and artisans; who from the first have been jointly teaching us how to think and how to act, how to rule over spiritual and over physical Nature. Well may we say that of our History the more important part is lost without recovery; and, — as thanksgivings were once wont to be offered 'for unrecognised mercies,' — look with reverence into the dark untenanted places of the Past, where, in formless oblivion, our chief benefactors, with all their sedulous endeavours, but not with the fruit of these, lie entombed.

So imperfect is that same Experience, by which Philosophy is to teach. Nay, even with regard to those occurrences which do stand recorded, which, at their origin have seemed worthy of record, and the summary of which constitutes what we now call History, is not our understanding of them altogether incomplete; is it even possible to represent them as they were? The old story of Sir Walter Raleigh's looking from his prison-window, on some street-tumult, which afterwards three witnesses reported in three different ways, himself differing from them all, is still a true lesson for us. Consider how it is that historical documents and records originate; even honest records, where the reporters were unbiased by personal regard; a case which, were nothing more wanted, must ever be among the rarest. The real leading features of a historical Transaction, those movements that essentially characterise it, and alone deserve to be recorded, are nowise the foremost to be noted. At first, among the various witnesses, who are also parties interested, there is only vague wonder, and fear or hope, and the noise of Rumour's thousand tongues; till, after a season, the conflict of testimonies has subsided into some general issue; and then it is settled, by majority of votes, that such and such a 'Crossing of the Rubicon,' an 'Impeachment of Strafford,' a

'Convocation of the Notables,' are epochs in the world's history, cardinal points on which grand world-revolutions have hinged. Suppose, however, that the majority of votes was all wrong; that the real cardinal points lay far deeper; and had been passed over unnoticed, because no Seer, but only mere Onlookers, chanced to be there! Our clock strikes when there is a change from hour to hour; but no hammer in the Horologe of Time peals through the universe, when there is a change from Era to Era. Men understand not what is among their hands: as calmness is the characteristic of strength, so the weightiest causes may be most silent. It is, in no case, the real historical Transaction, but only some more or less plausible scheme and theory of the Transaction, or the harmonised result of many such schemes, each varying from the other, and all varying from truth, that we can ever hope to behold.

Nay, were our faculty of insight into passing things never so complete, there is still a fatal discrepancy between our manner of observing these, and their manner of occurring. The most gifted man can observe, still more can record, only the *series* of his own impressions: his observation, therefore, to say nothing of its other imperfections, must be *successive*, while the things done were often *simultaneous;* the things done were not a series, but a group. It is not in acted, as it is in written History: actual events are nowise so simply related to each other as parent and offspring are; every single event is the offspring not of one, but of all other events, prior or contemporaneous, and will in its turn combine with all others to give birth to new: it is an ever-living, ever-working Chaos of Being, wherein shape after shape bodies itself forth from innumerable elements. And this Chaos, boundless as the habitation and duration of man, unfathomable as the soul and destiny of man, is what the historian will depict, and scientifically guage, we may say, by threading it with single lines of a few ells in length! For as all Action is, by its nature, to be figured as extended in breadth and in depth, as well as in length; that is to say, is based on Passion and Mystery, if we investigate its origin; and spreads abroad on all hands, modifying and modified; as well as advances towards completion, — so all Narrative is, by its nature, of only one dimension; only travels forward towards one, or towards successive points: Narrative is *linear*, Action is *solid.* Alas for our 'chains,' or chainlets of 'causes and effects,' which we so assiduously track through certain handbreadths of years and square miles, when the whole is a broad, deep Immensity, and each atom is 'chained' and complected with all! Truly, if History is Philosophy teaching by Experience, the writer fitted to compose History is hitherto an unknown man. The Experience itself would require All-knowledge to record it, — were the All-wisdom needful for such Philosophy as would interpret it, to be had for asking. Better were it that mere earthly Historians should lower such pretensions, more suitable for Omniscience than for human science; and aiming only at some picture of the things acted, which picture itself will at best be a poor approximation, leave the inscrutable purport of them an acknowledged secret: or at most, in reverent Faith, far different from that teaching of Philosophy, pause over the mysterious vestiges of Him, whose path is in the great deep of Time, whom History indeed reveals, but only all History, and in Eternity, will clearly reveal.

Such considerations truly were of small profit, did they, instead of teaching us vigilance and reverent humility in our inquiries into History, abate our esteem for them, or discourage us from unweariedly prosecuting them. Let us search more and more into the Past; let all men explore it, as the true fountain of knowledge; by whose light alone, consciously or unconsciously employed, can the Present and the Future be interpreted or guessed at. For though the whole meaning lies far beyond our ken; yet in that complex Manuscript, covered over with formless inextricably-entangled unknown characters, — nay which is a *Palimpsest*, and had once prophetic writing, still dimly legible there, — some letters, some words, may be deciphered; and if no complete Philosophy, here and there an intelligible precept, available in practice, be gathered: well understanding, in the mean while, that it is only a little portion we have deciphered; that much still remains to be interpreted; that History is a real Prophetic Manuscript, and can be fully interpreted by no man.

But the Artist in History may be distinguished from the Artisan in History; for here, as in all other provinces, there are Artists and Artisans; men who labour mechanically in a department, without eye for the Whole, not feeling that there is a Whole; and men who inform and ennoble the humblest department with an Idea of the Whole, and habitually know that only in the Whole is the Partial to be truly discerned. The proceedings and the duties of these two, in regard to History, must be altogether different. Not, indeed, that each has not a real worth, in his several degree. The simple husbandman can till his field, and by knowledge he has gained of its soil, sow it with the fit grain, though the deep rocks and central fires are unknown to him: his little crop hangs under and over the firmament of stars, and sails through whole untracked celestial spaces, between Aries and Libra; nevertheless, it ripens for him in due season, and he gathers it safe into his barn. As a husbandman he is blameless in disregarding those higher wonders; but as a thinker, and faithful inquirer into Nature, he were wrong. So likewise is it with the Historian, who examines some special aspect of History; and from this or that combination of circumstances, political, moral, economical, and the issues it has led to, infers that such and such properties belong to human society, and that the like circumstances will produce the like issue; which inference, if other trials confirm it, must be held true and practically valuable. He is wrong only, and an artisan, when he fancies that these properties, discovered or discoverable, exhaust the matter; and sees not, at every step, that it is inexhaustible.

However, that class of cause-and-effect speculators, with whom no wonder would remain wonderful, but all things in Heaven and Earth must be computed and 'accounted for;' and even the Unknown, the Infinite in man's Life, had, under the words *enthusiasm, superstition, spirit of the age* and so forth, obtained, as it were, an algebraical symbol and given value, — have now wellnigh played their part in European culture; and may be considered, as in most countries, even in England itself where they linger the latest, verging towards extinction. He who reads the inscrutable Book of Nature as if it were a Merchant's Ledger, is justly suspected of having never seen that Book, but only some school Synopsis thereof; from which, if taken for the real Book, more error than insight is to be derived.

Doubtless also, it is with a growing feeling of the infinite nature of History, that in these times, the old principle, division of labour, has been so widely applied to it. The Political Historian, once almost the sole cultivator of History, has now found various associates, who strive to elucidate other phases of human Life; of which, as hinted above, the political conditions it is passed under are but one, and though the primary, perhaps not the most important, of the many outward arrangements. Of this Historian himself, moreover, in his own special department, new and higher things are beginning to be expected. From of old, it was too often to be reproachfully observed of him, that he dwelt with disproportionate fondness in Senate-houses, in Battle-fields, nay even in Kings' Antechambers; forgetting, that far away from such scenes, the mighty tide of Thought and Action was still rolling on its wondrous course, in gloom and brightness; and in its thousand remote valleys, a whole world of Existence, with or without an earthly sun of Happiness to warm it, with or without a heavenly sun of Holiness to purify and sanctify it, was blossoming and fading, whether the 'famous victory' were won or lost. The time seems coming when much of this must be amended; and he who sees no world but that of courts and camps; and writes only how soldiers were drilled and shot, and how this ministerial conjuror out-conjured that other, and then guided, or at least held, something which he called the rudder of Government, but which was rather the spigot of Taxation, wherewith, in place of steering, he could tap, and the more cunningly the nearer the lees, — will pass for a more or less instructive Gazetteer, but will no longer be called a Historian.

However, the Political Historian, were his work performed with all conceivable perfection, can accomplish but a part, and still leaves room for numerous fellow-labourers. Foremost among these comes the Ecclesiastical Historian; endeavouring, with catholic or sectarian view, to trace the progress of the Church; of that portion of the social establishments, which respects our religious condition; as the other portion does our civil, or rather, in the long-run, our economical condition. Rightly conducted, this department were undoubtedly the more important of the two; inasmuch as it concerns us more to understand how man's moral well-being had been and might be promoted, than to understand in the like sort his physical well-being; which latter is ultimately the aim of all Political arrangements. For the physically happiest is simply the safest, the strongest; and, in all conditions of Government, Power (whether of wealth, as in these days, or of arms and adherents as in old days) is the only outward emblem and purchase-money of Good. True Good, however, unless we reckon Pleasure synonymous with it, is said to be rarely, or rather never, offered for sale in the market where that coin passes current. So that, for man's true advantage, not the outward condition of his life, but the inward and spiritual, is of prime influence; not the form of Government he lives under, and the power he can accumulate there, but the Church he is a member of, and the degree of moral elevation he can acquire by means of its instruction. Church History, then, did it speak wisely, would have momentous secrets to teach us: nay, in its highest degree, it were a sort of continued Holy Writ; our Sacred Books being, indeed, only a History of the primeval Church, as it first arose in man's soul, and symbolically embodied itself in his external life. How far our actual Church Historians fall below such unattainable standards, nay below quite attainable approximations thereto, we need not point out. Of the Ecclesiastical Historian we have to complain, as we did of his Political fellow-craftsman, that his inquiries turn rather on the outward mechanism, the mere hulls and superficial accidents of the object, than on the object itself: as if the Church lay in Bishops' Chapter-houses, and Ecumenic Council-halls, and Cardinals' Conclaves, and not far more in the hearts of Believing Men; in whose walk and conversation, as influenced thereby, its chief manifestations were to be looked for, and its progress or decline ascertained. The History of the Church is a History of the Invisible as well as of the Visible Church; which latter, if disjoined from the former, is but a vacant edifice; gilded, it may be, and overhung with old votive gifts, yet useless, nay pestilentially unclean; to write whose history is less important than to forward its downfall.

Of a less ambitious character are the Histories that relate to special separate provinces of human Action; to Sciences, Practical Arts, Institutions and the like; matters which do not imply an epitome of man's whole interest and form of life; but wherein, though each is still connected with all, the spirit of each, at least its material results, may be in some degree evolved without so strict a reference to that of the others. Highest in dignity and difficulty, under this head, would be our histories of Philosophy, of man's opinions and theories respecting the nature of his Being, and relations to the Universe Visible and Invisible: which History, indeed, were it fitly treated, or fit for right treatment, would be a province of Church History; the logical or dogmatical province thereof; for Philosophy, in its true sense, is or should be the soul, of which Religion, Worship is the body;

in the healthy state of things the Philosopher and Priest were one and the same. But Philosophy itself is far enough from wearing this character; neither have its Historians been men, generally speaking, that could in the smallest degree approximate it thereto. Scarcely since the rude era of the Magi and Druids has that same healthy identification of Priest and Philosopher had place in any country: but rather the worship of divine things, and the scientific investigation of divine things, have been in quite different hands, their relations not friendly but hostile. Neither have the Brückers and Bühles, to say nothing of the many unhappy Enfields who have treated of that latter department, been more than barren reporters, often unintelligent and unintelligible reporters, of the doctrine uttered; without force to discover how the doctrine originated, or what reference it bore to its time and country, to the spiritual position of mankind there and then. Nay, such a task did not perhaps lie before them, as a thing to be attempted.

Art also and Literature are intimately blended with Religion; as it were, outworks and abutments, by which that highest pinnacle in our inward world gradually connects itself with the general level, and becomes accessible therefrom. He who should write a proper History of Poetry, would depict for us the successive Revelations which man had obtained of the Spirit of Nature; under what aspects he had caught and endeavoured to body forth some glimpse of that unspeakable Beauty, which in its highest clearness is Religion, is the inspiration of a Prophet, yet in one or the other degree must inspire every true Singer, were his theme never so humble. We should see by what steps men had ascended to the Temple; how near they had approached; by what ill hap they had, for long periods, turned away from it, and grovelled on the plain with no music in the air, or blindly struggled towards other heights. That among all our Eichhorns and Wartons there is no such Historian, must be too clear to every one. Nevertheless let us not despair of far nearer approaches to that excellence. Above all, let us keep the Ideal of it ever in our eye; for thereby alone have we even a chance to reach it.

Our histories of Laws and Constitutions, wherein many a Montesquieu and Hallam has laboured with acceptance, are of a much simpler nature; yet deep enough if thoroughly investigated; and useful, when authentic, even with little depth. Then we have Histories of Medicine, of Mathematics, of Astronomy, Commerce, Chivalry, Monkery; and Goguets and Beckmanns have come forward with what might be the most bountiful contribution of all, a History of Inventions. Of all which sorts, and many more not here enumerated, not yet devised and put in practice, the merit and the proper scheme may require no exposition.

In this manner, though, as above remarked, all Action is extended three ways, and the general sum of human Action is a whole Universe, with all limits of it unknown, does History strive by running path after path, through the Impassable, in manifold directions and intersections, to secure for us some oversight of the Whole; in which endeavour, if each Historian look well around him from his path, tracking it out with the *eye*, not, as is more common, with the *nose*, she may at last prove not altogether unsuccessful. Praying only that increased division of labour do not here, as elsewhere, aggravate our already strong Mechanical tendencies, so that in the manual dexterity for parts we lose all command over the whole, and the hope of any Philosophy of History be farther off than ever, — let us all wish her great and greater success.

LUTHER'S PSALM.[1]

[1831.]

AMONG Luther's Spiritual Songs, of which various collections have appeared of late years,[2] the one entitled *Eine feste Burg ist unser Gott* is universally regarded as the best; and indeed still retains its place and devotional use in the Psalmodies of Protestant Germany. Of the Tune, which also is by Luther, we have no copy, and only a secondhand knowledge: to the original Words, probably never before printed in England, we subjoin the following Translation; which, if it possess the only merit it can pretend to, that of literal adherence to the sense, will not prove unacceptable to our readers. Luther's music is heard daily in our churches, several of our finest Psalm-tunes being of his composition. Luther's sentiments also are, or should be, present in many an English heart; the more interesting to us is any the smallest articulate expression of these.

The great Reformer's love of music, of poetry, it has often been remarked, is one of the most significant features in his character. But indeed, if every great man, Napoleon himself, is intrinsically a poet, an idealist, with more or less completeness of utterance, which of all our great men, in these modern ages, had such an endowment in that kind as Luther? He it was, emphatically, who stood based on the Spiritual World of man, and only by the footing and mi-

1 FRASER'S MAGAZINE, No. 12.

2 For example: *Luthers Geistliche Lieder, nebst dessen Gedanken über die Musica* (Berlin, 1817); *Die Lieder Luthers gesammelt von Kosegarten und Rambach, &c.*

raculous power he had obtained there, could work such changes in the Material World. As a participant and dispenser of divine influences, he shows himself among human affairs; a true connecting medium and visible Messenger between Heaven and Earth; a man, therefore, not only permitted to enter the sphere of Poetry, but to dwell in the purest centre thereof: perhaps the most inspired of all Teachers since the first Apostles of his faith; and thus not a Poet only, but a Prophet and god-ordained Priest, which is the highest form of that dignity, and of all dignity.

Unhappily, or happily, Luther's poetic feeling did not so much learn to express itself in fit Words that take captive every ear, as in fit Actions, wherein truly, under still more impressive manifestation, the spirit of spheral melody resides, and still audibly addresses us. In his written Poems we find little, save that strength of one 'whose words,' it has been said, 'were half battles;' little of that still harmony and blending softness of union, which is the last perfection of strength; less of it than even his conduct often manifested. With Words he had not learned to make pure music; it was by Deeds of love or heroic valour that he spoke freely; in tones, only through his Flute, amid tears, could the sigh of that strong soul find utterance.

Nevertheless, though in imperfect articulation, the same voice, if we will listen well, is to be heard also in his writings, in his Poems. The following, for example, jars upon our ears: yet there is something in it like the sound of Alpine avalanches, or the first murmur of earthquakes; in the very vastness of which dissonance a higher unison is revealed to us. Luther wrote this Song in a time of blackest threatenings, which however could in nowise become a time of despair. In those tones, rugged, broken as they are, do we not recognise the accent of that summoned man (summoned not by Charles the Fifth, but by God Almighty also), who answered his friends' warning not to enter Worms, in this wise: "Were there as many devils in Worms as there are roof-tiles, I would on;" — of him who, alone in that assemblage, before all emperors and principalities and powers, spoke forth these final and forever memorable words: "It is neither safe nor prudent to do aught against conscience. Here stand I, I cannot otherwise. God assist me. Amen!"[1] It is evident enough that to this man all Pope's Conclaves, and Imperial Diets, and hosts and nations, were but weak; weak as the forest, with all its strong *trees*, may be to the smallest spark of electric *fire*.

EINE FESTE BURG IST UNSER GOTT.

Eine feste Burg ist unser Gott,
Ein gutes Wehr und Waffen;
Er hilft uns frey aus aller Noth,
Die uns jetzt hat betroffen.
Der alte böse Feind,
Mit Ernst ers jetzt meint;
Gross Macht und viel List
Sein Grausam' Rüstzeuch ist,
Auf Erd'n ist nicht seins Gleichen.

Mit unsrer Macht ist Nichts gethan,
Wir sind gar bald verloren:
Es streit't für uns der rechte Mann,
Den Gott selbst hat erkoren.
Fragst du wer er ist?
Er heisst Jesus Christ,
Der Herre Zebaoth,
Und ist kein ander Gott,
Das Feld muss er behalten.

Und wenn die Welt voll Teufel wär,
Und wollt'n uns gar verschlingen,
So fürchten wir uns nicht so sehr,
Es soll uns doch gelingen.
Der Fürste dieser Welt,
Wie sauer er sich stellt,
Thut er uns doch Nichts;
Das macht er ist gerichtt,
Ein Wörtlein kann ihn fällen.

[1] 'Till such time as, either by proofs from Holy Scripture, or by fair 'reason or argument, I have been confuted and convicted, I cannot and 'will not recant, *weil weder sicher noch gerathen ist, etwas wider Gewissen 'zu thun. Hier stehe ich, ich kann nicht anders. Gott helfe mir. Amen!'*

Das Wort sie sollen lassen stahn,
Und keinen Dank dazu haben;
Er ist bey uns wohl auf dem Plan
Mit seinem Geist und Gaben.
Nehmen sie uns den Leib,
Gut', Ehr', Kind und Weib,
Lass fahren dahin.
Sie haben's kein Gewinn,
Das Reich Gottes muss uns bleiben.

A safe stronghold our God is still,
A trusty shield and weapon;
He'll help us clear from all the ill
That hath us now o'ertaken.
The ancient Prince of Hell
Hath risen with purpose fell;
Strong mail of Craft and Power
He weareth in this hour,
On Earth is not his fellow.

With force of arms we nothing can,
Full soon were we down-ridden;
But for us fights the proper Man,
Whom God himself hath bidden.
Ask ye, Who is this same?
Christ Jesus is his name,
The Lord Zebaoth's Son,
He and no other one
Shall conquer in the battle.

And were this world all Devils o'er,
And watching to devour us,
We lay it not to heart so sore,
Not they can overpower us.
And let the Prince of Ill
Look grim as e'er he will,
He harms us not a whit;
For why? His doom is writ:
A word shall quickly slay him.

God's Word, for all their craft and force,
One moment will not linger,
But spite of Hell, shall have its course,
'Tis written by his finger.
And though they take our life,
Goods, honour, children, wife,
Yet is their profit small;
These things shall vanish all,
The City of God remaineth.

SCHILLER.[1]

[1831.]

To the student of German Literature, or of Literature in general, these Volumes, purporting to lay open the private intercourse of two men eminent beyond all others of their time in that department, will doubtless be a welcome appearance. Neither Schiller nor Goethe has ever, that we have hitherto seen, written worthlessly on any subject; and the writings here offered us are confidential Letters, relating moreover to a highly important period in the spiritual history, not only of the parties themselves, but of their country likewise; full of topics, high and low, on which far meaner talents than theirs might prove interesting. We have heard and known so much of both these venerated persons; of their friendship, and true coöperation in so many noble endeavours, the fruit of which has long been plain to every one: and now are we to look into the secret constitution and conditions of all this; to trace the public result, which is Ideal, down to its roots in the Common; how Poets may live and work poetically among the Prose things of this world, and *Fausts* and *Tells* be written on rag-paper and with goose-quills, like mere Minerva Novels, and Songs by a Person of Quality! Virtuosos have glass bee-hives, which they curiously peep into; but here truly were a far stranger sort of honey-making.

[1] FRASER'S MAGAZINE, No. 14. — *Briefwechsel zwischen Schiller und Goethe, in den Jahren* 1794 *bis* 1805 (Correspondence between Schiller and Goethe, in the years 1794–1805). 1st–3d Volumes (1794–1797). Stuttgart and Tübingen, 1828–9.

Nay, apart from virtuosoship, or any technical object, what a hold have such things on our universal curiosity as men! If the sympathy we feel with one another is infinite, or nearly so, — in proof of which, do but consider the boundless ocean of Gossip (imperfect, undistilled Biography) which is emitted and imbibed by the human species daily; — if every secret-history, every closed-doors conversation, how trivial soever, has an interest for us; then might the conversation of a Schiller with a Goethe, so rarely do Schillers meet with Goethes among us, tempt Honesty itself into eaves-dropping.

Unhappily the conversation flits away forever with the hour that witnessed it; and the Letter and Answer, frank, lively, genial as they may be, are only a poor emblem and epitome of it. The living dramatic movement is gone; nothing but the cold historical net-product remains for us. It is true, in every confidential Letter, the writer will, in some measure, more or less directly depict himself: but nowhere is Painting, by pen or pencil, so inadequate as in delineating Spiritual Nature. The Pyramid can be measured in geometric feet, and the draughtsman represents it, with all its environment, on canvas, accurately to the eye; nay, Mont-Blanc is embossed in coloured stucco; and we have his very type, and miniature fac-simile, in our museums. But for great Men, let him who would know such, pray that he may see them daily face to face: for in the dim distance, and by the eye of the imagination, our vision, do what we may, will be too imperfect. How pale, thin, ineffectual do the great figures we would fain summon from History rise before us! Scarcely as palpable men does our utmost effort body them forth; oftenest only like Ossian's ghosts, in hazy twilight, with 'stars dim twinkling through their forms.' Our Socrates, our Luther, after all that we have talked and argued of them, are to most of us quite invisible; the Sage of Athens, the Monk of Eisleben; not Persons, but Titles. Yet such men, far more than any Alps or Coliseums are the true world-wonders, which it concerns us to behold clearly, and imprint forever on our remembrance. Great men are the Fire-pillars in this dark pilgrimage of mankind; they stand as heavenly Signs, everliving witnesses of what has been, prophetic tokens of what may still be, the revealed, embodied Possibilities of human nature; which greatness he who has never seen, or rationally conceived of, and with his whole heart passionately loved and reverenced, is himself forever doomed to be little. How many weighty reasons, how many innocent allurements attract our curiosity to such men! We would know them, see them visibly, even as we know and see our like: no hint, no notice that concerns them is superfluous or too small for us. Were Gulliver's Conjuror but here, to recall and sensibly bring back the brave Past, that we might look into it, and scrutinise it at will! But alas, in Nature there is no such conjuring: the great spirits that have gone before us can survive only as disembodied Voices; their form and distinctive aspect, outward and even in many respects inward, all whereby they were known as living, breathing men, has passed into another sphere; from which only History, in scanty memorials, can evoke some faint resemblance of it. The more precious, in spite of all imperfections, is such History, are such memorials, that still in some degree preserve what had otherwise been lost without recovery.

For the rest, as to the maxim, often enough inculcated on us, that close inspection will abate our admiration, that only the obscure can be sublime, let us put small faith in it. Here, as in other provinces, it is not knowledge, but a little knowledge, that puffeth up, and for wonder at the thing known substitutes mere wonder at the knower thereof: to a sciolist, the starry heavens revolving in dead mechanism may be less than a Jacob's vision; but to the Newton they are more; for the same God still dwells enthroned there, and holy Influences, like Angels, still ascend and descend; and this clearer vision of a little but renders the remaining mystery the deeper and more divine. So likewise is it with true spiritual greatness. On the whole, that theory of 'no man being a hero to his valet,' carries us but a little way into the real nature of the case. With a superficial meaning which is plain enough, it essentially holds good only of such heroes as are false, or else of such valets as are too genuine, as are shoulder-knotted and brass-lackered in soul as well as in body: of other sorts it does not hold. Milton was still a hero to the good Elwood. But we dwell not on that mean doctrine, which, true or false, may be left to itself the more safely, as in practice it is of little or no immediate import. For were it never so true, yet unless we preferred huge bugbears to small realities, our practical course were still the same: to inquire, to investigate by all methods, till we saw clearly.

What worth in this biographical point of view the *Correspondence of Schiller and Goethe* may have, we shall not attempt determining here; the rather as only a portion of the Work, and to judge by the space of time included in it, only a small portion, is yet before us. Nay perhaps its full worth will not become apparent till a future age, when the persons and concerns it treats of shall have assumed their proper relative magnitude, and stand disencumbered, and forever separated from contemporary trivialities, which, for the present, with their hollow transient bulk, so mar our estimate. Two centuries ago, Leicester and Essex might be the wonders of England; their Kenilworth Festivities and Cadiz Expeditions seemed the great occurrences of that day; — but what would we now give, were these all forgotten, and some 'Correspondence between Shakspeare and Ben Jonson' suddenly brought to light!

One valuable quality these Letters of Schiller and Goethe everywhere exhibit, that of truth: whatever we do learn from them, whether in the shape of fact or of opinion, may be relied on as genuine. There is a tone of entire sincerity in that style: a constant natural courtesy nowhere obstructs the right freedom of word or thought; indeed, no ends but honourable ones, and generally of a mutual interest, are before either party; thus neither needs to veil, still less to mask himself from the other; the two self-portraits, so far as they are filled up, may be looked upon as real likenesses. Perhaps, to most readers, some larger intermixture of what we should call domestic interest, of ordinary human concerns, and the hopes, fears and other feelings these excite, would have improved the Work; which as it is, not indeed without pleasant exceptions, turns mostly on compositions, and publications, and philosophies, and other such high matters. This, we believe, is a rare fault in modern Correspondences; where generally the opposite fault is complained of, and except mere temporalities, good and evil hap of the corresponding parties, their state of purse, heart and nervous system, and the moods and humours these give rise to, — little stands recorded for us. It may be, too, that native readers will feel such a want less than foreigners do, whose curiosity in this instance is equally minute, and to whom so many details, familiar enough in the country itself, must be unknown. At all events, it is to be remembered that Schiller and Goethe are, in strict speech, Literary Men; for whom their social life is only as the dwelling-place and outward tabernacle of their spiritual life; which latter is the one thing needful; the other, except in subserviency to this, meriting no attention, or the least possible. Besides, as cultivated men, perhaps even by natural temper, they are not in the habit of yielding to violent emotions of any kind, still less of unfolding and depicting such, by letter, even to closest intimates; a turn of mind which, if it diminished the warmth of their epistolary intercourse, must have increased their private happiness, and so, by their friends, can hardly be regretted. (He who wears his heart on his sleeve, will often have to lament aloud that daws peck at it: he who does not, will spare himself such lamenting.) Of Rousseau Confessions, whatever value we assign that sort of ware, there is no vestige in this Correspondence.

Meanwhile, many cheerful, honest little domestic touches are given here and there; which we can accept gladly, with no worse censure than wishing that there had been more. But this Correspondence has another and more proper aspect, under which, if rightly considered, it possesses a far higher interest than most domestic delineations could have imparted. It shows us two high, creative, truly poetic minds, unweariedly cultivating themselves, unweariedly advancing from one measure of strength and clearness to another; whereby to such as travel, we say not on the same road, for this few can do, but in the same direction, as all should do, the richest psychological and practical lesson is laid out; from which men of every intellectual degree may learn something, and he that is of the highest degree will probably learn the most. What value lies in this lesson, moreover, may be expected to increase in an increasing ratio as the Correspondence proceeds, and a larger space, with broader differences of advancement, comes into view; especially as respects Schiller, the younger and more susceptive of the two; for whom, in particular, these eleven years may be said to comprise the most important era of his culture; indeed, the whole history of his progress therein, from the time when he first found the right path, and properly became progressive.

But to enter farther on the merits and special qualities of these Letters, which, on all hands, will be regarded as a publication of real value, both intrinsic and extrinsic, is not our task now. Of the frank, kind, mutually-respectful relation that manifests itself between the two Correspondents; of their several epistolary styles, and the worth of each, and whatever else characterises this Work as a series of biographical documents, or of philosophical views, we may at some future period have occasion to speak: certain detached speculations and indications will of themselves come before us in the course of our present undertaking. Meanwhile, to British readers, the chief object is not the Letters, but the Writers of them. Of Goethe the public already know something: of Schiller less is known, and our wish is to bring him into closer approximation with our readers.

Indeed, had we considered only his importance in German, or we may now say, in European Literature, Schiller might well have demanded an earlier notice in our Journal. As a man of true poetical and philosophical genius, who proved this high endowment both in his conduct, and by a long series of Writings which manifest it to all; nay, even as a man so eminently admired by his nation, while he lived, and whose fame, there and abroad, during the twenty-five years since his decease, has been constantly expanding and confirming itself, he appears with such claims as can belong only to a small number of men. If we have seemed negligent of Schiller, want of affection was nowise the cause. Our admiration for him is of old standing, and has not abated, as it ripened into calm loving estimation. But to English expositors of Foreign Literature, at this epoch, there will be many more pressing duties than that of expounding Schiller. To a considerable extent, Schiller may be said to expound himself. His greatness is of a simple kind; his manner of displaying it is, for most part, apprehensible to every one. Besides, of all German Writers, ranking in any such class as his, Klopstock scarcely excepted, he has the least nationality: his character indeed is German, if German mean true, earnest, nobly-humane; but his mode of thought, and mode of utterance, all but the mere vocables of it, are European. Accordingly, it is to be observed, no German Writer has had such acceptance with foreigners; has been so instantaneously admitted into favour, at least any favour which proved permanent. Among the French, for example, Schiller is almost naturalised; translated, commented upon, by men of whom Constant is one; even brought upon the stage, and by a large class of critics vehemently extolled there. Indeed, to the Romanticist class, in all countries, Schiller is naturally the pattern man and great master; as it were, a sort of ambassador and mediator, were mediation possible, between the

Old School and the New; pointing to his own Works, as to a glittering bridge, that will lead pleasantly from the Versailles gardening and artificial hydraulics of the one, into the true Ginnistan and Wonderland of the other. With ourselves too, who are troubled with no controversies on Romanticism and Classicism, — the Bowles controversy on Pope having long since evaporated without result, and all critical guild-brethren now working diligently, with one accord, in the calmer sphere of Vapidism, or even Nullism, — Schiller is no less universally esteemed by persons of any feeling for poetry. To readers of German, and these are increasing everywhere a hundred-fold, he is one of the earliest studies; and the dullest cannot study him without some perception of his beauties. For the Un-German, again, we have Translations in abundance and superabundance; through which, under whatever distortion, however shorn of his beams, some image of this poetical sun must force itself; and in susceptive hearts awaken love, and a desire for more immediate insight. So that now, we suppose, anywhere in England, a man who denied that Schiller was a Poet would himself be, from every side, declared a Prosaist, and thereby summarily enough put to silence.

All which being so, the weightiest part of our duty, that of preliminary pleading for Schiller, of asserting rank and excellence for him while a stranger, and to judges suspicious of counterfeits, is taken off our hands. The knowledge of his works is silently and rapidly proceeding; in the only way by which true knowledge can be attained, by loving study of them in many an inquiring, candid mind. Moreover, as remarked above, Schiller's works, generally speaking, require little commentary: for a man of such excellence, for a true Poet, we should say that his worth lies singularly open; nay, in great part of his writings, beyond such open, universally recognisable worth, there is no other to be sought.

Yet doubtless if he is a Poet, a genuine interpreter of the Invisible, Criticism will have a greater duty to discharge for him. Every Poet, be his outward lot what it may, finds himself born in the midst of Prose; he has to struggle from the littleness and obstruction of an Actual world, into the freedom and infinitude of an Ideal; and the history of such struggle, which is the history of his life, cannot be other than instructive. His is a high, laborious, unrequited, or only self-requited endeavour; which, however, by the law of his being, he is compelled to undertake, and must prevail in, or be permanently wretched; nay the more wretched, the nobler his gifts are. For it is the deep, inborn claim of his whole spiritual nature, and will not and must not go unanswered. His youthful unrest, that 'unrest of genius,' often so wayward in its character, is the dim anticipation of this; the mysterious, all-powerful mandate, as from Heaven, to prepare himself, to purify himself, for the vocation wherewith he is called. And yet how few can fulfil this mandate, how few earnestly give heed to it! Of the thousand jingling dilettanti, whose jingle dies with the hour which it harmlessly or hurtfully amused, we say nothing here: to these, as to the mass of men, such calls for spiritual perfection speak only in whispers, drowned without difficulty in the din and dissipation of the world. But even for the Byron, for the Burns, whose ear is quick for celestial messages, in whom 'speaks the prophesying spirit,' in awful prophetic voice, how hard is it to 'take no counsel with flesh and blood,' and instead of living and writing for the Day that passes over them, live and write for the Eternity that rests and abides over them; instead of living commodiously in the Half, the Reputable, the Plausible, 'to live resolutely in the Whole, the Good, the True!'[1] Such Halfness, such halting between two opinions, such painful, altogether fruitless negotiating between Truth and Falsehood, has been the besetting sin, and chief misery, of mankind in all ages. Nay in our age, it has christened itself Moderation, a prudent taking of the middle course; and passes current among us as a virtue. How virtuous it is, the withered con-

[1] *Im Ganzen, Guten, Wahren resolut zu leben.* Goethe.

dition of many a once ingenuous nature that has lived by this method; the broken or breaking heart of many a noble nature that could not live by it, — speak aloud, did we but listen.

And now when, from among so many shipwrecks and misventures, one goodly vessel comes to land, we joyfully survey its rich cargo, and hasten to question the crew on the fortunes of their voyage. Among the crowd of uncultivated and miscultivated writers, the high, pure Schiller stands before us with a like distinction. We ask: How was this man successful? From what peculiar point of view did he attempt penetrating the secret of spiritual Nature? From what region of Prose rise into Poetry? Under what outward accidents; with what inward faculties; by what methods; with what result?

For any thorough or final answer to such questions, it is evident enough, neither our own means, nor the present situation of our readers in regard to this matter, are in any measure adequate. Nevertheless, the imperfect beginning must be made before the perfect result can appear. Some slight far-off glance over the character of the man, as he looked and lived, in Action and in Poetry, will not, perhaps, be unacceptable from us: for such as know little of Schiller, it may be an opening of the way to better knowledge; for such as are already familiar with him, it may be a stating in words of what they themselves have often thought, and welcome, therefore, as the confirming testimony of a second witness.

Of Schiller's personal history there are accounts in various accessible publications; so that, we suppose, no formal Narrative of his Life, which may now be considered generally known, is necessary here. Such as are curious on the subject, and still uninformed, may find some satisfaction in the *Life of Schiller* (London, 1824); in the *Vie de Schiller*, prefixed to the French Translation of his Dramatic Works; in the *Account of Schiller*, prefixed to the English Translation of his Thirty-Years War (Edinburgh, 1828); and, doubtless, in many other Essays, known to us only by title. Nay in the survey we propose to make of his character, practical as well as speculative, the main facts of his outward history will of themselves come to light.

Schiller's Life is emphatically a literary one; that of a man existing only for Contemplation; guided forward by the pursuit of ideal things, and seeking and finding his true welfare therein. A singular simplicity characterises it, a remoteness from whatever is called business; an aversion to the tumults of business, an indifference to its prizes, grows with him from year to year. He holds no office; scarcely for a little while an University Professorship; he covets no promotion; has no stock of money; and shows no discontent with these arrangements. Nay when permanent sickness, continual pain of body, is added to them, he still seems happy: these last fifteen years of his life are, spiritually considered, the clearest and most productive of all. We might say, there is something priest-like in that Life of his: under quite another colour and environment, yet with aims differing in form rather than in essence, it has a priest-like stillness, a priest-like purity; nay, if for the Catholic Faith we substitute the Ideal of Art, and for Convent Rules, Moral or Æsthetic Laws, it has even something of a monastic character. By the three monastic vows he was not bound: yet vows of as high and difficult a kind, both to do and to forbear, he had taken on him; and his happiness and whole business lay in observing them. Thus immured, not in cloisters of stone and mortar, yet in cloisters of the mind, which separate him as impassably from the vulgar, he works and meditates only on what we may call Divine things; his familiar talk, his very recreations, the whole actings and fancyings of his daily existence, tend thither.

As in the life of a Holy Man too, so in that of Schiller, there is but one great epoch: that of taking on him these

Literary Vows; of finally extricating himself from the distractions of the world, and consecrating his whole future days to Wisdom. What lies before this epoch, and what lies after it, have two altogether different characters. The former is worldly, and occupied with worldly vicissitudes; the latter is spiritual, of calm tenour; marked to himself only by his growth in inward clearness, to the world only by the peaceable fruits of this. It is to the first of these periods that we shall here chiefly direct ourselves.

In his parentage, and the circumstances of his earlier years, we may reckon him fortunate. His parents, indeed, are not rich, nor even otherwise independent: yet neither are they meanly poor; and warm affection, a true honest character, ripened in both into religion, not without an openness for knowledge, and even considerable intellectual culture, makes amends for every defect. The Boy, too, is himself of a character in which, to the observant, lies the richest promise. A modest, still nature, apt for all instruction in heart or head; flashes of liveliness, of impetuosity, from time to time breaking through. That little anecdote of the Thunder-storm is so graceful in its littleness, that one cannot but hope it may be authentic.

'Once, it is said, during a tremendous thunder-storm, his father missed him in the young group within doors; none of the sisters could tell what was become of Fritz, and the old man grew at length so anxious that he was forced to go out in quest of him. Fritz was scarcely past the age of infancy, and knew not the dangers of a scene so awful. His father found him at last, in a solitary place of the neighbourhood, perched on the branch of a tree, gazing at the tempestuous face of the sky, and watching the flashes as in succession they spread their lurid gleam over it. To the reprimands of his parent, the whimpering truant pleaded in extenuation, "that the Lightning was so beautiful, and he wished to see where it was coming from!"'

In his village-school he reads the Classics with diligence, without relish; at home, with far deeper feelings, the Bible; and already his young heart is caught with that mystic grandeur of the Hebrew Prophets. His devout nature, moulded by the pious habits of his parents, inclines him to be a clergyman: a clergyman, indeed, he proved; only the Church he ministered in was the Catholic, a far more Catholic than that false Romish one. But already in his ninth year, not without rapturous amazement, and a lasting remembrance, he had seen the 'splendours of the Ludwigsburg Theatre;' and so, unconsciously, cast a glimpse into that world, where, by accident or natural preference, his own genius was one day to work out its noblest triumphs.

Before the end of his boyhood, however, begins a far harsher era for Schiller; wherein, under quite other nurture, other faculties were to be developed in him. He must enter on a scene of oppression, distortion, isolation; under which, for the present, the fairest years of his existence are painfully crushed down. But this too has its wholesome influences on him; for there is in genius that alchemy which converts all metals into gold; which from suffering educes strength, from error clearer wisdom, from all things good.

'The Duke of Würtemberg had lately founded a free seminary for certain branches of professional education: it was first set up at Solitude, one of his country residences; and had now been transferred to Stuttgard, where, under an improved form, and with the name of *Karls-schule,* we believe it still exists. The Duke proposed to give the sons of his military officers a preferable claim to the benefits of this institution; and having formed a good opinion both of Schiller and his father, he invited the former to profit by this opportunity. The offer occasioned great embarrassment: the young man and his parents were alike determined in favour of the Church, a project with which this new one was inconsistent. Their embarrassment was but increased, when the Duke on learning the nature of their scruples, desired them to think well before they decided. It was out of fear, and with reluctance that his proposal was accepted. Schiller enrolled himself in 1773; and turned, with a heavy heart, from freedom and cherished hopes, to Greek, and seclusion, and Law.

'His anticipations proved to be but too just: the six years which he spent in this Establishment were the most harassing and comfortless of his life. The Stuttgard system of education seems to have been formed on the principle, not of cherishing and correcting nature, but of rooting it out, and supplying its place by something better. The process of teaching and living was conducted with the stiff formality of military drilling; everything went on by statute and ordinance; there was no scope for the exercise of free-will, no allowance for the varieties of original structure. A scholar might possess what instincts or capacities he pleased; the "regulations of the school" took no account of this; he must fit himself into the common mould, which, like the old Giant's bed, stood there, appointed by superior authority, to be filled alike by the great and the little. The same strict and narrow course of reading and composition was marked out for each beforehand, and it was by stealth if he read or wrote anything beside. Their domestic economy was regulated in the same spirit as their preceptorial: it consisted of the same sedulous exclusion of all that could border on pleasure, or give any exercise to choice. The pupils were kept apart from the conversation or sight of any person but their teachers; none ever got beyond the precincts of despotism to snatch even a fearful joy; their very amusements proceeded by the word of command.

'How grievous all this must have been it is easy to conceive. To Schiller it was more grievous than to any other. Of an ardent and impetuous yet delicate nature, whilst his discontentment devoured him internally, he was too modest to give it the relief of utterance by deeds or words. Locked up within himself, he suffered deeply, but without complaining. Some of his Letters written during this period have been preserved: they exhibit the ineffectual struggles of a fervid and busy mind, veiling its many chagrins under a certain dreary patience, which only shows them more painfully. He pored over his lexicons, and grammars, and insipid tasks, with an artificial composure; but his spirit pined within him like a captive's, when he looked forth into the cheerful world, or recollected the affection of parents, the hopes and frolicsome enjoyments of past years.'

Youth is to all the glad season of life; but often only by what it hopes, not by what it attains, or what it escapes. In these sufferings of Schiller's, many a one may say, there is nothing unexampled: could not the history of every Eton Scholar, of every poor Midshipman, with his rudely-broken domestic ties, his privations, persecutions and cheerless solitude of heart, equal or outdo them? In respect of these its palpable hardships perhaps it might; and be still very miserable. But the hardship which presses heaviest on Schiller lies deeper than all these; out of which the natural fire of almost any young heart will, sooner or later, rise victorious. His worst oppression is an oppression of the moral sense; a fettering not of the Desires only, but of the pure reasonable Will: for besides all outward sufferings, his mind is driven from its true aim, dimly yet invincibly felt to be the true one; and turned, by sheer violence, into one which it feels to be false. Not in Law, with its profits and dignities; not in Medicine, which he willingly, yet still hopelessly exchanges for Law; not in the routine of any marketable occupation, how gainful or honoured soever, can his soul find content and a home: only in some far purer and higher region of Activity; for which he has yet no name; which he once fancied to be the Church, which at length he discovers to be Poetry. Nor is this any transient boyish wilfulness, but a deep-seated, earnest, ineradicable longing, the dim purpose of his whole inner man. Nevertheless as a transient boyish wilfulness his teachers must regard it, and deal with it; and not till after the fiercest contest, and a clear victory, will its true nature be recognised. Herein lay the sharpest sting of Schiller's ill fortune; his whole mind is wrenched asunder; he has no rallying point in his misery; he is suffering and toiling for a wrong object. 'A singular miscal-'culation of Nature,' he says, long afterwards, 'had combined 'my poetical tendencies with the place of my birth. Any 'disposition to Poetry did violence to the laws of the Insti-'tution where I was educated, and contradicted the plan of 'its founder. For eight years, my enthusiasm struggled 'with military discipline; but the passion for Poetry is 'vehement and fiery as a first love. What discipline was 'meant to extinguish, it blew into a flame. To escape from 'arrangements that tortured me, my heart sought refuge in 'the world of ideas, when as yet I was unacquainted with 'the world of realities, from which iron bars excluded me.'

Doubtless Schiller's own prudence had already taught him

that in order to live poetically, it was first requisite to live; that he should and must, as himself expresses it, 'forsake the 'balmy climate of Pindus for the Greenland of a barren and 'dreary science of terms.' But the dull work of this Greenland once accomplished, he might rationally hope that his task was done; that the 'leisure gained by superior diligence' would be his own, for Poetry, or whatever else he pleased. Truly, it was 'intolerable and degrading to be hemmed-in 'still farther by the caprices of severe and formal peda-'gogues.' No wonder that Schiller 'brooded gloomily' over his situation. But what was to be done? 'Many plans he 'formed for deliverance: sometimes he would escape in 'secret to catch a glimpse of the free and busy world, to 'him forbidden: sometimes he laid schemes for utterly aban-'doning a place which he abhorred, and trusting to fortune 'for the rest.' But he is young, inexperienced, unprovided; without help or counsel: there is nothing to be done but endure.

'Under such corroding and continual vexations,' says his Biographer, 'an ordinary spirit would have sunk at length; would have gradually given up its loftier aspirations, and sought refuge in vicious indulgence, or at best have sullenly harnessed itself into the yoke, and plodded through existence; weary, discontented and broken, ever casting back a hankering look on the dreams of his youth, and ever without power to realise them. But Schiller was no ordinary character, and did not act like one. Beneath a cold and simple exterior, dignified with no artificial attractions, and marred in its native amiableness by the incessant obstruction, the isolation and painful destitutions under which he lived, there was concealed a burning energy of soul, which no obstruction could extinguish. The hard circumstances of his fortune had prevented the natural development of his mind; his faculties had been cramped and misdirected; but they had gathered strength by opposition and the habit of self-dependence which it encouraged. His thoughts, unguided by a teacher, had sounded into the depths of his own nature and the mysteries of his own fate; his feelings and passions, unshared by any other heart, had been driven back upon his own; where, like the volcanic fire that smoulders and fuses in secret, they accumulated till their force grew irresistible.

'Hitherto Schiller had passed for an unprofitable, a discontented and a disobedient Boy: but the time was now come when the gyves of school-discipline could no longer cripple and distort the giant might of his nature: he stood forth as a Man, and wrenched asunder his fetters with a force that was felt at the extremities of Europe. The publication of the *Robbers* forms an era not only in Schiller's history, but in the literature of the World; and there seems no doubt that, but for so mean a cause as the perverted discipline of the Stuttgard school, we had never seen this tragedy. Schiller commenced it in his nineteenth year; and the circumstances under which it was composed are to be traced in all its parts.

'Translations of the work soon appeared in almost all the languages of Europe,[1] and were read in almost all of them with a deep interest, compounded of admiration and aversion, according to the relative proportions of sensibility and judgment in the various minds, which contemplated the subject. In Germany, the enthusiasm which the *Robbers* excited was extreme. The young author had burst upon the world like a meteor; and surprise, for a time, suspended the power of cool and rational criticism. In the ferment produced by the universal discussion of this single topic, the poet was magnified above his natural dimensions, great as they were: and though the general sentence was loudly in his favour, yet he found detractors as well as praisers, and both equally beyond the limits of moderation.

'But the tragedy of the *Robbers* produced for its Author some consequences of a kind much more sensible than these. We have called it the signal of Schiller's deliverance from school-tyranny and military constraint; but its operation in this respect was not immediate. At first it seemed to involve him more deeply than before. He had finished the original sketch of it in 1778; but for fear of offence, he kept it secret till his medical studies were completed. These, in the mean time, he had pursued with sufficient assiduity to merit the usual honours. In 1780, he had, in consequence, obtained the post of Surgeon to the regiment *Augé*, in the Würtemberg army. This advancement enabled him to complete his project, — to print the *Robbers* at his own expense; not being able to find any bookseller that would undertake it. The nature of the work, and the universal interest it awakened, drew attention to the private circumstances of the Author, whom the *Robbers*, as well as other pieces of his writing that had found their way into the periodical publications of the time,

1 Our English translation, one of the washiest, was executed (we have been told) in Edinburgh by a 'Lord of Session,' otherwise not unknown in Literature; who went to work under deepest concealment, lest evil might befall him. The confidential Devil, now an Angel, who mysteriously carried him the proof-sheets, is our informant.

sufficiently showed to be no common man. Many grave persons were offended at the vehement sentiments expressed in the *Robbers;* and the unquestioned ability with which these extravagances were expressed but made the matter worse. To Schiller's superiors, above all, such things were inconceivable; he might perhaps be a very great genius, but was certainly a dangerous servant for His Highness the Grand Duke of Würtemberg. Officious people mingled themselves in the affair: nay the graziers of the Alps were brought to bear upon it. The Grisons magistrates, it appeared, had seen the book, and were mortally huffed at their people's being there spoken of, according to a Swabian adage, as *common highwaymen.*[1] They complained in the *Hamburg Correspondent;* and a sort of jackall, at Ludwigsburg, one Walter, whose name deserves to be thus kept in mind, volunteered to plead their cause before the Grand Duke.

'Informed of all these circumstances, the Grand Duke expressed his disapprobation of Schiller's poetical labours in the most unequivocal terms. Schiller was at length summoned before him; and it then turned out, that His Highness was not only dissatisfied with the moral or political errors of the work, but scandalised moreover at its want of literary merit. In this latter respect, he was kind enough to proffer his own services. But Schiller seems to have received the proposal with no sufficient gratitude; and the interview passed without advantage to either party. It terminated in the Duke's commanding Schiller to abide by medical subjects: or at least, to beware of writing any more poetry, without submitting it to *his* inspection.

* * * * *

'Various new mortifications awaited Schiller. It was in vain that he discharged the humble duties of his station with the most strict fidelity, and even, it is said, with superior skill: he was a suspected person, and his most innocent actions were misconstrued, his slightest faults were visited with the full measure of official severity. * * * His free spirit shrank at the prospect of wasting its strength in strife against the pitiful constraints, the minute and endless persecutions of men who knew him not, yet had his fortune in their hands: the

[1] The obnoxious passage has been carefully expunged from subsequent editions. It was in the third Scene of the second Act. Spiegelberg, discoursing with Razmann, observes, "An honest man you may form of windle-straws; but to make a rascal you must have grist: besides, there is a national genius in it, — a certain rascal-climate, so to speak." In the first Edition there was added, "*Go to the Grisons, for instance; that is what I call the Thief's Athens.*" The patriot who stood forth, on this occasion, for the honour of the Grisons, to deny this weighty charge, and denounce the crime of making it, was not Dogberry or Verges, but 'one of the noble family of Salis.'

idea of dungeons and jailors haunted and tortured his mind ; and the means of escaping them, the renunciation of poetry, the source of all his joy, if likewise of many woes, the radiant guiding-star of his turbid and obscure existence, seemed a sentence of death to all that was dignified, and delightful, and worth retaining, in his character. * * * With the natural feeling of a young author, he had ventured to go in secret, and witness the first representation of his Tragedy, at Manheim. His incognito did not conceal him ; he was put under arrest, during a week, for this offence : and as the punishment did not deter him from again transgressing in a similar manner, he learned that it was in contemplation to try more rigorous measures with him. Dark hints were given to him of some exemplary as well as imminent severity : and Dalberg's aid, the sole hope of averting it by quiet means, was distant and dubious. Schiller saw himself reduced to extremities. Beleaguered with present distresses, and the most horrible forebodings, on every side ; roused to the highest pitch of indignation, yet forced to keep silence and wear the face of patience, he could endure this maddening constraint no longer. He resolved to be free, at whatever risk ; to abandon advantages which he could not buy at such a price ; to quit his step-dame home, and go forth, though friendless and alone, to seek his fortune in the great market of life. Some foreign Duke or Prince was arriving at Stuttgard; and all the people were in movement, witnessing the spectacle of his entrance : Schiller seized this opportunity of retiring from the city, careless whither he went, so he got beyond the reach of turnkeys, and Grand Dukes, and commanding officers. It was in the month of October 1782, his twenty-third year.'[1]

Such were the circumstances under which Schiller rose to manhood. We see them permanently influence his character ; but there is also a strength in himself which on the whole triumphs over them. The kindly and the unkindly alike lead him towards the goal. In childhood, the most unheeded, but by far the most important era of existence, — as it were, the still Creation-days of the whole future man, — he had breathed the only wholesome atmosphere, a soft atmosphere of affection and joy: the invisible seeds which are one day to ripen into clear Devoutness, and all humane Virtue, are happily sown in him. Not till he has gathered force for resistance, does the time of contradiction, of being

[1] Life of Schiller, Part I.

'purified by suffering,' arrive. For this contradiction too we have to thank those Stuttgard Schoolmasters and their purblind Duke. Had the system they followed been a milder, more reasonable one, we should not indeed have altogether lost our Poet, for the Poetry lay in his inmost soul, and could not remain unuttered; but we might well have found him under a far inferior character: not dependent on himself and truth, but dependent on the world and its gifts; not standing on a native, everlasting basis, but on an accidental, transient one.

In Schiller himself, as manifested in these emergencies, we already trace the chief features which distinguish him through life. A tenderness, a sensitive delicacy, aggravated under that harsh treatment, issues in a certain shyness and reserve: which, as conjoined moreover with habits of internal and not of external activity, might in time have worked itself, had his natural temper been less warm and affectionate, into timorous self-seclusion, dissociality and even positive misanthropy. Nay generally viewed, there is much in Schiller at this epoch that to a careless observer might have passed for weakness; as indeed, for such observers, weakness and fineness of nature are easily confounded. One element of strength, however, and the root of all strength, he throughout evinces: he wills one thing, and knows what he wills. His mind has a purpose, and still better, a right purpose. He already loves true spiritual Beauty, with his whole heart and his whole soul; and for the attainment, for the pursuit of this, is prepared to make all sacrifices. As a dim instinct, under vague forms, this aim first appears; gains force with his force, clearness in the opposition it must conquer; and at length declares itself, with a peremptory emphasis which will admit of no contradiction.

As a mere piece of literary history, these passages of Schiller's life are not without interest: this is a 'persecution for conscience-sake,' such as has oftener befallen heresy in Religion than heresy in Literature; a blind struggle to extinguish, by physical violence, the inward celestial light of a human soul; and here in regard to Literature, as in regard to Religion it always is, an ineffectual struggle. Doubtless, as religious Inquisitors have often done, those secular Inquisitors meant honestly in persecuting; and since the matter went well in spite of them, their interference with it may be forgiven and forgotten. We have dwelt the longer on these proceedings of theirs, because they bring us to the grand crisis of Schiller's history, and for the first time show us his will decisively asserting itself, decisively pronouncing the law whereby his whole future life is to be governed. He himself says, he 'went empty away; empty in purse and hope.' Yet the mind that dwelt in him was still there with its gifts; and the task of his existence now lay undivided before him. He is henceforth a Literary Man; and need appear in no other character. 'All my connexions,' he could ere long say, 'are 'now dissolved. The public is now all to me; my study, my 'sovereign, my confidant. To the public alone I from this 'time belong; before this and no other tribunal will I place 'myself; this alone do I reverence and fear. Something 'majestic hovers before me, as I determine now to wear no 'other fetters but the sentence of the world, to appeal to no 'other throne but the soul of man.' [1]

In his subsequent life, with all varieties of outward fortune, we find a noble inward unity. That love of Literature, and that resolution to abide by it at all hazards, do not forsake him. He wanders through the world; looks at it under many phases; mingles in the joys of social life; is a husband, father; experiences all the common destinies of man; but the same 'radiant guiding-star' which, often obscured, had led him safe through the perplexities of his youth, now shines on him with unwavering light. In all relations and conditions, Schiller is blameless, amiable; he is even little tempted to err. That high purpose after spiritual perfection, which with him was a love of Poetry, and an unwearied

[1] Preface to the *Thalia*.

active love, is itself, when pure and supreme, the necessary parent of good conduct, as of noble feeling. With all men it should be pure and supreme, for in one or the other shape it is the true end of man's life. Neither in any man is it ever wholly obliterated; with the most, however, it remains a passive sentiment, an idle wish. And even with the small residue of men, in whom it attains some measure of activity, who would be Poets in act or word, how seldom is it the sincere and highest purpose, how seldom unmixed with vulgar ambition, and low, mere earthly aims, which distort or utterly pervert its manifestations! With Schiller, again, it was the one thing needful; the first duty, for which all other duties worked together, under which all other duties quietly prospered, as under their rightful sovereign. Worldly preferment, fame itself, he did not covet: yet of fame he reaps the most plenteous harvest; and of worldly goods what little he wanted is in the end made sure to him. His mild, honest character everywhere gains him friends: that upright, peaceful, simple life is honourable in the eyes of all; and they who know him the best love him the most.

Perhaps among all the circumstances of Schiller's literary life, there was none so important for him as his connexion with Goethe. To use our old figure, we might say, that if Schiller was a Priest, then was Goethe the Bishop from whom he first acquired clear spiritual light, by whose hands he was ordained to the priesthood. Their friendship has been much celebrated, and deserved to be so: it is a pure relation; unhappily too rare in Literature; where if a Swift and Pope can even found an imperious Duumvirate, on little more than mutually-tolerated pride, and part the spoils for some time without quarrelling, it is thought a credit. Seldom do men combine so steadily and warmly for such purposes, which when weighed in the economic balance are but gossamer. It appears also that preliminary difficulties stood in the way; prepossessions of some strength had to be conquered on both sides. For a number of years, the two, by accident or choice, never met, and their first interview scarcely promised any permanent approximation. 'On the whole,' says Schiller, 'this personal meeting has not at all dimin-'ished the idea, great as it was, which I had previously 'formed of Goethe; but I doubt whether we shall ever come 'into close communication with each other. Much that still 'interests me has already had its epoch with him. His 'whole nature is, from its very origin, otherwise constructed 'than mine; his world is not my world; our modes of con-'ceiving things appear to be essentially different. From 'such a combination no secure substantial intimacy can 'result.'

Nevertheless, in spite of far graver prejudices on the part of Goethe, — to say nothing of the poor jealousies which in another man so circumstanced would openly or secretly have been at work, — a secure substantial intimacy did result; manifesting itself by continual good offices, and interrupted only by death. If we regard the relative situation of the parties, and their conduct in this matter, we must recognise in both of them no little social virtue; at all events, a deep disinterested love of worth. In the case of Goethe, more especially, who, as the elder and everyway greater of the two, has little to expect in comparison with what he gives, this friendly union, had we space to explain its nature and progress, would give new proof that, as poor Jung Stilling also experienced, 'the man's heart, which few know, is 'as true and noble as his genius, which all know.' By Goethe, and this even before the date of their friendship, Schiller's outward interests had been essentially promoted: he was introduced, under that sanction, into the service of Weimar, to an academic office, to a pension; his whole way was made smooth for him. In spiritual matters, this help, or rather let us say coöperation, for it came not in the shape of help, but of reciprocal service, was of still more lasting consequence. By the side of his friend, Schiller rises into the highest regions of Art he ever reached; and in all worthy things is sure of sympathy, of one wise judgment amid a crowd of unwise ones, of one helpful hand amid many hostile. Thus outwardly and inwardly assisted and confirmed, he henceforth goes on his way with new stedfastness, turning neither to the right hand nor to the left; and while days are given him, devotes them wholly to his best duty. It is rare that one man can do so much for another, can permanently benefit another; so mournfully, in giving and receiving, as in most charitable affections and finer movements of our nature, are we all held-in by that paltry vanity, which, under reputable names, usurps, on both sides, a sovereignty it has no claim to. Nay many times, when our friend would honestly help us, and strives to do it, yet will he never bring himself to understand what we really need, and so to forward us on our own path; but insists more simply on our taking his path, and leaves us as incorrigible because we will not and cannot. Thus men are solitary among each other; no one will help his neighbour; each has even to assume a defensive attitude lest his neighbour hinder him!

Of Schiller's zealous, entire devotedness to Literature we have already spoken as of his crowning virtue, and the great source of his welfare. With what ardour he pursued this object, his whole life, from the earliest stage of it, had given proof: but the clearest proof, clearer even than that youthful self-exile, was reserved for his later years, when a lingering, incurable disease had laid on him its new and ever-galling burden. At no period of Schiller's history does the native nobleness of his character appear so decidedly, as now in this season of silent unwitnessed heroism, when the dark enemy dwelt within himself, unconquerable, yet ever, in all other struggles, to be kept at bay. We have medical evidence that during the last fifteen years of his life, not a moment could have been free of pain. Yet he utters no complaint. In this 'Correspondence with Goethe' we see him cheerful, laborious; scarcely speaking of his maladies, and then only historically, in the style of a third party, as it were, calculating what force and length of days might still remain at his disposal. Nay his highest poetical performances, we may say all that are truly poetical, belong to this era. If we recollect how many poor valetudinarians, Rousseaus, Cowpers and the like, men otherwise of fine endowments, dwindle under the influence of nervous disease, into pining wretchedness, some into madness itself; and then that Schiller, under the like influence, wrote some of his deepest speculations, and all his genuine dramas, from *Wallenstein* to *Wilhelm Tell*, we shall the better estimate his merit.

It has been said, that only in Religion, or something equivalent to Religion, can human nature support itself under such trials. But Schiller too had his Religion; was a Worshipper, nay, as we have often said, a Priest; and so in his earthly sufferings wanted not a heavenly stay. Without some such stay his life might well have been intolerable; stript of the Ideal, what remained for him in the Real was but a poor matter. Do we talk of his 'happiness?' Alas, what is the loftiest flight of genius, the finest frenzy that ever for moments united Heaven with Earth, to the perennial never-failing joys of a digestive-apparatus thoroughly eupeptic? Has not the turtle-eating man an eternal sunshine of the breast? Does not his Soul, — which, as in some Sclavonic dialects, means his Stomach, — sit forever at its ease, enwrapped in warm condiments, amid spicy odours; enjoying the past, the present and the future; and only awakening from its soft trance to the sober certainty of a still higher bliss each meal-time, — three, or even four visions of Heaven in the space of one solar day! While for the sick man of genius, 'whose world is of the mind, ideal, internal; when 'the mildew of lingering disease has struck that world, and 'begun to blacken and consume its beauty, what remains but 'despondency, and bitterness, and desolate sorrow felt and 'anticipated to the end?'

'Woe to him,' continues this Jeremiah, 'if his will likewise falter, if his resolution fail, and his spirit bend its neck to the yoke of this new enemy! Idleness and a disturbed imagination will gain the mastery of him, and let loose their thousand fiends to harass him, to torment him into madness. Alas, the bondage of Algiers is freedom compared with this of the sick man of genius, whose heart has fainted, and sunk beneath its load. His clay dwelling is changed into a gloomy prison; every nerve has become an avenue of disgust or anguish, and the soul sits within in her melancholy loneliness, a prey to the spectres of despair, or stupefied with excess of suffering; doomed, as it were, to a life-in-death, to a consciousness of agonised existence, without the consciousness of power which should accompany it. Happily death, or entire fatuity at length puts an end to such scenes of ignoble misery, which however, ignoble as they are, we ought to view with pity rather than contempt.'[1]

Yet on the whole, we say, it is a shame for the man of genius to complain. Has he not a 'light from Heaven' within him, to which the splendour of all earthly thrones and principalities is but darkness? And the head that wears such a crown grudges to lie uneasy? If that same 'light from Heaven,' shining through the falsest media, supported Syrian Simon through all weather on his sixty-feet Pillar, or the still more wonderful Eremite who walled himself, for life, up to the chin, in stone and mortar; how much more should it do, when shining direct, and pure from all intermixture? Let the modern Priest of Wisdom either suffer his small persecutions and inflictions, though sickness be of the number, in patience, or admit that ancient fanatics and bedlamites were truer worshippers than he.

A foolish controversy on this subject of Happiness now and then occupies some intellectual dinner-party; speculative gentlemen we have seen more than once almost forget their wine in arguing whether Happiness was the chief end of man. The most cry out, with Pope: 'Happiness, our being's end and aim;' and ask whether it is even conceivable that we should follow any other. How comes it, then, cry the Opposition, that the gross are happier than the re-

[1] Life of Schiller, p. 85.

fined; that even though we know them to be happier, we would not change places with them? Is it not written, Increase of knowledge is increase of sorrow? And yet also written, in characters still more ineffaceable, Pursue knowledge, attain clear vision, as the beginning of all good? Were your doctrine right, for what should we struggle with our whole might, for what pray to Heaven, if not that the 'malady of thought' might be utterly stifled within us, and a power of digestion and secretion, to which that of the tiger were trifling, be imparted instead thereof? Whereupon the others deny that thought is a malady; that increase of knowledge is increase of sorrow; that Aldermen have a sunnier life than Aristotle's, though the Stagyrite himself died exclaiming, *Fœde mundum intravi, anxius vixi, perturbatus morior*, &c.: and thus the argument circulates, and the bottles stand still.

So far as that Happiness-question concerns the symposia of speculative gentlemen, — the rather as it really is a good enduring hacklog whereon to chop logic, for those so minded, — we with great willingness leave it resting on its own bottom. But there are earnest natures for whom Truth is no plaything, but the staff of life; men whom the 'solid reality of things' will not carry forward; who, when the 'inward voice' is silent in them, are powerless, nor will the loud huzzaing of millions supply the want of it. To these men, seeking anxiously for guidance; feeling that did they once clearly see the right, they would follow it cheerfully to weal or to woe, comparatively careless which; to these men the question, what is the proper aim of man, has a deep and awful interest.

For the sake of such, it may be remarked that the origin this argument, like that of every other argument under the sun, lies in the confusion of language. If Happiness mean Welfare, there is no doubt but all men should and must pursue their Welfare, that is to say, pursue what is worthy of their pursuit. But if, on the other hand, Happiness mean, as for most men it does, 'agreeable sensations,' Enjoyment refined or not, then must we observe that there *is* a doubt; or rather that there is a certainty the other way. Strictly considered, this truth, that man has in him something higher than a Love of Pleasure, take Pleasure in what sense you will, has been the text of all true Teachers and Preachers, since the beginning of the world; and in one or another dialect, we may hope, will continue to be preached and taught till the world end. Neither is our own day without its assertors thereof: what, for example, does the astonished reader make of this little sentence from Schiller's *Æsthetic Letters?* It is on that old question, the 'improvement of the species;' which, however, is handled here in a very new manner:

> 'The first acquisitions, then, which men gathered in the Kingdom of Spirit were *Anxiety* and *Fear;* both, it is true, products of Reason, not of Sense; but of a Reason that mistook its object, and mistook its mode of application. Fruits of this same tree are all your Happiness-Systems (*Glückseligkeitssysteme*), whether they have for object the passing day, or the whole of life, or what renders them no whit more venerable, the whole of Eternity. A boundless duration of Being and Well-being (*Daseyns und Wohlseyns*) simply for Being and Well-being's sake, is an Ideal belonging to Appetite alone, and which only the struggle of mere Animalism (*Thierheit*), longing to be infinite, gives rise to. Thus without gaining anything for his Manhood, he, by this first effort of Reason, loses the happy limitation of the Animal; and has now only the unenviable superiority of missing the Present in an effort directed to the Distance, and whereby still, in the whole boundless Distance, nothing but the Present is sought for.'[1]

The *Æsthetic Letters,* in which this and many far deeper matters come into view, will one day deserve a long chapter to themselves. Meanwhile we cannot but remark, as a curious symptom of this time, that the pursuit of merely sensuous good, of personal Pleasure, in one shape or other, should be the universally admitted formula of man's whole duty. Once,

[1] Briefe über die æsthetische Erziehung des Menschen, b. 24.

Epicurus had his Zeno; and if the herd of mankind have at all times been the slaves of Desire, drudging anxiously for their mess of pottage, or filling themselves with swine's husks, — earnest natures were not wanting who, at least in theory, asserted for their kind a higher vocation than this; declaring as they could, that man's soul was no dead Balance for 'motives' to sway hither and thither, but a living, divine Soul, indefeasibly free, whose birthright it was to be the servant of Virtue, Goodness, God, and in such service to be blessed without fee or reward. Nowadays, however, matters are, on all hands, managed far more prudently. The choice of Hercules could not occasion much difficulty, in these times, to any young man of talent. On the one hand, — by a path which is steep, indeed, yet smoothed by much travelling, and kept in constant repair by many a moral Macadam, — smokes (in patent calefactors) a Dinner of innumerable courses; on the other, by a downward path, through avenues of very mixed character, frowns in the distance a grim Gallows, probably with 'improved drop.' Thus is Utility the only God of these days; and our honest Benthamites are but a small Provincial Synod of that boundless Communion. Without gift of prophecy we may predict, that the straggling bush-fire which is kept up here and there against that body of well-intentioned men, must one day become a universal battle; and the grand question, Mind *versus* Matter, be again under new forms judged of and decided. — But we wander too far from our task; to which, therefore, nothing doubtful of a prosperous issue in due time to that Utilitarian struggle, we hasten to return.

In forming for ourselves some picture of Schiller as a man, of what may be called his moral character, perhaps the very perfection of his manner of existence tends to diminish our estimate of its merits. What he aimed at he has attained in a singular degree. His life, at least from the period of manhood, is still, unruffled; of clear, even course. The completeness of the victory hides from us the magnitude of the struggle. On the whole, however, we may admit, that his character was not so much a great character as a holy one. We have often named him a Priest; and this title, with the quiet loftiness, the pure, secluded, only internal, yet still heavenly worth that should belong to it, perhaps best describes him. One high enthusiasm takes possession of his whole nature. Herein lies his strength, as well as the task he has to do; for this he lived, and we may say also he died for it. In his life we see not that the social affections played any deep part. As a son, husband, father, friend, he is ever kindly, honest, amiable; but rarely, if at all, do outward things stimulate him into what can be called passion. Of the wild loves and lamentations, and all the fierce ardour that distinguish, for instance, his Scottish contemporary Burns, there is scarcely any trace here. In fact, it was towards the Ideal, not towards the Actual, that Schiller's faith and hope was directed. His highest happiness lay not in outward honour, pleasure, social recreation, perhaps not even in friendly affection, such as the world could show it; but in the realm of Poetry, a city of the mind, where, for him, all that was true and noble had foundation. His habits, accordingly, though far from dissocial, were solitary; his chief business and chief pleasure lay in silent meditation.

'His intolerance of interruptions,' we are told, at an early period of his life, 'first put him on the plan of studying by night; an alluring, but pernicious practice, which began at Dresden, and was never afterwards given up. His recreations breathed a similar spirit: he loved to be much alone, and strongly moved. The banks of the Elbe were the favourite resort of his mornings: here, wandering in solitude, amid groves and lawns, and green and beautiful places, he abandoned his mind to delicious musings; or meditated on the cares and studies which had lately been employing, and were again soon to employ him. At times he might be seen floating on the river, in a gondola, feasting himself with the loveliness of earth and sky. He delighted most to be there when tempests were abroad; his unquiet spirit found a solace in the expression of its own unrest on the face of Nature; danger lent a charm to his situation; he felt in harmony with the scene, when the rack was sweeping stormfully across the heavens, and the forests were sounding in the breeze, and the river was rolling its chafed waters into wild eddying heaps.'

'During summer,' it is mentioned at a subsequent date, 'his place of study was in a garden, which he at length purchased, in the suburbs of Jena, not far from the Weselhofts' house, where, at that time, was the office of the *Allgemeine Litteraturzeitung*. Reckoning from the market-place of Jena, it lies on the south-west border of the town, between the Engelgatter and the Neuthor, in a hollow defile, through which a part of the Leutrabach flows round the city. On the top of the acclivity, from which there is a beautiful prospect into the valley of the Saal, and the fir mountains of the neighbouring forest, Schiller built himself a small house, with a single chamber. It was his favourite abode during hours of composition; a great part of the works he then wrote were written here. In winter he likewise dwelt apart from the tumult of men; — in the Griesbachs' house, on the outside of the city trench. On sitting down to his desk at night, he was wont to keep some strong coffee, or wine-chocolate, but more frequently a flask of old Rhenish or Champagne, standing by him, that he might from time to time repair the exhaustion of nature. Often the neighbours used to hear him earnestly declaiming in the silence of the night; and whoever had an opportunity of watching him on such occasions, — a thing very easy to be done, from the heights lying opposite his little garden-house, on the other side of the dale, — might see him now speaking aloud, and walking swiftly to and fro in his chamber, then suddenly throwing himself down into his chair, and writing; and drinking the while, sometimes more than once, from the glass standing near him. In winter he was to be found at his desk till four, or even five o'clock, in the morning; in summer till towards three. He then went to bed, from which he seldom rose till nine or ten.'

And again:

'At Weimar his present way of life was like his former one at Jena: his business was to study and compose; his recreations were in the circle of his family, where he could abandon himself to affections grave or trifling, and in frank cheerful intercourse with a few friends. Of the latter he had lately formed a social club, the meetings of which afforded him a regular and innocent amusement. He still loved solitary walks: in the Park at Weimar he might frequently be seen, wandering among the groves and remote avenues, with a note-book in his hand; now loitering slowly along, now standing still, now moving rapidly on: if any one appeared in sight, he would dart into another alley, that his dream might not be broken.

One of his favourite resorts, we are told, was the thickly-overshadowed, rocky path, which leads to the *Römische Haus,* a pleasure-house of the Duke's, built under the direction of Goethe. There he would often sit, in the gloom of the crags overgrown with cypresses and boxwood; shady thickets before him; not far from the murmur of a little brook, which there gushes in a smooth slaty channel, and where some verses of Goethe are cut upon a brown plate of stone, and fixed in the rock.'[1]

Such retirement, alike from the tumults and the pleasures of busy men, though it seems to diminish the merit of virtuous conduct in Schiller, is itself, as hinted above, the best proof of his virtue. No man is born without ambitious worldly desires; and for no man, especially for no man like Schiller, can the victory over them be too complete. His duty lay in that mode of life; and he had both discovered his duty, and addressed himself with his whole might to perform it. Nor was it in estrangement from men's interests that this seclusion originated; but rather in deeper concern for these. From many indications, we can perceive that to Schiller the task of the Poet appeared of far weightier import to mankind, in these times, than that of any other man whatever. It seemed to him that he was 'casting his bread upon the waters, and would find it after many days;' that when the noise of all conquerors, and demagogues, and political reformers had quite died away, some tone of heavenly wisdom that had dwelt even in him might still linger among men, and be acknowledged as heavenly and priceless, whether as his or not; whereby, though dead, he would yet speak, and his spirit would live throughout all generations, when the syllables that once formed his name had passed into forgetfulness forever. We are told, 'he was in the highest 'degree philanthropic and humane: and often said that he 'had no deeper wish than to know all men happy.' What was still more, he strove, in his public and private capacity, to do his utmost for that end. Honest, merciful, disinterested he is at all times found: and for the great duty laid on

[1] Life of Schiller.

him no man was ever more unweariedly ardent. It was his evening song and his morning prayer. He lived for it; and he died for it; 'sacrificing,' in the words of Goethe, 'his Life itself to this delineating of Life.'

In collision with his fellow-men, for with him as with others this also was a part of his relation to society, we find him no less noble than in friendly union with them. He mingles in none of the controversies of the time; or only like a god in the battles of men. In his conduct towards inferiors, even ill-intentioned and mean inferiors, there is everywhere a true, dignified, patrician spirit. Ever witnessing, and inwardly lamenting, the baseness of vulgar Literature in his day, he makes no clamorous attacks on it; alludes to it only from afar: as in Milton's writings, so in his, few of his contemporaries are named, or hinted at; it was not with men, but with things that he had a warfare. The *Review of Bürger*, so often descanted on, was doubtless highly afflicting to that down-broken, unhappy poet; but no hostility to Bürger, only love and veneration for the Art he professed, is to be discerned in it. With Bürger, or with any other mortal, he had no quarrel: the favour of the public, which he himself enjoyed in the highest measure, he esteemed at no high value. 'The Artist,' said he in a noble passage, already known to English readers, 'the Artist, it is 'true, is the son of his time; but pity for him if he is its 'pupil, or even its favourite! Let some beneficent divinity 'snatch him, when a suckling, from the breast of his mother, 'and nurse him with the milk of a better time; that he may 'ripen to his full stature beneath a distant Grecian sky. 'And having grown to manhood, let him return, a foreign 'shape, into his century; not, however, to delight it by his 'presence, but dreadful like the son of Agamemnon, to purify it!' On the whole, Schiller has no trace of vanity; scarcely of pride, even in its best sense, for the modest self-consciousness, which characterises genius, is with him rather implied than openly expressed. He has no hatred; no anger, save against Falsehood and Baseness, where it may be called a holy anger. Presumptuous triviality stood bared in his keen glance; but his look is the noble scowl that curls the lip of an Apollo, when, pierced with sun-arrows, the serpent expires before him. In a word, we can say of Schiller, what can be said only of few in any country or time: He was a high ministering servant at Truth's altar; and bore him worthily of the office he held. Let this, and that it was even in our age, be forever remembered to his praise.

Schiller's intellectual character has, as indeed is always the case, an accurate conformity with his moral one. Here too he is simple in his excellence; lofty rather than expansive or varied; pure, divinely ardent rather than great. A noble sensibility, the truest sympathy with Nature, in all forms, animates him; yet scarcely any creative gift altogether commensurate with this. If to his mind's eye all forms of Nature have a meaning and beauty, it is only under a few forms, chiefly of the severe or pathetic kind, that he can body forth this meaning, can represent as a Poet what as a Thinker he discerns and loves. We might say, his music is true spheral music; yet only with few tones, in simple modulation; no full choral harmony is to be heard in it. That Schiller, at least in his later years, attained a genuine poetic style, and dwelt, more or less, in the perennial regions of his Art, no one will deny: yet still his poetry shows rather like a partial than a universal gift; the laboured product of certain faculties rather than the spontaneous product of his whole nature. At the summit of the pyre, there is indeed white flame; but the materials are not all inflamed, perhaps not all ignited. Nay often it seems to us, as if poetry were, on the whole, not his essential gift; as if his genius were reflective in a still higher degree than creative; philosophical and oratorical rather than poetic. To the last, there is a stiffness in him, a certain infusibility. His genius is not an Æolian-harp for the common wind to play with, and make wild free melody; but a scientific harmonica, which being artfully touched will yield rich notes, though in limited measure. It may be, indeed, or rather it is highly probable, that of the gifts which lay in him only a small portion was unfolded: for we are to recollect that nothing came to him without a strenuous effort; and that he was called away at middle age. At all events, here as we find him, we should say, that of all his endowments the most perfect is understanding. Accurate, thorough insight is a quality we miss in none of his productions, whatever else may be wanting. He has an intellectual vision, clear, wide, piercing, methodical; a truly philosophic eye. Yet in regard to this also it is to be remarked, that the same simplicity, the same want of universality again displays itself. He looks aloft rather than around. It is in high, far-seeing philosophic views that he delights; in speculations on Art, on the dignity and destiny of Man, rather than on the common doings and interests of Men. Nevertheless these latter, mean as they seem, are boundless in significance; for every the poorest aspect of Nature, especially of living Nature, is a type and manifestation of the invisible spirit that works in Nature. There is properly no object trivial or insignificant: but every finite thing, could we look well, is as a window, through which solemn vistas are opened into Infinitude itself. But neither as a Poet nor as a Thinker, neither in delineation nor in exposition and discussion, does Schiller more than glance at such objects. For the most part, the Common is to him still the Common; or is idealised, rather as it were by mechanical art than by inspiration: not by deeper poetic or philosophic inspection, disclosing new beauty in its everyday features, but rather by deducting these, by casting them aside, and dwelling on what brighter features may remain in it. Herein Schiller, as indeed he himself was modestly aware, differs essentially from most great poets; and from none more than from his great contemporary, Goethe. Such intellectual preëminence as this, valuable though it be, is the easiest and the least valuable; a pre-eminence which, indeed, captivates the general eye, but may, after all, have little intrinsic grandeur. Less in rising into lofty abstractions lies the difficulty, than in seeing well and lovingly the complexities of what is at hand. He is wise who can instruct us and assist us in the business of daily virtuous living; he who trains us to see old truth under Academic formularies may be wise or not, as it chances; but we love to see Wisdom in unpretending forms, to recognise her royal features under week-day vesture. — There may be more true spiritual force in a Proverb than in a Philosophical System. A King in the midst of his body-guards, with all his trumpets, war-horses and gilt standard-bearers, will look great though he be little; but only some Roman Carus can give audience to satrap-ambassadors, while seated on the ground, with a woollen cap, and supping on boiled pease, like a common soldier.

In all Schiller's earlier writings, nay more or less in the whole of his writings, this aristocratic fastidiousness, this comparatively barren elevation, appears as a leading characteristic. In speculation he is either altogether abstract and systematic, or he dwells on old, conventionally-noble themes; never looking abroad, over the many-coloured stream of life, to elucidate and ennoble it; or only looking on it, so to speak, from a college window. The philosophy even of his Histories, for example, founds itself mainly on the perfectibility of man, the effect of constitutions, of religions, and other such high, purely scientific objects. In his Poetry we have a similar manifestation. The interest turns on prescribed, old-established matters; common love-mania, passionate greatness, enthusiasm for liberty and the like. This even in *Don Karlos;* a work of what may be called his transition-period, the turning-point between his earlier and his later period, where still we find Posa, the favourite hero, 'towering aloft, far-shining, clear, and also cold and vacant, as a sea-beacon.' In after years, Schiller himself saw well that the greatest lay not here. With unwearied effort he strove to lower and to widen his sphere; and not without success, as many of his Poems testify; for example, the *Lied der Glocke* (Song of the Bell), everyway a noble composition; and, in a still higher degree, the tragedy of *Wilhelm Tell*, the last, and, so far as spirit and style are concerned, the best of all his dramas.

Closely connected with this imperfection, both as cause and as consequence, is Schiller's singular want of Humour. Humour is properly the exponent of low things; that which first renders them poetical to the mind. The man of Humour sees common life, even mean life, under the new light of sportfulness and love; whatever has existence has a charm for him. Humour has justly been regarded as the finest perfection of poetic genius. He who wants it, be his other gifts what they may, has only half a mind; an eye for what is above him, not for what is about him or below him. Now, among all writers of any real poetic genius, we cannot recollect one who, in this respect, exhibits such total deficiency as Schiller. In his whole writings there is scarcely any vestige of it, scarcely any attempt that way. His nature was without Humour; and he had too true a feeling to adopt any counterfeit in its stead. Thus no drollery or caricature, still less any barren mockery, which, in the hundred cases are all that we find passing current as Humour, discover themselves in Schiller. His works are full of laboured earnestness; he is the gravest of all writers. Some of his critical discussions, especially in the *Æsthetische Briefe*, where he designates the ultimate height of a man's culture by the title *Spieltrieb* (literally, Sport-impulse), prove that he knew what Humour was, and how essential; as indeed, to his intellect, all forms of excellence, even the most alien to his own, were painted with a wonderful fidelity. Nevertheless, he himself attains not that height which he saw so clearly; to the last the *Spieltrieb* could be little more than a theory with him. With the single exception of *Wal-*

lenstein's Lager, where too, the Humour, if it be such, is not deep, his other attempts at mirth, fortunately very few, are of the heaviest. A rigid intensity, a serious enthusiastic ardour, majesty rather than grace, still more than lightness or sportfulness, characterises him. Wit he had, such wit as keen intellectual insight can give; yet even of this no large endowment. Perhaps he was too honest, too sincere, for the exercise of wit; too intent on the deeper relations of things to note their more transient collisions. Besides, he dealt in Affirmation, and not in Negation; in which last, it has been said, the material of wit chiefly lies.

These observations are to point out for us the special department and limits of Schiller's excellence; nowise to call in question its reality. Of his noble sense for Truth, both in speculation and in action; of his deep genial insight into Nature; and the living harmony in which he renders back what is highest and grandest in Nature, no reader of his works need be reminded. In whatever belongs to the pathetic, the heroic, the tragically elevating, Schiller is at home; a master; nay perhaps the greatest of all late poets. To the assiduous student, moreover, much else that lay in Schiller, but was never worked into shape, will become partially visible: deep, inexhaustible mines of thought and feeling; a whole world of gifts, the finest produce of which was but beginning to be realised. To his high-minded, unwearied efforts what was impossible, had length of years been granted him! There is a tone in some of his later pieces, which here and there breathes of the very highest region of Art. Nor are the natural or accidental defects we have noticed in his genius, even as it stands, such as to exclude him from the rank of great Poets. Poets whom the whole world reckons great have, more than once, exhibited the like. Milton, for example, shares most of them with him: like Schiller, he dwells, with full power, only in the high and earnest; in all other provinces exhibiting a certain inaptitude, an elephantine unpliancy: he too has little Humour; his coarse invective has in it contemptuous emphasis enough, yet scarcely any graceful sport. Indeed, on the positive side also, these two worthies are not without a resemblance. Under far other circumstances, with less massiveness and vehement strength of soul, there is in Schiller the same intensity; the same concentration, and towards similar objects, towards whatever is Sublime in Nature and in Art; which sublimities they both, each in his several way, worship with undivided heart. There is not in Schiller's nature the same rich complexity of rhythm as in Milton's, with its depths of linked sweetness; yet in Schiller too there is something of the same pure swelling force, some tone which, like Milton's, is deep, majestic, solemn.

It was as a Dramatic Author that Schiller distinguished himself to the world: yet often we feel as if chance rather than a natural tendency had led him into this province; as if his talent were essentially, in a certain style, lyrical, perhaps even epic, rather than dramatic. He dwelt within himself, and could not without effort, and then only within a certain range, body forth other forms of being. Nay much of what is called his poetry seems to us, as hinted above, oratorical rather than poetical; his first bias might have led him to be a speaker, rather than a singer. Nevertheless, a pure fire dwelt deep in his soul; and only in Poetry, of one or the other sort, could this find utterance. The rest of his nature, at the same time, has a certain prosaic rigour; so that not without strenuous and complex endeavours, long persisted in, could its poetic quality evolve itself. Quite pure, and as the all-sovereign element, it perhaps never did evolve itself; and among such complex endeavours, a small accident might influence large portions of its course.

Of Schiller's honest, undivided zeal in this great problem of self-cultivation, we have often spoken. What progress he had made, and in spite of what difficulties, appears if we contrast his earlier compositions with those of his later years. A few specimens of both sorts we shall here present. By this means too, such of our readers as are unacquainted with Schiller may gain some clearer notion of his poetic individuality than any description of ours could give. We shall take the *Robbers*, as his first performance, what he himself calls 'a monster produced by the unnatural union of Genius with Thraldom;' the fierce fuliginous fire that burns in that singular piece will still be discernible in separated passages. The following Scene, even in the yeasty vehicle of our common English version, has not wanted its admirers; it is the Second of the Third Act:

Country on the Danube.

THE ROBBERS.

(*Camped on a Height, under Trees: the Horses are grazing on the Hill farther down.*)

MOOR. I can no farther (*throws himself on the ground*). My limbs ache as if ground in pieces. My tongue parched as a potsherd. (SCHWEITZER *glides away unperceived.*) I would ask you to fetch me a handful of water from the stream; but ye all are wearied to death.

SCHWARZ. And the wine too is all down there, in our jacks.

MOOR. See, how lovely the harvest looks! The trees almost breaking under their load. The vine full of hope.

GRIMM. It is a plentiful year.

MOOR. Think'st thou? — And so *one* toil in the world will be repaid. *One?* — Yet overnight there may come a hailstorm, and shatter it all to ruin.

SCHWARZ. Possible enough. It might all be ruined two hours before reaping.

MOOR. Ay, so say I. It will all be ruined. Why should man prosper in what he has from the Ant; when he fails in what makes him like the Gods? — Or is this the true aim of his Destiny?

SCHWARZ. I know it not.

MOOR. Thou hast said well; and done still better, if thou never tri'dst to know it! — Brother, — I have looked at men, at their insect-anxieties and giant-projects — their godlike schemes and mouselike occupations, their wondrous race-running after Happiness; — he trusting to the gallop of his horse, — he to the nose of his ass, — a third to his own legs; this whirling lottery of life, in which so many a creature stakes his innocence, and — his Heaven! all trying for a prize, and — blanks are the whole drawing, — there was not a prize in the batch. It is a drama, Brother, to bring tears into thy eyes, if it tickle thy midriff to laughter.

SCHWARZ. How gloriously the sun is setting yonder!

MOOR (*lost in the view*). So dies a hero! To be worshipped!

GRIMM. It seems to move thee.

MOOR. When I was a lad — it was my darling thought to live so, to die so — (*with suppressed pain*). It was a lad's thought!

GRIMM. I hope so, truly.

MOOR (*draws his hat down on his face*). There was a time — Leave me alone, comrades.

SCHWARZ. Moor! Moor! What, Devil? — How his colour goes!

GRIMM. Ha! What ails him? Is he ill?

MOOR. There was a time when I could not sleep, if my evening prayer had been forgotten —

GRIMM. Art thou going crazed? Will Moor let such milksop fancies tutor him?

MOOR (*lays his head on* GRIMM'S *breast*). Brother! Brother!

GRIMM. Come! don't be a child, — I beg —

MOOR. Were I a child! — O, were I one!

GRIMM. Pooh! Pooh!

SCHWARZ. Cheer up. Look at the brave landscape, — the fine evening.

MOOR. Yes, Friends, this world is all so lovely.

SCHWARZ. There now — that's right.

MOOR. This Earth so glorious.

GRIMM. Right, — Right — that is it.

MOOR (*sinking back*). And I so hideous in this lovely world, and I a monster in this glorious Earth.

GRIMM. Out on it!

MOOR. My innocence! My innocence! — See, all things are gone forth to bask in the peaceful beam of the Spring, — why must I alone inhale the torments of Hell out of the joys of Heaven? — That all should be so happy, all so married together by the spirit of peace! — The whole world *one* family, its Father above — that Father not *mine!* — I alone the castaway, — I alone struck out from the company of the just; — for me no child to lisp my name, — never for me the languishing look of one whom I love, — never, never, the embracing of a bosom-friend (*dashing wildly back*). Encircled with murderers, — serpents hissing round me, — rushing down to the gulf of perdition on the eddying torrent of wickedness, — amid the flowers of the glad world, a howling Abaddon!

SCHWARZ (*to the rest*). How *is* this? I never saw him so.

MOOR (*with piercing sorrow*). O, that I might return into my mother's womb, — that I might be born a beggar! — No! I durst not pray,

O Heaven, to be as one of these day-labourers — Oh! I would toil till the blood ran down my temples to buy myself the pleasure of one noontide sleep, — the blessedness of a single tear.

Grimm (*to the rest*). Patience, a moment. The fit is passing.

Moor. There *was* a time too when I could weep — O ye days of peace, thou castle of my father, ye green lovely valleys! O all ye Elysian scenes of my childhood! will ye never come again, never with your balmy sighing cool my burning bosom? Mourn with me, Nature! They will never come again, never cool my burning bosom with their balmy sighing. They are gone! gone! and will not return!

Or take that still wilder monologue of Moor's on the old subject of suicide; in the midnight Forest, among the sleeping Robbers:

(*He lays aside the lute, and walks up and down in deep thought.*)

Who shall warrant me? —— 'Tis all so dark, — perplexed labyrinths, — no outlet, no loadstar — Were it but *over* with this last draught of breath — *Over*, like a sorry farce. — But whence this fierce *Hunger* after *Happiness?* whence this ideal of a *never-reached* perfection? this *continuation* of uncompleted plans? — if the pitiful pressure of this pitiful thing (*holding out a Pistol*) makes the wise man equal with the fool, the coward with the brave, the noble-minded with the caitiff? — There is so divine a harmony in all irrational Nature, why should there be this dissonance in rational? — No! No! there is somewhat beyond, for I have yet never known happiness.

Think ye, I will tremble? spirits of my murdered ones! I will not tremble (*trembling violently*). — Your feeble dying moan, — your black-choked faces, — your frightfully gaping wounds are but links of an unbreakable chain of Destiny; and depend at last on my childish sports, on the whims of my nurses and pedagogues, on the temperament of my father, on the blood of my mother — (*shaken with horror*). Why has my Perillus made of me a Brazen Bull to roast mankind in my glowing belly?

(*Gazing on the Pistol.*) Time and Eternity — linked together by a single moment! — Dread key, that shuttest behind me the prison of Life, and before me openest the dwelling of eternal Night — say — O say, — *whither*, — *whither* wilt thou lead me? Foreign, never circumnavigated Land! — See, manhood waxes faint under *this* image; the effort of the finite gives up, and Fancy, the capricious ape of Sense, juggles our credulity with strange shadows. — No! No! It becomes not a man to waver. Be what thou wilt, *nameless Yonder* — so this Me keep but true. Be what thou wilt, so I take *myself* along with me — ! — Outward things are but the colouring of the man — I am my Heaven and my Hell.

What if Thou shouldst send me *companionless* to some burnt and blasted circle of the Universe; which Thou hast banished from Thy sight; where the lone darkness and the motionless desert were my prospects — forever ? — I would people the silent wilderness with my fantasies ; I should have Eternity for leisure to unravel the perplexed image of the boundless woe. — Or wilt Thou lead me through still other births ; still other scenes of pain, from stage to stage — onwards to Annihilation ? The life-threads that are to be woven for me Yonder, cannot I tear them asunder, as I do these ? — Thou canst make me Nothing ; — but *this* freedom canst Thou not take from me. (*He loads the Pistol. Suddenly he stops.*) And shall I for terror of a miserable life — die ? — Shall I give wretchedness the victory over me ? — No, I will endure it (*he throws the Pistol away*). Let misery blunt itself on my pride ! I will go through with it.[1]

And now with these ferocities, and Sibylline frenzies, compare the placid strength of the following delineation, also of a stern character, from the *Maid of Orleans ;* where Talbot, the gray veteran, dark, unbelieving, indomitable, passes down, as he thinks, to the land of utter Nothingness, contemptuous even of the Fate that destroys him, and —

In death reposes on the soil of France,
Like hero on his unsurrender'd shield.

It is the sixth Scene of the third Act ; in the heat of a Battle :

(*The scene changes to an open Space encircled with Trees. During the music, Soldiers are seen hastily retreating across the Background.*)

TALBOT, *leaning on* FASTOLF, *and accompanied by Soldiers. Soon after*, LIONEL.

TALBOT.

Here, set me down beneath this tree, and you
Betake yourselves again to battle: quick!
I need no help to die.

FASTOLF.

O day of woe! [*Lionel enters.*
Look what a sight awaits you, Lionel!
Our leader wounded, dying!

[1] Act iv. Scene 6.

LIONEL.

God forbid!
O noble Talbot, this is not a time to die:
Yield not to Death; force faltering Nature
By your strength of soul, that life depart not!

TALBOT.

In vain! the day of Destiny is come
That levels with the dust our power in France.
In vain, in the fierce clash of desp'rate battle,
Have I risk'd my utmost to withstand it:
The bolt has smote and crush'd me, and I lie
To rise no more forever. Rheims is lost;
Make haste to rescue Paris.

LIONEL.

Paris is the Dauphin's:
A post arrived even now with th' evil news
It had surrender'd.

TALBOT (*tears away his bandages*).

Then flow out, ye life-streams;
This Sun is growing loathsome to me.

LIONEL.

Fastolf,
Convey him to the rear: this post can hold
Few instants more; yon coward knaves fall back,
Resistless comes the Witch, and havoc round her.

TALBOT.

Madness, thou conquerest, and I must yield:
Against Stupidity the Gods themselves are powerless.
High Reason, radiant Daughter of the head of God,
Wise Foundress of the system of the Universe,
Conductress of the Stars, who art thou, then,
If tied to th' tail o' th' wild horse, Superstition,
Thou must plunge, eyes open, vainly shrieking,
Sheer down with that drunk Beast to the Abyss?
Cursed who sets his life upon the great
And dignified; and with forecasting spirit
Lays out wise plans! The Fool-King's is this World.

LIONEL.

Oh! Death is near! Think of your God, and pray!

TALBOT.

Were we, as brave men, worsted by the brave,

'T had been but Fortune's common fickleness.
But that a paltry Farce should tread us down! —
Did toil and peril, all our earnest life,
Deserve no graver issue?

LIONEL (*grasps his hand*).
Talbot, farewell!
The meed of bitter tears I'll duly pay you,
When the fight is done, should I outlive it.
But now Fate calls me to the field, where yet
She wav'ring sits, and shakes her doubtful urn.
Farewell! we meet beyond the unseen shore.
Brief parting for long friendship! God be with you! [*Exit.*

TALBOT.
Soon it is over, and to th' Earth I render,
To th' everlasting Sun, the transient atoms
Which for pain and pleasure join'd to form me;
And of the mighty Talbot, whose renown
Once fill'd the world, remains naught but a handful
Of flitting dust. Thus man comes to his end;
And all our conquest in the fight of Life
Is knowledge that 'tis Nothing, and contempt
For hollow shows which once we chas'd and worship'd.

SCENE VII.

Enter CHARLES, BURGUNDY, DUNOIS, DU CHATEL, *and Soldiers.*

BURGUNDY.
The trench is stormed.

DUNOIS.
Bravo! The fight is ours.

CHARLES (*observing* TALBOT).
Ha! who is this that to the light of day
Is bidding his constrained and sad farewell?
His bearing speaks no common man: go, haste,
Assist him, if assistance yet avail.
[*Soldiers from the Dauphin's suite step forward.*

FASTOLF.
Back! Keep away! Approach not the Departing,
Him whom in life ye never wished too near.

BURGUNDY.
What do I see? Great Talbot in his blood!
[*He goes towards him.* TALBOT *gazes fixedly at him, and dies.*

FASTOLF.

Off, Burgundy! With th' aspect of a Traitor
Disturb not the last moment of a Hero.

The 'Power-words and Thunder-words,' as the Germans call them, so frequent in the *Robbers*,[1] are altogether wanting here; that volcanic fury has assuaged itself; instead of smoke and red lava, we have sunshine and a verdant world. For still more striking examples of this benignant change, we might refer to many scenes (too long for our present purposes) in *Wallenstein*, and indeed in all the Dramas which followed this, and most of all in *Wilhelm Tell*, which is the latest of them. The careful, and in general truly poetic structure of these works, considered as complete Poems, would exhibit it infinitely better; but for this object, larger limits than ours at present, and studious Readers as well as a Reviewer, were essential.

In his smaller Poems the like progress is visible. Schiller's works should all be dated, as we study them; but indeed the most, by internal evidence, date themselves.— Besides the *Lied der Glocke*, already mentioned, there are many lyrical pieces of high merit; particularly a whole series of *Ballads*, nearly every one of which is true and poetical. The *Ritter Toggenburg*, the *Dragon-fight*, the *Diver*, are all well known; the *Cranes of Ibycus* has in it, under this simple form, something Old-Grecian, an emphasis, a prophetic gloom which might seem borrowed even from the spirit of Æschylus. But on these, or any farther on the other poetical works of Schiller, we must not dilate at present. One little piece, which lies by us translated, we may give, as a specimen of his style in this lyrical province, and therewith terminate this part of our subject. It is entitled *Alpenlied* (Song of the Alps), and seems to require no commentary. Perhaps something of the clear, melodious, yet still somewhat metallic, tone of the original may penetrate even through our version.

[1] Thus, to take one often-cited instance, Moor's simple question, 'Whether there is any powder left?' receives this emphatic answer: 'Powder enough to blow the Earth into the Moon!'

SONG OF THE ALPS.

By the edge of the chasm is a slippery Track,
The torrent beneath, and the mist hanging o'er thee;
The cliffs of the mountain, huge, rugged and black,
Are frowning like giants before thee:
And, wouldst thou not waken the sleeping Lawine,
Walk silent and soft through the deadly ravine.

That Bridge, with its dizzying, perilous span
Aloft o'er the gulf and its flood suspended,
Think'st thou it was built by the art of man,
By his hand that grim old arch was bended?
Far down in the jaws of the gloomy abyss
The water is boiling and hissing, — forever will hiss.

That Gate through the rocks is as darksome and drear,
As if to the region of Shadows it carried:
Yet enter! A sweet laughing landscape is here,
Where the Spring with the Autumn is married.
From the world with its sorrows and warfare and wail,
O could I but hide in this bright little vale!

Four Rivers rush down from on high,
Their spring will be hidden forever;
Their course is to all the four points of the sky,
To each point of the sky is a river;
And fast as they start from their old Mother's feet,
They dash forth, and no more will they meet.

Two Pinnacles rise to the depths of the Blue:
Aloft on their white summits glancing,
Bedeck'd in their garments of golden dew,
The Clouds of the sky are dancing;
There threading alone their lightsome maze,
Uplifted apart from all mortals' gaze.

And high on her ever-enduring throne
The Queen of the mountains reposes;
Her head serene, and azure, and lone,
A diamond crown encloses;
The Sun with his darts shoots round it keen and hot,
He gilds it always, he warms it not.

Of Schiller's Philosophic talent, still more of the results he had arrived at in philosophy, there were much to be said and thought; which we must not enter upon here. As hinted above, his primary endowment seems to us fully as much philosophical as poetical: his intellect, at all events, is peculiarly of that character; strong, penetrating, yet systematic and scholastic, rather than intuitive; and manifesting this tendency both in the objects it treats, and in its mode of treating them. The Transcendental Philosophy, which arose in Schiller's busiest era, could not remain without influence on him: he had carefully studied Kant's System, and appears to have not only admitted but zealously appropriated its fundamental doctrines; remoulding them, however, into his own peculiar forms, so that they seem no longer borrowed, but permanently acquired, not less Schiller's than Kant's. Some, perhaps little aware of his natural wants and tendencies, are of opinion that these speculations did not profit him: Schiller himself, on the other hand, appears to have been well contented with his Philosophy; in which, as harmonised with his Poetry, the assurance and safe anchorage for his moral nature might lie.

'From the opponents of the New Philosophy,' says he, 'I expect not that tolerance, which is shown to every other system, no better seen into than this: for Kant's Philosophy itself, in its leading points, practises no tolerance; and bears much too rigorous a character, to leave any room for accommodation. But in my eyes this does it honour; proving how little it can endure to have truth tampered with. Such a Philosophy will not be discussed with a mere shake of the head. In the open, clear, accessible field of Inquiry it builds up its system; seeks no shade, makes no reservation: but even as it treats its neighbours, so it requires to be treated; and may be forgiven for lightly esteeming everything but Proofs. Nor am I terrified to think that the Law of Change, from which no human and no divine work finds grace, will operate on this Philosophy, as on every other, and one day its Form will be destroyed: but its Foundations will not have this destiny to fear; for ever since mankind has existed, and any Reason among mankind, these same first principles have been admitted, and on the whole acted upon.'[1]

Schiller's philosophical performances relate chiefly to matters of Art; not, indeed, without significant glances into still more important regions of speculation: nay Art, as he viewed

[1] Correspondence with Goethe, i. 58.

it, has its basis on the most important interests of man, and of itself involves the harmonious adjustment of these. We have already undertaken to present our readers, on a future occasion, with some abstract of the *Æsthetic Letters*, one of the deepest, most compact pieces of reasoning we are anywhere acquainted with: by that opportunity, the general character of Schiller, as a Philosopher, will best fall to be discussed. Meanwhile, the two following brief passages, as some indication of his views on the highest of all philosophical questions, may stand here without commentary. He is speaking of *Wilhelm Meister*, and in the first extract, of the *Fair Saint's Confessions*, which occupy the Sixth Book of that work:

'The transition from Religion in general to the Christian Religion, by the experience of sin, is excellently conceived. * * * I find virtually in the Christian System the rudiments of the Highest and Noblest; and the different phases of this System, in practical life, are so offensive and mean, precisely because they are bungled representations of that same Highest. If you study the specific character of Christianity, what distinguishes it from all monotheistic Religions, it lies in nothing else than in that *making-dead of the Law*, the removal of that Kantean Imperative, instead of which Christianity requires a free Inclination. It is thus, in its pure form, a representing of Moral Beauty, or the Incarnation of the Holy; and in this sense, the only *æsthetic* Religion: hence, too, I explain to myself why it so prospers with female natures, and only in women is now to be met with under a tolerable figure.'[1]

'But in seriousness,' he says elsewhere, 'whence may it proceed that you have had a man educated, and in all points equipt, without ever coming upon certain wants which only Philosophy can meet? I am convinced, it is entirely attributable to the *æsthetic direction* you have taken, through the whole Romance. Within the æsthetic temper there arises no want of those grounds of comfort, which are to be drawn from speculation: such a temper has self-subsistence, has infinitude, within itself; only when the Sensual and the Moral in man strive hostilely together, need help be sought of pure Reason. A healthy poetic nature wants, as you yourself say, no Moral Law, no Rights of Man, no Political Metaphysics. You might have added as well, it wants no Deity, no Immortality, to stay and uphold itself

[1] Correspondence, i. 195.

withal. Those three points round which, in the long-run, all speculation turns, may in truth afford such a nature matter for poetic play, but can never become serious concerns and necessities for it.'[1]

This last seems a singular opinion; and may prove, if it be correct, that Schiller himself was no 'healthy poetic nature;' for undoubtedly with him those three points were 'serious concerns and necessities;' as many portions of his works, and various entire treatises, will testify. Nevertheless, it plays an important part in his theories of Poetry; and often, under milder forms, returns on us there.

But, without entering farther on those complex topics, we must here for the present take leave of Schiller. Of his merits we have all along spoken rather on the negative side; and we rejoice in feeling authorised to do so. That any German writer, especially one so dear to us, should already stand so high with British readers that, in admiring him, the critic may also, without prejudice to right feeling on the subject, coolly judge of him, cannot be other than a gratifying circumstance. Perhaps there is no other true Poet of that nation with whom the like course would be suitable.

Connected with this there is one farther observation we must make before concluding. Among younger students of German Literature, the question often arises, and is warmly mooted: Whether Schiller or Goethe is the greater Poet? Of this question we must be allowed to say that it seems rather a slender one, and for two reasons. First, because Schiller and Goethe are of totally dissimilar endowments and endeavours, in regard to all matters intellectual, and cannot well be compared together as Poets. Secondly, because if the question mean to ask, which Poet is on the whole the rarer and more excellent, as probably it does, it must be considered as long ago abundantly answered. To the clear-sighted and modest Schiller, above all, such a question would have appeared surprising. No one knew better

[1] Correspondence, ii. 131.

than himself, that as Goethe was a born Poet, so he was in great part a made Poet; that as the one spirit was intuitive, all-embracing, instinct with melody, so the other was scholastic, divisive, only partially and as it were artificially melodious. Besides, Goethe has lived to perfect his natural gift, which the less happy Schiller was not permitted to do. The former accordingly is the national Poet; the latter is not, and never could have been. We once heard a German remark that readers till their twenty-fifth year usually prefer Schiller; after their twenty-fifth year, Goethe. This probably was no unfair illustration of the question. Schiller can seem higher than Goethe only because he is narrower. Thus to unpractised eyes, a Peak of Teneriffe, nay a Strasburg Minster, when we stand on it, may seem higher than a Chimborazo; because the former rise abruptly, without abutment or environment; the latter rises gradually, carrying half a world aloft with it; and only the deeper azure of the heavens, the widened horizon, the 'eternal sunshine,' disclose to the geographer that the 'Region of Change' lies far below him.

However, let us not divide these two Friends, who in life were so benignantly united. Without asserting for Schiller any claim that even enemies can dispute, enough will remain for him. We may say that, as a Poet and Thinker, he attained to a perennial Truth, and ranks among the noblest productions of his century and nation. Goethe may continue *the* German Poet, but neither through long generations can Schiller be forgotten. 'His works too, the memory of what 'he did and was, will arise afar off like a towering landmark 'in the solitude of the Past, when distance shall have dwarfed 'into invisibility many lesser people that once encompassed 'him, and hid him from the near beholder.'

THE NIBELUNGEN LIED.[1]

[1831.]

In the year 1757, the Swiss Professor Bodmer printed an ancient poetical manuscript, under the title of *Chriemhilden Rache und die Klage* (Chriemhilde's Revenge, and the Lament); which may be considered as the first of a series, or stream of publications and speculations still rolling on, with increased current, to the present day. Not, indeed, that all these had their source or determining cause in so insignificant a circumstance; their source, or rather thousand sources, lay far elsewhere. As has often been remarked, a certain antiquarian tendency in literature, a fonder, more earnest looking back into the Past, began about that time to manifest itself in all nations (witness our own *Percy's Reliques*): this was among the first distinct symptoms of it in Germany; where, as with ourselves, its manifold effects are still visible enough.

Some fifteen years after Bodmer's publication, which, for the rest, is not celebrated as an editorial feat, one C. H. Müller undertook a *Collection of German Poems from the Twelfth, Thirteenth and Fourteenth Centuries;* wherein, among other articles, he reprinted Bodmer's *Chriemhilde* and *Klage*, with a highly remarkable addition prefixed to the former, essential indeed to the right understanding of it; and the whole now stood before the world as one Poem,

[1] Westminster Review, No. 29. — *Das Nibelungen Lied, übersetzt von Karl Simrock* (The Nibelungen Lied, translated by Karl Simrock). 2 vols. 12mo. Berlin, 1827.

under the name of the *Nibelungen Lied*, or Lay of the Nibelungen. It has since been ascertained that the *Klage* is a foreign inferior appendage; at best, related only as epilogue to the main work: meanwhile out of this *Nibelungen*, such as it was, there soon proceeded new inquiries, and kindred enterprises. For much as the Poem, in the shape it here bore, was defaced and marred, it failed not to attract observation: to all open-minded lovers of poetry, especially where a strong patriotic feeling existed, the singular antique *Nibelungen* was an interesting appearance. Johannes Müller, in his famous *Swiss History*, spoke of it in warm terms: subsequently, August Wilhelm Schlegel, through the medium of the *Deutsche Museum*, succeeded in awakening something like a universal popular feeling on the subject; and, as a natural consequence, a whole host of Editors and Critics, of deep and of shallow endeavour, whose labours we yet see in progress. The *Nibelungen* has now been investigated, translated, collated, commented upon, with more or less result, to almost boundless lengths: besides the Work named at the head of this Paper, and which stands there simply as one of the latest, we have Versions into the modern tongue by Von der Hagen, by Hinsberg, Lachmann, Büsching, Zeune, the last in Prose, and said to be worthless; Criticisms, Introductions, Keys, and so forth, by innumerable others, of whom we mention only Docen and the Brothers Grimm.

By which means, not only has the Poem itself been elucidated with all manner of researches, but its whole environment has come forth in new light: the scene and personages it relates to, the other fictions and traditions connected with it, have attained a new importance and coherence. Manuscripts, that for ages had lain dormant, have issued from their archives into public view; books that had circulated only in mean guise for the amusement of the people, have become important, not to one or two virtuosos, but to the general body of the learned: and now a whole System of antique Teutonic Fiction and Mythology unfolds itself, shedding here and there a real though feeble and uncertain glimmer over what was once the total darkness of the old Time. No fewer than Fourteen ancient Traditionary Poems, all strangely intertwisted, and growing out of and into one another, have come to light among the Germans; who now, in looking back, find that they too, as well as the Greeks, have their Heroic Age, and round the old Valhalla, as their Northern Pantheon, a world of demi-gods and wonders.

Such a phenomenon, unexpected till of late, cannot but interest a deep-thinking, enthusiastic people. For the *Nibelungen* especially, which lies as the centre and distinct keystone of the whole too chaotic System, — let us say rather, blooms as a firm sunny island in the middle of these cloud-covered, ever-shifting sand-whirlpools, — they cannot sufficiently testify their love and veneration. Learned professors lecture on the *Nibelungen* in public schools, with a praiseworthy view to initiate the German youth in love of their fatherland; from many zealous and nowise ignorant critics we hear talk of a 'great Northern Epos,' of a 'German Iliad;' the more saturnine are shamed into silence, or hollow-mouth-homage: thus from all quarters comes a sound of joyful acclamation; the *Nibelungen* is welcomed as a precious national possession, recovered after six centuries of neglect, and takes undisputed place among the sacred books of German literature.

Of these curious transactions some rumour has not failed to reach us in England, where our minds, from their own antiquarian disposition, were willing enough to receive it. Abstracts and extracts of the *Nibelungen* have been printed in our language; there have been disquisitions on it in our Reviews: hitherto, however, such as nowise to exhaust the subject. On the contrary, where so much was to be told at once, the speaker might be somewhat puzzled where to begin: it was a much readier method to begin with the end, or with any part of the middle, than like Hamilton's Ram (whose example is too little followed in literary narrative) to begin with the beginning. Thus has our stock of intelligence come rushing out on us quite promiscuously and pell-mell; whereby the whole matter could not but acquire a tortuous, confused, altogether inexplicable and even dreary aspect; and the class of 'well-informed persons' now find themselves in that uncomfortable position, where they are obliged to profess admiration, and at the same time feel that, except by name, they know not what the thing admired is. Such a position towards the venerable *Nibelungen*, which is no less bright and graceful than historically significant, cannot be the right one. Moreover, as appears to us, it might be somewhat mended by very simple means. Let any one that had honestly read the *Nibelungen*, which in these days is no surprising achievement, only tell us what he found there, and nothing that he did not find: we should then know something, and, what were still better, be ready for knowing more. To search out the secret roots of such a production, ramified through successive layers of centuries, and drawing nourishment from each, may be work, and too hard work, for the deepest philosopher and critic; but to look with natural eyes on what part of it stands visibly above ground, and record his own experiences thereof, is what any reasonable mortal, if he will take heed, can do.

Some such slight service we here intend proffering to our readers: let them glance with us a little into that mighty maze of Northern Archæology; where, it may be, some pleasant prospects will open. If the *Nibelungen* is what we have called it, a firm sunny island amid the weltering chaos of antique tradition, it must be worth visiting on general grounds; nay, if the primeval rudiments of it have the antiquity assigned them, it belongs specially to us English *Teutones* as well as to the German.

Far be it from us, meanwhile, to venture rashly, or farther than is needful, into that same traditionary chaos, fondly named the 'Cycle of Northern Fiction,' with its Fourteen Sectors (or separate Poems), which are rather Fourteen shoreless Limbos, where we hear of pieces containing 'a hundred thousand verses,' and 'seventy thousand verses,' as of a quite natural affair! How travel through that inane country; by what art discover the little grain of Substance that casts such multiplied immeasurable Shadows? The primeval Mythus, were it at first philosophical truth, or were it historical incident, floats too vaguely on the breath of men: each successive Singer and Redactor furnishes it with new personages, new scenery, to please a new audience; each has the privilege of inventing, and the far wider privilege of borrowing and new-modelling from *all* that have preceded him. Thus though Tradition may have but one root, it grows like a Banian, into a whole overarching labyrinth of trees. Or rather might we say, it is a Hall of Mirrors, where in pale light each mirror reflects, convexly or concavely, not only some real Object, but the Shadows of this in other mirrors; which again do the like for it: till in such reflection and re-reflection the whole immensity is filled with dimmer and dimmer shapes; and no firm scene lies round us, but a dislocated, distorted chaos, fading away on all hands, in the distance, into utter night. Only to some brave Von der Hagen, furnished with indefatigable ardour, and a deep, almost religious love, is it given to find sure footing there, and see his way. All those *Dukes of Aquitania*, therefore, and *Etzel's Court-holdings*, and *Dietrichs* and *Sigenots* we shall leave standing where they are. Such as desire farther information, will find an intelligible account of the whole Series or Cycle, in Messrs. Weber and Jamieson's *Illustrations of Northern Antiquities;* and all possible furtherance, in the numerous German works above alluded to; among which Von der Hagen's writings, though not the readiest, are probably the safest guides. But for us, our business here is with the *Nibelungen*, the inhabited poetic country round which all these wildernesses lie; only as environments of which, as routes to which, are they of moment to us. Perhaps our shortest and smoothest route will be through the *Heldenbuch* (Hero-book) ; which is greatly the most important of these subsidiary Fictions, not without interest of its own, and closely related to the *Nibelungen.* This *Heldenbuch,* therefore, we must now address ourselves to traverse with all despatch. At the present stage of the business too, we shall forbear any historical inquiry and argument concerning the date and local habitation of those Traditions ; reserving what little is to be said on that matter till the Traditions themselves have become better known to us. Let the reader, on trust for the present, transport himself into the twelfth or thirteenth century ; and therefrom looking back into the sixth or fifth, see what presents itself.

Of the *Heldenbuch,* tried on its own merits, and except as illustrating that other far worthier Poem, or at most as an old national, and still in some measure popular book, we should have felt strongly inclined to say, as the Curate in *Don Quixote* so often did, *Al corral con ello,* Out of window with it ! Doubtless there are touches of beauty in the work, and even a sort of heartiness and antique quaintness in its wildest follies ; but on the whole that George-and-Dragon species of composition has long ceased to find favour with any one ; and except for its groundwork, more or less discernible, of old Northern Fiction, this *Heldenbuch* has little to distinguish it from these. Nevertheless, what is worth remark, it seems to have been a far higher favourite than the *Nibelungen,* with ancient readers : it was printed soon after the invention of printing ; some think in 1472, for there is no place or date on the first edition ; at all events, in 1491, in 1509, and repeatedly since ; whereas the *Nibelungen,* though written earlier, and in worth immeasurably superior, had to remain in manuscript three centuries longer. From which, for the thousandth time, inferences might be drawn as to the infallibility of popular taste, and its value as a criterion for poetry. However, it is probably in virtue of this neglect, that the *Nibelungen* boasts of its actual purity; that it now comes before us, clear and graceful as it issued from the old Singer's head and heart; not overloaded with Ass-eared Giants, Fiery Dragons, Dwarfs and Hairy Women, as the *Heldenbuch* is, many of which, as charity would hope, may be the produce of a later age than that famed *Swabian Era*, to which these poems, as we now see them, are commonly referred. Indeed, one Casper von Roen is understood to have passed the whole *Heldenbuch* through his limbec, in the fifteenth century; but like other rectifiers, instead of purifying it, to have only drugged it with still fiercer ingredients to suit the sick appetite of the time.

Of this drugged and adulterated *Hero-book* (the only one we yet have, though there is talk of a better) we shall quote the long Title-page of Lessing's Copy, the edition of 1560; from which, with a few intercalated observations, the reader's curiosity may probably obtain what little satisfaction it wants:

Das Heldenbuch, welchs auffs new corrigirt und gebessert ist, mit shönen Figuren geziert. Gedrückt zu Frankfurt am Mayn, durch Weygand Han und Sygmund Feyerabend, &c. That is to say:

'The *Hero-book*, which is of new corrected and improved, 'adorned with beautiful Figures. Printed at Frankfurt on 'the Mayn, through Weygand Han and Sygmund Feyera- 'bend.

'*Part First* saith of Kaiser Ottnit and the little King 'Elberich, how they with great peril, over sea, in Heathen- 'dom, won from a king his daughter (and how he in lawful 'marriage took her to wife).'

From which announcement the reader already guesses the contents: how this little King Elberich was a Dwarf, or Elf, some half-span long, yet full of cunning practices, and the most helpful activity; nay, stranger still, had been Kaiser Ottnit of *Lampartei* or Lombardy's father, — having had his own ulterior views in that indiscretion. How they sailed with Messina ships, into Paynim land; fought with that unspeakable Turk, King Machabol, in and about his fortress and metropolis of Montebur, which was all stuck round with christian heads; slew from seventy to a hundred thousand of the Infidels at one heat; saw the lady on the battlements; and at length, chiefly by Dwarf Elberich's help, carried her off in triumph; wedded her in Messina; and without difficulty, rooting out the Mahometan prejudice, converted her to the creed of Mother Church. The fair runaway seems to have been of a gentle, tractable disposition, very different from old Machabol; concerning whom it is here chiefly to be noted that Dwarf Elberich, rendering himself invisible on their first interview, plucks out a handful of hair from his chin; thereby increasing to a tenfold pitch the royal choler; and, what is still more remarkable, furnishing the poet Wieland, six centuries afterwards, with the critical incident in his *Oberon*. As for the young lady herself, we cannot but admit that she was well worth sailing to Heathendom for; and shall here, as our sole specimen of that old German doggerel, give the description of her, as she first appeared on the battlements during the fight; subjoining a version as verbal and literal as the plainest prose can make it. Considered as a detached passage, it is perhaps the finest we have met with in the *Heldenbuch*.

Ihr herz brann also schone,
Recht als ein rot rubein,
Gleich dem vollen mone
Gaben ihr äuglein schein.
Sich hett die maget reine
Mit rosen wohl bekleid
Und auch mit berlin kleine ;
Niemand da tröst die meid.

Her heart burnt (with anxiety) as beautiful
Just as a red ruby,
Like the full moon
Her eyes (eyelings, pretty eyes) gave sheen.
Herself had the maiden pure
Well adorned with roses,

And also with pearls small :
No one there comforted the maid.

Sie war schön an dem leibe,
Und zu den seiten schmal;
Recht als ein kertze scheibe
Wohlgeschaffen überall:
Ihr beyden händ gemeine
Dars ihr gentz nichts gebrach;
Ihr näglein schön und reine,
Das man sich darin besach.

She was fair of body,
And in the waist slender;
Right as a (golden) candlestick
Well-fashioned everywhere:
Her two hands proper,
So that she wanted naught;
Her little nails fair and pure,
That you could see yourself therein.

Ihr har war schön umbfangen
Mit elder seiden fein;
Das liess sie nieder hangen,
Das hübsche magedlein.
Sie trug ein kron mit steinen,
Sie war von gold so rot;
Elberich dem viel kleinen
War zu der magte not.

Her hair was beautifully girt
With noble silk (band) fine;
She let it flow down,
The lovely maidling.
She wore a crown with jewels,
It was of gold so red:
For Elberich the very small
The maid had need (to console her).

Da vornen in den kronen
Lag ein karfunkelstein,
Der in dem pallast schonen
Aecht als ein kertz erschein,
Auf jrem haupt das hare
War lauter und auch fein,
Es leuchtet also klare
Recht als der sonnen schein.

There in front of the crown
Lay a carbuncle-stone,
Which in the palace fair
Even as a taper seemed;
On her head the hair
Was glossy and also fine,
It shone as bright
Even as the sun's sheen.

Die magt die stand alleine,
Gar trawrig war jr mut;
Ihr farb und die war reine,
Lieblich-we milch und blut:
Her durch jr zöpffe reinen
Schien jr hals als der schnee:
Elberich dem viel kleinen
That der maget jammer weh.

The maid she stood alone,
Right sad was her mind;
Her colour it was pure,
Lovely as milk and blood:
Out through her pure locks
Shone her neck like the snow.
Elberich the very small
Was touched with the maiden's sorrow.

Happy man was Kaiser Ottnit, blessed with such a wife, after all his travail;—had not the Turk Machabol cunningly sent him, in revenge, a box of young Dragons, or Dragon-eggs, by the hands of a caitiff Infidel, contriver of the mischief; by whom in due course of time they were hatched and nursed, to the infinite woe of all Lampartei, and ultimately to the death of Kaiser Ottnit himself, whom they swallowed and attempted to digest, once without effect, but the next time too fatally, crown and all!

'*Part Second* announceth (*meldet*) of Herr Hugdietrich 'and his son Wolfdietrich; how they for justice-sake, oft by 'their doughty acts succoured distressed persons, with other 'bold heroes that stood by them in extremity.'

Concerning which Hugdietrich, Emperor of Greece, and his son Wolfdietrich, one day the renowned Dietrich of Bern, we can here say little more than that the former trained himself to sempstress-work; and for many weeks plied his needle, before he could get wedded and produce Wolfdietrich; who coming into the world in this clandestine manner, was let down into the castle-ditch, and like Romulus and Remus nursed by a Wolf, whence his name. However, after never-imagined adventures, with enchanters and enchantresses, pagans and giants, in all quarters of the globe, he finally, with utmost effort, slaughtered those Lombardy Dragons; then married Kaiser Ottnit's widow, whom he had rather flirted with before; and so lived universally respected in his new empire, performing yet other notable achievements. One strange property he had, sometimes useful to him, sometimes hurtful: that his breath, when he became angry, grew flame, red-hot, and would take the temper out of swords. We find him again in the *Nibelungen*, among King Etzel's (Attila's) followers; a staid, cautious, yet still invincible man; on which occasion, though with great reluctance, he is forced to interfere, and does so with effect. Dietrich is the favourite hero of all those Southern Fictions, and well acknowledged in the Northern also, where the chief man, however, as we shall find, is not he but Siegfried.

'*Part Third* showeth of the Rose-garden at Worms, 'which was planted by Chrimhilte, King Gibich's daughter; 'whereby afterwards most part of those Heroes and Giants 'came to destruction and were slain.'

In this Third Part the Southern or Lombard Heroes come into contact and collision with another as notable Northern class, and for us much more important. Chriemhild, whose ulterior history makes such a figure in the *Nibelungen*, had, it would seem, near the ancient City of Worms, a Rose-garden, some seven English miles in circuit; fenced only by a silk thread; wherein, however, she maintained Twelve stout fighting men; several of whom, as Hagen, Volker, her three Brothers, above all the gallant Siegfried her betrothed, we shall meet with again: these, so unspeakable was their prowess, sufficed to defend the silk-thread Garden against all mortals. Our good antiquary, Von der Hagen, imagines that this Rose-garden business (in the primeval Tradition) glances obliquely at the Ecliptic with its Twelve Signs, at Jupiter's fight with the Titans, and we know not what confused skirmishing in the Utgard, or Asgard, or Midgard of the Scandinavians. Be this as it may, Chriemhild, we are here told, being very beautiful, and very wilful, boasts, in the pride of her heart, that no heroes on earth are to be compared with hers; and hearing accidentally that Dietrich of Bern has a high character in this line, forthwith challenges him to visit Worms, and with eleven picked men to do battle there against those other Twelve champions of Christendom that watch her Rose-garden. Dietrich, in a towering passion at the style of the message, which was 'surly and stout,' instantly pitches upon his eleven seconds, who also are to be principals; and with a retinue of other sixty thousand, by quick stages, in which obstacles enough are overcome, reaches Worms, and declares himself ready. Among these eleven Lombard heroes of his are likewise several whom we meet with again in the *Nibelungen;* beside Dietrich himself, we have the old Duke Hildebrand, Wolfhart, Ortwin. Notable among them, in another way, is Monk Ilsan, a truculent, gray-bearded fellow, equal to any Friar Tuck in *Robin Hood.*

The conditions of fight are soon agreed on: there are to be twelve successive duels, each challenger being expected to find his match; and the prize of victory is a Rose-garland from Chriemhild, and *ein Helssen und ein Küssen*, that is to say virtually, one kiss from her fair lips to each. But here as it ever should do, Pride gets a fall; for Chriemhild's bully-hectors are, in divers ways, all successively felled to the ground by the Berners; some of whom, as old Hildebrand, will not even take her Kiss when it is due: even Siegfried himself, most reluctantly engaged with by Dietrich, and for a while victorious, is at last forced to seek shelter in her lap. Nay, Monk Ilsan, after the regular fight is over, and his part in it well performed, calls out in succession, fifty-two other idle Champions of the Garden, part of them Giants, and routs the whole fraternity; thereby earning, besides his own regular allowance, fifty-two spare Garlands, and fifty-two several Kisses; in the course of which latter, Chriemhild's cheek, a just punishment as seemed, was scratched to the drawing of blood by his rough beard. It only remains to be added, that King Gibich, Chriemhild's Father, is now fain to do homage for his kingdom to Dietrich; who returns triumphant to his own country; where also, Monk Ilsan, according to promise, distributes these fifty-two Garlands among his fellow Friars, crushing a garland on the bare crown of each, till 'the red blood ran over their ears.' Under which hard, but not undeserved treatment, they all agreed to pray for remission of Ilsan's sins: indeed, such as continued refractory he tied together by the beards, and hung pair-wise over poles; whereby the stoutest soon gave in.

So endeth here this ditty
Of strife from woman's pride:
God on our griefs take pity,
And Mary still by us abide.

'In *Part Fourth* is announced (*gemelt*) of the little King 'Laurin, the Dwarf, how he encompassed his Rose-garden 'with so great manhood and art-magic, till at last he was 'vanquished by the heroes, and forced to become their Jug- 'gler, with &c. &c.'

Of which Fourth and happily last part we shall here say nothing; inasmuch as, except that certain of our old heroes again figure there, it has no coherence or connexion with the rest of the *Heldenbuch;* and is simply a new tale, which by way of episode Heinrich von Ofterdingen, as we learn from his own words, had subsequently appended thereto. He says:

Heinrich von Ofterdingen
This story hath been singing,
To the joy of Princes bold,
They gave him silver and gold,

Moreover pennies and garments rich:
Here endeth this Book the which
Doth sing our noble Heroes' story:
God help us all to heavenly glory.

Such is some outline of the famous *Heldenbuch;* on which it is not our business here to add any criticism. The fact that it has so long been popular betokens a certain worth in it; the kind and degree of which is also in some measure apparent. In poetry 'the rude man,' it has been said, 'requires only to see something going on; the man of more 'refinement wishes to feel; the truly refined man must be 'made to reflect.' For the first of these classes our *Hero-book*, as has been apparent enough, provides in abundance; for the other two scantily, indeed for the second not at all. Nevertheless our estimate of this work, which as a series of Antique Traditions may have considerable meaning, is apt rather to be too low. Let us remember that this is not the original *Heldenbuch* which we now see; but only a version of it into the Knight-errant dialect of the thirteenth, indeed partly of the fourteenth and fifteenth centuries, with all the fantastic monstrosities, now so trivial, pertaining to that style; under which disguises the really antique earnest groundwork, interesting as old Thought, if not as old Poetry, is all but quite obscured from us. But Antiquarian diligence is now busy with the *Heldenbuch* also, from which what light is in it will doubtless be elicited, and here and there a deformity removed. Though the Ethiop cannot change his skin, there is no need that even he should go abroad unwashed.[1]

Casper von Roen, or whoever was the ultimate redactor

[1] Our inconsiderable knowledge of the *Heldenbuch* is derived from various secondary sources; chiefly from Lessing's *Werke* (b. xiii.), where the reader will find an epitome of the whole Poem, with Extracts by Herr Fülleborn, from which the above are taken. A still more accessible and larger Abstract, with long specimens translated into verse, stands in the *Illustrations of Northern Antiquities* (pp. 45–167). Von der Hagen has since been employed specially on the *Heldenbuch;* with what result we have not yet learned.

of the *Heldenbuch*, whom Lessing designates as 'a highly ill-informed man,' would have done better had he quite omitted that little King Laurin, 'and his little Rose-garden,' which properly is no Rose-garden at all; and instead thereof introduced the *Gehörnte Siegfried* (Behorned Siegfried), whose history lies at the heart of the whole Northern Traditions; and, under a rude prose dress, is to this day a real child's-book and people's-book among the Germans. Of this Siegfried we have already seen somewhat in the Rose-garden at Worms; and shall erelong see much more elsewhere; for he is the chief hero of the *Nibelungen:* indeed nowhere can we dip into those old Fictions, whether in Scandinavia or the Rhine-land, but under one figure or another, whether as Dragon-killer and Prince-royal, or as Blacksmith and Horse-subduer, as Sigurd, Sivrit, Siegfried, we are sure to light on him. As his early adventures belong to the strange sort, and will afterwards concern us not a little, we shall here endeavour to piece together some consistent outline of them; so far indeed as that may be possible; for his biographers, agreeing in the main points, differ widely in the details.

First, then, let no one from the title *Gehörnte* (Horned, Behorned), fancy that our brave Siegfried, who was the loveliest as well as the bravest of men, was actually cornuted, and had horns on his brow, though like Michael Angelo's Moses; or even that his skin, to which the epithet *Behorned* refers, was hard like a crocodile's, and not softer than the softest shamoy: for the truth is, his Hornedness means only an Invulnerability, like that of Achilles, which he came by in the following manner. All men agree that Siegfried was a king's son; he was born, as we here have good reason to know, 'at Santen in Netherland,' of Siegemund and the fair Siegelinde; yet by some family misfortune or discord, of which the accounts are very various, he came into singular straits during boyhood; having passed that happy period of life, not under the canopies of costly state, but by the sooty stithy, in one Mimer a Blacksmith's shop. Here, however, he was nowise in his proper element; ever quarrelling with his fellow-apprentices; nay, as some say, breaking the hardest anvils into shivers by his too stout hammering. So that Mimer, otherwise a first-rate Smith, could by no means do with him there. He sends him, accordingly, to the neighbouring forest, to fetch charcoal; well aware that a monstrous Dragon, one Regin, the Smith's own Brother, would meet him and devour him. But far otherwise it proved; Siegfried by main force slew this Dragon, or rather Dragonised Smith's-Brother; made broth of him; and, warned by some significant phenomena, bathed therein; or, as others assert, bathed directly in the monster's blood, without cookery; and hereby attained that Invulnerability, complete in all respects, save that between his shoulders, where a lime-tree leaf chanced to settle and stick during the process, there was one little spot, a fatal spot as afterwards turned out, left in its natural state.

Siegfried, now seeing through the craft of the Smith, returned home and slew him; then set forth in search of adventures, the bare catalogue of which were long to recite. We mention only two, as subsequently of moment both for him and for us. He is by some said to have courted, and then jilted, the fair and proud Queen Brunhild of Isenland; nay to have thrown down the seven gates of her Castle; and then ridden off with her wild-horse Gana, having mounted him in the meadow, and instantly broken him. Some cross passages between him and Queen Brunhild, who understood no jesting, there must clearly have been, so angry is her recognition of him in the *Nibelungen;* nay, she bears a lasting grudge against him there; as he, and indeed she also, one day too sorely felt.

His other grand adventure is with the two sons of the deceased King Nibelung, in Nibelungen-land: these two youths, to whom their father had bequeathed a Hoard or Treasure beyond all price or computation, Siegfried, 'riding by alone,' found on the side of a mountain, in a state of great perplexity. They had brought out the Treasure from the cave where it usually lay; but how to part it was the difficulty; for, not to speak of gold, there were as many jewels alone 'as twelve wagons in four days and nights, each going 'three journeys, could carry away;' nay, 'however much 'you took from it there was no diminution:' besides in real property, a Sword, Balmung, of great potency; a Divining-rod, 'which gave power over every one;' and a *Tarnkappe* (or Cloak of Darkness), which not only rendered the wearer invisible, but also gave him twelve men's strength. So that the two Princes Royal, without counsel save from their Twelve stupid Giants, knew not how to fall upon any amicable arrangement; and, seeing Siegfried ride by so opportunely, requested him to be arbiter; offering also the Sword Balmung for his trouble. Siegfried, who readily undertook the impossible problem, did his best to accomplish it; but, of course, without effect; nay the two Nibelungen Princes, being of choleric temper, grew impatient, and provoked him; whereupon, with the Sword Balmung he slew them both, and their Twelve Giants (perhaps originally Signs of the Zodiac) to boot. Thus did the famous *Nibelungen Hort* (Hoard), and indeed the whole Nibelungen-land, come into his possession: wearing the Sword Balmung, and having slain the two Princes and their Champions, what was there farther to oppose him? Vainly did the Dwarf Alberich, our old friend Elberich of the *Heldenbuch*, who had now become special keeper of this Hoard, attempt some resistance with a Dwarf Army; he was driven back into the cave; plundered of his *Tarnkappe;* and obliged with all his myrmidons to swear fealty to the conqueror, whom indeed thenceforth he and they punctually obeyed.

Whereby Siegfried might now farther style himself King of the Nibelungen; master of the infinite Nibelungen Hoard (collected doubtless by art-magic in the beginning of Time, in the deep bowels of the Universe), with the *Wünschelruthe*

(Wishing or Divining Rod) pertaining thereto; owner of the *Tarnkappe*, which he ever after kept by him, to put on at will; and though last not least, Bearer and Wielder of the Sword Balmung,[1] by the keen edge of which all this gain had come to him. To which last acquisitions adding his previously acquired Invulnerability, and his natural dignities as Prince of Netherland, he might well show himself before the foremost at Worms or elsewhere; and attempt any the highest adventure that fortune could cut out for him. However, his subsequent history belongs all to the *Nibelungen Song;* at which fair garden of poesy we are now, through all these shaggy wildernesses and enchanted woods, finally arrived.

[1] By this Sword Balmung also hangs a tale. Doubtless it was one of those invaluable weapons sometimes fabricated by the old Northern Smiths, compared with which our modern Foxes, and Ferraras, and Toledos, are mere leaden tools. Von der Hagen seems to think it simply the Sword Mimung under another name; in which case Siegfried's old master, Mimer, had been the maker of it, and called it after himself, as if it had been his son. In Scandinavian chronicles, veridical or not, we have the following account of that transaction. Mimer (or, as some have it, surely without ground, one Velint, once an apprentice of his) was challenged by another Craftsman, named Amilias, who boasted that he had made a suit of armour which no stroke could dint, — to equal that feat, or own himself the second Smith then extant. This last the stout Mimer would in no case do, but proceeded to forge the Sword Mimung; with which, when it was finished, he, 'in presence of the King,' cut asunder 'a thread of wool floating on water.' This would have seemed a fair fire-edge to most smiths: not so to Mimer; he sawed the blade in pieces, welded it in 'a red-hot fire for three days,' tempered it 'with milk and oatmeal,' and by much other cunning, brought out a sword that severed 'a ball of wool floating on water.' But neither would this suffice him; he returned to his smithy, and by means known only to himself, produced, in the course of seven weeks, a third and final edition of Mimung, which split asunder a whole floating pack of wool. The comparative trial now took place forthwith. Amilias, cased in his impenetrable coat of mail, sat down on a bench, in presence of assembled thousands, and bade Mimer strike him. Mimer fetched of course his best blow, on which Amilias observed, that there was a strange feeling of cold iron in his inwards. "Shake thyself," said Mimer; the luckless wight did so, and fell in two halves, being cleft sheer through from collar to haunch, never more to swing hammer in this world. — See *Illustrations of Northern Antiquities*, p. 31.

Apart from its antiquarian value, and not only as by far the finest monument of old German art; but intrinsically, and as a mere detached composition, this *Nibelungen* has an excellence that cannot but surprise us. With little preparation, any reader of poetry, even in these days, might find it interesting. It is not without a certain Unity of interest and purport, and internal coherence and completeness; it is a Whole, and some spirit of Music informs it: these are the highest characteristics of a true Poem. Considering farther what intellectual environment we now find it in, it is doubly to be prized and wondered at; for it differs from those *Hero-books*, as molten or carved metal does from rude agglomerated ore; almost as some Shakspeare from his fellow Dramatists, whose *Tamburlaines* and *Island Princesses*, themselves not destitute of merit, first show us clearly in what pure loftiness and loneliness the *Hamlets* and *Tempests* reign.

The unknown Singer of the *Nibelungen*, though no Shakspeare, must have had a deep poetic soul; wherein things discontinuous and inanimate shaped themselves together into life, and the Universe with its wondrous purport stood significantly imaged; overarching as with heavenly firmaments and eternal harmonies, the little scene where men strut and fret their hour. His Poem, unlike so many old and new pretenders to that name, has a basis and organic structure, a beginning, middle and end; there is one great principle and idea set forth in it, round which all its multifarious parts combine in living union. Remarkable it is, moreover, how along with this essence and primary condition of all poetic virtue, the minor external virtues of what we call Taste and so forth, are, as it were, presupposed; and the living soul of Poetry being there, its body of incidents, its garment of language, come of their own accord. So too in the case of Shakspeare: his feeling of propriety, as compared with that of the Marlowes and Fletchers, his quick sure sense of what is fit and unfit, either in act or word, might astonish us, had he no other superiority. But true Inspiration, as it may well do, includes that same Taste, or rather a far higher and heartfelt Taste, of which that other 'elegant' species is but an ineffectual, irrational apery: let us see the herald Mercury actually descend from his Heaven, and the bright wings, and the graceful movement of these, will not be wanting.

With an instinctive art, far different from acquired artifice, this Poet of the *Nibelungen*, working in the same province with his contemporaries of the *Heldenbuch*, on the same material of tradition, has, in a wonderful degree, possessed himself of what these could only strive after; and with his 'clear feeling of fictitious truth,' avoided as false the errors and monstrous perplexities in which they vainly struggled. He is of another species than they; in language, in purity and depth of feeling, in fineness of invention, stands quite apart from them.

The language of the *Heldenbuch*, as we saw above, was a feeble half-articulate child's-speech, the metre nothing better than a miserable doggerel; whereas here in the old Frankish (*Oberdeutsch*) dialect of the *Nibelungen*, we have a clear decisive utterance, and in a real system of verse, not without essential regularity, great liveliness, and now and then even harmony of rhythm. Doubtless we must often call it a diffuse diluted utterance; at the same time it is genuine, with a certain antique garrulous heartiness, and has a rhythm in the thoughts as well as the words. The simplicity is never silly; even in that perpetual recurrence of epithets, sometimes of rhymes, as where two words, for instance *lip* (body, life, *leib*) and *wip* (woman, wife, *weib*) are indissolubly wedded together, and the one never shows itself without the other following, — there is something which reminds us not so much of poverty, as of trustfulness and childlike innocence. Indeed a strange charm lies in those old tones, where, in gay dancing melodies, the sternest tidings are sung to us; and deep floods of Sadness and Strife play lightly in little curling billows, like seas in summer. It is as a meek smile, in whose still, thoughtful depths a whole infinitude of patience, and love, and heroic strength lie revealed. But in other cases too, we have seen this outward sport and inward earnestness offer grateful contrast, and cunning excitement; for example, in Tasso; of whom, though otherwise different enough, this old Northern Singer has more than once reminded us. There too, as here, we have a dark solemn meaning in light guise; deeds of high temper, harsh self-denial, daring and death, stand embodied in that soft, quick-flowing, joyfully-modulated verse. Nay farther, as if the implement, much more than we might fancy, had influenced the work done, these two Poems, could we trust our individual feeling, have in one respect the same poetical result for us: in the *Nibelungen* as in the *Gerusalemme*, the persons and their story are indeed brought vividly before us, yet not near and palpably present; it is rather as if we looked on that scene through an inverted telescope, whereby the whole was carried far away into the distance, the life-large figures compressed into brilliant miniatures, so clear, so real, yet tiny, elf-like and beautified as well as lessened, their colours being now closer and brighter, the shadows and trivial features no longer visible. This, as we partly apprehend, comes of *singing* Epic Poems; most part of which only pretend to be sung. Tasso's rich melody still lives among the Italian people; the *Nibelungen* also is what it professes to be, a *Song*.

No less striking than the verse and language is the quality of the invention manifested here. Of the Fable, or narrative material of the *Nibelungen*, we should say that it had high, almost the highest merit; so daintily yet firmly is it put together; with such felicitous selection of the beautiful, the essential, and no less felicitous rejection of whatever was unbeautiful or even extraneous. The reader is no longer afflicted with that chaotic brood of Fire-drakes, Giants, and malicious turbaned Turks, so fatally rife in the *Heldenbuch*: all this is swept away, or only hovers in faint shadows afar off; and free field is open for legitimate perennial interests.

Yet neither is the *Nibelungen* without its wonders; for it is poetry and not prose; here too, a supernatural world encompasses the natural, and, though at rare intervals and in calm manner, reveals itself there. It is truly wonderful with what skill our simple untaught Poet deals with the marvellous; admitting it without reluctance or criticism, yet precisely in the degree and shape that will best avail him. Here, if in no other respect, we should say, that he has a decided superiority to Homer himself. The whole story of the *Nibelungen* is fateful, mysterious, guided on by unseen influences; yet the actual marvels are few, and done in the far distance; those Dwarfs, and Cloaks of Darkness, and charmed Treasure-caves, are heard of rather than beheld, the tidings of them seem to issue from unknown space. Vain were it to inquire where that Nibelungen-land specially is: its very name is *Nebel-land* or *Nifl-land*, the land of Darkness, of Invisibility. The 'Nibelungen Heroes' that muster in thousands and tens of thousands, though they march to the Rhine or Danube, and we see their strong limbs and shining armour, we could almost fancy to be children of the air. Far beyond the firm horizon, that wonder-bearing region swims on the infinite waters; unseen by bodily eye, or at most discerned as a faint streak, hanging in the blue depths, uncertain whether island or cloud. And thus the *Nibelungen Song*, though based on the bottomless foundations of Spirit, and not unvisited of skyey messengers, is a real, rounded, habitable Earth, where we find firm footing, and the wondrous and the common live amicably together. Perhaps it would be difficult to find any Poet of ancient or modern times, who in this trying problem has steered his way with greater delicacy and success.

To any of our readers who may have personally studied the *Nibelungen*, these high praises of ours will not seem exaggerated: the rest, who are the vast majority, must endeavour to accept them with some degree of faith, at least of curiosity; to vindicate, and judicially substantiate them would far exceed our present opportunities. Nay in any case, the criticism, the alleged Characteristics of a Poem are so many Theorems, which are indeed enunciated, truly or falsely, but the Demonstration of which must be sought for in the reader's own study and experience. Nearly all that can be attempted here, is some hasty epitome of the mere Narrative; no substantial image of the work, but a feeble outline and shadow. To which task, as the personages and their environment have already been in some degree illustrated, we can now proceed without obstacle.

The *Nibelungen* has been called the Northern Epos; yet it has, in great part, a Dramatic character: those thirty-nine *Aventiuren* (Adventures), which it consists of, might be so many scenes in a Tragedy. The catastrophe is dimly prophesied from the beginning; and, at every fresh step, rises more and more clearly into view. A shadow of coming Fate, as it were, a low inarticulate voice of Doom falls, from the first, out of that charmed Nibelungen-land: the discord of two women is as a little spark of evil passion, which erelong enlarges itself into a crime; foul murder is done; and now the Sin rolls on like a devouring fire, till the guilty and the innocent are alike encircled with it, and a whole land is ashes, and a whole race is swept away.

Uns ist in alten mæren Wunders vil geseit,
Von helden lobebæren Von grozer chuonheit;
Von vrouden und hoch-geziten, Von weinen und von chlagen,
Von chuner rechen striten, Muget ir nu wunder hören sagen.

We find in ancient story Wonders many told,
Of heroes in great glory With spirit free and bold;
Of joyances and high-tides, Of weeping and of woe,
Of noble Recken striving, Mote ye now wonders know.

This is the brief artless Proem; and the promise contained in it proceeds directly towards fulfilment. In the very second stanza, we learn:

Es wühs in Burgonden Ein vil edel magedin,
Das in allen landen Niht schoners mohte sin;

Chriemhilt was si geheien, Si wart ein schone wip;
Darumbe müsen degene Vil verliesen den lip.

A right noble maiden Did grow in Burgundy,
That in all lands of earth Naught fairer mote there be;
Chriemhild of Worms she hight, She was a fairest *wife;*
For the which must warriors A many lose their life.[1]

Chriemhild, this world's-wonder, a king's daughter and king's sister, and no less coy and proud than fair, dreams one night that 'she had petted a falcon, strong, beautiful and 'wild; which two eagles snatched away from her: this she 'was forced to see; greater sorrow felt she never in the 'world.' Her mother, Ute, to whom she relates the vision, soon redes it for her; the falcon is a noble husband, whom, God keep him, she must suddenly lose. Chriemhild declares warmly for the single state; as, indeed, living there at the Court of Worms, with her brothers, Gunther, Gernot, Geiselher, 'three kings noble and rich,' in such pomp and renown, the pride of Burgunden-land and Earth, she might readily enough have changed for the worse. However, dame Ute bids her not be toò emphatical; for 'if ever she 'have heartfelt joy in life, it will be from man's love, and she 'shall be a fair wife (*wip*), when God sends her a right 'worthy Ritter's *lip*.' Chriemhild is more in earnest than maidens usually are when they talk thus; it appears, she guarded against love, 'for many a lief-long day;' nevertheless, she too must yield to destiny. 'Honourably she was to

[1] This is the first of a thousand instances, in which the two inseparables, *wip* and *lip*, or in modern tongue, *weib* and *leib*, as mentioned above, appear together. From these two opening stanzas of the *Nibelungen Lied*, in its purest form, the reader may obtain some idea of the versification; it runs on in more or less regular Alexandrines, with a cæsural pause in each, where the capital letter occurs; indeed, the lines seem originally to have been divided into two at that point, for sometimes, as in Stanza First, the middle words (*mæren, lobebæren; geziten, striten*) also rhyme; but this is rather a rare case. The word *rechen* or *recken*, used in the First Stanza, is the constant designation for bold fighters, and has the same root with *rich* (thus in old French, *hommes riches;* in Spanish, *ricos hombres*), which last is here also synonymous with *powerful*, and is applied to kings, and even to the Almighty, *Got dem richen.*

become a most noble Ritter's wife.' 'This,' adds the old Singer, 'was that same falcon she dreamed of: how sorely 'she since revenged him on her nearest kindred! For that 'one death died full many a mother's son.'

It may be observed, that the Poet here, and at all times, shows a marked partiality for Chriemhild; ever striving, unlike his fellow-singers, to magnify her worth, her faithfulness and loveliness; and softening, as much as may be, whatever makes against her. No less a favourite with him is Siegfried, the prompt, gay, peaceably fearless hero; to whom, in the Second *Aventiure*, we are here suddenly introduced, at Santen (Xanten), the Court of Netherland; whither, to his glad parents, after achievements (to us partially known) 'of which one might sing and tell forever,' that noble prince has returned. Much as he has done and conquered, he is but just arrived at man's years: it is on occasion of this joyful event, that a high-tide (*hochgezit*) is now held there, with infinite joustings, minstrelsy, largesses and other chivalrous doings, all which is sung with utmost heartiness. The old King Siegemund offers to resign his crown to him; but Siegfried has other game a-field: the unparalleled beauty of Chriemhild has reached his ear and his fancy; and now he will to Worms and woo her, at least 'see how it stands with her.' Fruitless is it for Siegemund and the mother Siegelinde to represent the perils of that enterprise, the pride of those Burgundian Gunthers and Gernots, the fierce temper of their uncle Hagen; Siegfried is as obstinate as young men are in these cases, and can hear no counsel. Nay he will not accept the much more liberal proposition, to take an army with him, and conquer the country, if it must be so; he will ride forth, like himself, with twelve champions only, and so defy the future. Whereupon, the old people finding that there is no other course, proceed to make him clothes;[1]

[1] This is a never-failing preparative for all expeditions, and always specified and insisted on with a simple, loving, almost female impressiveness.

— at least, the good queen with 'her fair women sitting night and day,' and sewing, does so, the father furnishing noblest battle and riding gear; — and so dismiss him with many blessings and lamentations. 'For him wept sore the king 'and his *wife*, but he comforted both their bodies (*lip*); he 'said, "Ye must not weep, for my body ever shall ye be 'without care."'

> Sad was it to the Recken, Stood weeping many a maid;
> I ween their heart had them The tidings true foresaid,
> That of their friends so many Death thereby should find;
> Cause had they of lamenting, Such boding in their mind.

Nevertheless, on the seventh morning, that adventurous company 'ride up the sand,' on the Rhinebeach, to Worms; in high temper, in dress and trappings, aspect and bearing more than kingly.

Siegfried's reception at King Gunther's court, and his brave sayings and doings there for some time, we must omit. One fine trait of his chivalrous delicacy it is that, for a whole year, he never hints at his errand; never once sees or speaks of Chriemhild, whom, nevertheless, he is longing day and night to meet. She, on her side, has often through her lattices noticed the gallant stranger, victorious in all tiltings and knightly exercises; whereby it would seem, in spite of her rigorous predeterminations, some kindness for him is already gliding in. Meanwhile, mighty wars and threats of invasion arise, and Siegfried does the state good service. Returning victorious, both as general and soldier, from Hessen (Hessia), where, by help of his own courage and the sword Balmung, he has captured a Danish king, and utterly discomfited a Saxon one; he can now show himself before Chriemhild without other blushes than those of timid love. Nay the maiden has herself inquired pointedly of the messengers, touching his exploits; and 'her fair face grew rose-red when she heard them.' A gay High-tide, by way of triumph, is appointed; several kings, and two-and-thirty princes, and knights enough with 'gold-red saddles,' come to joust; and better than whole infinities of kings and princes with their saddles, the fair Chriemhild herself, under guidance of her mother, chiefly too in honour of the victor, is to grace that sport. 'Ute the full rich' fails not to set her needle-women to work, and 'clothes of price are taken from their presses,' for the love of her child, 'wherewith to deck many women and maids.' And now, 'on the Whitsun-morning,' all is ready, and glorious as heart could desire it; brave Ritters, 'five thousand or more,' all glancing in the lists; but grander still, Chriemhild herself is advancing beside her mother, with a hundred body-guards, all sword-in-hand, and many a noble maid 'wearing rich raiment,' in her train!

'Now issued forth the lovely one (*minnechliche*), as the red morning doth from troubled clouds; much care fled away from him who bore her in his heart, and long had done; he saw the lovely one stand in her beauty.

'There glanced from her garments full many precious stones, her rose-red colour shone full lovely: try what he might, each man must confess that in this world he had not seen aught so fair.

'Like as the light moon stands before the stars, and its sheen so clear goes over the clouds, even so stood she now before many fair women; whereat cheered was the mind of the hero.

'The rich chamberlains you saw go before her, the high-spirited Recken would not forbear, but pressed on where they saw the lovely maiden. Siegfried the lord was both glad and sad.

'He thought in his mind, How could this be that I should woo thee? That was a foolish dream; yet must I forever be a stranger, I were rather (*sanfter*, softer) dead. He became, from these thoughts, in quick changes, pale and red.

'Thus stood so lovely the child of Siegelinde, as if he were limned on parchment by a master's art; for all granted that hero so beautiful they had never seen.'

In this passage, which we have rendered, from the Fifth *Aventiure*, into the closest prose, it is to be remarked, among other singularities, that there are two similes: in which figure of speech our old Singer deals very sparingly. The first, that comparison of Chriemhild to the moon among stars with its sheen going over the clouds, has now for many centuries had little novelty or merit: but the second, that of Siegfried to a Figure in some illuminated Manuscript, is graceful in itself; and unspeakably so to antiquaries, seldom honoured, in their Black-letter stubbing and grubbing, with such a poetic windfall!

A prince and a princess of this quality are clearly made for one another. Nay, on the motion of young Herr Gernot, fair Chriemhild is bid specially to salute Siegfried, she who had never before saluted man; which unparalleled grace the lovely one, in all courtliness, openly does him. "Be welcome," said she, "Herr Siegfried, a noble Ritter good;" from which salute, for this seems to have been all, 'much raised was his mind.' He bowed with graceful reverence, as his manner was with women; she took him by the hand, and with fond stolen glances they looked at each other. Whether in that ceremonial joining of hands there might not be some soft, slight pressure, of far deeper import, is what our Singer will not take upon him to say; however, he thinks the affirmative more probable. Henceforth, in that bright May weather, the two were seen constantly together: nothing but felicity around and before them. — In these days, truly, it must have been that the famous Prize-fight, with Dietrich of Bern and his Eleven Lombardy champions took place, little to the profit of the two Lovers; were it not rather that the whole of that Rose-garden transaction, as given in the *Heldenbuch*, might be falsified and even imaginary; for no mention or hint of it occurs here. War or battle is not heard of; Siegfried the peerless walks wooingly by the side of Chriemhild the peerless; matters, it is evident, are in the best possible course.

But now comes a new side-wind, which, however, in the long-run also forwards the voyage. Tidings, namely, reached over the Rhine, not so surprising we might hope, 'that there was many a fair maiden;' whereupon Gunther the King 'thought with himself to win one of them.' It was an honest purpose in King Gunther, only his choice was not the discreetest. For no fair maiden will content him but Queen Brunhild, a lady who rules in *Isenland*, far over sea, famed indeed for her beauty, yet no less so for her caprices. Fables we have met with of this Brunhild being properly a *Valkyr*, or Scandinavian Houri, such as were wont to lead old northern warriors from their last battle-field into Valhalla; and that her castle of *Isenstein* stood amidst a lake of fire: but this, as we said, is fable and groundless calumny, of which there is not so much as notice taken here. Brunhild, it is plain enough, was a flesh-and-blood maiden, glorious in look and faculty, only with some preternatural talents given her, and the strangest wayward habits. It appears, for example, that any suitor proposing for her has this brief condition to proceed upon: he must try the adorable in the three several games of hurling the Spear (at one another), Leaping, and throwing the Stone; if victorious, he gains her hand; if vanquished, he loses his own head; which latter issue, such is the fair Amazon's strength, frequent fatal experiment has shown to be the only probable one.

Siegfried, who knows something of Brunhild and her ways, votes clearly against the whole enterprise; however, Gunther has once for all got the whim in him, and must see it out. The prudent Hagen von Troneg, uncle to love-sick Gunther, and ever true to him, then advises that Siegfried be requested to take part in the adventure; to which request Siegfried readily accedes on one condition: that, should they prove fortunate, he himself is to have Chriemhild to wife when they return. This readily settled, he now takes charge of the business, and throws a little light on it for the others. They must lead no army thither; only two, Hagen and Dankwart, besides the king and himself, shall go. The grand subject of *waete*[1] (clothes) is next hinted at, and in general terms elucidated; whereupon a solemn consultation with Chriemhild ensues; and a great cutting-out, on her part, of white

[1] Hence our English *weeds*, and Scotch *wad* (pledge); and, say the etymologists, *wadding*, and even *wedding*.

silk from Araby, of green silk from Zazemang, of strange fish-skins covered with morocco silk; a great sewing thereof for seven weeks, on the part of her maids; lastly, a fitting-on of the three suits by each hero, for each had three; and heartiest thanks in return, seeing all fitted perfectly, and was of grace and price unutterable. What is still more to the point, Siegfried takes his Cloak of Darkness with him, fancying he may need it there. The good old Singer, who has hitherto alluded only in the faintest way to Siegfried's prior adventures and miraculous possessions, introduces this of the *Tarnkappe* with great frankness and simplicity. 'Of wild 'dwarfs (*getwergen*),' says he, 'I have heard tell, they are in 'hollow mountains, and for defence wear somewhat called '*Tarnkappe*, of wondrous sort;' the qualities of which garment, that it renders invisible, and gives twelve men's strength, are already known to us.

The voyage to Isenstein, Siegfried steering the ship thither, is happily accomplished in twenty days. Gunther admires to a high degree the fine masonry of the place; as indeed he well might, there being some eighty-six towers, three immense palaces and one immense hall, the whole built of 'marble green as grass;' farther he sees many fair women looking from the windows down on the bark, and thinks the loveliest is she in the snow-white dress; which, Siegfried informs him, is a worthy choice; the snow-white maiden being no other than Brunhild. It is also to be kept in mind that Siegfried, for reasons known best to himself, had previously stipulated that, though a free king, they should all treat him as vassal of Gunther, for whom accordingly he holds the stirrup, as they mount on the beach; thereby giving rise to a misconception, which in the end led to saddest consequences.

Queen Brunhild, who had called back her maidens from the windows, being a strict disciplinarian, and retired into the interior of her green marble Isenstein, to dress still better, now inquires of some attendant, Who these strangers of such lordly aspect are, and what brings them? The attendant professes himself at a loss to say; one of them looks like Siegfried, the other is evidently by his port a noble king. His notice of Von Troneg Hagen is peculiarly vivid:

> The third of those companions He is of aspect stern,
> And yet with lovely body, Rich queen, as ye might discern;
> From those *his rapid glances*, For the eyes naught rest in him,
> Meseems this foreign Recke Is of temper fierce and grim.

This is one of those little graphic touches, scattered all over our Poem, which do more for picturing out an object, especially a man, than whole pages of enumeration and mensuration. Never after do we hear of this stout indomitable Hagen, in all the wild deeds and sufferings he passes through, but those *swinden blicken* of his come before us, with the restless, deep, dauntless spirit that looks through them.

Brunhild's reception of Siegfried is not without tartness; which, however, he, with polished courtesy, and the nimblest address, ever at his command, softens down, or hurries over: he is here, without will of his own, and so forth, only as attendant on his master, the renowned King Gunther, who comes to sue for her hand, as the summit and keystone of all earthly blessings. Brunhild, who had determined on fighting Siegfried himself, if so he willed it, makes small account of this King Gunther or his prowess; and instantly clears the ground, and equips her for battle. The royal wooer must have looked a little blank when he saw a shield brought in for his fair one's handling, 'three spans thick with gold and iron,' which four chamberlains could hardly bear, and a spear or javelin she meant to shoot or hurl, which was a burden for three. Hagen, in angry apprehension for his king and nephew, exclaims that they shall all lose their life (*lip*), and that she is the *tiuvels wip*, or Devil's wife. Nevertheless Siegfried is already there in his Cloak of Darkness, twelve men strong, and privily whispers in the ear of royalty to be of comfort; takes the shield to himself, Gunther only affecting to hold it, and so fronts the edge of battle. Brunhild performs prodigies of spear-hurling, of leaping, and stone-pitching; but Gunther, or rather Siegfried, 'who does the work, he only acting the gestures,' nay who even snatches him up into the air, and leaps carrying him, — gains a decided victory, and the lovely Amazon must own with surprise and shame, that she is fairly won. Siegfried presently appears without *Tarnkappe*, and asks with a grave face, When the games then are to begin?

So far well; yet somewhat still remains to be done. Brunhild will not sail for Worms, to be wedded, till she have assembled a fit train of warriors: wherein the Burgundians, being here without retinue, see symptoms or possibilities of mischief. The deft Siegfried, ablest of men, again knows a resource. In his *Tarnkappe* he steps on board the bark, which seen from the shore, appears to drift-off of its own accord; and therein, stoutly steering towards *Nibelungen-land*, he reaches that mysterious country and the mountain where his Hoard lies, before the second morning; finds Dwarf Alberich and all his giant sentinels at their post, and faithful almost to the death; these soon rouse him thirty thousand Nibelungen Recken, from whom he has only to choose one thousand of the best; equip them splendidly enough; and therewith return to Gunther, simply as if they were that sovereign's own body-guard, that had been delayed a little by stress of weather.

The final arrival at Worms; the bridal feasts, for there are two, Siegfried also receiving his reward; and the joyance and splendour of man and maid, at this lordliest of high-tides; and the joustings, greater than those at Aspramont or Montauban, — every reader can fancy for himself. Remarkable only is the evil eye with which Queen Brunhild still continues to regard the noble Siegfried. She cannot understand how Gunther, the Landlord of the Rhine,[1] should have

[1] *Der Wirt von Rine:* singular enough, the word *Wirth*, often applied to royalty in that old dialect, is now also the title of innkeepers. To such base uses may we come.

bestowed his sister on a vassal: the assurance that Siegfried also is a prince and heir-apparent, the prince namely of Netherland, and little inferior to Burgundian majesty itself, yields no complete satisfaction; and Brunhild hints plainly that, unless the truth be told her, unpleasant consequences may follow. Thus is there ever a ravelled thread in the web of life! But for this little cloud of spleen, these bridal feasts had been all bright and balmy as the month of June. Unluckily too, the cloud is an electric one; spreads itself in time into a general earthquake; nay that very night becomes a thunder-storm, or tornado, unparalleled we may hope in the annals of connubial happiness.

The Singer of the *Nibelungen*, unlike the Author of *Roderick Random*, cares little for intermeddling with 'the chaste mysteries of Hymen.' Could we, in the corrupt ambiguous modern tongue, hope to exhibit any shadow of the old simple, true-hearted, merely historical spirit, with which, in perfect purity of soul, he describes things unattempted yet in prose or rhyme, — we could a tale unfold! Suffice it to say, King Gunther, Landlord of the Rhine, falling sheer down from the third heaven of hope, finds his spouse the most athletic and intractable of women; and himself, at the close of the adventure, nowise encircled in her arms, but tied hard and fast, hand and foot, in her girdle, and hung thereby, at considerable elevation, on a nail in the wall. Let any reader of sensibility figure the emotions of the royal breast, there as he vibrates suspended on his peg, and his inexorable bride sleeping sound in her bed below! Towards morning he capitulates; engaging to observe the prescribed line of conduct with utmost strictness, so he may but avoid becoming a laughing-stock to all men.

No wonder the dread king looked rather grave next morning, and received the congratulations of mankind in a cold manner. He confesses to Siegfried, who partly suspects how it may be, that he has brought the 'evil devil' home to his house in the shape of wife, whereby he is wretched enough. However, there are remedies for all things but death. The ever-serviceable Siegfried undertakes even here to make the crooked straight. What may not an honest friend with Tarnkappe and twelve men's strength perform? Proud Brunhild, next night, after a fierce contest, owns herself again vanquished; Gunther is there to reap the fruits of another's victory; the noble Siegfried withdraws, taking nothing with him but the luxury of doing good, and the proud queen's Ring and Girdle gained from her in that struggle; which small trophies he, with the last infirmity of a noble mind, presents to his own fond wife, little dreaming that they would one day cost him and her, and all of them, so dear. Such readers as take any interest in poor Gunther will be gratified to learn, that from this hour Brunhild's preternatural faculties quite left her, being all dependent on her maidhood; so that any more spear-hurling, or other the like extraordinary work, is not to be apprehended from her.

If we add, that Siegfried formerly made over to his dear Chriemhild the Nibelungen Hoard, by way of *Morgengabe* (or, as we may say, Jointure); and the high-tide, though not the honeymoon being past, returned to Netherland with his spouse, to be welcomed there with infinite rejoicings, — we have gone through as it were the First Act of this Tragedy; and may here pause to look round us for a moment. The main characters are now introduced on the scene, the relations that bind them together are dimly sketched out: there is the prompt, cheerfully heroic, invulnerable and invincible Siegfried, now happiest of men; the high Chriemhild, fitly-mated, and if a moon, revolving glorious round her sun, or *Friedel* (joy and darling); not without pride and female aspirings, yet not prouder than one so gifted and placed is pardonable for being. On the other hand, we have King Gunther, or rather let us say king's-mantle Gunther, for never except in that one enterprise of courting Brunhild, in which too, without help, he would have cut so poor a figure, does the worthy sovereign show will of his own, or character other than that of good potter's clay; farther, the suspicious, forecasting, yet stout and reckless Hagen, him with the *rapid glances*, and these turned not too kindly on Siegfried, whose prowess he has used yet dreads, whose Nibelungen Hoard he perhaps already covets; lastly, the rigorous and vigorous Brunhild, of whom also more is to be feared than hoped. Considering the fierce nature of these now mingled ingredients; and how, except perhaps in the case of Gunther, there is no menstruum of placid stupidity to soften them; except in Siegfried, no element of heroic truth to master them and bind them together, — unquiet fermentation may readily be apprehended.

Meanwhile, for a season all is peace and sunshine. Siegfried reigns in Netherland, of which his father has surrendered him the crown; Chriemhild brings him a son, whom in honor of the uncle he christens Gunther, which courtesy the uncle and Brunhild repay in kind. The Nibelungen Hoard is still open and inexhaustible; Dwarf Alberich and all the Recken there still loyal; outward relations friendly, internal supremely prosperous: these are halcyon days. But, alas, they cannot last. Queen Brunhild, retaining with true female tenacity her first notion, right or wrong, reflects one day that Siegfried, who is and shall be nothing but her husband's vassal, has for a long while paid him no service; and, determined on a remedy, manages that Siegfried and his queen shall be invited to a high-tide at Worms, where opportunity may chance for enforcing that claim. Thither accordingly, after ten years' absence, we find these illustrious guests returning; Siegfried escorted by a thousand Nibelungen Ritters, and farther by his father Siegemund who leads a train of Netherlanders. Here for eleven days, amid infinite joustings, there is a true heaven-on-earth: but the apple of discord is already lying in the knightly ring, and two Women, the proudest and keenest-tempered of the world, simultaneously stoop to lift it. *Aventiure* Fourteenth is entitled 'How the two queens rated one another.' Never was courtlier Billingsgate uttered, or which came more directly home to the business and bosoms of women. The subject is that old story of Precedence, which indeed, from the time of Cain and Abel downwards, has wrought such effusion of blood and bile both among men and women; lying at the bottom of all armaments and battle-fields, whether Blenheims and Waterloos, or only plate-displays, and tongue-and-eye skirmishes, in the circle of domestic Tea: nay, the very animals have it; and horses, were they but the miserablest Shelties and Welsh ponies, will not graze together till it has been ascertained, by clear fight, who is master of whom, and a proper drawing-room etiquette established.

Brunhild and Chriemhild take to arguing about the merits of their husbands: the latter, fondly expatiating on the pre-eminence of her *Friedel*, how he walks 'like the moon among stars' before all other men, is reminded by her sister that one man at least must be excepted, the mighty King Gunther of Worms, to whom by his own confession long ago at Isenstein, he is vassal and servant. Chriemhild will sooner admit that clay is above sunbeams, than any such proposition; which therefore she, in all politeness, requests of her sister nevermore to touch upon while she lives. The result may be foreseen: rejoinder follows reply, statement grows assertion; flint-sparks have fallen on the dry flax, which from smoke bursts into conflagration. The two queens part in hottest, though still clear-flaming anger. Not, however, to let their anger burn out, but only to feed it with more solid fuel. Chriemhild dresses her forty maids in finer than royal apparel; orders out all her husband's Recken; and so attended, walks foremost to the Minster, where mass is to be said; thus practically asserting that she is not only a true queen, but the worthier of the two. Brunhild, quite outdone in splendour, and enraged beyond all patience, overtakes her at the door of the Minster, with peremptory order to stop: "before king's wife shall vassal's never go."

Then said the fair Chriemhild, Right angry was her mood:
"Couldest thou but hold thy peace, It were surely for thy good;
Thyself hast all polluted With shame thy fair bodye;
How can a Concubine By right a King's wife be?"

"Whom hast thou Concubined?" The King's wife quickly spake;
"That do I thee," said Chriemhild; "For thy pride and vaunting's sake;
Who first had thy fair body Was Siegfried my beloved Man;
My Brother it was not That thy maidhood from thee wan."

In proof of which outrageous saying, she produces that Ring and Girdle; the innocent conquest of which, as we well know, had a far other origin. Brunhild bursts into tears; 'sadder day she never saw.' Nay, perhaps a new light now rose on her over much that had been dark in her late history; 'she rued full sore that ever she was born.'

Here, then, is the black injury, which only blood will wash away. The evil fiend has begun his work; and the issue of it lies beyond man's control. Siegfried may protest his innocence of that calumny, and chastise his indiscreet spouse for uttering it even in the heat of anger: the female heart is wounded beyond healing; the old springs of bitterness against this hero unite into a fell flood of hate; while he sees the sunlight, she cannot know a joyful hour. Vengeance is soon offered her: Hagen, who lives only for his prince, undertakes this bad service; by treacherous professions of attachment, and anxiety to guard Siegfried's life, he gains from Chriemhild the secret of his vulnerability; Siegfried is carried out to hunt; and in the hour of frankest gaiety is stabbed through the fatal spot; and, felling the murderer to the ground, dies upbraiding his false kindred, yet, with a touching simplicity, recommending his child and wife to their protection. '"Let her feel that she is your 'sister; was there ever virtue in princes, be true to her: 'for me my Father and my men shall long wait." The 'flowers all around were wetted with blood, then he strug-

'gled with death ; not long did he this, the weapon cut him 'too keen ; so he could speak naught more, the Recke bold 'and noble.'

At this point, we might say, ends the Third Act of our Tragedy; the whole story henceforth takes a darker character ; it is as if a tone of sorrow and fateful boding became more and more audible in its free, light music. Evil has produced new evil in fatal augmentation : injury is abolished ; but in its stead there is guilt and despair. Chriemhild, an hour ago so rich, is now robbed of all : her grief is boundless as her love has been. No glad thought can ever more dwell in her ; darkness, utter night has come over her, as she looked into the red of morning. The spoiler took walks abroad unpunished ; the bleeding corpse witnesses against Hagen, nay he himself cares not to hide the deed. But who is there to avenge the friendless ? Siegfried's Father has returned in haste to his own land ; Chriemhild is now alone on the earth, her husband's grave is all that remains to her ; there only can she sit, as if waiting at the threshold of her own dark home ; and in prayers and tears pour out the sorrow and love that have no end. Still farther injuries are heaped on her : by advice of the crafty Hagen, Gunther, who had not planned the murder, yet permitted and witnessed it, now comes with whining professions of repentance and good-will ; persuades her to send for the Nibelungen Hoard to Worms ; where no sooner is it arrived, than Hagen and the rest forcibly take it from her ; and her last trust in affection or truth from mortal is rudely cut away. Bent to the earth, she weeps only for her lost Siegfried, knows no comfort, but will weep forever.

One lurid gleam of hope, after long years of darkness, breaks in on her, in the prospect of revenge. King Etzel sends from his far country to solicit her hand : the embassy she hears at first, as a woman of ice might do ; the good Rudiger, Etzel's spokesman, pleads in vain that his king is the richest of all earthly kings ; that he is so lonely 'since

Frau Helke died;' that though a heathen, he has Christians about him, and may one day be converted: till at length, when he hints distantly at the power of Etzel to avenge her injuries, she on a sudden becomes all attention. Hagen, foreseeing such possibilities, protests against the match; but is overruled: Chriemhild departs with Rudiger for the land of the Huns; taking cold leave of her relations; only two of whom, her brothers Gernot and Geiselher, innocent of that murder, does she admit near her as convoy to the Donau.

The Nibelungen Hoard has hitherto been fatal to all its possessors; to the two sons of Nibelung; to Siegfried its conqueror: neither does the Burgundian Royal House fare better with it. Already, discords threatening to arise, Hagen sees prudent to sink it in the Rhine; first taking oath of Gunther and his brothers, that none of them shall reveal the hiding-place, while any of the rest is alive. But the curse that clave to it could not be sunk there. The Nibelungen-land is now theirs: they themselves are henceforth called Nibelungen; and this history of their fate is the Nibelungen Song, or *Nibelungen Noth* (Nibelungen's Need, extreme need, or final wreck and abolition).

The Fifth Act of our strange eventful history now draws on. Chriemhild has a kind husband, of hospitable disposition, who troubles himself little about her secret feelings and intents. With his permission, she sends two minstrels, inviting the Burgundian Court to a high-tide at Etzel's: she has charged the messengers to say that she is happy, and to bring all Gunther's champions with them. Her eye was on Hagen, but she could not single him from the rest. After seven days' deliberation, Gunther answers that he will come. Hagen has loudly dissuaded the journey, but again been overruled. 'It is his fate,' says a commentator, 'like Cassandra's, ever to foresee the evil, and ever to be disregarded. 'He himself shut his ear against the inward voice; and now 'his warnings are uttered to the deaf.' He argues long, but in vain: nay young Gernot hints at last that this aversion originates in personal fear:

Then spake Von Troneg Hagen: "Nowise is it through fear;
So you command it, Heroes, Then up, gird on your gear;
I ride with you the foremost Into King Etzel's land."
Since then full many a helm Was shivered by his hand.

Frau Ute's dreams and omens are now unavailing with him; "whoso heedeth dreams," said Hagen, "of the right story wotteth not:" he has computed the worst issue, and defied it.

Many a little touch of pathos, and even solemn beauty lies carelessly scattered in these rhymes, had we space to exhibit such here. As specimen of a strange, winding, diffuse, yet innocently graceful style of narrative, we had translated some considerable portion of this Twenty-fifth *Aventiure*, 'How the Nibelungen marched (fared) to the Huns,' into verses as literal as might be; which now, alas, look mournfully different from the original; almost like Scriblerus's shield when the barbarian housemaid had scoured it! Nevertheless, to do for the reader what we can, let somewhat of that modernised ware, such as it is, be set before him. The brave Nibelungen are on the eve of departure; and about ferrying over the Rhine: and here it may be noted that Worms,[1] with our old Singer, lies not in its true position,

[1] This City of Worms, had we a right imagination, ought to be as venerable to us Moderns, as any Thebes or Troy was to the Ancients. Whether founded by the Gods or not, it is of quite unknown antiquity, and has witnessed the most wonderful things. Within authentic times, the Romans were here; and if tradition may be credited, Attila also; it was the seat of the Austrasian kings; the frequent residence of Charlemagne himself; innumerable Festivals, High-tides, Tournaments and Imperial Diets were held in it, of which latter, one at least, that where Luther appeared in 1521, will be forever remembered by all mankind. Nor is Worms more famous in history than, as indeed we may see here, it is in romance; whereof many monuments and vestiges remain to *this day*. 'A pleasant 'meadow there,' says Von der Hagen, 'is still called Chriemhild's *Rosen-* '*garten*. The name *Worms* itself is derived (by Legendary Etymology) 'from the Dragon, or *Worm*, which Siegfried slew, the figure of which 'once formed the City Arms; in past times, there was also to be seen here

but at some distance from the river; a proof at least that he was never there, and probably sang and lived in some very distant region:

The boats were floating ready, And many men there were;
What clothes of price they had They took and stow'd them there,
Was never a rest from toiling Until the eventide,
Then they took the flood right gaily, Would longer not abide.

Brave tents and hutches You saw raised on the grass,
Other side the Rhine-stream That camp it pitched was:
The king to stay a while Was besought of his fair wife;
That night she saw him with her, And never more in life.

Trumpets and flutes spoke out, At dawning of the day,
That time was come for parting, So they rose to march away:
Who loved-one had in arms Did kiss that same, I ween;
And fond farewells were bidden By cause of Etzel's Queen.

Frau Ute's noble sons They had a serving-man,
A brave one and a true: Or ever the march began,
He speaketh to King Gunther, What for his ear was fit,
He said: "Woe for this journey, I grieve because of it."

He Rumold hight, the Sewer, Was known as hero true;
He spake: "Whom shall this people And land be trusted to?
Woe on't, will naught persuade ye, Brave Recken, from this road!
Frau Chriemhild's flattering message No good doth seem to bode."

'an ancient strong *Riesen-Haus* (Giant's house), and many a memorial of 'Siegfried: his Lance, 66 feet long (almost 80 English feet), in the Cathe-'dral; his Statue, of gigantic size, on the *Neue Thurm* (New Tower) on 'the Rhine;' &c. &c. 'And lastly the Siegfried's Chapel, in primeval, 'Pre-Gothic architecture, not long since pulled down. In the time of the '*Meistersängers* too, the Stadtrath was bound to give every Master, who 'sang the Lay of Siegfried (*Meisterlied von Siegfrieden*, the purport of 'which is now unknown) without mistake, a certain gratuity.' — *Glossary* to the *Nibelungen*, § *Worms*.

One is sorry to learn that this famed Imperial City is no longer Imperial, but much fallen in every way from its palmy state; the 30,000 inhabitants, to be found there in Gustavus Adolphus' time, having now declined into some 6,800, — 'who maintain themselves by wine-growing, Rhine-boats, tobacco-manufacture, and making sugar-of-lead.' So hard has war, which respects nothing, pressed on Worms, ill-placed for safety, on the hostile border: Louvois, or Louis XIV., in 1689, had it utterly devastated; whereby in the interior, 'spaces that were once covered with buildings are now gardens.' — See *Conv. Lexicon*, § *Worms*.

"The land to thee be trusted, And my fair boy also,
And serve thou well the women, I tell thee ere I go;
Whomso thou findest weeping Her heart give comfort to;
No harm to one of us King Etzel's wife will do."

The steeds were standing ready, For the Kings and for their men;
With kisses tenderest Took leave full many then,
Who, in gallant cheer and hope, To march were naught afraid:
Them since that day bewaileth Many a noble wife and maid.

But when the rapid Recken Took horse and prickt away,
The women shent in sorrow You saw behind them stay;
Of parting all too long Their hearts to them did tell;
When grief so great is coming, The mind forbodes not well.

Nathless the brisk Burgonden All on their way did go,
Then rose the country over A mickle dole and woe;
On both sides of the hills Woman and man did weep:
Let their folk do how they list, These gay their course did keep.

The Nibelungen Recken [1] Did march with them as well,
In a thousand glittering hauberks, Who at home had ta'en farewell
Of many a fair woman Should see them never more:
The wound of her brave Siegfried Did grieve Chriemhilde sore.

Then 'gan they shape their journey Towards the River Maine,
All on through East-Franconia, King Gunther and his train;
Hagen he was their leader, Of old did know the way;
Dankwart did keep, as marshal, Their ranks in good array.

As they, from East-Franconia, The Salfield rode along,
Might you have seen them prancing, A bright and lordly throng,
The Princes and their vassals, All heroes of great fame:
The twelfth morn brave King Gunther Unto the Donau came.

There rode Von Troneg Hagen, The foremost of that host,
He was to the Nibelungen The guide they lov'd the most:
The Ritter keen dismounted, Set foot on the sandy ground,
His steed to a tree he tied, Look'd wistful all around.

"Much scaith," Von Troneg said, "May lightly chance to thee,
King Gunther, by this tide, As thou with eyes mayst see:

[1] These are the Nibelungen proper who had come to Worms with Siegfried, on the famed bridal journey from Isenstein, long ago. Observe, at the same time, that ever since the *Nibelungen Hoard* was transferred to Rhine-land, the whole subjects of King Gunther are often called Nibelungen, and their subsequent history is this *Nibelungen Song*.

The river is overflowing, Full strong runs here its stream,
For crossing of this Donau Some counsel might well beseem."

" What counsel hast thou, brave Hagen," King Gunther then did say,
" Of thy own wit and cunning? Dishearten me not, I pray:
Thyself the ford wilt find us, If knightly skill it can,
That safe to yonder shore We may pass both horse and man."

" To me, I trow," spake Hagen, " Life hath not grown so cheap,
To go with will and drown me In riding these waters deep;
But first, of men some few By this hand of mine shall die,
In great King Etzel's country, As best good-will have I.

But bide ye here by the River, Ye Ritters brisk and sound,
Myself will seek some boatman, If boatman here be found,
To row us at his ferry, Across to Gelfrat's land:"
The Troneger grasped his buckler, Fared forth along the strand.

He was full bravely harness'd, Himself he knightly bore,
With buckler and with helmet, Which bright enough he wore;
And, bound above his hauberk, A weapon broad was seen,
That cut with both its edges, Was never sword so keen.

Then hither he and thither Search'd for the Ferryman,
He heard a splashing of waters, To watch the same he 'gan,
It was the white Mer-women, That in a fountain clear,
To cool their fair bodyes, Were merrily bathing here.

From these Mer-women, who 'skimmed aloof like white cygnets' at sight of him, Hagen snatches up 'their wondrous raiment;' on condition of returning which, they rede him his fortune; how this expedition is to speed. At first favourably:

She said: " To Etzel's country, Of a truth ye well may hie,
For here I pledge my hand, Now kill me if I lie,
That heroes seeking honour Did never arrive thereat
So richly as ye shall do, Believe thou surely that."

But no sooner is the wondrous raiment restored them, than they change their tale; for in spite of that matchless honour, it appears every one of the adventurous Recken is to perish.

Outspake the wild Mer-woman: " I tell thee it will arrive,
Of all your gallant host No man shall be left alive,

Except King Gunther's chaplain, As we full well do know;
He only, home returning, To the Rhine-land back shall go."

Then spake Von Troneg Hagen, His wrath did fiercely swell:
"Such tidings to my master I were right loath to tell,
That in King Etzel's country We all must lose our life:
Yet show me over the water, Thou wise all-knowing *wife*."

Thereupon, seeing him bent on ruin, she gives directions how to find the ferry, but withal counsels him to deal warily; the ferry-house stands on the other side of the river; the boatman, too, is not only the hottest-tempered of men, but rich and indolent; nevertheless, if nothing else will serve, let Hagen call himself Amelrich, and that name will bring him. All happens as predicted: the boatman, heedless of all shouting and offers of gold clasps, bestirs him lustily at the name of Amelrich; but the more indignant is he, on taking-in his fare, to find it a counterfeit. He orders Hagen, if he loves his life, to leap out.

"Now say not that," spake Hagen; "Right hard am I bested,
Take from me for good friendship This clasp of gold so red;
And row our thousand heroes And steeds across this river."
Then spake the wrathful boatman, "That will I surely never."

Then one of his oars he lifted, Right broad it was and long,
He struck it down on Hagen, Did the hero mickle wrong,
That in the boat he staggered, And alighted on his knee;
Other such wrathful boatman Did never the Troneger see.

His proud unbidden guest He would now provoke still more,
He struck his head so stoutly That it broke in twain the oar,
With strokes on head of Hagen; He was a sturdy wight:
Nathless had Gelfrat's boatman Small profit of that fight.

With fiercely raging spirit, The Troneger turn'd him round,
Clutch'd quick enough his scabbard, And a weapon there he found;
He smote his head from off him, And cast it on the sand,
Thus had that wrathful boatman His death from Hagen's hand.

Even as Von Troneg Hagen The wrathful boatman slew,
The boat whirl'd round to the river, He had work enough to do;
Or ever he turn'd it shorewards, To weary he began,
But kept full stoutly rowing, The bold King Gunther's man.

He wheel'd it back, brave Hagen, With many a lusty stroke,
The strong oar, with such rowing, In his hand asunder broke;
He fain would reach the Recken, All waiting on the shore,
No tackle now he had; Hei,[1] how deftly he spliced the oar,

With thong from off his buckler! It was a slender band;
Right over against a forest He drove the boat to land;
Where Gunther's Recken waited, In crowds along the beach;
Full many a goodly hero Moved down his boat to reach.

Hagen ferries them over himself 'into the unknown land,' like a right yare steersman; yet ever brooding fiercely on that prediction of the wild Mer-woman, which had outdone even his own dark forebodings. Seeing the Chaplain, who alone of them all was to return, standing in the boat beside his *chappelsoume* (pyxes and other sacred furniture), he determines to belie at least this part of the prophecy, and on a sudden hurls the chaplain overboard. Nay as the poor priest swims after the boat, he pushes him down, regardless of all remonstrance, resolved that he shall die. Nevertheless it proved not so: the chaplain made for the other side; when his strength failed, 'then God's hand helped him,' and at length he reached the shore. Thus does the stern truth stand revealed to Hagen, by the very means he took for eluding it: 'he thought with himself these Recken must all lose their lives.' From this time, a grim reckless spirit takes possession of him; a courage, an audacity, waxing more and more into the fixed strength of desperation. The passage once finished, he dashes the boat in pieces, and casts it in the stream, greatly as the others wonder at him.

"Why do ye this, good brother?" Said the Ritter Dankwart then;
"How shall we cross this river, When the road we come again?

[1] These apparently insignificant circumstances, down even to mending the oar from his shield, are preserved with a singular fidelity in the most distorted editions of the Tale: see, for example, the Danish ballad, *Lady Grimhild's Wrack* (translated in the *Northern Antiquities*, p. 275, by Mr. Jamieson). This '*Hei!*' is a brisk interjection, whereby the worthy old Singer now and then introduces his own person, when anything very eminent is going forward.

Returning home from Hunland, Here must we lingering stay?" —
Not then did Hagen tell him That return no more could they.

In this shipment 'into the unknown land,' there lies, for the more penetrating sort of commentators, some hidden meaning and allusion. The destruction of the unreturning Ship, as of the Ship Argo, of Æneas's Ships, and the like, is a constant feature of such traditions: it is thought, this ferrying of the Nibelungen has a reference to old Scandinavian Mythuses; nay, to the oldest, most universal emblems shaped out by man's Imagination; Hagen the ferryman being, in some sort, a type of Death, who ferries over his thousands and tens of thousands into a Land still more unknown.[1]

But leaving these considerations, let us remark the deep fearful interest, which, in gathering strength, rises to a really tragical height in the close of this Poem. Strangely has the old Singer, in these his loose melodies, modulated the wild narrative into a poetic whole, with what we might call true art, were it not rather an instinct of genius still more unerring. A fateful gloom now hangs over the fortunes of the Nibelungen, which deepens and deepens as they march onwards to the judgment-bar, till all are engulfed in utter night.

Hagen himself rises in tragic greatness; so helpful, so prompt and strong is he, and true to the death, though without hope. If sin can ever be pardoned, then that one act of his is pardonable; by loyal faith, by free daring and heroic constancy, he has made amends for it. Well does he know what is coming; yet he goes forth to meet it, offers to Ruin his sullen welcome. Warnings thicken on him, which he treats lightly, as things now superfluous. Spite of our love for Siegfried, we must pity and almost respect the lost Hagen, now in his extreme need, and fronting it so nobly. 'Mixed was his hair with a gray colour, his limbs strong, 'and threatening his look.' Nay, his sterner qualities are

[1] See Von der Hagen's *Nibelungen ihre Bedeutung*, &c.

beautifully tempered by another feeling, of which till now we understood not that he was capable, — the feeling of friendship. There is a certain Volker of Alsace here introduced, not for the first time, yet first in decided energy, who is more to Hagen than a brother. This Volker, a courtier and noble, is also a *Spielmann* (minstrel), a *Fidelere gut* (fiddler good); and surely the prince of all *Fideleres;* in truth a very phœnix, melodious as the soft nightingale, yet strong as the royal eagle: for also in the brunt of battle he can play tunes; and, with a *Steel Fiddlebow,* beats strange music from the cleft helmets of his enemies. There is, in this continual allusion to Volker's *Schwert-fidelbogen* (Sword-fiddlebow), as rude as it sounds to us, a barbaric greatness and depth; the light minstrel of kingly and queenly halls is gay also in the storm of Fate, its dire rushing pipes and whistles to him: is he not the image of every brave man fighting with Necessity, be that duel when and where it may; smiting the fiend with giant strokes, yet every stroke *musical?* — This Volker and Hagen are united inseparably, and defy death together. 'Whatever Volker said pleased Hagen; whatever Hagen did pleased Volker.'

But into these last Ten *Aventiures,* almost like the image of a Doomsday, we must hardly glance at present. Seldom, perhaps, in the poetry of that or any other age, has a grander scene of pity and terror been exhibited than here, could we look into it clearly. At every new step new shapes of fear arise. Dietrich of Bern meets the Nibelungen on their way, with ominous warnings: but warnings, as we said, are now superfluous, when the evil itself is apparent and inevitable. Chriemhild, wasted and exasperated here into a frightful Medea, openly threatens Hagen, but is openly defied by him; he and Volker retire to a seat before her palace, and sit there, while she advances in angry tears, with a crowd of armed Huns, to destroy them. But Hagen has Siegfried's Balmung lying naked on his knee, the Minstrel also has drawn his keen Fiddlebow, and the Huns dare not provoke the battle. Chriemhild would fain single out Hagen for vengeance; but Hagen, like other men, stands not alone; and sin is an infection which will not rest with one victim. Partakers or not of his crime, the others also must share his punishment. Singularly touching, in the mean while, is King Etzel's ignorance of what every one else understands too well; and how, in peaceful hospitable spirit, he exerts himself to testify his joy over these royal guests of his, who are bidden hither for far other ends. That night the way-worn Nibelungen are sumptuously lodged; yet Hagen and Volker see good to keep watch: Volker plays them to sleep: 'under the porch of the house he sat on the stone: bolder 'fiddler was there never any; when the tones flowed so 'sweetly, they all gave him thanks. Then sounded his 'strings till all the house rang; his strength and the art 'were great; sweeter and sweeter he began to play, till 'flitted forth from him into sleep full many a careworn soul.' It was their last lullaby; they were to sleep no more. Armed men appear, but suddenly vanish, in the night; assassins sent by Chriemhild, expecting no sentinel: it is plain that the last hour draws nigh.

In the morning the Nibelungen are for the Minster to hear mass; they are putting on gay raiment; but Hagen tells them a different tale: '"ye must take other garments, 'Recken; instead of silk shirts hauberks, for rich mantles 'your good shields: and, beloved masters, moreover squires 'and men, ye shall full earnestly go to the church, and plain 'to God the powerful (*Got dem richen*) of your sorrow and 'utmost need; and know of a surety that death for us is 'nigh."' In Etzel's Hall, where the Nibelungen appear at the royal feast in complete armour, the Strife, incited by Chriemhild, begins; the first answer to her provocation is from Hagen, who hews off the head of her own and Etzel's son, making it bound into the mother's bosom: 'then began among the Recken, a murder grim and great.' Dietrich, with a voice of preternatural power, commands pause; retires with Etzel and Chriemhild; and now the bloody work has free course. We have heard of battles, and massacres, and deadly struggles in siege and storm; but seldom has even the poet's imagination pictured anything so fierce and terrible as this. Host after host, as they enter that huge vaulted Hall, perish in conflict with the doomed Nibelungen; and ever after the terrific uproar, ensues a still more terrific silence. All night, and through morning it lasts. They throw the dead from the windows; blood runs like water; the Hall is set fire to, they quench it with blood, their own burning thirst they slake with blood. It is a tumult like the Crack of Doom, a thousand-voiced, wild-stunning hubbub; and, frightful like a Trump of Doom, the *Sword-fiddlebow* of Volker, who guards the door, makes music to that death-dance. Nor are traits of heroism wanting, and thrilling tones of pity and love; as in that act of Rudiger, Etzel's and Chriemhild's champion, who, bound by oath, 'lays his soul in God's hand,' and enters that Golgotha to die fighting against his friends; yet first changes shields with Hagen, whose own, also given him by Rudiger in a far other hour, had been shattered in the fight. 'When he so lovingly bade 'give him the shield, there were eyes enough red with hot 'tears; it was the last gift which Rudiger of Bechelaren 'gave to any Recke. As grim as Hagen was, and as hard 'of mind, he wept at this gift which the hero good, so near 'his last times, had given him; full many a noble Ritter 'began to weep.'

At last Volker is slain; they are all slain, save only Hagen and Gunther, faint and wounded, yet still unconquered among the bodies of the dead. Dietrich the wary, though strong and invincible, whose Recken too, except old Hildebrand, he now finds are all killed, though he had charged them strictly not to mix in the quarrel, at last arms himself to finish it. He subdues the two wearied Nibelungen, binds them, delivers them to Chriemhild; 'and Herr Dietrich went 'away with weeping eyes, worthily from the heroes.' These never saw each other more. Chriemhild demands of Hagen, Where the Nibelungen Hoard is? But he answers her, that he has sworn never to disclose it, while any of her brothers live. "I bring it to an end," said the infuriated woman; orders her brother's head to be struck off, and holds it up to Hagen. '"Thou hast it now according to thy will," said Hagen; '"of the Hoard knoweth none but God and I; from thee, 'she-devil (*valendinne*), shall it forever be hid."' She kills him with his own sword, once her husband's; and is herself struck dead by Hildebrand, indignant at the woe she has wrought; King Etzel, there present, not opposing the deed. Whereupon the curtain drops over that wild scene: 'the full 'highly honoured were lying dead; the people all had sor-'row and lamentation; in grief had the king's feast ended, 'as all love is wont to do:'

Ine chan iu nicht bescheiden Waz sider da geschach,
Wan ritter unde wrovven Weinen man do sach,
Dar-zuo die edeln chnechte Ir lieben vriunde tot:
Da hat das mære ein ende; Diz ist der Nibelunge not.

I cannot say you now What hath befallen since;
The women all were weeping, And the Ritters and the prince,
Also the noble squires, Their dear friends lying dead:
Here hath the story ending; This is the *Nibelungen's Need.*

We have now finished our slight analysis of this Poem; and hope that readers, who are curious in this matter, and ask themselves, What is the *Nibelungen?* may have here found some outlines of an answer, some help towards farther researches of their own. To such readers another question will suggest itself: Whence this singular production comes to us, When and How it originated? On which point also, what little light our investigation has yielded may be summarily given.

The worthy Von der Hagen, who may well understand the *Nibelungen* better than any other man, having rendered it into the modern tongue, and twice edited it in the original, not without collating some eleven manuscripts, and travelling several thousands of miles to make the last edition perfect, — writes a Book some years ago, rather boldly denominated *The Nibelungen, its Meaning for the present and forever;* wherein, not content with any measurable antiquity of centuries, he would fain claim an antiquity beyond all bounds of dated time. Working his way with feeble mine-lamps of etymology and the like, he traces back the rudiments of his beloved *Nibelungen*, 'to which the flower of his whole life has been consecrated,' into the thick darkness of the Scandinavian *Niflheim* and *Muspelheim*, and the Hindoo Cosmogony; connecting it farther (as already in part we have incidentally pointed out) with the Ship Argo, with Jupiter's goatskin Ægis, the fire-creed of Zerdusht, and even with the heavenly Constellations. His reasoning is somewhat abstruse; yet an honest zeal, very considerable learning and intellectual force bring him tolerably through. So much he renders plausible or probable: that in the *Nibelungen*, under more or less defacement, lie fragments, scattered like mysterious Runes, yet still in part decipherable, of the earliest Thoughts of men; that the fiction of the Nibelungen was at first a religious or philosophical Mythus; and only in later ages, incorporating itself more or less completely with vague traditions of real events, took the form of a story, or mere Narrative of earthly transactions; in which last form, moreover, our actual *Nibelungen Lied* is nowise the original Narrative, but the second, or even the third redaction of one much earlier.

At what particular era the primeval fiction of the *Nibelungen* passed from its Mythological into its Historical shape; and the obscure spiritual elements of it wedded themselves to the obscure remembrances of the Northern Immigrations; and the Twelve Signs of the Zodiac became Twelve Champions of Attila's Wife, — there is no fixing with the smallest certainty. It is known from history that Eginhart, the secretary of Charlemagne, compiled, by order of that monarch, a collection of the ancient German Songs; among which, it is fondly believed by antiquaries, this *Nibelungen* (not indeed our actual *Nibelungen Lied*, yet an older one of similar purport), and the main traditions of the *Heldenbuch* connected therewith, may have had honourable place. Unluckily Eginhart's Collection has quite perished, and only his Life of the Great Charles, in which this circumstance stands noted, survives to provoke curiosity. One thing is certain, Fulco, Archbishop of Rheims, in the year 885, is introduced as 'citing certain German books,' to enforce some argument of his by instance of 'King Ermerich's crime toward his relations;' which King Ermerich and his crime are at this day part and parcel of the 'Cycle of German Fiction,' and presupposed in the *Nibelungen*.[1] Later notices, of a more decisive sort, occur in abundance. Saxo Grammaticus, who flourished in the twelfth century, relates that about the year 1130, a Saxon minstrel being sent to Seeland, with a treacherous invitation from one royal Dane to another; and not daring to violate his oath, yet compassionating the victim, sang to him by way of indirect warning 'the Song of Chriemhild's Treachery to her Brothers;' that is to say, the latter portion of the Story which we still read at greater length in the existing *Nibelungen Lied.* To which direct evidence, that these traditions were universally known in the twelfth century, nay had been in some shape committed to writing, as 'German Books,' in the ninth or rather in the eighth, — we have still to add the probability of their being 'ancient songs,' even at that earliest date; all which may perhaps carry us back into the seventh or even sixth century; yet not farther, inasmuch as certain of the poetic personages that figure in them belong historically to the fifth.

Other and more open proof of antiquity lies in the fact, that these Traditions are so universally diffused. There are Danish and Icelandic versions of them, externally more or less altered and distorted, yet substantially real copies, pro-

[1] Von der Hagen's *Nibelungen*, Einleitung, § vii.

fessing indeed to be borrowed from the German; in particular we have the *Niflinga* and the *Wilkina Saga*, composed in the thirteenth century, which still in many ways illustrate the German original. Innumerable other songs and sagas point more remotely in the same direction. Nay, as Von der Hagen informs us, certain rhymed tales, founded on these old adventures, have been recovered from popular recitation, in the Faroe Islands, within these few years.

If we ask now, What lineaments of Fact still exist in these Traditions; what are the Historical events and persons which our primeval Mythuses have here united with, and so strangely metamorphosed? the answer is unsatisfactory enough. The great Northern Immigrations, unspeakably momentous and glorious as they were for the Germans, have wellnigh faded away utterly from all vernacular records. Some traces, nevertheless, some names and dim shadows of occurrences in that grand movement, still linger here; which, in such circumstances, we gather with avidity. There can be no doubt, for example, but this 'Etzel, king of Hunland,' is the Attila of history; several of whose real achievements and relations are faintly yet still recognisably pictured forth in these Poems. Thus his first queen is named Halke, and in the Scandinavian versions, Herka; which last (Erca) is also the name that Priscus gives her, in the well-known account of his Embassy to Attila. Moreover, it is on his second marriage, which had in fact so mysterious and tragical a character, that the whole catastrophe of the *Nibelungen* turns. It is true, the 'Scourge of God' plays but a tame part here; however, his great acts, though all past, are still visible in their fruits: besides, it is on the Northern or German personages that the tradition chiefly dwells.

Taking farther into account the general 'Cycle,' or System of Northern Tradition, whereof this *Nibelungen* is the centre and keystone, there is, as indeed we saw in the *Heldenbuch*, a certain Kaiser Ottnit and a Dietrich of Bern; to whom also it seems unreasonable to deny historical existence. This

Bern (Verona), as well as the *Rabenschlacht* (Battle of Ravenna), is continually figuring in these fictions; though whether under Ottnit we are to understand Odoacer the vanquished, and under Dietrich of Bern Theodoricus Veronensis, the victor both at Verona and Ravenna, is by no means so indubitable. Chronological difficulties stand much in the way. For our Dietrich of Bern, as we saw in the *Nibelungen*, is represented as one of Etzel's Champions: now Attila died about the year 450; and this Ostrogoth Theodoric did not fight his great Battle at Verona till 489; that of Ravenna, which was followed by a three years' siege, happening next year. So that before Dietrich could become Dietrich *of Bern*, Etzel had been gone almost half a century from the scene. Startled by this anachronism, some commentators have fished out another Theodoric, eighty years prior to him of Verona, and who actually served in Attila's hosts, with a retinue of Goths and Germans; with which new Theodoric, however, the old Ottnit, or Odoacer, of the *Heldenbuch* must, in his turn, part company; whereby the case is no whit mended. Certain it seems, in the mean time, that *Dietrich*, which signifies *Rich in People*, is the same name which in Greek becomes Theodoricus; for at first (as in Procopius) this very *Theodoricus* is always written Θεύδεριχ, which almost exactly corresponds with the German sound. But such are the inconsistencies involved in both hypotheses, that we are forced to conclude one of two things: either that the Singers of those old Lays were little versed in the niceties of History, and unambitious of passing for authorities therein; which seems a remarkably easy conclusion: or else, with Lessing, that they meant some quite other series of persons and transactions, some Kaiser Otto, and his two Anti-Kaisers (in the twelfth century); which, from what has come to light since Lessing's day, seems now an untenable position.

However, as concerns the *Nibelungen*, the most remarkable coincidence, if genuine, remains yet to be mentioned.

'Thwortz,' a Hungarian Chronicler (or perhaps Chronicle), of we know not what authority, relates, 'that Attila left his 'kingdom to his two sons Chaba and Aladar, the former by 'a Grecian mother, the latter by Kremheilch (Chriemhild) a 'German; that Theodoric, one of his followers, sowed dis-'sension between them; and, along with the Teutonic hosts, 'took part with his half-countryman the younger son; where-'upon rose a great slaughter, which lasted for fifteen days, 'and terminated in the defeat of Chaba (the Greek), and his 'flight into Asia.'[1] Could we but put faith in this Thwortz, we might fancy that some vague rumour of that Kremheilch tragedy, swoln by the way, had reached the German ear and imagination; where, gathering round older Ideas and Mythuses, as Matter round its Spirit, the first rude form of *Chriemhilde's Revenge and the Wreck of the Nibelungen* bodied itself forth in Song.

Thus any historical light emitted by these old Fictions is little better than darkness visible; sufficient at most to indicate that great Northern Immigrations, and wars and rumours of war have been; but nowise how and what they have been. Scarcely clearer is the special history of the Fictions themselves; where they were first put together, who have been their successive redactors and new-modellers. Von der Hagen, as we said, supposes that there may have been three several series of such. Two, at all events, are clearly indicated. In their present shape, we have internal evidence that none of these poems can be older than the twelfth century; indeed, great part of the *Hero-book* can be proved to be considerably later. With this last it is understood that Wolfram von Eschenbach and Heinrich von Ofterdingen, two singers otherwise noted in that era, were largely concerned; but neither is there any demonstration of this vague belief: while again, in regard to the Author of our

[1] Weber (*Illustrations of Northern Antiquities*, p. 39), who cites Görres (*Zeitung für Einsiedler*) as his authority.

actual *Nibelungen* not so much as a plausible conjecture can be formed.

Some vote for a certain Conrad von Würzburg; others for the above-named Eschenbach and Ofterdingen; others again for Klingsohr of Ungerland, a minstrel who once passed for a magician. Against all and each of which hypotheses there are objections; and for none of them the smallest conclusive evidence. Who this gifted singer may have been, only in so far as his Work itself proves that there was but One, and the style points to the latter half of the twelfth century, — remains altogether dark: the unwearied Von der Hagen himself, after fullest investigation, gives for verdict, 'we know it not.' Considering the high worth of the *Nibelungen*, and how many feeble balladmongers of that *Swabian Era* have transmitted us their names, so total an oblivion, in this infinitely more important case, may seem surprising. But those *Minnelieder* (Love-songs) and Provençal Madrigals were the Court Poetry of that time, and gained honour in high places; while the old National Traditions were common property and plebeian, and to sing them an unrewarded labour.

Whoever he may be, let him have our gratitude, our love. Looking back with a farewell glance, over that wondrous old Tale, with its many-coloured texture 'of joyances and high-tides, of weeping and of woe,' so skilfully yet artlessly knit up into a whole, we cannot but repeat that a true epic spirit lives in it; that in many ways it has meaning and charms for us. Not only as the oldest Tradition of Modern Europe, does it possess a high antiquarian interest; but farther, and even in the shape we now see it under, unless the 'Epics of the Son of Fingal' had some sort of authenticity, it is our oldest Poem also; the earliest product of these New Ages, which on its own merits, both in form and essence, can be named Poetical. Considering its chivalrous, romantic tone, it may rank as a piece of literary composition, perhaps considerably higher than the Spanish *Cid;* taking in its historical significance, and deep ramifications into the remote Time, it ranks indubitably and greatly higher.

It has been called a Northern *Iliad;* but except in the fact that both poems have a narrative character, and both sing 'the destructive rage' of men, the two have scarcely any similarity. The Singer of the *Nibelungen* is a far different person from Homer; far inferior both in culture and in genius. Nothing of the glowing imagery, of the fierce bursting energy, of the mingled fire and gloom, that dwell in the old Greek, makes its appearance here. The German Singer is comparatively a simple nature; has never penetrated deep into life; never 'questioned Fate;' or struggled with fearful mysteries; of all which we find traces in Homer, still more in Shakspeare; but with meek believing submission, has taken the Universe as he found it represented to him; and rejoices with a fine childlike gladness in the mere outward shows of things. He has little power of delineating character; perhaps he had no decisive vision thereof. His persons are superficially distinguished, and not altogether without generic difference; but the portraiture is imperfectly brought out; there lay no true living original within him. He has little Fancy; we find scarcely one or two similitudes in his whole Poem; and these one or two, which moreover are repeated, betoken no special faculty that way. He speaks of the 'moon among stars;' says often, of sparks struck from steel armour in battle, and so forth, that they were *wie es wehte der wind*, 'as if the wind were blowing them.' We have mentioned Tasso along with him; yet neither in this case is there any close resemblance; the light playful grace, still more the Italian pomp and sunny luxuriance of Tasso are wanting in the other. His are humble wood-notes wild; no nightingale's, but yet a sweet sky-hidden lark's. In all the rhetorical gifts, to say nothing of rhetorical attainments, we should pronounce him even poor.

Nevertheless, a noble soul he must have been, and furnished with far more essential requisites for Poetry than these are; namely, with the heart and feeling of a Poet. He has a clear eye for the Beautiful and True; all unites itself gracefully and compactly in his imagination: it is strange with what careless felicity he winds his way in that complex Narrative, and be the subject what it will, comes through it unsullied, and with a smile. His great strength is an unconscious instinctive strength; wherein truly lies his highest merit. The whole spirit of Chivalry, of Love, and heroic Valour, must have lived in him, and inspired him. Everywhere he shows a noble Sensibility; the sad accents of parting friends, the lamentings of women, the high daring of men, all that is worthy and lovely prolongs itself in melodious echoes through his heart. A true old Singer, and taught of Nature herself! Neither let us call him an inglorious Milton, since now he is no longer a mute one. What good were it that the four or five Letters composing his Name could be printed, and pronounced, with absolute certainty? All that was mortal in him is gone utterly; of his life, and its environment, as of the bodily tabernacle he dwelt in, the very ashes remain not: like a fair heavenly Apparition, which indeed he *was*, he has melted into air, and only the Voice he uttered, in virtue of its inspired gift, yet lives and will live.

To the Germans this *Nibelungen Song* is naturally an object of no common love; neither if they sometimes overvalue it, and vague antiquarian wonder is more common than just criticism, should the fault be too heavily visited. After long ages of concealment, they have found it in the remote wilderness, still standing like the trunk of some almost antediluvian oak; nay with boughs on it still green, after all the wind and weather of twelve hundred years. To many a patriotic feeling, which lingers fondly in solitary places of the Past, it may well be a rallying-point, and 'Lovers' *Trysting-tree*.'

For us also it has its worth. A creation from the old

ages, still bright and balmy, if we visit it; and opening into the first History of Europe, of Mankind. Thus all is not oblivion; but on the edge of the abyss, that separates the Old world from the New, there hangs a fair Rainbow-land; which also, in curious repetitions of itself (*twice* over, say the critics), as it were in a secondary and even a ternary reflex, sheds some feeble twilight far into the deeps of the primeval Time.

GERMAN LITERATURE OF THE FOURTEENTH AND FIFTEENTH CENTURIES.[1]

[1831.]

It is not with Herr Soltau's work, and its merits or demerits, that we here purpose to concern ourselves. The old Low-German Apologue was already familiar under many shapes; in versions into Latin, English and all modern tongues: if it now comes before our German friends under a new shape, and they can read it not only in Gottsched's prosaic Prose, and Goethe's poetic Hexameters, but also 'in the metre of the original,' namely, in Doggerel; and this, as would appear, not without comfort, for it is 'the second edition;' — doubtless the Germans themselves will look to it, will direct Herr Soltau aright in his praiseworthy labours, and, with all suitable speed, forward him from his second edition into a third. To us strangers the fact is chiefly interesting, as another little memento of the indestructible vitality there is in worth, however rude; and to stranger Reviewers, as it brings that wondrous old Fiction, with so much else that holds of it, once more specifically into view.

The Apologue of *Reynard the Fox* ranks undoubtedly among the most remarkable Books, not only as a German, but, in all senses, as a European one; and yet for us perhaps its extrinsic, historical character is even more noteworthy than its intrinsic. In Literary History it forms, so

[1] Foreign Quarterly Review, No. 16. — *Reinecke der Fuchs, übersetzt von D. W. Soltau* (Reynard the Fox, translated by D. W. Soltau). 2d edition, 8vo. Lüneburg, 1830.

to speak, the culminating point, or highest manifestation of a Tendency which had ruled the two prior centuries: ever downwards from the last of the Hohenstauffen Emperors, and the end of their Swabian Era, to the borders of the Reformation, rudiments and fibres of this singular Fable are seen, among innumerable kindred things, fashioning themselves together; and now, after three other centuries of actual existence, it still stands visible and entire, venerable in itself, and the enduring memorial of much that has proved more perishable. Thus, naturally enough, it figures as the representative of a whole group that historically cluster round it; in studying its significance, we study that of a whole intellectual period.

As this section of German Literature closely connects itself with the corresponding section of European Literature, and indeed offers an expressive, characteristic epitome thereof, some insight into it, were such easily procurable, might not be without profit. No Literary Historian that we know of, least of all any in England, having looked much in this direction, either as concerned Germany or other countries, whereby a long space of time, once busy enough and full of life, now lies barren and void in men's memories, — we shall here endeavour to present, in such clearness as first attempts may admit, the result of some slight researches of our own in regard to it.

The *Troubadour Period* in general Literature, to which the *Swabian Era* in German answers, has, especially within the last generation, attracted inquiry enough; the French have their Raynouards, we our Webers, the Germans their Haugs, Gräters, Langs, and numerous other Collectors and Translators of *Minnelieder;* among whom Ludwig Tieck, the foremost in far other provinces, has not disdained to take the lead. We shall suppose that this Literary Period is partially known to all readers. Let each recall whatever he has learned or figured regarding it; represent to himself that brave young heyday of Chivalry and Minstrelsy, when a stern Barbarossa, a stern Lion-heart, sang *sirventes*, and with the hand that could wield the sword and sceptre twanged the melodious strings; when knights-errant tilted, and ladies' eyes rained bright influences; and suddenly, as at sunrise, the whole Earth had grown vocal and musical. Then truly was the time of singing come; for princes and prelates, emperors and squires, the wise and the simple, men, women and children, all sang and rhymed, or delighted in hearing it done. It was a universal noise of Song; as if the Spring of Manhood had arrived, and warblings from every spray, not indeed without infinite twitterings also, which, except their gladness, had no music, were bidding it welcome. This was the *Swabian Era;* justly reckoned not only superior to all preceding eras, but properly the First Era of German Literature. Poetry had at length found a home in the life of men; and every pure soul was inspired by it; and in words, or still better, in actions, strove to give it utterance. 'Believers,' says Tieck, 'sang of Faith; Lovers of Love; 'Knights described knightly actions and battles; and loving, 'believing knights were their chief audience. The Spring, 'Beauty, Gaiety, were objects that could never tire; great 'duels and deeds of arms carried away every hearer, the 'more surely the stronger they were painted; and as the 'pillars and dome of the Church encircled the flock, so did Religion, as the Highest, encircle Poetry and Reality; and 'every heart, in equal love, humbled itself before her.'[1]

Let the reader, we say, fancy all this, and moreover that, as earthly things do, it is all passing away. And now, from this extreme verge of the *Swabian Era,* let us look forward into the inane of the next two centuries, and see whether there also some shadows and dim forms, significant in their kind, may not begin to grow visible. Already, as above indicated, *Reinecke de Fos* rises clear in the distance, as the goal of our survey: let us now, restricting ourselves to the German aspects of the matter, examine what may lie between.

[1] *Minnelieder aus dem Schwäbischen Zeitalter.* (Vorrede, x.)

Conrad the Fourth, who died in 1254, was the last of the Swabian Emperors; and Conradin his son, grasping too early at a Southern Crown, perished on the scaffold at Naples in 1268; with which stripling, more fortunate in song than in war, and whose death, or murder, with fourteen years of other cruelty, the *Sicilian Vespers* so frightfully avenged, the imperial line of the Hohenstauffen came to an end. Their House, as we have seen, gives name to a Literary Era; and truly, if dates alone were regarded, we might reckon it much more than a name. For with this change of dynasty, a great change in German Literature begins to indicate itself; the fall of the Hohenstauffen is close followed by the decay of Poetry; as if that fair flowerage and umbrage, which blossomed far and wide round the Swabian Family, had in very deed depended on it for growth and life; and now, the stem being felled, the leaves also were languishing, and soon to wither and drop away. Conradin, as his father and his grandfather had been, was a singer; some lines of his, though he died in his sixteenth year, have even come down to us; but henceforth no crowned poet, except, long afterwards, some few with cheap laurel-crowns, is to be met with: the Gay Science was visibly declining. In such times as now came, the court and the great could no longer patronise it; the polity of the Empire was, by one convulsion after another, all but utterly dismembered; ambitious nobles, a sovereign without power; contention, violence, distress, everywhere prevailing. Richard of Cornwall, who could not so much as keep hold of his sceptre, not to speak of swaying it wisely; or even the brave Rudolf of Hapsburg, who manfully accomplished both these duties, had other work to do than sweet singing. Gay *Wars of the Wartburg* were now changed to stern *Battles of the Marchfeld;* in his leisure hours a good Emperor, instead of twanging harps, must hammer from his helmet the dints it had got in his working and fighting hours.[1] Amid such rude

[1] It was on this famous plain of the Marchfeld that Ottocar, King of Bohemia, conquered Bela of Hungary, in 1260; and was himself, in 1278,

tumults the Minne-Song could not but change its scene and tone: if, indeed, it continued at all, which, however, it scarcely did; for now, no longer united in courtly choir, it seemed to lose both its sweetness and its force, gradually became mute, or in remote obscure corners lived on, feeble and inaudible, till after several centuries, when under a new title, and with far inferior claims, it again solicits some notice from us.

Doubtless, in this posture of affairs political, the progress of Literature could be little forwarded from without; in some directions, as in that of Court-Poetry, we may admit that it was obstructed or altogether stopped. But why not only Court-Poetry, but Poetry of all sorts should have declined, and as it were gone out, is quite another question; to which, indeed, as men must have their theory on everything, answer has often been attempted, but only with partial success. To most of the German Literary Historians this so ungenial condition of the Court and Government appears enough: by the warlike, altogether practical character of Rudolf, by the imbecile ambition of his successors, by the general prevalence of feuds and lawless disorder, the death of Poetry seems fully accounted for. In which conclusion of theirs, allowing all force to the grounds it rests on, we cannot but perceive that there lurks some fallacy: the fallacy namely, so common in these times, of deducing the inward and spiritual exclusively from the outward and material; of tacitly, perhaps unconsciously, denying all independent force, or even life, to the former, and looking out for the secret of its vicissitudes solely in some circumstance belonging to the latter. Now it cannot be too often repeated, where it continues still unknown or forgotten, that man has a soul as certainly as he

conquered and slain by Rudolf of Hapsburg, at that time much left to his own resources; whose talent for mending helmets, however, is perhaps but a poetical tradition. Curious, moreover: it was here again, after more than five centuries, that the House of Hapsburg received its worst overthrow, and from a new and greater Rudolf, namely, from Napoleon, at Wagram, which lies in the middle of this same Marchfeld.

has a body ; nay, much more certainly ; that properly it is the course of his unseen, spiritual life, which informs and rules his external visible life, rather than receives rule from it; in which spiritual life, indeed, and not in any outward action or condition arising from it, the true secret of his history lies, and is to be sought after, and indefinitely approached. Poetry above all, we should have known long ago, is one of those mysterious things whose origin and developments never can be what we call explained; often it seems to us like the wind, blowing where it lists, coming and departing with little or no regard to any the most cunning theory that has yet been devised of it. Least of all does it seem to depend on court-patronage, the form of government, or any modification of politics or economics, catholic as these influences have now become in our philosophy : it lives in a snow-clad sulphurous Iceland, and not in a sunny wine-growing France; flourishes under an arbitrary Elizabeth, and dies out under a constitutional George; Philip II. has his Cervantes, and in prison; Washington and Jackson have only their Coopers and Browns. Why did Poetry appear so brightly after the Battles of Thermopylæ and Salamis, and quite turn away her face and wings from those of Lexington and Bunker's Hill? We answer, the Greeks were a poetical people, the Americans are not; that is to say, it appeared because it did appear! On the whole, we could desire that one of two things should happen : Either that our theories and genetic histories of Poetry should henceforth cease, and mankind rest satisfied, once for all, with Dr. Cabanis' theory, which seems to be the simplest, that 'Poetry is a product of the smaller intestines,' and must be cultivated medically by the exhibition of castor-oil: Or else that, in future speculations of this kind, we should endeavour to start with some recognition of the fact, once well known, and still in words admitted, that Poetry is Inspiration; has in it a certain spirituality and divinity which no dissecting-knife will discover; arises in the most secret and most sacred region of man's soul, as it were in our Holy of Holies; and as for external things, depends only on such as can operate in that region; among which it will be found that Acts of Parliament, and the state of the Smithfield Markets, nowise play the chief part.

With regard to this change in German Literature especially, it is to be remarked, that the phenomenon was not a German, but a European one; whereby we easily infer so much at least, that the roots of it must have lain deeper than in any change from Hohenstauffen Emperors to Hapsburg ones. For now the Troubadours and Trouvères, as well as the Minnesingers, were sinking into silence; the world seems to have rhymed itself out; those chivalrous roundelays, heroic tales, mythologies, and quaint love-sicknesses, had grown unprofitable to the ear. In fact, Chivalry itself was in the wane; and with it that gay melody, like its other pomp. More earnest business, not sportfully, but with harsh endeavour, was now to be done. The graceful minuet-dance of Fancy must give place to the toilsome, thorny pilgrimage of Understanding. Life and its appurtenances and possessions, which had been so admired and besung, now disclosed, the more they came to be investigated, the more contradictions. The Church no longer rose with its pillars, 'like a venerable dome over the united flock;' but, more accurately seen into, was a strait prison, full of unclean creeping things; against which thraldom all better spirits could not but murmur and struggle. Everywhere greatness and littleness seemed so inexplicably blended: Nature, like the Sphinx, her emblem, with her fair woman's face and neck, showed also the claws of a lioness. Now too her Riddle had been propounded; and thousands of subtle, disputatious Schoolmen were striving earnestly to rede it, that they might live, morally live, that the monster might not devour them. These, like strong swimmers, in boundless bottomless vortices of Logic, swam manfully, but could not get to land.

On a better course, yet with the like aim, Physical Science was also unfolding itself. A Roger Bacon, an Albert the

Great, are cheering appearances in this era; not blind to the greatness of Nature, yet no longer with poetic reverence of her, but venturing fearlessly into her recesses, and extorting from her many a secret; the first victories of that long series which is to make man more and more her King. Thus everywhere we have the image of contest, of effort. The spirit of man, which once, in peaceful, loving communion with the Universe, had uttered forth its gladness in Song, now feels hampered and hemmed-in, and struggles vehemently to make itself room. Power is the one thing needful, and that Knowledge which is Power: thus also Intellect becomes the grand faculty, in which all the others are well-nigh absorbed.

Poetry, which has been defined as 'the harmonious unison of Man with Nature,' could not flourish in this temper of the times. The number of poets, or rather versifiers, henceforth greatly diminishes; their style also, and topics, are different and less poetical. Men wish to be practically instructed rather than poetically amused: Poetry itself must assume a preceptorial character, and teach wholesome saws and moral maxims, or it will not be listened to. Singing for the song's sake is now nowhere practised; but in its stead there is everywhere the jar and bustle of argument, investigation, contentious activity. Such throughout the fourteenth century is the general aspect of mind over Europe. In Italy alone is there a splendid exception; the mystic song of Dante, with its stern indignant moral, is followed by the light love-rhymes of Petrarch, the Troubadour of Italy, when this class was extinct elsewhere: the master minds of that country, peculiar in its social and moral condition, still more in its relations to classical Antiquity, pursue a course of their own. But only the master minds; for Italy too has its Dialecticians, and projectors, and reformers; nay, after Petrarch, these take the lead; and there as elsewhere, in their discords and loud assiduous toil, the voice of Poetry dies away.

To search out the causes of this great revolution, which lie not in Politics nor Statistics, would lead us far beyond our depth. Meanwhile let us remark that the change is nowise to be considered as a relapse, or fall from a higher state of spiritual culture to a lower; but rather, so far as we have objects to compare it with, as a quite natural progress and higher development of culture. In the history of the universal mind, there is a certain analogy to that of the individual. Our first self-consciousness is the first revelation to us of a whole universe, wondrous and altogether good; it is a feeling of joy and new-found strength, of mysterious infinite hope and capability; and in all men, either by word or act, expresses itself poetically. The world without us and within us, beshone by the young light of Love, and all instinct with a divinity, is beautiful and great; it seems for us a boundless happiness that we are privileged to live. This is the season of generous deeds and feelings; which also, on the lips of the gifted, form themselves into musical utterance, and give spoken poetry as well as acted. Nothing is calculated and measured, but all is loved, believed, appropriated. All action is spontaneous, high sentiment a sure, imperishable good; and thus the youth stands, like the First Man, in his fair Garden, giving Names to the bright Appearances of this Universe which he has inherited, and rejoicing in it as glorious and divine. Erelong, however, comes a harsher time. Under the first beauty of man's life appears an infinite, earnest rigour: high sentiment will not avail, unless it can continue to be translated into noble action; which problem, in the destiny appointed for man born to toil, is difficult, interminable, capable of only approximate solution. What flowed softly in melodious coherence when seen and sung from a distance, proves rugged and unmanageable when practically handled. The fervid, lyrical gladness of past years gives place to a collected thoughtfulness and energy; nay often, — so painful, so unexpected are the contradictions everywhere met with, — to gloom, sadness and anger; and not till after long struggles and hard-contested victories is the youth changed into a man.

Without pushing the comparison too far, we may say that in the culture of the European mind, or in Literature which is the symbol and product of this, a certain similarity of progress is manifested. That tuneful Chivalry, that high cheerful devotion to the Godlike in heaven, and to Women, its emblems on earth; those Crusades and vernal Love-songs were the heroic doings of the world's youth; to which also a corresponding manhood succeeded. Poetic recognition is followed by scientific examination: the reign of Fancy, with its gay images, and graceful, capricious sports, has ended; and now Understanding, which when reunited to Poetry, will one day become Reason and a nobler Poetry, has to do its part. Meantime, while there is no such union, but a more and more widening controversy, prosaic discord and the unmusical sounds of labour and effort are alone audible.

The era of the Troubadours, who in Germany are the Minnesingers, gave place in that country, as in all others, to a period which we might name the Didactic; for Literature now ceased to be a festal melody, and addressing itself rather to the intellect than to the heart, became as it were a school-lesson. Instead of that cheerful, warbling Song of Love and Devotion, wherein nothing was taught, but all was believed and worshipped, we have henceforth only wise Apologues, Fables, Satires, Exhortations and all manner of edifying Moralities. Poetry, indeed, continued still to be the form of composition for all that can be named Literature; except Chroniclers, and others of that genus, valuable not as doers of the work, but as witnesses of the work done, these Teachers all wrote in verse: nevertheless, in general there are few elements of Poetry in their performances; the internal structure has nothing poetical, is a mere business-like prose: in the rhyme alone, at most in the occasional graces of expression, could we discover that it reckoned itself poetical. In fact, we may say that Poetry, in the old sense, had now altogether gone out of sight: instead of her heavenly vesture and Ariel-harp, she had put on earthly weeds, and walked abroad with ferula and horn-book. It was long before this new guise would sit well on her; only in late centuries that she could fashion it into beauty, and learn to move with it, and mount with it, gracefully as of old.

Looking now more specially to our historical task, if we inquire how far into the subsequent time this Didactic Period extended, no precise answer can well be given. On this side there seem no positive limits to it; with many superficial modifications, the same fundamental element pervades all spiritual efforts of mankind through the following centuries. We may say that it is felt even in the Poetry of our own time; nay, must be felt through all time; inasmuch as Inquiry once awakened cannot fall asleep, or exhaust itself; thus Literature must continue to have a didactic character; and the Poet of these days is he who, not indeed by mechanical but by poetical methods, can instruct us, can more and more evolve for us the mystery of our Life. However, after a certain space, this Didactic Spirit in Literature cannot, as a historical partition and landmark, be available here. At the era of the Reformation, it reaches its acme; and, in singular shape, steps forth on the high places of Public Business, and amid storms and thunder, not without brightness and true fire from Heaven, convulsively renovates the world. This is, as it were, the apotheosis of the Didactic Spirit, where it first attains a really poetical concentration, and stimulates mankind into heroism of word and of action also. Of the latter, indeed, still more than of the former; for not till a much more recent time, almost till our own time, has Inquiry in some measure again reconciled itself to Belief; and Poëtry, though in detached tones, arisen on us, as a true musical Wisdom. Thus is the deed, in certain circumstances, readier and greater than the word: Action strikes fiery light from the rocks it has to hew through;

Poetry reposes in the skyey splendour which that rough passage has led to. But after Luther's day, this Didactic Tendency again sinks to a lower level; mingles with manifold other tendencies; among which, admitting that it still forms the main stream, it is no longer so preëminent, positive and universal, as properly to characterise the whole. For minor Periods and subvisions in Literary History, other more superficial characteristics must, from time to time, be fixed on.

Neither, examining the other limit of this Period, can we say specially where it begins; for, as usual in these things, it begins not at once, but by degrees: Kings' reigns and changes in the form of Government have their day and date; not so changes in the spiritual condition of a people. The Minnesinger Period and the Didactic may be said to commingle, as it were, to overlap each other, for above a century: some writers partially belonging to the latter class occur even prior to the times of Friedrich II.; and a certain echo of the Minne-song had continued down to Manesse's day, under Ludwig the Bavarian.

Thus from the Minnesingers to the Church Reformers we have a wide space of between two and three centuries; in which, of course, it is impossible for us to do more than point out one or two of the leading appearances; a minute survey and exposition being foreign from our object.

Among the Minnesingers themselves, as already hinted, there are not wanting some with an occasionally didactic character: Gottfried of Strasburg, known also as a translator of *Sir Tristrem*, and two other Singers, Reinmar von Zweter and Walter von der Vogelweide, are noted in this respect; the last two especially, for their oblique glances at the Pope and his Monks, the unsound condition of which body could not escape even a Love-minstrel's eye.[1] But per-

[1] Reinmar von Zweter, for example, says once:

Har und bart nach klostersitten gesnitten
Des vind ich gennog,

haps the special step of transition may be still better marked in the works of a rhymer named the *Stricker*, whose province was the epic, or narrative; into which he seems to have introduced this new character in unusual measure. As the *Stricker* still retains some shadow of a place in Literary History, the following notice of him may be borrowed here. Of his personal history, it may be premised, nothing whatever is known; not even why he bears this title; unless it be, as some have fancied, that *Stricker*,

Ich vinde aber der nit vil dies rehte tragen;
Halb visch halb man ist visch noch man,
Gar visch ist visch, gar man ist man,
Als ich erkennen kan:
Von hofmunchen und von klosterrittern
Kan ich niht gesagen:
Hofmunchen, klosterrittern, diesen beiden
Wolt ich reht ze rehte wol bescheiden,
Ob sie sich wolten lassen vinden,
Da sie ze rehte solten wesen;
In kloster munche solten genesen,
So suln des hofs sich ritter unterwinden.

Hair and beard cut in the cloister fashion
Of this I find enough,
But of those that wear it well I find not many;
Half-fish half-man is neither fish nor man,
Whole fish is fish, whole man is man,
As I discover can:
Of court-monks and of cloister-knights
Can I not speak:
Court-monks, cloister-knights, these both
Would I rightly put to rights,
Whether they would let themselves be found
Where they by right should be;
In their cloister monks should flourish,
And knights obey at court.

See also in Flögel (*Geschichte der Komischen Litteratur*, b. iii. s. 11), immediately following this Extract, a formidable dinner-course of *Lies*, — boiled lies, roasted lies, lies with saffron, forced-meat lies, and other varieties, arranged by this same artist; — farther (in page 9), a rather gallant onslaught from Walter von der Vogelweide, on the *Babest* (Pope, *Papst*) himself. All this was before the middle of the thirteenth century.

which now signifies *Knitter*, in those days meant *Schreiber* (Writer):

'In truth,' says Bouterwek, 'this painstaking man was more a writer than a Poet, yet not altogether without talent in that latter way. Voluminous enough, at least, is his redaction of an older epic work on the *War of Charlemagne with the Saracens in Spain*, the old German original of which is perhaps nothing more than a translation from the Latin or French. Of a Poet in the Stricker's day, when the romantic epos had attained such polish among the Germans, one might have expected that this ancient Fiction, since he was pleased to remodel it, would have served as the material to a new poetic creation; or at least, that he would have breathed into it some new and more poetic spirit. But such a development of these Charlemagne Fables was reserved for the *Italian* Poets. The Stricker has not only left the matter of the old Tale almost unaltered, but has even brought out its unpoetical lineaments in stronger light. The fanatical piety with which it is overloaded probably appeared to him its chief merit. To convert these castaway Heathens, or failing this, to annihilate them, Charlemagne takes the field. Next to him, the hero Roland plays a main part there. Consultations are held, ambassadors negotiate; war breaks out with all its terrors: the Heathen fight stoutly: at length comes the well-known defeat of the Franks at Ronceval, or Roncevaux; where, however, the Saracens also lose so many men, that their King Marsilies dies of grief. The Narrative is divided into chapters, each chapter again into sections, an epitome of which is always given at the outset. Miracles occur in the story, but for most part only such as tend to evince how God himself inspirited the Christians against the Heathen. Of anything like free, bold flights of imagination there is little to be met with: the higher features of the genuine romantic epos are altogether wanting. In return, it has a certain didactic temper, which, indeed, announces itself even in the Introduction. The latter, it should be added, prepossesses us in the Poet's favour; testifying with what warm interest the noble and great in man's life affected him.' [1]

The *Wälsche Gast* (Italian Guest) of Zirkler or Tirkeler, who professes, truly or not, to be from Friuli, and, as a benevolent stranger, or *Guest*, tells the Germans hard truths

[1] Bouterwek, ix. 245. Other versified Narratives by this worthy *Stricker* still exist, but for the most part only in manuscript. Of these the History of *Wilhelm von Blumethal*, a Round-table adventurer, appears to be the principal. The Poem on Charlemagne stands printed in Schilter's *Thesaurus;* its exact date is matter only of conjecture.

somewhat in the spirit of Juvenal; even the famous *Meister Freidank* (Master Freethought), with his wise Book of rhymed Maxims, entitled *Die Bescheidenheit* (Modesty); still more the sagacious *Tyro, King of Scots*, quite omitted in history, but who teaches *Friedebrand his Son*, with some discrimination, how to choose a good priest; — all these, with others of still thinner substance, rise before us only as faint shadows, and must not linger in our field of vision. Greatly the most important figure in the earlier part of this era is Hugo von Trimberg, to whom we must now turn; author of various poetico-preceptorial works, one of which, named the *Renner* (Runner), has long been known not only to antiquarians, but, in some small degree, even to the general reader. Of Hugo's Biography he has himself incidentally communicated somewhat. His surname he derives from Trimberg, his birthplace, a village on the Saale, not far from Würzburg, in Franconia. By profession he appears to have been a Schoolmaster: in the conclusion of his *Renner*, he announces that 'he kept school for forty years at Thürstadt, near Bamberg;' farther, that his Book was finished in 1300, which date he confirms by other local circumstances.

Der dies Buch gedichtet hat,
Vierzig jar vor Babenberg,
Der pflag der schulen zu Thürstat.
Und hiess Hugo von Trymberg.
Es ward follenbracht das ist wahr,
Da tausent und dreyhundert jar
Nach Christus Geburt vergangen waren,
Drithalbs jar gleich vor den jaren
Da die Juden in Franken wurden erschlagen.
Bey der zeit und in den tagen,
Da bischoff Leupolt bischoff was
Zu Babenberg.

Some have supposed that the Schoolmaster dignity, claimed here, refers not to actual wielding of the birch, but to a Mastership and practice of instructing in the art of Poetry, which about this time began to have its scholars and even guild brethren, as the feeble remnants of Minne-song gradually took the new shape, in which we afterwards see it, of *Meistergesang* (Master-song): but for this hypothesis, so plain are Hugo's own words, there seems little foundation. It is uncertain whether he was a clerical personage, certain enough that he was not a monk: at all events, he must have been a man of reading and knowledge; industrious in study, and superior in literary acquirement to most in that time. By a collateral account, we find that he had gathered a library of two hundred Books, among which were a whole dozen by himself, five in Latin, seven in German; hoping that by means of these, and the furtherance they would yield in the pedagogic craft, he might live at ease in his old days; in which hope, however, he had been disappointed; seeing, as himself rather feelingly complains 'no one now cares to study 'knowledge (*Kunst*), which, nevertheless, deserves honour 'and favour.' What these twelve Books of Hugo's own writing were, can, for most part, only be conjectured. Of one, entitled the *Sammler* (Collector), he himself makes mention in the *Renner:* he had begun it above thirty years before this latter: but having by ill accident lost great part of his manuscript, abandoned it in anger. Of another work Flögel has discovered the following notice to Johann Wolf: 'About this time (1599) did that virtuous and learned noble-'man, Conrad von Liebenstein, present to me a manuscript of 'Hugo von Trimberg, who flourished about the year 1300. 'It sets forth the shortcomings of all ranks, and especially 'complains of the clergy. It is entitled *Reu ins Land* (Re-'pentance to the Land); and now lies with the Lord of Zill-'hart.'[1] The other ten appear to have vanished even to the last vestige.

Such is the whole sum-total of information which the assiduity of commentators has collected touching worthy Hugo's life and fortunes. Pleasant it were to see him face to face; gladly would we penetrate through that long vista of five hundred years, and peep into his book-presses, his frugal fire-

[1] Flögel (iii. 15), who quotes for it *Wolfii Lexicon Memorab.* t. ii. p. 1061.

side, his noisy mansion with its disobedient urchins, now that it is all grown so silent: but the distance is too far, the intervening medium intercepts our light; only in uncertain fluctuating dusk, will Hugo and his environment appear to us. Nevertheless Hugo, as he had in Nature, has in History, an immortal part: as to his inward man, we can still see that he was no mere bookworm, or simple Parson Adams; but of most observant eye ; shrewd, inquiring, considerate, who from his Thürstadt school-chair, as from a *sedes exploratoria*, had looked abroad into the world's business, and formed his own theory about many things. A cheerful, gentle heart had been given him; a quiet, sly humour; light to see beyond the garments and outer hulls of Life into Life itself: the long-necked purse, the threadbare gabardine, the languidly-simmering pot of his pedagogic household establishment were a small matter to him: he was a man to look on these things with a meek smile; to nestle down quietly, as the lark, in the lowest furrow; nay to mount therefrom singing, and soar above all mere earthly heights. How many potentates, and principalities, and proud belligerents have evaporated into utter oblivion, while the poor Thürstadt Schoolmaster still holds together!

This *Renner*, which seems to be his final work, probably comprises the essence of all those lost Volumes ; and indeed a synopsis of Hugo's whole Philosophy of Life, such as his two hundred Books and long decades of quiet observation and reflection had taught him. Why it has been named the *Renner*, whether by Hugo himself, or by some witty Editor and Transcriber, there are two guesses forthcoming, and no certain reason. One guess is, that this Book was to *run* after the lost Tomes, and make good to mankind the deficiency occasioned by want of them; which happy-thought, hide-bound though it be, might have seemed sprightly enough to Hugo and that age. The second guess is, that our Author, in the same style of easy wit, meant to say, this Book must *hasten* and run out into the world, and do him a good turn quickly, while it was yet time, he being so very old. But leaving this, we may remark, with certainty enough, that what we have left of Hugo was first printed under this title of *Renner*, at Frankfort on the Mayn, in 1549; and quite incorrectly, being modernised to all lengths, and often without understanding of the sense; the Edition moreover is now rare, and Lessing's project of a new one did not take effect; so that, except in Manuscripts, of which there are many, and in printed Extracts, which also are numerous, the *Renner* is to most readers a sealed book.

In regard to its literary merit opinions seem to be nearly unanimous. The highest merit, that of poetical unity, or even the lower merit of logical unity, is not ascribed to it by the warmest panegyrist. Apparently this work had been a sort of store-chest, wherein the good Hugo had, from time to time, deposited the fruits of his meditation as they chanced to ripen for him; here a little, and there a little, in all varieties of kind; till the chest being filled, or the fruits nearly exhausted, it was sent forth and published to the world, by the easy process of turning up the bottom.

'No theme,' says Bouterwek, 'leads with certainty to the other: satirical descriptions, proverbs, fables, jests and other narratives, all huddled together at random, to teach us in a poetical way a series of moral lessons. A strained and frosty Allegory opens the work; then follow the Chapters of *Meyden* (Maids); of Wicked Masters; of Pages; of Priests, Monks and Friars, with great minuteness; then of a Young Minx with an Old Man; then of Bad Landlords, and of Robbers. Next come divers Virtues and Vices, all painted out, and judged of. Towards the end, there follows a sort of Moral Natural History; Considerations on the dispositions of various Animals; a little Botany and Physiology; then again all manner of didactic Narratives; and finally a Meditation on the Last Day.'

Whereby it would appear clearly, as hinted, that Hugo's *Renner* pursues no straight course; and only through the most labyrinthic mazes, here wandering in deep thickets, or even sinking in moist bogs, there panting over mountain-tops by narrow sheep-tracks; but for most part jigging lightly on sunny greens, accomplishes his wonderful journey.

Nevertheless, as we ourselves can testify, there is a certain charm in the worthy man; his Work, such as it is, seems to flow direct from the heart, in natural, spontaneous abundance; is at once cheerful and earnest; his own simple, honest, mildly decided character is everywhere visible. Besides Hugo, as we said, is a person of understanding; has looked over many provinces of Life, not without insight; in his quiet, sly way, can speak forth a shrewd word on occasion. There is a genuine though slender vein of Humour in him; nor in his satire does he ever lose temper, but rebukes sportfully; not indeed laughing aloud, scarcely even sardonically smiling, yet with a certain subdued roguery and patriarchal knowingness. His fancy too, if not brilliant, is copious almost beyond measure; no end to his crotchets, suppositions, minute specifications. Withal he is original: his maxims, even when professedly borrowed, have passed through the test of his own experience; all carries in it some stamp of his personality. Thus the *Renner*, though in its whole extent perhaps too boundless and planless for ordinary nerves, makes in the fragmentary state no unpleasant reading: that old doggerel is not without significance; often in its straggling, broken, entangled strokes some vivid antique picture is strangely brought out for us.

As a specimen of Hugo's general manner, we select a small portion of his Chapter on *The Maidens;* that passage where he treats of the highest enterprise a maiden can engage in, the choosing of a husband. It will be seen at once that Hugo is no Minnesinger, glozing his fair audience with madrigals and hypocritical gallantry; but a quiet Natural Historian, reporting such facts as he finds, in perfect good nature, it is true, yet not without an undercurrent of satirical humour. His quaint style of thought, his garrulous minuteness of detail are partly apparent here. The first few lines we may give in the original also; not as they stand in the

Frankfort Edition, but as professing to derive themselves from a genuine ancient source:

Kortzyn mut und lange haar
han die meyde sunderbar
dy zu yren jaren kommen synt
dy wal machen yn daz hertze blynt
dy auchgn wysen yn den weg
von den auchyn get eyn steg
tzu dem hertzen nit gar lang
uff deme stege ist vyl mannig gedang
wen sy woln nemen oder nit.[1]

Short of sense and long of hair,
Strange enough the maidens are;
Once they to their teens have got,
Such a choosing, this or that:
Eyes they have that ever spy,
From the Eyes a Path doth lie
To the Heart, and is not long,
Hereon travel thoughts a throng,
Which one they will have or not.

'Woe's me,' continues Hugo, 'how often this same is repeated; till they grow all confused how to choose, from so many, whom they have brought in without number. First they bethink them so: This one is short, that one is long; he is courtly and old, the other young and ill-favoured; this is lean, that is bald; here is one fat, there one thin; this is noble, that is weak; he never yet broke a spear: one is white, another black; that other is named Master Hack (*hartz*); this is pale, that again is red; he seldom eateth cheerful bread;'

and so on, through endless other varieties, in new streams of soft-murmuring doggerel, whereon, as on the Path it would represent, do travel thoughts a throng, which one these fair irresolutes will have or not.

Thus, for Hugo, the age of Minstrelsy is gone: not soft Love-ditties, and hymns of Lady-worship, but sceptical criticism, importunate animadversion, not without a shade of mockery, will he indite. The age of Chivalry is gone also. To a Schoolmaster, with empty larder, the pomp of tournaments could never have been specially interesting; but now

[1] Horn, *Geschichte und Kritik der deutschen Poesie*, s. 44.

such passages of arms, how free and gallant soever, appear to him no other than the probable product of delirium. 'God might well laugh, could it be,' says he, 'to see his 'mannikins live so wondrously on this Earth: two of them 'will take to fighting, and nowise let it alone; nothing serves 'but with two long spears they must ride and stick at one 'another: greatly to their hurt; for when one is by the 'other skewered through the bowels or through the weasand, 'he hath small profit thereby. But who forced them to such 'straits?' The answer is too plain: some modification of Insanity. Nay, so contemptuous is Hugo of all chivalrous things, that he openly grudges any time spent in reading of them; in Don Quixote's Library he would have made short work:

How Master Dietrich fought with Ecken,
And how of old the stalwart Recken
Were all by women's craft betrayed:
Such things you oft hear sung and said,
And wept at, like a case of sorrow; —
Of our own Sins we'll think to-morrow.

This last is one of Hugo's darker strokes; for commonly, though moral perfection is ever the one thing needful with him, he preaches in a quite cheerful tone; nay, ever and anon, enlivens us with some timely joke. Considerable part, and apparently much the best part, of his work is occupied with satirical Fables, and *Schwänke* (jests, comic tales); of which latter class we have seen some possessing true humour, and the simplicity which is their next merit. These, however, we must wholly omit; and indeed, without farther parleying, here part company with Hugo. We leave him, not without esteem, and a touch of affection, due to one so true-hearted, and, under that old humble guise, so gifted with intellectual talent. Safely enough may be conceded him the dignity of chief moral Poet of his time; nay perhaps, for his solid character, and modest manly ways, a much higher dignity. Though his Book can no longer be considered, what the Frankfort Editor describes it in his interminable title-page, as a universal *vade-mecum* for mankind, it is still 'so adorned with many fine sayings,' and in itself of so curious a texture, that it seems well worth preserving. A proper Edition of the *Renner* will one day doubtless make its appearance among the Germans. Hugo is farther remarkable as the precursor and prototype of Sebastian Brandt, whose *Narrenschiff* (Ship of Fools) has, with perhaps less merit, had infinitely better fortune than the *Renner.*

Some half century later in date, and no less didactic in character than Hugo's *Renner*, another Work, still rising visible above the level of those times, demands some notice from us. This is the *Edelstein* (Gem) of Bonerius or Boner, which at one time, to judge by the number of Manuscripts, whereof fourteen are still in existence, must have enjoyed great popularity; and indeed, after long years of oblivion, it has, by recent critics and redactors, been again brought into some circulation. Boner's *Gem* is a collection of a Hundred Fables done into German rhyme; and derives its proud designation not more perhaps from the supposed excellence of the work, than from a witty allusion to the title of Fable First, which, in the chief Manuscript, chances to be that well-known one of the Cock scraping for Barleycorns, and finding instead thereof a precious stone (*Edelstein*) or Gem: *Von einem Hanen und dem edelen Steine;* whereupon the author, or some kind friend, remarks in a sort of Prologue:

Dies Büchlein mag der Edelstein
Wol heiszen, wand es in treit (*in sich trägt*)
Bischaft (*Beispiel*) *manger kluogheit.*

'This Bookling may well be called the Gem, sith it includes examples of many a prudence;'—which name, accordingly, as we see, it bears even to this day.

Boner and his Fables have given rise to much discussion among the Germans: scattered at short distances throughout the last hundred years, there is a series of Selections, Editions, Translations, Critical Disquisitions, some of them in the shape of Academic Program; among the labourers in which enterprise we find such men as Gellert and Lessing. A *Bonerii Gemma*, or Latin version of the work, was published by Oberlin, in 1782; Eschenburg sent forth an Edition in modern German, in 1810; Benecke a reprint of the antique original, in 1816. So that now a faithful duty has been done to Boner; and what with bibliographical inquiries, what with vocabularies, and learned collations of texts, he that runs may read whatever stands written in the *Gem.*

Of these diligent lucubrations, with which we strangers are only in a remote degree concerned, it will be sufficient here to report in few words the main results, — not indeed very difficult to report. First then, with regard to Boner himself, we have to say that nothing whatever has been discovered: who, when, or what that worthy moralist was, remains, and may always remain, entirely uncertain. It is merely conjectured, from the dialect, and other more minute indications, that his place of abode was the northwest quarter of Switzerland; with still higher probability, that he lived about the middle of the fourteenth century; from his learning and devout pacific temper, some have inferred that he was a monk or priest; however, in one Manuscript of his *Gem*, he is designated, apparently by some ignorant Transcriber, a knight, *ein Ritter gotz alsus:* from all which, as above said, our only conclusion is, that nothing can be concluded.

Johann Scherz, about the year 1710, in what he called *Philosophiæ moralis Germanorum medii ævi Specimen*, sent forth certain of these Fables, with expositions, but apparently without naming the Author; to which *Specimen* Gellert in his *Dissertatio de Poesi Apologorum* had again, some forty years afterwards, invited attention. Nevertheless, so total was the obscurity which Boner had fallen into, that Bodmer, already known as the resuscitator of the *Nibelungen Lied*, in printing the *Edelstein* from an old Manuscript, in

1752, mistook its probable date by about a century, and gave his work the title of *Fables from the Minnesinger Period,*[1] without naming the Fabulist, or guessing whether there were one or many. In this condition stood the matter, when several years afterwards, Lessing, pursuing another inquiry, came across the track of this Boner; was allured into it; proceeded to clear it; and moving briskly forward, with a sure eye and sharp critical axe, hewed away innumerable entanglements; and so opened out a free avenue and vista, where strangely, in remote depth of antiquarian woods, the whole ancient Fable-manufactory, with Boner and many others working in it, becomes visible, in all the light which probably will ever be admitted to it. He who has perplexed himself with *Romulus and Rimicius*, and Nevelet's *Anonymus*, and *Avianus*, and still more, with the false guidance of their many commentators, will find help and deliverance in this light, thorough-going Inquiry of Lessing's.[2]

Now, therefore, it became apparent: first, that those supposed *Fables from the Minnesinger Period*, of Bodmer, were in truth written by one Boner, in quite another Period; secondly, that Boner was not properly the author of them, but the borrower and free versifier from certain Latin originals; farther, that the real title was *Edelstein;* and strangest of all, that the work had been printed three centuries before Bodmer's time, namely, at Bamberg, in 1461; of which Edition, indeed, a tattered copy, typographically curious, lay, and probably lies, in the Wolfenbüttel Library, where Lessing then waited, and wrote. The other discoveries, touching Boner's personality and locality, are but conjectures, due also to Lessing, and have been stated already.

As to the *Gem* itself, about which there has been such scrambling, we may say, now when it is cleaned and laid out

[1] Koch also, with a strange deviation from his usual accuracy, dates Boner, in one place, 1220; and in another, 'towards the latter half of the fourteenth century.' See his *Compendium*, pp. 28 and 200, vol. i.

[2] *Sämmtliche Schriften*, b. viii.

before us, that, though but a small seed-pearl, it has a genuine value. To us Boner is interesting by his antiquity, as the speaking witness of many long-past things; to his contemporaries again he must have been still more interesting as the reporter of so many new things. These Fables of his, then for the first time rendered out of inaccessible Latin[1] into German metre, contain no little edifying matter, had we not known it before; our old friends, the Fox with the musical Raven; the Man and Boy taking their Ass to market, and so inadequate to please the public in their method of transporting him; the Bishop that gave his Nephew a Cure of Souls, but durst not trust him with a Basket of Pears; all these and many more figure here. But apart from the material of his Fables, Boner's style and manner has an abiding merit. He is not so much a Translator as a free Imitator: he tells the story in his own way; appends his own moral, and, except that in the latter department he is apt to be a little prolix, acquits himself to high satisfaction. His narrative, in those old limping rhymes, is cunningly enough brought out: artless, lively, graphic, with a spicing of innocent humour, a certain childlike archness, which is the chief merit of a Fable. Such is the German Æsop; a character whom in the northwest district of Swit-

[1] The two originals to whom Lessing has traced all his Fables are *Avianus* and Nevelet's *Anonymus;* concerning which personages the following brief notice by Jördens (*Lexicon*, i. 161) may be inserted here: 'Flavius 'Avianus (who must not be confounded with another Latin Poet, *Avie-'nus*) lived, as is believed, under the two Antonines in the second cen-'tury: he has left us forty-two Fables in elegiac measure, the best Editions 'of which are that by Kannegiesser (Amsterdam, 1731), that by' &c. &c. With respect to the *Anonymus* again: 'Under this designation is under-'stood the half-barbarous Latin Poet, whose sixty Fables, in elegiac meas-'ure, stand in the collection, which Nevelet, under the title *Mythologia 'Æsopica*, published at Frankfort in 1610, and which directly follow those 'of Avianus in that work. They are nothing else than versified transla-'tions of the Fables written in prose by *Romulus*, a noted Fabulist, whose 'era cannot be fixed, nor even his name made out to complete satisfaction.' — The reader who wants deeper insight into these matters may consult Lessing, as cited above.

zerland, at that time of day, we should hardly have looked for.

Could we hope that to many of our readers the old rough dialect of Boner would be intelligible, it were easy to vindicate these praises. As matters stand, we can only venture on one translated specimen, which in this shape claims much allowance; the Fable, also, is nowise the best, or perhaps the worst, but simply one of the shortest. For the rest, we have rendered the old doggerel into new, with all possible fidelity:

THE FROG AND THE STEER.

Of him that striveth after more honour than he should.

A Frog with Frogling by his side
Came hopping through the plain, one tide:
There he an Ox at grass did spy,
Much anger'd was the Frog thereby;
He said: "Lord God, what was my sin
Thou madest me so small and thin?
Likewise I have no handsome feature,
And all dishonoured is my nature,
To other creatures far and near,
For instance, this same grazing Steer."
The Frog would fain with Bullock cope,
'Gan brisk outblow himself in hope.
Then spake his Frogling: "Father o' me,
It boots not, let thy blowing be;
Thy nature hath forbid this battle,
Thou canst not vie with the black-cattle."
Nathless let be the Frog would not,
Such prideful notion had he got;
Again to blow right sore 'gan he,
And said: "Like Ox could I but be
In size, within this world there were
No Frog so glad, to thee I swear."
The Son spake: "Father, me is woe
Thou shouldst torment thy body so,
I fear thou art to lose thy life;
Come follow me and leave this strife;
Good Father, take advice of me,
And let thy boastful blowing be."
Frog said: "Thou need'st not beck and nod,
I will not do't, so help me God;

Big as this Ox is I must turn,
Mine honour now it doth concern."
He blew himself, and burst in twain,
Such of that blowing was his gain.

The like hath oft been seen of such
Who grasp at honour overmuch;
They must with none at all be doing,
But sink full soon and come to ruin.
He that, with wind of Pride accurs'd,
Much puffs himself, will surely burst;
He men miswishes and misjudges,
Inferiors scorns, superiors grudges,
Of all his equals is a hater,
Much griev'd he is at any better;
Wherefore it were a sentence wise
Were his whole body set with Eyes,
Who envy hath, to see so well
What lucky hap each man befell,
That so he filled were with fury,
And burst asunder in a hurry;
And so full soon betid him this
Which to the Frog betided is.

Readers to whom such stinted twanging of the true Poetic Lyre, such cheerful fingering, though only of one and its lowest string, has any melody, may find enough of it in Benecke's *Boner*, a reproduction, as above stated, of the original *Edelstein;* which Edition we are authorised to recommend as furnished with all helps for such a study: less adventurous readers may still, from Eschenburg's half-modernised Edition, derive some contentment and insight.

Hugo von Trimberg and Boner, who stand out here as our chief Literary representatives of the Fourteenth Century, could play no such part in their own day, when the great men, who shone in the world's eye, were Theologians and Jurists, Politicians at the Imperial Diet; at best Professors in the new Universities; of whom all memory has long since perished. So different is universal from temporary importance, and worth belonging to our manhood from that merely of our station or calling. Nevertheless, as every writer, of any true gifts, is 'citizen both of his time and of his country,' and the more completely the greater his gifts; so in the works of these two secluded individuals, the characteristic tendencies and spirit of their age may best be discerned.

Accordingly, in studying their commentators, one fact that cannot but strike us is, the great prevalence and currency which this species of Literature, cultivated by them, had obtained in that era. Of Fable Literature especially, this was the summer-tide and highest efflorescence. The Latin originals which Boner partly drew from, descending, with manifold transformations and additions, out of classical times, were in the hands of the learned; in the living memories of the people were numerous fragments of primeval Oriental Fable, derived perhaps through Palestine; from which two sources, curiously intermingled, a whole stream of Fables evolved itself; whereat the morally athirst, such was the genius of that time, were not slow to drink. Boner, as we have seen, worked in a field then zealously cultivated: nay, was not Æsop himself, what we have for Æsop, a contemporary of his; the Greek Monk Planudes and the Swiss Monk Boner might be chanting their Psalter at one and the same hour!

Fable, indeed, may be regarded as the earliest and simplest product of Didactic Poetry, the first attempt of Instruction clothing itself in Fancy: hence the antiquity of Fables, their universal diffusion in the childhood of nations, so that they have become a common property of all: hence also their acceptance and diligent culture among the Germans, among the Europeans, in this the first stage of an era when the whole bent of Literature was Didactic. But the Fourteenth Century was the age of Fable in a still wider sense: it was the age when whatever Poetry there remained took the shape of Apologue and moral Fiction: the higher spirit of Imagination had died away, or withdrawn itself into Religion; the lower and feebler not only took continual counsel of Understanding, but was content to walk in its leading-strings. Now was the time when human life and its relations were looked at with an earnest practical eye; and the moral perplexities that occur there, when man, hemmed-in between the Would and the Should, or the Must, painfully hesitates, or altogether sinks in that collision, were not only set forth in the way of precept, but embodied, for still clearer instruction, in Examples, and edifying Fictions. The Monks themselves, such of them as had any talent, meditated and taught in this fashion: witness that strange *Gesta Romanorum*, still extant, and once familiar over all Europe; — a Collection of Moral Tales, expressly devised for the use of Preachers, though only the Shakspeares, and in subsequent times, turned it to right purpose.[1] These and the like old *Gests*, with most of which the *Romans* had so little to do, were the staple Literature of that period; cultivated with great assiduity, and so far as mere invention, or compilation, of incident goes, with no little merit; for already almost all the grand destinies, and fundamental ever-recurring entanglements of human life, are laid hold of and depicted here; so that, from the first, our modern Novelists and Dramatists could find nothing new under the sun, but everywhere, in contrivance of their Story, saw themselves forestalled. The boundless abundance of Narratives then current, the singular derivations and transmigrations of these, surprise antiquarian commentators: but, indeed, it was in this same century that Boccaccio, refining the gold from that so copious dross, produced his *Decamerone*, which still indicates the same fact in more pleasant fashion, to all readers. That in these universal tendencies of the time the Germans participated and coöperated, Boner's Fables, and Hugo's many Narrations, serious and comic, may, like two specimens from a great multitude, point out to us. The Madrigal had passed into the Apologue; the Heroic Poem, with its supernatural machinery and sentiment, into the Fiction of

[1] See an account of this curious Book in Douce's learned and ingenious *Illustrations of Shakspeare.*

practical Life: in which latter species a prophetic eye might have discerned the coming *Tom Joneses* and *Wilhelm Meisters;* and with still more astonishment, the *Minerva Presses* of all nations, and this their huge transit-trade in Rags, all lifted from the dunghill, printed on, and returned thither, to the comfort of parties interested.

The Drama, as is well known, had an equally Didactic origin; namely, in those *Mysteries* contrived by the clergy for bringing home religious truth, with new force, to the universal comprehension. That this cunning device had already found its way into Germany, we have proof in a document too curious to be omitted here:

'In the year 1322, there was a play shown at Eisenach, which had a tragical enough effect. Markgrat Friedrich of Misnia, Landgraf also of Thuringia, having brought his tedious warfares to a conclusion, and the country beginning now to revive under peace, his subjects were busy repaying themselves for the past distresses by all manner of diversions; to which end, apparently by the Sovereign's order, a dramatic representation of the *Ten Virgins* was schemed, and at Eisenach, in his presence, duly executed. This happened fifteen days after Easter, by indulgence of the Preaching Friars. In the *Chronicon Sampetrinum* stands recorded that the play was enacted in the Bear-garden (*in horto ferarum*), by the clergy and their scholars. But now, when it came to pass that the Wise Virgins would give the Foolish no oil, and these latter were shut out from the Bridegroom, they began to weep bitterly, and called on the Saints to intercede for them; who, however, even with Mary at their head, could effect nothing from God; but the Foolish Virgins were all sentenced to damnation. Which things the Landgraf seeing and hearing, he fell into a doubt, and was very angry; and said, "What then is the Christian Faith, if God will not take pity on us, for intercession of Mary and all the Saints?" In this anger he continued five days; and the learned men could hardly enlighten him to understand the Gospel. Thereupon he was struck with apoplexy, and became speechless and powerless; in which sad state he continued bed-rid, two years and seven months, and so died, being then fifty-five.' [1]

Surely a serious warning, would they but take it, to Dra-

[1] Flögel (*Geschichte der komischen Litteratur*, iv. 287), who founds on that old *Chronicon Sampetrinum Erfurtense*, contained in Menke's Collection.

matic Critics, not to venture beyond their depth! Had this fiery old Landgraf given up the reins of his imagination into his author's hands, he might have been pleased he knew not why: whereas the meshes of Theology, in which he kicks and struggles, here strangle the life out of him; and the Ten Virgins at Eisenach are more fatal to warlike men than Æschylus's Furies at Athens were to weak women.

Neither were the unlearned People without their Literature, their Narrative Poetry; though how, in an age without printing and bookstalls, it was circulated among them; whether by strolling *Fideleres* (Minstrels), who might recite as well as fiddle, or by other methods, we have not learned. However, its existence and abundance in this era is sufficiently evinced by the multitude of *Volksbücher* (People's-Books) which issued from the Press, next century, almost as soon as there was a Press. Several of these, which still languidly survive among the people, or at least the children, of all countries, were of German composition; of most, so strangely had they been sifted and winnowed to and fro, it was impossible to fix the origin. But borrowed or domestic, they nowhere wanted admirers in Germany: the *Patient Helena*, the *Fair Magelone*, *Bluebeard*, *Fortunatus;* these, and afterwards the *Seven Wise Masters*, with other more directly Æsopic ware, to which the introduction of the old Indian stock, or *Book of Wisdom*, translated from John of Capua's Latin,[1] one day formed a rich accession, were in all memories and on all tongues.

Beautiful traits of Imagination and a pure genuine feeling, though under the rudest forms, shine forth in some of these old Tales: for instance, in *Magelone* and *Fortunatus;* which two, indeed, with others of a different stamp, Ludwig Tieck has, with singular talent, ventured, not unsuccessfully, to reproduce in our own time and dialect. A second class distinguish

[1] In 1483, by command of a certain Eberhard, Duke of Würtemberg. What relation this old *Book of Wisdom* bears to our actual *Pilpay*, we have not learned.

themselves by a homely, honest-hearted Wisdom, full of character and quaint devices; of which class the *Seven Wise Masters*, extracted chiefly from that *Gesta Romanorum* above mentioned, and containing 'proverb-philosophy, anecdotes, 'fables and jests, the seeds of which, on the fertile German 'soil, spread luxuriantly through several generations,' is perhaps the best example. Lastly, in a third class, we find in full play that spirit of broad drollery, of rough saturnine Humour, which the Germans claim as a special characteristic; among these, we must not omit to mention the *Schiltbürger*, correspondent to our own *Wise Men of Gotham;* still less, the far-famed *Tyll Eulenspiegel* (Tyll Owlglass), whose rogueries and waggeries belong, in the fullest sense, to this era.

This last is a true German work; for both the man Tyll Eulenspiegel, and the Book which is his history, were produced there. Nevertheless, Tyll's fame has gone abroad into all lands: this, the Narrative of his exploits, has been published in innumerable editions, even with all manner of learned glosses, and translated into Latin, English, French, Dutch, Polish; nay, in several languages, as in his own, an *Eulenspiegelerei*, an *Espièglerie*, or dog's-trick, so named after him, still, by consent of lexicographers, keeps his memory alive. We may say, that to few mortals has it been granted to earn such a place in Universal History as Tyll: for now after five centuries, when Wallace's birthplace is unknown even to the Scots; and the Admirable Crichton still more rapidly is grown a shadow; and Edward Longshanks sleeps unregarded save by a few antiquarian English,—Tyll's native village is pointed out with pride to the traveller, and his tombstone, with a sculptured pun on his name, an Owl, namely, and a Glass, still stands, or pretends to stand, 'at Möllen, near Lubeck,' where, since 1350, his once nimble bones have been at rest. Tyll, in the calling he had chosen, naturally led a wandering life, as place after place became too hot for him; by which means he saw into many things with his own eyes: having been not only over all Westphalia and Saxony, but even in Poland, and as far as Rome. That in his old days, like other great men, he became an Autobiographer, and in trustful winter evenings, not on paper, but on air, and to the laughter-lovers of Möllen, composed this work himself, is purely a hypothesis; certain only that it came forth originally in the dialect of this region, namely the *Platt-Deutsch;* and was therefrom translated, probably about a century afterwards, into its present High German, as Lessing conjectures, by one Thomas Mürner, who on other grounds is not unknown to antiquaries. For the rest, write it who might, the Book is here, 'abounding,' as a wise Critic remarks, 'in inventive humour, in rough 'merriment and broad drollery, not without a keen rugged 'shrewdness of insight; which properties must have made it 'irresistibly captivating to the popular sense; and, with all 'its fantastic extravagancies and roguish crotchets, in many 'points instructive.'

From Tyll's so captivating achievements, we shall here select one to insert some account of; the rather as the tale is soon told, and by means of it we catch a little trait of manners, and, through Tyll's spectacles, may peep into the interior of a Household, even of a Parsonage, in those old days.

'It chanced after so many adventures, that Eulenspiegel came to a Parson, who promoted him to be his Sacristan, or as we now say, Sexton. Of this Parson it is recorded that he kept a Concubine, who had but one eye; she also had a spite at Tyll, and was wont to speak evil of him to his master, and report his rogueries. Now while Eulenspiegel held this Sextoncy, the Easter-season came, and there was to be a play set forth of the Resurrection of Our Lord. And as the people were not learned, and could not read, the Parson took his Concubine and stationed her in the holy Sepulchre by way of Angel. Which thing Eulenspiegel seeing, he took to him three of the simplest persons that could be found there, to enact the Three Marys; and the Parson himself, with a flag in his hand, represented Christ. Thereupon spake Eulenspiegel to the simple persons: "When the Angel asks you, Whom ye seek, ye must answer: The

Parson's one-eyed Concubine." Now it came to pass that the time arrived when they were to act, and the Angel asked them: "Whom seek ye here?" and they answered, as Eulenspiegel had taught and bidden them, and said: "We seek the Parson's one-eyed Concubine." Whereby did the Parson observe that he was made a mock of. And when the Parson's Concubine heard the same, she started out of the Grave, and aimed a box at Eulenspiegel's face, but missed him, and hit one of the simple persons, who were representing the Three Marys. This latter then returned her a slap on the mouth, whereupon she caught him by the hair. But his Wife seeing this, came running thither, and fell upon the Parson's Harlot. Which thing the Parson discerning, he threw down his flag, and sprang forward to his Harlot's assistance. Thus gave they one another hearty thwacking and basting, and there was great uproar in the Church. But when Eulenspiegel perceived that they all had one another by the ears in the Church, he went his ways, and came no more back."[1]

These and the like pleasant narratives were the People's Comedy in those days. Neither was their Tragedy wanting; as indeed both spring up spontaneously in all regions of human Life; however, their chief work of this latter class, the wild, deep and now world-renowned *Legend of Faust*, belongs to a somewhat later date.[2]

[1] Flögel, iv. 290. For more of Eulenspiegel, see Görres *Ueber die Volksbücher*.

[2] To the fifteenth century, say some who fix it on Johann Faust, the Goldsmith and partial Inventor of Printing: to the sixteenth century, say others, referring it to Johann Faust, Doctor in Philosophy; which individual did actually, as the Tradition also bears, study first at Wittenberg (where he might be one of Luther's pupils), then at Ingolstadt, where also he taught, and had a *Famulus* named Wagner, son of a clergyman at Wasserberg. Melancthon, Tritheim and other credible witnesses, some of whom had seen the man, vouch sufficiently for these facts. The rest of the Doctor's history is much more obscure. He seems to have been of a vehement, unquiet temper; skilled in Natural Philosophy, and perhaps in the occult science of Conjuring, by aid of which two gifts, a much shallower man, wandering in Need and Pride over the world in those days, might, without any Mephistopheles, have worked wonders enough. Nevertheless, that he rode off through the air on a wine-cask, from Auerbach's Keller at Leipsig, in 1523, seems questionable; though an old carving, in that venerable Tavern, still mutely asserts it to the toper of this day. About 1560, his term of Thaumaturgy being over, he disappeared: whether, under feigned name, by the rope of some hangman; or 'frightfully torn in

Thus, though the Poetry which spoke in rhyme was feeble enough, the spirit of Poetry could nowise be regarded as extinct; while Fancy, Imagination and all the intellectual faculties necessary for that art, were in active exercise. Neither had the Enthusiasm of heart, on which it still more intimately depends, died out; but only taken another form. In lower degrees it expressed itself as an ardent zeal for Knowledge and Improvement; for spiritual excellence such as the time held out and prescribed. This was no languid, low-minded age; but of earnest busy effort; in all provinces of culture resolutely struggling forward. Classical Literature, after long hindrances, had now found its way into Germany also: old Rome was open, with all its wealth, to the intelligent eye; scholars of Chrysoloras were fast unfolding the treasures of Greece. School Philosophy, which had never obtained firm footing among the Germans, was in all countries drawing to a close; but the subtle, piercing vision, which it had fostered and called into activity, was henceforth to employ itself with new profit on more substantial interests. In such manifold praiseworthy endeavours the most ardent mind had ample arena.

A higher, purer enthusiasm, again, which no longer found its place in chivalrous Minstrelsy, might still retire to meditate and worship in religious Cloisters, where, amid all the corruption of monkish manners, there were not wanting men who aimed at, and accomplished, the highest problem of

'pieces by the Devil, near the village of Rimlich, between Twelve and One 'in the morning,' let each reader judge for himself. The latter was clearly George Rudolf Wiedemann's opinion, whose *Veritable History of the abominable Sins of Dr. Johann Faust* came out at Hamburg in 1599; and is no less circumstantially announced in the old People's-Book, *That everywhere-infamous Arch-Black-Artist and Conjuror, Dr. Faust's Compact with the Devil, wonderful Walk and Conversation, and terrible End*, printed, seemingly without date, at Köln (Cologne) and Nürnberg; read by every one; written by we know not whom. See again, for farther insight, Görres *Ueber die deutschen Volksbücher*. Another Work (Leipsig, 1824), expressly 'On Faust and the Wandering Jew,' which latter, in those times, wandered much in Germany, is also referred to. — *Conv. Lexicon*, § *Faust*.

manhood, a life of spiritual Truth. Among the Germans especially, that deep-feeling, deep-thinking, devout temper, now degenerating into abstruse theosophy, now purifying itself into holy eloquence and clear apostolic light, was awake in this era; a temper which had long dwelt, and still dwells there; which erelong was to render that people worthy the honour of giving Europe a new Reformation, a new Religion. As an example of monkish diligence and zeal, if of nothing more, we here mention the German Bible of Mathias von Behaim, which, in his Hermitage at Halle, he rendered from the Vulgate, in 1343; the Manuscript of which is still to be seen in Leipzig. Much more conspicuous stand two other German Priests of this Period; to whom, as connected with Literature also, a few words must now be devoted.

Johann Tauler is a name which fails in no Literary History of Germany: he was a man famous in his own day as the most eloquent of preachers; is still noted by critics for his intellectual deserts; by pious persons, especially of the class called Mystics, is still studied as a practical instructor; and by all true inquirers prized as a person of high talent and moral worth. Tauler was a Dominican Monk; seems to have lived and preached at Strasburg; where, as his gravestone still testifies, he died in 1361. His devotional works have been often edited: one of his modern admirers has written his biography; wherein perhaps this is the strangest fact, if it be one, that once in the pulpit, 'he grew suddenly 'dumb, and did nothing but weep; in which despondent state 'he continued for two whole years.' Then, however, he again lifted up his voice, with new energy and new potency. We learn farther, that he 'renounced the dialect of Philosophy, and spoke direct to the heart in language of the heart.' His Sermons, composed in Latin and delivered in German, in which language, after repeated renovations and changes of dialect, they are still read, have, with his other writings, been characterised, by a native critic worthy of confidence, in these terms:

'They contain a treasure of meditations, hints, indications, full of heart-felt piety, which still speak to the inmost longings and noblest wants of man's mind. His style is abrupt, compressed, significant in its conciseness; the nameless depth of feelings struggles with the phraseology. He was the first that wrested from our German speech the fit expression for ideas of moral Reason and Emotion, and has left us riches in that kind, such as the zeal for purity and fulness of language in our own days cannot leave unheeded.'—Tauler, it is added, 'was a man who, imbued with genuine Devoutness, as it springs from the depths of a soul strengthened in self-contemplation, and, free and all powerful, rules over Life and Effort,—attempted to train and win the people for a duty which had hitherto been considered as that of the learned class alone: to raise the Lay-world into moral study of Religion for themselves, that so, enfranchised from the bonds of unreflecting custom, they might regulate Creed and Conduct by strength self-acquired. He taught men to look within; by spiritual contemplation to feel the secret of their higher Destiny; to seek in their own souls what from without is never, or too scantily afforded; self-believing, to create what, by the dead letter of foreign Tradition, can never be brought forth.'[1]

Known to all Europe, as Tauler is to Germany, and of a class with him, as a man of antique Christian walk, of warm devoutly-feeling poetic spirit, and insight and experience in the deepest regions of man's heart and life, follows, in the next generation, Thomas Hamerken, or Hammerlein (*Malleolus*); usually named *Thomas à Kempis*, that is, *Thomas of Kempen*, a village near Cologne, where he was born in 1388. Others contend that Kampen in Overyssel was his birthplace; however, in either case, at that era, more especially considering what he did, we can here regard him as a *Deutscher*, a German. For his spiritual and intellectual character we may refer to his works, written in the Latin tongue, and still known; above all, to his far-famed work *De Imitatione Christi*, which has been praised by such men as Luther, Leibnitz, Haller; and, what is more, has been read, and continues to be read, with moral profit, in all Christian languages and communions, having passed through up-

[1] Wachler, *Vorlesungen über die Geschichte der deutschen National-litteratur* (Lectures on the History of German National Literature), b. i. s. 131.

wards of a thousand editions, which number is yet daily increasing. A new English *Thomas à Kempis* was published only the other year. But the venerable man deserves a word from us, not only as a high, spotless Priest, and father of the Church, at a time when such were rare, but as a zealous promoter of learning, which, in his own country, he accomplished much to forward. Hammerlein, the son of poor parents, had been educated at the famous school of Deventer; he himself instituted a similar one at Zwoll, which long continued the grand classical seminary of the North. Among his own pupils we find enumerated Moritz von Spiegelberg, Rudolf von Lange, Rudolf Agricola, Antonius Liber, Ludwig Dringenberg, Alexander Hegius; of whom Agricola, with other two, by advice of their teacher, visited Italy to study Greek; the whole six, united through manhood and life, as they had been in youth and at school, are regarded as the founders of true classical literature among the Germans. Their scholastico-monastic establishments at Deventer, with Zwoll and its other numerous offspring, which rapidly extended themselves over the northwest of Europe from Artois to Silesia, and operated powerfully both in a moral and intellectual view, are among the characteristic redeeming features of that time; but the details of them fall not within our present limits.[1]

If now, quitting the Cloister and Library, we look abroad over active Life, and the general state of culture and spiritual endeavour as manifested there, we have on all hands the cheering prospect of a society in full progress. The Practical Spirit, which had pressed forward into Poetry itself, could not but be busy and successful in those provinces where its home specially lies. Among the Germans, it is true, so far as political condition was concerned, the aspect of affairs had not changed for the better. The Imperial Constitution was weakened and loosened into the mere semblance of a Government; the head of which had still the

[1] See Eichhorn's *Geschichte der Litteratur*, b. ii. s. 134.

title, but no longer the reality of sovereign power; so that Germany, ever since the times of Rudolf, had, as it were, ceased to be one great nation, and become a disunited, often conflicting aggregate of small nations. Nay, we may almost say, of petty districts, or even of households: for now, when every pitiful Baron claimed to be an independent potentate, and exercised his divine right of peace and war too often in plundering the industrious Burgher, public Law could no longer vindicate the weak against the strong: except the venerable unwritten code of *Faustrecht* (Club-Law), there was no other valid. On every steep rock, or difficult fastness, these dread sovereigns perched themselves; studding the country with innumerable *Raubschlösser* (Robber-Towers), which now in the eye of the picturesque tourist look interesting enough, but in those days were interesting on far other grounds. Herein dwelt a race of persons, proud, ignorant, hungry; who, boasting of an endless pedigree, talked familiarly of living on the produce of their 'Saddles' (*vom Sattel zu leben*), that is to say, by the profession of highwayman; for which unluckily, as just hinted, there was then no effectual gallows. Some, indeed, might plunder as the eagle, others as the vulture and crow; but, in general, from men cultivating that walk of life, no profit in any other was to be looked for. Vain was it, however, for the Kaiser to publish edict on edict against them; nay, if he destroyed their Robber-Towers, new ones were built; was the old wolf hunted down, the cub had escaped, who reappeared when his teeth were grown. Not till industry and social cultivation had everywhere spread, and risen supreme, could that brood, in detail, be extirpated or tamed.

Neither was this miserable defect of police the only misery in such a state of things. For the saddle-eating Baron, even in pacific circumstances, naturally looked down on the fruit-producing Burgher; who, again, feeling himself a wiser, wealthier, better and in time a stronger man, ill brooked this procedure, and retaliated, or, by quite declining such communications, avoided it. Thus, throughout long centuries, and after that old Code of Club-Law had been wellnigh abolished, the effort of the nation was still divided into two courses; the Noble and the Citizen would not work together, freely imparting and receiving their several gifts; but the culture of the polite arts, and that of the useful arts, had to proceed with mutual disadvantage, each on its separate footing. Indeed that supercilious and too marked distinction of ranks, which so ridiculously characterised the Germans, has only in very recent times disappeared.

Nevertheless here, as it ever does, the strength of the country lay in the middle classes; which were sound and active, and, in spite of all these hindrances, daily advancing. The Free Towns, which, in Germany as elsewhere, the sovereign favoured, held within their walls a race of men as brave as they of the Robber-Towers, but exercising their bravery on fitter objects; who, by degrees, too, ventured into the field against even the greatest of these kinglets, and in many a stout fight taught them a juristic doctrine, which no head with all its helmets was too thick for taking in. The Four Forest Cantons had already testified in this way; their Tells and Stauffachers preaching, with apostolic blows and knocks, like so many Luthers; whereby, from their remote Alpine glens, all lands and all times have heard them, and believed them. By dint of such logic it began to be understood everywhere, that a Man, whether clothed in purple cloaks or in tanned sheepskins, wielding the sceptre or the oxgoad, is neither Deity nor Beast, but simply a Man, and must comport himself accordingly.

But Commerce of itself was pouring new strength into every peaceable community; the Hanse League, now in full vigour, secured the fruits of industry over all the North. The havens of the Netherlands, thronged with ships from every sea, transmitted or collected their wide-borne freight over Germany; where, far inland, flourished market-cities, with their cunning workmen, their spacious warehouses, and merchants who in opulence vied with the richest. Except perhaps in the close vicinity of Robber-Towers, and even there not always nor altogether, Diligence, good Order, peaceful Abundance were everywhere conspicuous in Germany. Petrarch has celebrated, in warm terms, the beauties of the Rhine, as he witnessed them; the rich, embellished, cultivated aspect of land and people: Æneas Sylvius, afterwards Pope Pius the Second, expresses himself, in the next century, with still greater emphasis: he says, and he could judge, having seen both, 'that the King of Scotland 'did not live so handsomely as a moderate Citizen of Nürn-'berg:' indeed Conrad Celtes, another contemporary witness, informs us, touching these same citizens, that their wives went abroad loaded with the richest jewels, that 'most of their household utensils were of silver and gold.' For, as Æneas Sylvius adds, 'their mercantile activity is astonishing; the greater part of the German nation consists of merchants.' Thus too, in Augsburg, the Fugger family which sprang, like that of the Medici, from smallest beginnings, were fast rising into that height of commercial greatness, such that Charles V., in viewing the Royal Treasury at Paris, could say, "I have a weaver in Augsburg able to buy it all with his own gold."[1] With less satisfaction the same haughty

[1] Charles had his reasons for such a speech. This same Anton Fugger, to whom he alluded here, had often stood by him in straits; showing a munificence and even generosity worthy of the proudest princes. During the celebrated Diet of Augsburg, in 1530, the Emperor lodged for a whole year in Anton's house; and Anton was a man to warm his Emperor 'at a fire of cinnamon wood,' and to burn therein 'the bonds for large sums owing him by his majesty.' For all which, Anton and his kindred had countships and princeships in abundance; also the right to coin money, but no solid bullion to exercise such right on; which, however, they repeatedly did on bullion of their own. This Anton left six millions of gold-crowns in cash; 'besides precious articles, jewels, properties in all countries of Europe, and both the Indies.' The Fuggers had ships on every sea, wagons on every highway; they worked the Carinthian Mines; even Albrecht Dürer's Pictures must pass through their warehouses to the Italian market. However, this family had other merits than their mountains of metal,

Monarch had to see his own Nephew wedded to the fair Philippine Welser, daughter of another merchant in that city, and for wisdom and beauty the paragon of her time.[1]

In this state of economical prosperity, Literature and Art, such kinds of them at least as had a practical application, could not want encouragement. It is mentioned as one of the furtherances to Classical Learning among the Germans, that these Free Towns, as well as numerous petty Courts of Princes, exercising a sovereign power, required individuals of some culture to conduct their Diplomacy; one man able at least to write a handsome Latin style was an indispensable requisite. For a long while even this small accomplishment was not to be acquired in Germany; where, such had been

their kindness to needy Sovereigns, and even their all-embracing spirit of commercial enterprise. They were famed for acts of general beneficence, and did much charity where no imperial thanks were to be looked for. To found Hospitals and Schools, on the most liberal scale, was a common thing with them. In the sixteenth century, three benevolent brothers of the House purchased a suburb of Augsburg; rebuilt it with small commodious houses, to be let to indigent industrious burghers for a trifling rent: this is the well-known *Fuggerei*, which still existing, with its own walls and gate, maintains their name in daily currency there. — The founder of this remarkable family did actually drive the shuttle in the village of Göggingen, near Augsburg, about the middle of the Fourteenth Century; 'but in 1619,' says the *Spiegel der Ehren* (Mirror of Honour), 'the noble stem 'had so branched out, that there were forty-seven Counts and Countesses 'belonging to it, and of young descendants as many as there are days in 'the year.' Four stout boughs of this same noble stem, in the rank of Princes, still subsist and flourish. 'Thus in the generous Fuggers,' says that above-named *Mirror*, 'was fulfilled our Saviour's promise: Give, and 'it shall be given you.' — *Conv. Lexicon*, § *Fugger-Geschlecht.*

[1] The Welsers were of patrician descent, and had for many centuries followed commerce at Augsburg, where, next only to the Fuggers, they played a high part. It was they, for example, that, at their own charges, first colonised Venezuela; that equipped the first German ship to India, 'the Journal of which still exists;' they united with the Fuggers to lend Charles V. twelve *Tonnen Gold*, 1,200,000 Florins. The fair Philippine, by her pure charms and honest wiles, worked out a reconciliation with Kaiser Ferdinand the First, her Father-in-law; lived thirty happy years with her husband; and had medals struck by him, *Divæ Philippinæ*, in honour of her, when (at Inspruck in 1580) he became a widower. — *Conv. Lexicon*, § *Welser*.

the troublous condition of the Governments, there were yet, in the beginning of the fourteenth century, no Universities: however, a better temper and better fortune began at length to prevail among the German Sovereigns; the demands of the time insisted on fulfilment. The University of Prague was founded in 1348, that of Vienna in 1364;[1] and now, as if to make up for the delay, princes and communities on all hands made haste to establish similar Institutions; so that before the end of the century we find three others, Heidelberg, Cologne, Erfurt; in the course of the next, no fewer than eight more, of which Leipsig (in 1404) is the most remarkable. Neither did this honourable zeal grow cool in the sixteenth century, or even down to our own, when Germany, boasting of some forty great Schools and twenty-two Universities, four of which date within the last thirty years, may fairly reckon itself the best school-provided country in Europe; as, indeed, those who in any measure know it, are aware that it is also indisputably the best educated.

Still more decisive are the proofs of national activity, of progressive culture, among the Germans, if we glance at what concerns the practical Arts. Apart from Universities and learned show, there has always dwelt, in those same Nürnbergs and Augsburgs, a solid, quietly-perseverant spirit, full of old Teutonic character and old Teutonic sense; whereby, ever and anon, from under the bonnet of some rugged German artisan or staid burgher, this and the other World-Invention has been starting forth, where such

[1] There seems to be some controversy about the precedence here: Bouterwek gives Vienna, with a date 1333, as the earliest; Koch again puts Heidelberg, 1346, in front; the dates in the Text profess to be taken from Meiner's *Geschichte der Entstehung und Entwickelung der Hohen Schulen unsers Erdtheils* (History of the Origin and Development of High Schools in Europe), Göttingen, 1802. The last-established University is that of München (Munich), in 1826. Prussia alone has 21,000 Public Schoolmasters, specially trained to their profession, sometimes even sent to travel for improvement, at the cost of Government. What says 'the most enlightened nation in the world' to this? — Eats its pudding, and says little or nothing.

was least of all looked for. Indeed, with regard to practical Knowledge in general, if we consider the present history and daily life of mankind, it must be owned that while each nation has contributed a share, — the largest share, at least of such shares as can be appropriated and fixed on any special contributor, belongs to Germany. Copernic, Hevel, Kepler, Otto Guericke, are of other times; but in this era also the spirit of Inquiry, of Invention, was especially busy. Gunpowder (of the thirteenth century), though Milton gives the credit of it to Satan, has helped mightily to lessen the horrors of War: thus much at least must be admitted in its favour, that it secures the dominion of civilised over savage man: nay hereby, in personal contests, not brute Strength, but Courage and Ingenuity, can avail; for the Dwarf and the Giant are alike strong with pistols between them. Neither can Valour now find its best arena in War, in Battle, which is henceforth a matter of calculation and strategy, and the soldier a chess-pawn to shoot and be shot at; whereby that noble quality may at length come to reserve itself for other more legitimate occasions, of which, in this our Life-Battle with Destiny, there are enough. And thus Gunpowder, if it spread the havoc of War, mitigates it in a still higher degree; like some Inoculation, — to which may an extirpating Vaccination one day succeed! It ought to be stated, however, that the claim of Schwartz to the original invention is dubious; to the sole invention altogether unfounded: the recipe stands, under disguise, in the writings of Roger Bacon; the article itself was previously known in the East.

Far more indisputable are the advantages of Printing: and if the story of Brother Schwartz's mortar giving fire and driving his pestle through the ceiling, in the city of Mentz, as the painful Monk and Alchymist was accidentally pounding the ingredients of our first Gunpowder, is but a fable, — that of our first Book being printed there is much better ascertained. Johann Gutenberg was a native of Mentz; and there, in company with Faust and Schöffer, appears to have completed his invention between the years 1440 and 1449: the famous 'Forty-two line Bible' was printed there in 1455.[1] Of this noble art, which is like an infinitely intensated organ of Speech, whereby the Voice of a small transitory man may reach not only through all earthly Space, but through all earthly Time, it were needless to repeat the often-repeated praises; or speculate on the practical effects, the most momentous of which are, perhaps, but now becoming visible. On this subject of the Press, and its German origin, a far humbler remark may be in place here; namely, that Rag-paper, the material on which Printing works and lives, was also invented in Germany some hundred and fifty years before. 'The oldest specimens of this 'article yet known to exist,' says Eichhorn, 'are some Docu-'ments, of the year 1318, in the Archives of the Hospital at 'Kaufbeuern. Breitkopf (*Vom Ursprung der Spielkarten*, 'On the Origin of Cards) has demonstrated our claim to 'the invention; and that France and England borrowed it 'from Germany, and Spain from Italy.'[2]

On the invention of Printing there followed naturally a multiplication of Books, and a new activity, which has ever since proceeded at an accelerating rate, in the business of Literature; but for the present, no change in its character or objects. Those Universities, and other Establishments and Improvements, were so many tools which the spirit of the time had devised, not for working out new paths, which were their ulterior issue, but in the mean while for proceeding more commodiously on the old path. In the Prague University, it is true, whither Wickliffe's writings had found their way, a Teacher of more earnest tone had risen, in the person of John Huss, Rector there; whose Books, *Of the*

[1] As to the Dutch claim, it rests only on vague local traditions, which were never heard of publicly till their Lorenz Coster had been dead almost a hundred and fifty years; so that, out of Holland, it finds few partisans.

[2] B. ii. s. 91.—'The first German Paper-mill we have sure account of,' says Koch, 'worked at Nürnberg in 1390.'—Vol. i. p. 35.

Six Errors and *Of the Church*, still more his energetic, zealously polemical Discourses to the people, were yet unexampled on the Continent. The shameful murder of this man, who lived and died as beseemed a Martyr; and the stern vengeance which his countrymen took for it, unhappily not on the Constance Cardinals, but on less offensive Bohemian Catholics, kept up during twenty years, on the Eastern Border of Germany, an agitating tumult, not only of opinion, but of action: however, the fierce, indomitable Zisca being called away, and the pusillanimous Emperor offering terms, which, indeed, he did not keep, this uproar subsided, and the national activity proceeded in its former course.

In German Literature, during those years, nothing presents itself as worthy of notice here. Chronicles were written; Class-books for the studious, edifying Homilies, in varied guise, for the busy, were compiled: a few Books of Travels make their appearance, among which Translations from our too fabulous countryman, Mandeville, are perhaps the most remarkable. For the rest, Life continued to be looked at less with poetic admiration, than in a spirit of observation and comparison: not without many a protest against clerical and secular error; such, however, seldom rising into the style of grave hate and hostility, but playfully expressing themselves in satire. The old effort towards the Useful; in Literature, the old prevalence of the Didactic, especially of the Æsopic, is everywhere manifest. Of this Æsopic spirit, what phases it successively assumed, and its significance in these, there were much to be said. However, in place of multiplying smaller instances and aspects, let us now take up the highest; and with the best of all Apologues, *Reynard the Fox*, terminate our survey of that Fable-loving time.

The story of *Reinecke Fuchs*, or, to give it the original Low-German name, *Reineke de Fos*, is, more than any other, a truly European performance: for some centuries, a universal household possession and secular Bible, read everywhere, in the palace and the hut: it still interests us, moreover, by its intrinsic worth, being, on the whole, the most poetical and meritorious production of our Western World in that kind; or perhaps of the whole World, though, in such matters, the West has generally yielded to, and learned from, the East.

Touching the origin of this Book, as often happens in like cases, there is a controversy, perplexed not only by inevitable ignorance, but also by anger and false patriotism. Into this vexed sea we have happily no call to venture; and shall merely glance for a moment, from the firm land, where all that can specially concern us in the matter stands rescued and safe. The oldest printed Edition of our actual *Reynard* is that of Lübeck, in 1498; of which there is a copy, understood to be the only one, still extant in the Wolfenbüttel Library. This oldest Edition is in the Low-German or Saxon tongue, and appears to have been produced by Hinrek van Alkmer, who in the preface calls himself 'School-'master and Tutor of that noble virtuous Prince and Lord, 'the Duke of Lorraine;' and says farther, that by order of this same worthy sovereign, he 'sought out and rendered the 'present Book from Walloon and French tongue into Ger-'man, to the praise and honour of God, and wholesome 'edification of whoso readeth therein.' Which candid and business-like statement would doubtless have continued to yield entire satisfaction; had it not been that, in modern days, and while this first Lübeck Edition was still lying in its dusty recess unknown to Bibliomaniacs, another account, dated some hundred years later, and supported by a little subsequent hearsay, had been raked up: how the real Author was Nicholas Baumann, Professor at Rostock; how he had been Secretary to the Duke of Juliers, but was driven from his service by wicked cabals; and so in revenge composed this satirical adumbration of the Juliers Court; putting on the title-page, to avoid consequences, the feigned tale of its being rendered from the French and Walloon tongue, and the feigned name of Hinrek van Alkmer, who, for the rest, was never Schoolmaster and Tutor at Lorraine, or anywhere else, but a mere man of straw, created for the nonce out of so many Letters of the Alphabet. Hereupon excessive debate, and a learned sharp-shooting, with victory-shouts on both sides; into which we nowise enter. Some touch of human sympathy does draw us towards Hinrek, whom, if he was once a real man, with bones and sinews, stomach and provender-scrip, it is mournful to see evaporated away into mere vowels and consonants: however, beyond a kind wish, we can give him no help. In Literary History, except on this one occasion, as seems indisputable enough, he is nowhere mentioned or hinted at.

Leaving Hinrek and Nicolaus, then, to fight out their quarrel as they may, we remark that the clearest issue of it would throw little light on the origin of *Reinecke.* The victor could at most claim to be the first German redactor of this Fable, and the happiest; whose work had superseded and obliterated all preceding ones whatsoever; but nowise to be the inventor thereof, who must be sought for in a much remoter period. There are even two printed versions of the Tale, prior in date to this of Lübeck: a Dutch one, at Delft, in 1484; and one by Caxton in English, in 1481, which seems to be the earliest of all.[1] These two differ essentially from Hinrek's; still more so does the French *Roman du nou-*

[1] Caxton's Edition, a copy of which is in the British Museum, bears title: *Hystorye of Reynart the Foxe;* and begins thus: 'It was aboute the 'tyme of Pentecoste or Whytsontyde that the wodes comynly be lusty 'and gladsome, and the trees clad with levys and blossoms, and the 'grounds with herbes and flowers sweete smellyng;'— where, as in many other passages, the fact that Caxton and Alkmer had the same original before them is manifest enough. Our venerable Printer says in conclusion: 'I have not added ne mynnsshed but have followed as nyghe as I can my 'copye whych was in dutche; and by me Willm Caxton translated in to 'this rude and symple englyssh in thabbey of Westminster, and fyn-'nyshed the vi daye of Juyn the yere of our lord 1481, the 21 yere of the 'regne of Kynge Edward the iiijth.'

veau Renard, composed 'by Jacquemars Gielée at Lisle, about the year 1290,' which yet exists in manuscript: however, they sufficiently verify that statement, by some supposed to be feigned, of the German redactor's having 'sought and rendered' his work from the Walloon and French; in which latter tongue, as we shall soon see, some shadow of it had been known and popular, long centuries before that time. For besides Gielée's work, we have a *Renard Couronné* of still earlier, a *Renard Contrefait* of somewhat later date: and Chroniclers inform us that, at the noted Festival given by Philip the Fair, in the beginning of the fourteenth century, among the dramatic entertainments, was a whole Life of Reynard; wherein it must not surprise us that he 'ended by becoming Pope, and still, under the Tiara, continued to eat poultry.' Nay, curious inquirers have discovered, on the French and German borders, some vestige of the Story even in Carlovingian times; which, indeed, again makes it a German original: they will have it that a certain Reinhard, or Reinecke, Duke of Lorraine, who, in the ninth century, by his craft and exhaustless stratagems worked strange mischief in that region, many times overreaching King Zwentibald himself, and at last, in his stronghold of Durfos, proving impregnable to him,—had in satirical songs of that period been celebrated as a *fox*, as *Reinhard the Fox*, and so given rise afar off to this Apologue, at least to the title of it. The name *Isegrim*, as applied to the Wolf, these same speculators deduce from an Austrian Count Isengrin, who, in those old days, had revolted against Kaiser Arnulph, and otherwise exhibited too wolfish a disposition. Certain it is, at least, that both designations were in universal use during the twelfth century; they occur, for example, in one of the two *sirventes* which our Cœur-de-Lion has left us: 'Ye have promised me fidelity,' says he, 'but ye have kept it as the Wolf did to the Fox,' as *Isangrin* did to *Reinhart*.[1] Nay, perhaps the

[1] Flögel (iii. 31), who quotes the *Histoire Littéraire des Troubadours* t. i. p. 63.

ancient circulation of some such Song or Tale, among the French, is best of all evinced by the fact that this same *Reinhart*, or *Renard*, is still the only word in their language for *Fox;* and thus, strangely enough, the Proper may have become an Appellative; and sly Duke Reinhart, at an era when the French tongue was first evolving itself from the rubbish of Latin and German, have insinuated his name into Natural as well as Political History.

From all which, so much at least would appear: That the Fable of *Reynard the Fox*, which in the German version we behold completed, nowise derived its completeness from the individual there named Hinrek van Alkmer, or from any other individual or people; but rather, that being in old times universally current, it was taken up by poets and satirists of all countries; from each received some accession or improvement; and properly has no single author. We must observe, however, that as yet it had attained no fixation or consistency; no version was decidedly preferred to every other. Caxton's and the Dutch appear, at best, but as the skeleton of what afterwards became a body; of the old Walloon version, said to have been discovered lately, we are taught to entertain a similar opinion:[1] in the existing French versions, which are all older, either in Gielée's, or in the others, there is even less analogy. Loosely conjoined, therefore, and only in the state of dry bones, was it that Hinrek, or Nicolaus, or some Lower-Saxon whoever he might be, found the story; and blowing on it with the breath of genius, raised it up into a consistent Fable. Many additions and some exclusions he must have made; was probably enough assisted by personal experience of a Court, whether that of Juliers or some other; perhaps also he admitted personal allusions, and doubtless many an oblique glance at existing things: and thus was produced the Low-German *Reineke de Fos;* which version, shortly after its appearance, had extinguished all the rest, and come to be,

[1] See Scheller: *Reineke de Fos, To Brunswyk*, 1825; Vorrede.

what it still is, the sole veritable representative of *Reynard*, inasmuch as all subsequent translations and editions have derived themselves from it.

The farther history of *Reinecke* is easily traced. In this new guise, it spread abroad over all the world, with a scarcely exampled rapidity; fixing itself also as a firm possession in most countries, where, indeed, in this character, we still find it. It was printed and rendered, innumerable times: in the original dialect alone, the last Editor has reckoned up more than twenty Editions; on one of which, for example, we find such a name as that of Heinrich Voss. It was first translated into High-German in 1545; into Latin in 1567, by Hartmann Schopper, whose smooth style and rough fortune keep him in memory with Scholars:[1] a new version into short German verse appeared next century; in our own times, Goethe has not disdained to reproduce it, by means of his own, in a third shape: of Soltau's version, into literal doggerel, we have already testified. Long generations before, it had been manufactured into Prose, for the

[1] While engaged in this Translation, at Freiburg in Baden, he was impressed as a soldier, and carried, apparently in fetters, to Vienna, having given his work to another to finish. At Vienna he stood not long in the ranks; having fallen violently sick, and being thrown out in the streets to recover there. He says, 'he was without bed, and had to seek quarters on the muddy pavement in a Barrel.' Here too, in the night, some excessively straitened individual stole from him his cloak and sabre. However, men were not all hyænas: one Josias Hufnagel, unknown to him, but to whom by his writings he was known, took him under his roof, procured medical assistance, equipped him anew; so that 'in the 'harvest-season, being half-cured, he could return or rather recrawl to 'Frankfort on the Mayn.' There too 'a Magister Johann Cuipius, Chris-'tian Egenolph's son-in-law, kindly received him,' and encouraged him to finish his Translation; as accordingly he did, dedicating it to the Emperor, with doleful complaints, fruitless or not is unknown. For now poor Hartmann, no longer an Autobiographer, quite vanishes, and we can understand only that he laid his wearied back one day in a most still bed, where the blanket of the Night softly enwrapped him and all his woes.—— His Book is entitled *Opus poeticum de admirabili Fallaciâ et Astutiâ Vulpeculæ Reinekes*, &c. &c.; and in the Dedication and Preface contains all these details.

use of the people, and was sold on stalls; where still, with the needful changes in spelling, and printed on grayest paper, it tempts the speculative eye.

Thus has our old Fable, rising like some River in the remote distance, from obscure rivulets, gathered strength out of every valley, out of every country, as it rolled on. It is European in two senses; for as all Europe contributed to it, so all Europe has enjoyed it. Among the Germans, *Reinecke Fuchs* was long a House-book and universal Best-companion: it has been lectured on in the Universities, quoted in Imperial Council-halls; it lay on the toilette of Princesses; and was thumbed to pieces on the bench of the Artisan; we hear of grave men ranking it only next to the Bible. Neither, as we said, was its popularity confined to home; Translations erelong appeared in French, Italian, Danish, Swedish, Dutch, English:[1] nor was that same stall-honour, which has been reckoned the truest literary celebrity, refused it here; perhaps many a reader of these pages may, like the writer of them, recollect the hours, when, hidden from unfeeling gaze of pedagogue, he swallowed *The most pleasant and delightful History of Reynard the Fox*, like stolen waters, with a timorous joy.

So much for the outward fortunes of this remarkable Book. It comes before us with a character such as can belong only to a very few; that of being a true World's-Book, which through centuries was everywhere at home, the spirit of which diffused itself into all languages and all

[1] Besides Caxton's original, of which little is known among us but the name, we have two versions; one in 1667, 'with excellent Morals and Expositions,' which was reprinted in 1681, and followed in 1684 by a Continuation, called the *Shifts of Reynardine the son of Reynard*, of English growth; another in 1708, slightly altered from the former, explaining what appears doubtful or allegorical; 'it being originally written,' says the brave Editor elsewhere, 'by an eminent Statesman of the German Em-'pire, to show some Men their Follies, and correct the Vices of the Times 'he lived in.' Not only *Reynardine*, but a second Appendix, *Cawood the Rook*, appears here; also there are 'curious Devices, or Pictures.' — Of Editions 'printed for the Flying-Stationers' we say nothing.

minds. These quaint Æsopic figures have painted themselves in innumerable heads; that rough, deep-lying humour has been the laughter of many generations. So that, at worst, we must regard this *Reinecke* as an ancient Idol, once worshipped, and still interesting for that circumstance, were the sculpture never so rude. We can love it, moreover, as being indigenous, wholly of our own creation: it sprang up from European sense and character, and was a faithful type and organ of these.

But independently of all extrinsic considerations, this Fable of *Reinecke* may challenge a judgment on its own merits. Cunningly constructed, and not without a true poetic life, we must admit it to be: great power of conception and invention, great pictorial fidelity, a warm, sunny tone of colouring, are manifest enough. It is full of broad rustic mirth; inexhaustible in comic devices; a World-Saturnalia, where Wolves tonsured into Monks, and nigh starved by short commons, Foxes pilgriming to Rome for absolution, Cocks pleading at the judgment-bar, make strange mummery. Nor is this wild Parody of Human Life without its meaning and moral: it is an air-pageant from Fancy's dream-grotto, yet wisdom lurks in it; as we gaze, the vision becomes poetic and prophetic. A true Irony must have dwelt in the Poet's heart and head; here, under grotesque shadows, he gives us the sadder picture of Reality; yet for us without sadness; his figures mask themselves in uncouth, bestial vizards, and enact, gambolling; their Tragedy dissolves into sardonic grins. He has a deep, heartfelt Humour, sporting with the world and its evils in kind mockery: this is the poetic *soul*, round which the outward *material* has fashioned itself into living coherence. And so, in that rude old Apologue, we have still a mirror, though now tarnished and timeworn, of true magic reality; and can discern there, in cunning reflex, some image both of our destiny and of our duty: for now, as then, Prudence is the only virtue sure of its reward, and Cunning triumphs where Honesty is worsted; and now, as then, it is the wise man's part to know this, and cheerfully look for it, and cheerfully defy it:

Ut vulpis adulatio
Here through his own world moveth,
Sic hominis et ratio
Most like to Reynard's proveth.

Ut vulpis adulatio
Nu in de werlde blikket:
Sic hominis et ratio
Gelyk dem Fos sik shikket.
Motto to *Reineke.*

If *Reinecke* is nowise a perfect Comic Epos, it has various features of such, and above all, a genuine Epic spirit, which is the rarest feature.

Of the Fable, and its incidents and structure, it is perhaps superfluous to offer any sketch; to most readers the whole may be already familiar. How Noble, King of the Beasts, holding a solemn Court one Whitsuntide, is deafened on all hands with complaints against Reinecke; Hinze the Cat, Lampe the Hare, Isegrim the Wolf, with innumerable others, having suffered from his villany, Isegrim especially, in a point which most keenly touches honour; nay, Chanticleer the Cock (*Henning de Hane*), amid bitterest wail, appearing even with the *corpus delicti*, the body of one of his children, whom that arch-knave has feloniously murdered with intent to eat. How his indignant Majesty thereupon despatches Bruin the Bear to cite the delinquent in the King's name; how Bruin, inveigled into a Honey-expedition, returns without his errand, without his ears, almost without his life; Hinze the Cat, in a subsequent expedition, faring no better. How at last Reinecke, that he may not have to stand actual siege in his fortress of Malapertus, does appear for trial, and is about to be hanged, but on the gallows-ladder makes a speech unrivalled in forensic eloquence, and saves his life; nay, having incidentally hinted at some Treasures, the hiding-place of which is well known to him, rises into high favour; is permitted to depart on that pious pilgrimage to Rome he has so much at heart, and furnished even with shoes, cut from the living hides of Isegrim and Isegrim's much-injured spouse, his worst enemies. How, the Treasures not making their appearance, but only new misdeeds, he is again haled to judgment; again glozes the general ear with sweetest speeches; at length, being challenged to it, fights Isegrim in knightly tourney, and by the cunningest, though the most unchivalrous method, not to be further specified in polite writing, carries off a complete victory; and having thus, by wager of battle, manifested his innocence, is overloaded with royal favour, created Chancellor, and Pilot to weather the Storm; and so, in universal honour and authority, reaps the fair fruit of his gifts and labours:

Whereby shall each to wisdom turn,
Evil eschew and virtue learn,
Therefore was this same story wrote,
That is its aim, and other not.
This Book for little price is sold,
But image clear of world doth hold;
Whoso into the world would look,
My counsel is, — he buy this book.
So endeth Reynard Fox's story:
God help us all to heavenly glory!

It has been objected that the Animals in *Reinecke* are not Animals, but Men disguised; to which objection, except in so far as grounded on the necessary indubitable fact that this is an Apologue or emblematic Fable, and no Chapter of Natural History, we cannot in any considerable degree accede. Nay, that very contrast between Object and Effort, where the Passions of men develop themselves on the Interests of animals, and the whole is huddled together in chaotic mockery, is a main charm of the picture. For the rest, we should rather say, these bestial characters were moderately well sustained: the vehement, futile vociferation of Chanticleer; the hysterical promptitude, and earnest profession and protestation of poor Lampe the Hare; the thickheaded ferocity of Isegrim; the sluggish, gluttonous opacity of Bruin; above all, the craft, the tact and inexhaustible knavish adroitness of Reinecke himself, are in strict accuracy of costume. Often also their situations and occupations are bestial enough. What quantities of bacon and other proviant do Isegrim and Reinecke forage; Reinecke contributing the scheme, — for the two were then in partnership, — and Isegrim paying the shot in broken bones! What more characteristic then the fate of Bruin, when ill-counselled, he introduces his stupid head into Rustefill's half-split log; has the wedges whisked away, and stands clutched there, as in a vice, and uselessly roaring; disappointed of honey, sure only of a beating without parallel! Not to forget the Mare, whom, addressing her by the title of Goodwife, with all politeness, Isegrim, sore-pinched with hunger, asks whether she will sell her foal: she answers, that the price is written on her hinder hoof; which document the intending purchaser, being 'an Erfurt graduate,' declares his full ability to read; but finds there no writing, or print, — save only the *print* of six horsenails on his own mauled visage. And abundance of the like; sufficient to excuse our old Epos on this head, or altogether justify it. Another objection, that, namely, which points to the great and excessive coarseness of the work here and there, it cannot so readily turn aside; being indeed rude, old-fashioned, and homespun, apt even to draggle in the mire: neither are its occasional dulness and tediousness to be denied; but only to be set against its frequent terseness and strength, and pardoned as the product of poor humanity, from whose hands nothing, not even a *Reineke de Fos*, comes perfect.

He who would read, and still understand this old Apologue, must apply to Goethe, whose version, for poetical use, we have found infinitely the best; like some copy of an ancient, bedimmed, half-obliterated woodcut, but new-done on steel, on India-paper, with all manner of graceful yet appropriate appendages. Nevertheless, the old Low-German original has also a certain charm, and simply as the original, would claim some notice. It is reckoned greatly the best performance that was ever brought out in that dialect; interesting, moreover, in a philological point of view, especially to us English; being properly the language of our old Saxon Fatherland; and still curiously like our own, though the two, for some twelve centuries, have had no brotherly communication. One short specimen, with the most verbal translation, we shall insert here, and then have done with *Reinecke:*

'De Greving was Reinken broder's söne,
The Badger was Reinke's brother's son,
De sprak do, un was sêr köne.
He spoke there, and was (sore) very (keen) bold.
He forantworde in dem Hove den Fos,
He (for-answered) defended in the Court the Fox,
De dog was sêr falsh un lôs.
That (though) yet was very false and loose.
He sprak to deme Wulve also fôrd:
He spoke to the Wolf so forth:
Here Isegrim, it is ein ôldspräken wôrd,
Master Isegrim, it is an old-spoken word,
Des fyendes mund shaffet selden frôm!
The (fiend's) enemy's mouth (shapeth) bringeth seldom advantage!
So do ji ôk by Reinken, minem ôm.
So do ye (eke) too by Reinke, mine (eme) uncle.
Were he so wol alse ji hyr to Hove,
Were he as well as ye here at Court,
Un stunde he also in des Koninge's love,
And stood he so in the King's favour,
Here Isegrim, alse ji dôt,
Master Isegrim, as ye do,
It sholde ju nigt dünken gôd,
It should you not (think) seem good,
Dat ji en hyr alsus forspräken
That ye him here so forspake
Un de ôlden stükke hyr fôrräken.
And the old tricks here forth-raked.
Men dat kwerde, dat ji Reinken hävven gedân,
But the ill that ye Reinke have done,
Dat late ji al agter stan.
That let ye all (after stand) stand by.
It is nog etliken heren wol kund,
It is yet to some gentlemen well known,

Wo ji mid Reinken maken den ferbund,
How ye with Reinke made (bond) alliance,
Un wolden wären twe like gesellen:
And would be two (like) equal partners:
Dat mot ik dirren heren fortällen.
That mote I these gentlemen forth-tell.
Wente Reinke, myn ôm in wintersnôd,
Since Reinke, mine uncle, in winter's-need,
Umme Isegrim's willen, fylna was dôd.
For Isegrim's (will) sake, full-nigh was dead.
Wente it geshag dat ein kwam gefaren,
For it chanced that one came (faring) driving,
De hadde grote fishe up ener karen:
Who had many fishes upon a car:
Isegrim hadde geren der fishe gehaled,
Isegrim had fain the fishes (have haled) have got,
Men he hadde nigt, darmid se wörden betaled.
But he had not wherewith they should be (betold) paid.
He bragte minen ôm in de grote nôd,
He brought mine uncle into great (need) straits,
Um sinen willen ging he liggen for dôd,
For his sake went he to (lig) lie for dead,
Regt in den wäg, un stund äventur.
Right in the way, and stood (adventure) chance.
Market, worden em ôk de fishe sûr?
Mark, were him eke the fishes (sour) dear-bought?
Do jenne mid der kare gefaren kwam
When (yond) he with the car driving came
Un minen ôm darsülvest fornem,
And mine uncle (there-self) even there perceived,
Hastigen tôg he syn swërd un snel,
Hastily (took) drew he his sword and (snell) quick,
Un wolde mineme ome torrükken en fel.
And would my uncle (tatter in fell) tear in pieces.
Men he rögede sik nigt klên nog grôt;
But he stirred himself not (little nor great) more or less;
Do mênde he dat he were dôd;
Then (meaned) thought he that he was dead;
He läde ön up de kar, und dayte en to fillen,
He laid him upon the car, and thought him to skin,
Dat wagede he all dorg Isegrim's willen!
That risked he all through Isegrim's will!
Do he fordan begunde to faren,
When he forth-on began to fare,
Wärp Reinke etlike fishe fan der karen,
Cast Reinke some fishes from the car,

Isegrim fan ferne agteona kwam
Isegrim from far after came
Un derre fishe al to sik nam.
And these fishes all to himself took.
Reinke sprang wedder fan der karen;
Reinke sprang again from the car;
Em lüstede to nigt länger to faren.
Him listed not longer to fare.
He hadde ôk gêrne der fishe begërd,
He (had) would have also fain of the fishes required,
Men Isegrim hadde se alle fortêrd.
But Isegrim had them all consumed.
He had de geten dat he wolde barsten,
He had eaten so that he would burst,
Un moste darumme gên torn arsten.
And must thereby go to the doctor.
Do Isegrim der graden nigt en mogte,
As Isegrim the fish-bones not liked,
Der sülven he em ein weinig brogte.
Of these (self) same he him a little brought.

Whereby it would appear, if we are to believe Grimbart the Badger, that Reinecke was not only the cheater in this case, but also the cheatee: however, he makes matters straight again in that other noted fish-expedition, where Isegrim, minded not to steal but to catch fish, and having no fishing-tackle, by Reinecke's advice inserts his tail into the lake, in winter-season; but before the promised string of trouts, all hooked to one another and to him, will bite, — is frozen in, and left there to his own bitter meditations.

We here take leave of *Reineke de Fos*, and of the whole Æsopic genus, of which it is almost the last, and by far the most remarkable example. The Age of Apologue, like that of Chivalry and Love-singing, is gone; for nothing in this Earth has continuance. If we ask, Where are now our People's-Books? the answer might give room for reflections. Hinrek van Alkmer has passed away, and Dr. Birkbeck has risen in his room. What good and evil lie in that little sentence! — But doubtless the day is coming when what is wanting here will be supplied; when as the Logical, so likewise the Poetical susceptibility and faculty of the people, — their Fancy, Humour, Imagination, wherein lie the main elements of spiritual life, — will no longer be left uncultivated, barren, or bearing only spontaneous thistles, but in new and finer harmony with an improved Understanding, will flourish in new vigour; and in our inward world there will again be a sunny Firmament and verdant Earth, as well as a Pantry and culinary Fire; and men will learn not only to recapitulate and compute, but to worship, to love; in tears or in laughter, hold mystical as well as logical communion with the high and the low of this wondrous Universe; and read, as they should live, with their whole being. Of which glorious consummation there is at all times, seeing these endowments are indestructible, nay essentially supreme in man, the firmest ulterior certainty, but, for the present, only faint prospects and far-off indications. Time brings Roses!

TAYLOR'S HISTORIC SURVEY OF GERMAN POETRY.[1]

[1831.]

GERMAN Literature has now for upwards of half a century been making some way in England; yet by no means at a constant rate, rather in capricious flux and reflux, — deluge alternating with desiccation: never would it assume such moderate, reasonable currency, as promised to be useful and lasting. The history of its progress here would illustrate the progress of more important things; would again exemplify what obstacles a new spiritual object, with its mixture of truth and of falsehood, has to encounter from unwise enemies, still more from unwise friends; how dross is mistaken for metal, and common ashes are solemnly labelled as fell poison; how long, in such cases, blind Passion must vociferate before she can awaken Judgment; in short, with what tumult, vicissitude and protracted difficulty, a foreign doctrine adjusts and locates itself among the homeborn. Perfect ignorance is quiet, perfect knowledge is quiet; not so the transition from the former to the latter. In a vague, all-exaggerating twilight of wonder, the new has to fight its battle with the old; Hope has to settle accounts with Fear: thus the scales strangely waver; public opinion, which is as yet baseless, fluctuates without limit; periods of foolish admiration and foolish execration must elapse, before that of true inquiry and zeal according to knowledge can begin.

[1] EDINBURGH REVIEW, No. 105. — Historic Survey of German Poetry, interspersed with various Translations. By W. Taylor, of Norwich. 3 vols. 8vo. London, 1830.

Thirty years ago, for example, a person of influence and understanding thought good to emit such a proclamation as the following: 'Those ladies, who take the lead in society, 'are loudly called upon to act as guardians of the public 'taste as well as of the public virtue. They are called upon, 'therefore, to oppose, with the whole weight of their influ-'ence, the irruption of those swarms of Publications now 'daily issuing from the banks of the Danube, which, like 'their ravaging predecessors of the darker ages, though 'with far other and more fatal arms, are overrunning civ-'ilised society. Those readers, whose purer taste has been 'formed on the correct models of the old classic school, see 'with indignation and astonishment the Huns and Vandals 'once more overpowering the Greeks and Romans. They 'behold our minds, with a retrograde but rapid motion, 'hurried back to the reign of Chaos and old Night, by dis-'torted and unprincipled Compositions, which, in spite of 'strong flashes of genius, unite the taste of the Goths with 'the morals of Bagshot.' — 'The newspapers announce that 'Schiller's *Tragedy of the Robbers*, which inflamed the young 'nobility of Germany to enlist themselves into a band of 'highwaymen to rob in the forests of Bohemia, is now acting 'in England by persons of quality!' [1]

Whether our fair Amazons, at sound of this alarm-trumpet, drew up in array of war to discomfit those invading Compositions, and snuff-out the lights of that questionable private theatre, we have not learned; and see only that, if so, their campaign was fruitless and needless. Like the old Northern Immigrators, those new Paper Goths marched on resistless whither they were bound; some to honour, some to dishonour, the most to oblivion and the impalpable inane; and no weapon or artillery, not even the glances of bright eyes, but only the omnipotence of Time, could tame and assort them. Thus, Kotzebue's truculent armaments, once so threatening,

[1] *Strictures on the Modern System of Female Education.* By Hannah More. The Eighth Edition, p. 41.

all turned out to be mere Phantasms and Night-apparitions; and so rushed onwards, like some Spectre-Hunt, with loud howls indeed, yet hurrying nothing into Chaos but themselves. While again, Schiller's *Tragedy of the Robbers*, which did not inflame either the young or the old nobility of Germany to rob in the forests of Bohemia. or indeed to do anything, except perhaps yawn a little less, proved equally innocuous in England, and might still be acted without offence, could living individuals, idle enough for that end, be met with here. Nay, this same Schiller, not indeed by *Robbers*, yet by *Wallensteins*, by *Maids of Orleans*, and *Wilhelm Tells*, has actually conquered for himself a fixed dominion among us, which is yearly widening; round which other German kings, of less intrinsic prowess, and of greater, are likewise erecting thrones. And yet, as we perceive, civilised society still stands in its place; and the public taste, as well as the public virtue, live on, though languidly, as before. For, in fine, it has become manifest that the old Cimmerian Forest is now quite felled and tilled; that the true Children of Night, whom we have to dread, dwell not on the banks of the Danube, but nearer hand.

Could we take our progress in knowledge of German Literature since that diatribe was written, as any measure of our progress in the science of Criticism, above all, in the grand science of national Tolerance, there were some reason for satisfaction. With regard to Germany itself, whether we yet stand on the right footing, and know at last how we are to live in profitable neighbourhood and intercourse with that country; or whether the present is but one other of those capricious tides, which also will have its reflux, may seem doubtful: meanwhile, clearly enough, a rapidly growing favour for German Literature comes to light; which favour too is the more hopeful, as it now grounds itself on better knowledge, on direct study and judgment. Our knowledge is better, if only because more general. Within the last ten years, independent readers of German have multiplied perhaps a hundredfold; so that now this acquirement is almost expected as a natural item in liberal education. Hence, in a great number of minds, some immediate personal insight into the deeper significance of German Intellect and Art; — everywhere, at least a feeling that it has some such significance. With independent readers, moreover, the writer ceases to be independent, which of itself is a considerable step. Our British Translators, for instance, have long been unparalleled in modern literature, and, like their country, 'the envy of surrounding nations:' but now there are symptoms that, even in the remote German province, they must no longer range quite at will; that the butchering of a *Faust* will henceforth be accounted literary homicide, and practitioners of that quality must operate on the dead subject only. While there are Klingemanns and Claurens in such abundance, let no merely ambitious, or merely hungry Interpreter fasten on Goethes and Schillers. Remark too, with satisfaction, how the old-established British Critic now feels that it has become unsafe to speak delirium on this subject; wherefore he prudently restricts himself to one of two courses: either to acquire some understanding of it, or, which is the still surer course, altogether to hold his peace. Hence freedom from much babble that was wont to be oppressive: probably no watchhorn with such a note as that of Mrs. More's can again be sounded, by male or female Dogberry, in these Islands. Again, there is no one of our younger, more vigorous Periodicals, but has its German craftsman, gleaning what he can: we have seen Jean Paul quoted in English Newspapers. Nor, among the signs of improvement, at least of extended curiosity, let us omit our British Foreign Reviews, a sort of merchantmen that regularly visit the Continental, especially the German Ports, and bring back such ware as luck yields them, with the hope of better. Last, not least among our evidences of Philo-Germanism, here is a whole *Historic Survey of German Poetry*, in three sufficient octavos; and this not merely in the eulogistic and recommendatory vein, but proceeding in the way of criticism, and indifferent, impartial narrative: a man of known character, of talent, experience, penetration, judges that the English public is prepared for such a service, and likely to reward it.

These are appearances, which, as advocates for the friendly approximation of all men and all peoples, and the readiest possible interchange of whatever each produces of advantage to the others, we must witness gladly. Free literary intercourse with other nations, what is it but an extended Freedom of the Press; a liberty to read (in spite of Ignorance, of Prejudice, which is the worst of Censors) what our foreign teachers also have printed for us? Ultimately, therefore, a liberty to speak and to hear, were it with men of all countries and of all times; to use, in utmost compass, those precious natural organs, by which not Knowledge only but mutual Affection is chiefly generated among mankind! It is a natural wish in man to know his fellow-passengers in this strange Ship, or Planet, on this strange Life-voyage: neither need his curiosity restrict itself to the cabin where he himself chances to lodge; but may extend to all accessible departments of the vessel. In all he will find mysterious beings, of Wants and Endeavours like his own; in all he will find Men; with these let him comfort and manifoldly instruct himself. As to German Literature, in particular, which professes to be not only new, but original, and rich in curious information for us; which claims, moreover, nothing that we have not granted to the French, Italian, Spanish, and in a less degree to far meaner literatures, we are gratified to see that such claims can no longer be resisted. In the present fallow state of our English Literature, when no Poet cultivates his own poetic field, but all are harnessed into Editorial teams, and ploughing in concert, for Useful Knowledge, or Bibliopolic Profit, we regard this renewal of our intercourse with poetic Germany, after twenty years of languor or suspension, as among the most remarkable and even promising features of our recent intellectual history. In the absence of better tendencies, let this, which is no idle, but in some points of view a deep and earnest one, be encouraged. For ourselves, in the midst of so many louder and more exciting interests, we feel it a kind of duty to cast some glances now and then on this little stiller interest: since the matter is once for all to be inquired into, sound notions on it should be furthered, unsound ones cannot be too speedily corrected. It is on such grounds that we have taken up this *Historic Survey.*

Mr. Taylor is so considerable a person, that no Book deliberately published by him, on any subject, can be without weight. On German Poetry, such is the actual state of public information and curiosity, his guidance will be sure to lead or mislead a numerous class of inquirers. We are therefore called on to examine him with more than usual strictness and minuteness. The Press, in these times, has become so active; Literature, what is still called Literature, has so dilated in volume, and diminished in density, that the very Reviewer feels at a nonplus, and has ceased to review. Why thoughtfully examine what was written without thought; or note faults and merits, where there is neither fault nor merit? From a Nonentity, embodied, with innocent deception, in foolscap and printers' ink, and named Book; from the common wind of Talk, even when it is conserved by such mechanism, for days, in the shape of Froth, — how shall the hapless Reviewer filter aught in that once so profitable colander of his? He has ceased, as we said, to attempt the impossible, — cannot review, but only discourse; he dismisses his too unproductive Author, generally with civil words, not to quarrel needlessly with a fellow-creature; and must try, as he best may, to grind from his own poor garner. Authors long looked with an evil, envious eye on the Reviewer, and strove often to blow out his light, which only burnt the clearer for such blasts; but now, cunningly altering their tactics, they have extinguished it by want of oil.

Unless for some unforeseen change of affairs, or some new-contrived machinery, of which there is yet no trace, the trade of the Reviewer is wellnigh done.

The happier are we that Mr. Taylor's Book is of the old stamp, and has substance in it for our uses. If no honour, there will be no disgrace, in having carefully examined it; which service, indeed, is due to our readers, not without curiosity in this matter, as well as to the Author. In so far as he seems a safe guide, and brings true tidings from the promised land, let us proclaim that fact, and recommend him to all pilgrims: if, on the other hand, his tidings are false, let us hasten to make this also known; that the German Canaan suffer not, in the eyes of the fainthearted, by spurious samples of its produce and reports of bloodthirsty sons of Anak dwelling there, which this harbinger and spy brings out of it. In either case, we may hope, our Author, who loves the Germans in his way, and would have his countrymen brought into closer acquaintance with them, will feel that, in purpose at least, we are coöperating with him.

First, then, be it admitted without hesitation, that Mr. Taylor, in respect of general talent and acquirement, takes his place above all our expositors of German things; that his Book is greatly the most important we yet have on this subject. Here are upwards of fourteen hundred solid pages of commentary, narrative and translation, submitted to the English reader; numerous statements and personages, hitherto unheard of, or vaguely heard of, stand here in fixed shape; there is, if no map of intellectual Germany, some first attempt at such. Farther, we are to state that our Author is a zealous, earnest man; no hollow dilettante hunting after shadows, and prating he knows not what; but a substantial, distinct, remarkably decisive man; has his own opinion on many subjects, and can express it adequately. We should say, precision of idea was a striking quality of his: no vague transcendentalism, or mysticism of any kind; nothing but what is measurable and tangible, and has a meaning which he that runs may read, is to be apprehended here. He is a man of much classical and other reading; of much singular reflection; stands on his own basis, quiescent yet immovable: a certain rugged vigour of natural power, interesting even in its distortions, is everywhere manifest. Lastly, we venture to assign him the rare merit of honesty: he speaks out in plain English what is in him; seems heartily convinced of his own doctrines, and preaches them because they are his own; not for the sake of sale, but of truth; at worst, for the sake of making proselytes.

On the strength of which properties, we reckon that this *Historic Survey* may, under certain conditions, be useful and acceptable to two classes. First, to incipient students of German Literature in the original; who in any History of their subject, even in a bare catalogue, will find help; though for that class, unfortunately, Mr. Taylor's help is much diminished in value by several circumstances; by this one, were there no other, that he nowhere cites any authority: the path he has opened may be the true or the false one; for farther researches and lateral surveys there is no direction or indication. But, secondly, we reckon that this Book may be welcome to many of the much larger miscellaneous class, who read less for any specific object than for the sake of reading; to whom any book that will, either in the way of contradiction or of confirmation, by new wisdom or new perversion of wisdom, stir up the stagnant inner man, is a windfall; the rather if it bring some historic tidings also, fit for remembering, and repeating; above all, if, as in this case, the style with many singularities have some striking merits, and so the book be a light exercise, even an entertainment.

To such praise and utility the Work is justly entitled; but this is not all it pretends to; and more cannot without many limitations be conceded it. Unluckily the *Historic Survey* is not what it should be, but only what it would be. Our Author hastens to correct in his Preface any false hopes his Title-page may have excited: 'A complete History of Ger-

'man Poetry,' it seems, 'is hardly within reach of his local 'command of library: so comprehensive an undertaking 'would require another residence in a country from which 'he has now been separated more than forty years:' and which various considerations render it unadvisable to revisit. Nevertheless, 'having long been in the practice of importing the productions of its fine literature,' and of working in that material, as critic, biographer and translator, for more than one 'periodic publication of this country,' he has now composed 'introductory and connective sections,' filled up deficiencies, retrenched superfluities; and so, collecting and remodelling those 'successive contributions,' cements them together into the 'new and entire work' here offered to the public. 'With fragments,' he concludes, 'long since 'hewn, as it were, and sculptured, I attempt to construct an 'English Temple of Fame to the memory of those German 'Poets.'

There is no doubt but a Complete History of German Poetry exceeds any local or universal command of books which a British man can at this day enjoy; and, farther, presents obstacles of an infinitely more serious character than this. A History of German, or of any national Poetry, would form, taken in its complete sense, one of the most arduous enterprises any writer could engage in. Poetry, were it the rudest, so it be sincere, is the attempt which man makes to render his existence harmonious, the utmost he can do for that end: it springs therefore from his whole feelings, opinions, activity, and takes its character from these. It may be called the music of his whole manner of being; and, historically considered, is the test how far Music, or Freedom, existed therein; how far the feeling of Love, of Beauty and Dignity, could be elicited from that peculiar situation of his, and from the views he there had of Life and Nature, of the Universe, internal and external. Hence, in any measure to understand the Poetry, to estimate its worth and historical meaning, we ask as a quite fundamental inquiry: What that situation was? Thus the History of a nation's Poetry is the essence of its History, political, economic, scientific, religious. With all these the complete Historian of a national Poetry will be familiar; the national physiognomy, in its finest traits, and through its successive stages of growth, will be clear to him: he will discern the grand spiritual Tendency of each period, what was the highest Aim and Enthusiasm of mankind in each, and how one epoch naturally evolved itself from the other. He has to record the highest Aim of a nation, in its successive directions and developments; for by this the Poetry of the nation modulates itself; this *is* the Poetry of the nation.

Such were the primary essence of a true History of Poetry; the living principle round which all detached facts and phenomena, all separate characters of Poems and Poets, would fashion themselves into a coherent whole, if they are by any means to cohere. To accomplish such a work for any Literature would require not only all outward aids, but an excellent inward faculty: all telescopes and observatories were of no avail, without the seeing eye and the understanding heart.

Doubtless, as matters stand, such models remain in great part ideal; the stinted result of actual practice must not be too rigidly tried by them. In our language, we have yet no example of such a performance. Neither elsewhere, except perhaps in the well-meant, but altogether ineffectual, attempt of Denina, among the Italians, and in some detached, though far more successful, sketches by German writers, is there any that we know of. To expect an English History of German Literature in this style were especially unreasonable; where not only the man to write it, but the people to read and enjoy it are wanting. Some *Historic Survey*, wherein such an ideal standard, if not attained, if not approached, might be faithfully kept in view, and endeavoured after, would suffice us. Neither need such a Survey, even as a British Surveyor might execute it, be deficient in striking objects, and views of a general interest. There is the spectacle of a great people, closely related to us in blood, language, character, advancing through fifteen centuries of culture; with the eras and changes that have distinguished the like career in other nations. Nay, perhaps, the intellectual history of the Germans is not without peculiar attraction, on two grounds: first, that they are a separate unmixed people; that in them one of the two grand stem-tribes, from which all modern European countries derive their population and speech, is seen growing up distinct, and in several particulars following its own course: secondly, that by accident and by desert, the Germans have more than once been found playing the highest part in European culture; at more than one era the grand Tendencies of Europe have first embodied themselves into action in Germany, the main battle between the New and the Old has been fought and gained there. We mention only the Swiss Revolt, and Luther's Reformation. The Germans have not indeed so many classical works to exhibit as some other nations; a Shakspeare, a Dante, has not yet been recognised among them; nevertheless, they too have had their Teachers and inspired Singers; and in regard to popular Mythology, traditionary possessions and spirit, what we may call the *inarticulate* Poetry of a nation, and what is the element of its spoken or written Poetry, they will be found superior to any other modern people.

The Historic Surveyor of German Poetry will observe a remarkable nation struggling out of Paganism; fragments of that stern Superstition, saved from the general wreck, and still, amid the new order of things, carrying back our view, in faint reflexes, into the dim primeval time. By slow degrees the chaos of the Northern Immigrations settles into a new and fairer world; arts advance; little by little, a fund of Knowledge, of Power over Nature, is accumulated by man; feeble glimmerings, even of a higher knowledge, of a poetic, break forth; till at length in the *Swabian Era*, as it is named, a blaze of true though simple Poetry bursts over Germany, more splendid, we might say, than the Troubadour Period of any other nation; for that famous *Nibelungen Song*, produced, at least ultimately fashioned in those times, and still so significant in these, is altogether without parallel elsewhere.

To this period, the essence of which was young Wonder, and an enthusiasm for which Chivalry was still the fit exponent, there succeeds, as was natural, a period of Inquiry, a Didactic period; wherein, among the Germans, as elsewhere, many a Hugo von Trimberg delivers wise saws, and moral apophthegms, to the general edification: later, a Town-clerk of Strasburg sees his *Ship of Fools* translated into all living languages, twice into Latin, and read by Kings; the Apologue of *Reynard the Fox* gathering itself together, from sources remote and near, assumes its Low-German vesture, and becomes the darling of high and low; nay still lives with us, in rude genial vigour, as one of the most remarkable indigenous productions of the Middle Ages. Nor is acted poetry of this kind wanting; the Spirit of Inquiry translates itself into Deeds which are poetical, as well as into words: already at the opening of the fourteenth century, Germany witnesses the first assertion of political right, the first vindication of Man against Nobleman; in the early history of the German Swiss. And again, two centuries later, the first assertion of intellectual right, the first vindication of Man against Clergyman; in the history of Luther's Reformation. Meanwhile the Press has begun its incalculable task; the indigenous Fiction of the Germans, what we have called their inarticulate Poetry, issues in innumerable *Volksbücher* (People's-Books), the progeny and kindred of which still live in all European countries: the People have their Tragedy and their Comedy; *Tyll Eulenspiegel* shakes every diaphragm with laughter; the rudest heart quails with awe at the wild mythus of *Faust.*

With Luther, however, the Didactic Tendency has reached

its poetic acme; and now we must see it assume a prosaic character, and Poetry for a long while decline. The Spirit of Inquiry, of Criticism, is pushed beyond the limits, or too exclusively cultivated: what had done so much, is supposed capable of doing all; Understanding is alone listened to, while Fancy and Imagination languish inactive, or are forcibly stifled; and all poetic culture gradually dies away. As if with the high resolute genius, and noble achievements, of its Luthers and Huttens, the genius of the country had exhausted itself, we behold generation after generation of mere Prosaists succeed these high Psalmists. Science indeed advances, practical manipulation in all kinds improves; Germany has its Copernics, Hevels, Guerickes, Keplers; later, a Leibnitz opens the path of true Logic, and teaches the mysteries of Figure and Number: but the finer Education of mankind seems at a stand. Instead of Poetic recognition and worship, we have stolid Theologic controversy, or still shallower Freethinking; pedantry, servility, mode-hunting, every species of Idolatry and Affectation holds sway. The World has lost its beauty, Life its infinite majesty, as if the Author of it were no longer divine: instead of admiration and creation of the True, there is at best criticism and denial of the False; to Luther there has succeeded Thomasius. In this era, so unpoetical for all Europe, Germany, torn in pieces by a Thirty-Years' War, and its consequences, is preëminently prosaic; its few Singers are feeble echoes of foreign models little better than themselves. No Shakspeare, no Milton appears there; such, indeed, would have appeared earlier, if at all, in the current of German history: but instead, they have only at best Opitzes, Flemmings, Logaus, as we had our Queen Anne Wits; or, in their Lohensteins, Gryphs, Hoffmannswaldaus, though in inverse order, an unintentional parody of our Drydens and Lees.

Nevertheless from every moral death there is a new birth; in this wondrous course of his, man may indeed linger, but cannot retrograde or stand still. In the middle of last century, from among Parisian Erotics, rickety Sentimentalism, Court aperies, and hollow Dulness striving in all hopeless courses, we behold the giant spirit of Germany awaken as from long slumber; shake away these worthless fetters, and by its Lessings and Klopstocks, announce, in true German dialect, that the Germans also are men. Singular enough in its circumstances was this resuscitation; the work as of a 'spirit on the waters,' a movement agitating the great popular mass; for it was favoured by no court or king: all sovereignties, even the pettiest, had abandoned their native Literature, their native language, as if to irreclaimable barbarism. The greatest king produced in Germany since Barbarossa's time, Frederick the Second, looked coldly on the native endeavour, and saw no hope but in aid from France. However, the native endeavour prospered without aid: Lessing's announcement did not die away with him, but took clearer utterance, and more inspired modulation from his followers; in whose works it now speaks, not to Germany alone, but to the whole world. The results of this last Period of German Literature are of deep significance, the depth of which is perhaps but now becoming visible. Here too, it may be, as in other cases, the Want of the Age has first taken voice and shape in Germany; that change from Negation to Affirmation, from Destruction to Re-construction, for which all thinkers in every country are now prepared, is perhaps already in action there. In the nobler Literature of the Germans, say some, lie the rudiments of a new spiritual era, which it is for this and for succeeding generations to work out and realise. The ancient creative Inspiration, it would seem, is still possible in these ages; at a time when Scepticism, Frivolity, Sensuality had withered Life into a sand-desert, and our gayest prospect was but the *false mirage*, and even our Byrons could utter but a death-song or despairing howl, the Moses'-wand has again struck from that Horeb refreshing streams, towards which the better spirits of all nations are hastening, if not to drink, yet wistfully and hopefully to examine. If the older Literary History of Germany has the common attractions, which in a greater or a less degree belong to the successive epochs of other such Histories; its newer Literature, and the historical delineation of this, has an interest such as belongs to no other.

It is somewhat in this way, as appears to us, that the growth of German Poetry must be construed and represented by the historian: these are the general phenomena and vicissitudes, which, if elucidated by proper individual instances, by specimens fitly chosen, presented in natural sequence, and worked by philosophy into union, would make a valuable book; on any and all of which the observations and researches of so able an inquirer as Mr. Taylor would have been welcome. Sorry are we to declare that of all this, which constitutes the essence of anything calling itself *Historic Survey*, there is scarcely a vestige in the Book before us. The question, What is the German mind; what is the culture of the German mind; what course has Germany followed in that matter; what are its national characteristics as manifested therein? appears not to have presented itself to the Author's thought. No theorem of Germany and its intellectual progress, not even a false one, has he been at pains to construct for himself. We believe, it is impossible for the most assiduous reader to gather from these three Volumes any portraiture of the national mind of Germany, not to say in its successive phases and the historical sequence of these, but in any one phase or condition. The Work is made up of critical, biographical, bibliographical dissertations, and notices concerning this and the other individual poet; interspersed with large masses of translation; and except that all these are strung together in the order of time, has no historical feature whatever. Many literary lives as we read, the nature of literary life in Germany, what sort of moral, economical, intellectual element it is that a German writer lives in and works in, — will nowhere manifest itself. Indeed, far from depicting Germany, scarcely on more than one or two occasions does our Author even look at it, or so much as remind us that it were capable of being depicted. On these rare occasions too, we are treated with such philosophic insight as the following: 'The Germans are not an imitative, 'but they are a listening people: they can do nothing without 'directions, and anything with them. As soon as Gottsched's 'rules for writing German correctly had made their appear-'ance, everybody began to write German.' Or we have theoretic hints, resting on no basis, about some new tribunal of taste which at one time had formed itself 'in the mess-rooms of the Prussian officers!'

In a word, the 'connecting sections,' or indeed by what alchymy such a congeries could be connected into a *Historic Survey*, have not become plain to us. Considerable part of it consists of quite detached little Notices, mostly of altogether insignificant men; heaped together as separate fragments; fit, had they been unexceptionable in other respects, for a Biographical Dictionary, but nowise for a *Historic Survey*. Then we have dense masses of Translation, sometimes good, but seldom of the characteristic pieces; an entire *Iphigenia*, an entire *Nathan the Wise;* nay worse, a *Sequel to Nathan*, which when we have conscientiously struggled to peruse, the Author turns round, without any apparent smile, and tells that it is by a nameless writer, and worth nothing. Not only Mr. Taylor's own Translations, which are generally good, but contributions from a whole body of labourers in that department are given: for example, near sixty pages, very ill rendered by a Miss Plumtre, of a *Life of Kotzebue*, concerning whom, or whose life, death or burial, there is now no curiosity extant among men. If in that 'English Temple of Fame,' with its hewn and sculptured stones, those Biographical-Dictionary fragments and fractions are so much dry *rubble-work* of whinstone, is not this quite despicable *Autobiography of Kotzebue* a rood or two of mere *turf;* which, as ready-cut, our architect, to make up measure, has packed in among his marble ashlar; whereby the whole wall will the sooner bulge? But indeed, generally speaking, symmetry is not one of his architectural rules. Thus, in Volume First, we have a long story translated from a German Magazine, about certain antique Hyperborean *Baresarks*, amusing enough, but with no more reference to Germany than to England; while in return the *Nibelungen Lied* is despatched in something less than one line, and comes no more to light. Tyll Eulenspiegel, who was not an 'anonymous Satire, entitled the *Mirror of Owls*,' but a real flesh-and-blood hero of that name, whose tombstone is standing to this day near Lübeck, has some four lines for his share; *Reineke de Fos* about as many, which also are inaccurate. Again, if Wieland have his half-volume, and poor Ernst Schulze, poor Zacharias Werner, and numerous other poor men, each his chapter; Luther also has his two sentences, and is in these weighed against — Dr. Isaac Watts. Ulrich Hutten does not occur here; Hans Sachs and his Master-singers escape notice, or even do worse; the poetry of the Reformation is not alluded to. The name of Jean Paul Friedrich Richter appears not to be known to Mr. Taylor; or, if want of rhyme was to be the test of a Prosaist, how comes Salomon Gesner here? Stranger still, Ludwig Tieck is not once mentioned; neither is Novalis; neither is Maler Müller. But why dwell on these omissions and commissions? Is not all included in this one wellnigh incredible fact, that one of the largest articles in the Book, a tenth part of the whole *Historic Survey of German Poetry*, treats of that delectable genius, August von Kotzebue?

The truth is, this *Historic Survey* has not anything historical in it; but is a mere aggregate of Dissertations, Translations, Notices and Notes, bound together indeed by the circumstance that they are all about German Poetry, 'about it and about it;' also by the sequence of time, and still more strongly by the Bookbinder's pack-thread; but by no other sufficient tie whatever. The authentic title, were not some mercantile varnish allowable in such cases, might be: 'Gen-

'eral Jail-delivery of all Publications and Manuscripts, orig- 'inal or translated, composed or borrowed, on the subject of 'German Poetry; by' &c.

To such Jail-delivery, at least when it is from the prison of Mr. Taylor's Desk at Norwich, and relates to a subject in the actual predicament of German Poetry among us, we have no fundamental objection: and for the name, now that it is explained, there is nothing in a name; a rose by any other name would smell as sweet. However, even in this lower and lowest point of view, the *Historic Survey* is liable to grave objections; its worth is of no unmixed character. We mentioned that Mr. Taylor did not often cite authorities: for which doubtless he may have his reasons. If it be not from French Prefaces, and the *Biographie Universelle*, and other the like sources, we confess ourselves altogether at a loss to divine whence any reasonable individual gathered such notices as these. Books indeed are scarce; but the most untoward situation may command Wachler's *Vorlesungen*, Horn's *Poesie und Beredsamkeit*, Meister's *Characteristiken*, Koch's *Compendium*, or some of the thousand-and-one compilations of that sort, numerous and accurate in German, more than in any other literature: at all events, Jördens's *Lexicon Deutscher Dichter und Prosaisten*, and the world-renowned Leipzig *Conversations-Lexicon*. No one of these appears to have been in Mr. Taylor's possession; — Bouterwek alone, and him he seems to have consulted perfunctorily. A certain proportion of errors in such a work is pardonable and unavoidable: scarcely so the proportion observed here. The *Historic Survey* abounds with errors, perhaps beyond any book it has ever been our lot to review. Of these indeed many are harmless enough: as, for instance, where we learn that Görres was born in 1804 (not in 1776): though in that case he must have published his *Shah-Nameh* at the age of three years: or where it is said that Werner's epitaph 'begs Mary Magdalene to pray for his soul,' which it does not do, if indeed any one cared what it did. Some are of a quite mysterious nature; either impregnated with a wit which continues obstinately latent, or indicating that, in spite of Railways and Newspapers, some portions of this Island are still singularly impermeable. For example: 'It (*Götz* '*von Berlichingen*) was admirably translated into English, in '1799, at Edinburgh, by *William* Scott, Advocate; no doubt, 'the same person who, under the poetical but assumed name 'of *Walter*, has since become the most extensively popular of 'the British writers.' — Others again are the fruit of a more culpable ignorance; as when we hear that Goethe's *Dichtung und Wahrheit* is literally meant to be a fictitious narrative, and no genuine Biography; that his *Stella* ends quietly in Bigamy (to Mr. Taylor's satisfaction), which, however the French translation may run, in the original it certainly does not. Mr. Taylor likewise complains that his copy of *Faust* is incomplete: so, we grieve to state, is ours. Still worse is it when speaking of distinguished men, who probably have been at pains to veil their sentiments on certain subjects, our Author takes it upon him to lift such veil, and with perfect composure pronounces this to be a Deist, that a Pantheist, that other an Atheist, often without any due foundation. It is quite erroneous, for example, to describe Schiller by any such unhappy term as that of Deist: it is very particularly erroneous to say that Goethe anywhere 'avows himself an Atheist,' that he 'is a Pantheist;' — indeed, that he is, was, or is like to be any *ist* to which Mr. Taylor would attach just meaning.

But on the whole, what struck us most in these errors is their surprising number. In the way of our calling, we at first took pencil, with intent to mark such transgressions; but soon found it too appalling a task, and so laid aside our black-lead and our art (*cæstus artemque*). Happily, however, a little natural invention, assisted by some tincture of arithmetic, came to our aid. Six pages, studied for that end, we did mark; finding therein thirteen errors: the pages are 167–173 of Volume Third, and still in our copy have their marginal stigmas, which can be vindicated before a jury of Authors. Now if 6 give 13, who sees not that 1455, the entire number of pages, will give 3152 and a fraction? Or, allowing for Translations, which are freer from errors, and for philosophical Discussions, wherein the errors are of another sort; nay, granting with a perhaps unwarranted liberality, that these six pages may yield too high an average, which we know not that they do, — may not, in round numbers, Fifteen Hundred be given as the approximate amount, not of errors, indeed, yet of mistakes and misstatements, in these three octavos?

Of errors in doctrine, false critical judgments and all sorts of philosophical hallucination, the number, more difficult to ascertain, is also unfortunately great. Considered, indeed, as in any measure a picture of what is remarkable in German Poetry, this *Historic Survey* is one great Error. We have to object to Mr. Taylor on all grounds; that his views are often partial and inadequate, sometimes quite false and imaginary; that the highest productions of German Literature, those works in which properly its characteristic and chief worth lie, are still as a sealed book to him; or what is worse, an open book that he will not read, but pronounces to be filled with blank paper. From a man of such intellectual vigour, who has studied his subject so long, we should not have expected such a failure.

Perhaps the main principle of it may be stated, if not accounted for, in this one circumstance, that the *Historic Survey*, like its Author, stands separated from Germany by 'more than forty years.' During this time Germany has been making unexampled progress; while our Author has either advanced in the other direction, or continued quite stationary. Forty years, it is true, make no difference in a classical Poem; yet much in the readers of that Poem, and its position towards these. Forty years are but a small period in some Histories, but in the history of German Literature, the most rapidly extending, incessantly fluctuating object even in the spiritual world, they make a great period. In Germany, within these forty years, how much has been united, how much has fallen asunder! Kant has superseded Wolf; Fichte, Kant; Schelling, Fichte; and now, it seems, Hegel is bent on superseding Schelling. Baumgarten has given place to Schlegel; the *Deutsche Bibliothek* to the Berlin *Hermes:* Lessing still towers in the distance like an Earth-born Atlas; but in the poetical Heaven, Wieland and Klopstock burn fainter, as new and more radiant luminaries have arisen. Within the last forty years, German Literature has become national, idiomatic, distinct from all others; by its productions during that period, it is either something or nothing.

Nevertheless it is still at the distance of forty years, sometimes we think it must be fifty, that Mr. Taylor stands. 'The fine Literature of Germany,' no doubt he has 'imported;' yet only with the eyes of 1780 does he read it. Thus Sulzer's *Universal Theory* continues still to be his roadbook to the temple of German taste; almost as if the German critic should undertake to measure *Waverley* and *Manfred* by the scale of Blair's *Lectures.* Sulzer was an estimable man, who did good service in his day; but about forty years ago sank into a repose, from which it would now be impossible to rouse him. The superannuation of Sulzer appears not once to be suspected by our Author; as indeed little of all the great work that has been done or undone in Literary Germany, within that period, has become clear to him. The far-famed *Xenien* of Schiller's *Musenalmanach* are once mentioned, in some half-dozen lines, wherein also there are more than half-a-dozen inaccuracies, and one rather egregious error. Of the results that followed from these *Xenien;* of Tieck, Wackenroder, the two Schlegels and Novalis, whose critical Union, and its works, filled all Germany with tumult, discussion, and at length with new conviction, no whisper transpires here. The *New School,* with all that it taught, untaught and mistaught, is not so much as alluded to. Schiller and Goethe, with all the poetic world they created, remain invisible, or dimly seen: Kant is a sort of Political Reformer. It must be stated with all distinctness, that of the newer and higher German Literature, no reader will obtain the smallest understanding from these Volumes.

Indeed, quite apart from his inacquaintance with actual Germany, there is that in the structure or habit of Mr. Taylor's mind which singularly unfits him for judging of such matters well. We must complain that he reads German Poetry, from first to last, with English eyes; will not accommodate himself to the spirit of the Literature he is investigating, and do his utmost, by loving endeavour, to win its secret from it; but plunges in headlong, and silently assuming that all this was written for him and for his objects, makes short work with it, and innumerable false conclusions. It is sad to see an honest traveller confidently gauging all foreign objects with a measure that will not mete them; trying German Sacred Oaks by their fitness for British shipbuilding; walking from Dan to Beersheba, and finding so little that he did not bring with him. This, we are too well aware, is the commonest of all errors, both with vulgar readers and with vulgar critics; but from Mr. Taylor we had expected something better; nay let us confess, he himself now and then seems to attempt something better, but too imperfectly succeeds in it.

The truth is, Mr. Taylor, though a man of talent, as we have often admitted, and as the world well knows, though a downright, independent and to all appearance most praiseworthy man, is one of the most peculiar critics to be found in our times. As we construe him from these Volumes, the basis of his nature seems to be Polemical; his whole view of the world, of its Poetry, and whatever else it holds, has a militant character. According to this philosophy, the whole duty of man, it would almost appear, is to lay aside the opinion of his grandfather. Doubtless, it is natural, it is indispensable, for a man to lay aside the opinion of his grandfather, when it will no longer hold together on him ; but we had imagined that the great and infinitely harder duty was : To turn the opinion that does hold together to some account. However, it is not in receiving the New, and creating good with it, but solely in pulling to pieces the Old, that Mr. Taylor will have us employed. Often, in the course of these pages, might the British reader sorrowfully exclaim : " Alas ! is this the year of grace 1831, and are we still *here ?* Armed with the hatchet and tinder-box ; still no symptom of the sower's-sheet and plough ? " These latter, for our Author, are implements of the dark ages ; the ground is full of thistles and jungle ; cut down and spare not. A singular aversion to Priests, something like a natural horror and hydrophobia, gives him no rest night nor day ; the gist of all his speculations is to drive down more or less effectual palisades against that class of persons ; nothing that he does but they interfere with or threaten : the first question he asks of every passer-by, be it German Poet, Philosopher, Farce-writer, is : " Arian or Trinitarian ? Wilt thou help me or not ? " Long as he has now laboured, and though calling himself Philosopher, Mr. Taylor has not yet succeeded in sweeping his arena clear ; but still painfully struggles in the questions of Naturalism and Supernaturalism, Liberalism and Servilism.

Agitated by this zeal, with its fitful hope and fear, it is that he goes through Germany ; scenting out Infidelity with the nose of an ancient Heresy-hunter, though for opposite purposes ; and, like a recruiting-sergeant, beating aloud for recruits ; nay, where in any corner he can spy a tall man, clutching at him, to crimp him or impress him. Goethe's and Schiller's creed we saw specified above ; those of Lessing and Herder are scarcely less edifying ; but take rather this sagacious exposition of Kant's Philosophy :

'The Alexandrian writings do not differ so widely as is commonly apprehended from those of the Königsberg School ; for they abound with passages, which, while they seem to flatter the popular credulity, resolve into allegory the stories of the gods, and into an illustrative personification the soul of the world; thus insinuating, to the more alert and penetrating, the speculative rejection of opinions with which they are encouraged and commanded in action to comply. With analogous spirit, Professor Kant studiously introduces a distinction between Practical and Theoretical Reason; and while he teaches that rational conduct will indulge the hypothesis of a God, a revelation, and a future state (this, we presume, is meant by calling them *inferences of Practical Reason*), he pretends that Theoretical Reason can adduce no one satisfactory argument in their behalf: so that his morality amounts to a defence of the old adage, "Think with the wise, and act with the vulgar;" a plan of behaviour which secures to the vulgar an ultimate victory over the wise. * * * Philosophy is to be withdrawn within a narrower circle of the initiated; and these must be induced to conspire in favouring a vulgar superstition. This can best be accomplished by enveloping with enigmatic jargon the topics of discussion; by employing a cloudy phraseology, which may intercept from below the war-whoop of impiety, and from above the evulgation of infidelity; by contriving a kind of "cipher of illuminism," in which public discussions of the most critical nature can be carried on from the press, without alarming the prejudices of the people, or exciting the precautions of the magistrate. Such a cipher, in the hands of an adept, is the dialect of Kant. Add to this, the notorious Gallicanism of his opinions, which must endear him to the patriotism of the philosophers of the Lyceum; and it will appear probable that the reception of his forms of syllogising should extend from Germany to France; should completely and exclusively establish itself on the Continent; entomb with the Reasonings the Reason of the modern world; and form the tasteless fretwork which seems about to convert the halls of liberal Philosophy into churches of mystical Supernaturalism.'

These are indeed fearful symptoms, and enough to quicken the diligence of any recruiting officer that has the good cause at heart. Reasonably may such officer, beleaguered with 'witchcraft and demonology, trinitarianism, intolerance,' and a considerable list of *et-ceteras*, and still seeing no hearty followers of his flag, but a mere Falstaff regiment, smite upon his thigh, and, in moments of despondency, lament that Christianity had ever entered, or as we here have it, 'intruded' into Europe at all; that, at least, some small slip of heathendom, 'Scandinavia, for instance,' had not been 'left 'to its natural course, unmisguided by ecclesiastical missionaries and monastic institutions. Many superstitions, which 'have fatigued the credulity, clouded the intellect and impaired the security of man, and which, alas! but too naturally followed in the train of the Sacred Books, would there, 'perhaps, never have struck root; and in one corner of the 'world, the inquiries of reason might have found an earlier 'asylum, and asserted a less circumscribed range.' Nevertheless, there is still hope, preponderating hope. 'The general tendency of the German school,' it would appear, could we but believe such tidings, 'is to teach French opinions in English forms.' Philosophy can now look down with some approving glances on Socinianism. Nay, the literature of Germany, 'very liberal and tolerant,' is gradually overflowing, even into the Slavonian nations, 'and will found, in 'new languages and climates, those latest inferences of a 'corrupt but instructed refinement, which are likely to rebuild the morality of the Ancients on the ruins of Christian Puritanism.'

Such retrospections and prospections bring to mind an absurd rumour which, confounding our Author with his namesake, the celebrated Translator of Plato and Aristotle, represented him as being engaged in the repair and re-establishment of the Pagan Religion. For such rumour, we are happy to state, there is not and was not the slightest foundation. Wieland may, indeed, at one time, have put some whims into his disciple's head; but Mr. Taylor is too solid a man to embark in speculations of that nature. Prophetic daydreams are not practical projects; at all events, as we here see, it is not the old Pagan gods that we are to bring back, but only the ancient Pagan morality, a refined and reformed Paganism; — as some middle-aged householder, if distressed by tax-gatherers and duns, might resolve on becoming thirteen again, and a bird-nesting schoolboy. Let no timid layman apprehend any overflow of priests from Mr. Taylor, or even of gods. Is not this commentary on the hitherto so inexplicable conversion of Friedrich Leopold Count Stolberg enough to quiet every alarmist?

'On the Continent of Europe, the gentleman, and Frederic Leopold was emphatically so, is seldom brought up with much solicitude for any positive doctrine: among the Catholics, the moralist insists on the duty of conforming to the religion of one's ancestors; among the Protestants, on the duty of conforming to the religion of the magistrate: but Frederic Leopold seems to have invented a new point of honour, and a most rational one, — the duty of conforming to the religion of one's father-in-law.

'A young man is the happier, while single, for being unencumbered with any religious restraints; but when the time comes for submitting to matrimony, he will find the precedent of Frederic Leopold well entitled to consideration. A predisposition to conform to the religion of the father-in-law facilitates advantageous matrimonial connexions; it produces in a family the desirable harmony of religious profession; it secures the sincere education of the daughters in the faith of their mother; and it leaves the young men at liberty to apostatise in their turn, to exert their right of private judgment, and to choose a worship for themselves. Religion, if a blemish in the male, is surely a grace in the female sex: courage of mind may tend to acknowledge nothing above itself; but timidity is ever disposed to look upwards for protection, for consolation and for happiness.'

With regard to this latter point, whether Religion is 'a blemish in the male, and surely a grace in the female sex,' it is possible judgments may remain suspended: Courage of mind, indeed, will prompt the squirrel to set itself in posture against an armed horseman; yet whether for men and women, who seem to stand, not only under the Galaxy and Stellar system, and under Immensity and Eternity, but even under any bare bodkin or drop of prussic acid, 'such courage of mind as may tend to acknowledge nothing above itself,' were ornamental or the contrary; whether, lastly, religion is grounded on Fear, or on something infinitely higher and inconsistent with Fear, — may be questions. But they are of a kind we are not at present called to meddle with.

Mr. Taylor promulgates many other strange articles of faith, for he is a positive man, and has a certain quiet wilfulness; these, however, cannot henceforth much surprise us. He still calls the Middle Ages, during which nearly all the inventions and social institutions, whereby we yet live as civilised men, were originated or perfected, 'a Millennium of Darkness;' on the faith chiefly of certain long-past Pedants, who reckoned everything barren, because Chrysoloras had not yet come, and no Greek Roots grew there. Again, turning in the other direction, he criticises Luther's Reformation, and repeats that old and indeed quite foolish story of the Augustine Monk's having a merely commercial grudge against the Dominican; computes the quantity of blood shed for Protestantism; and, forgetting that men shed blood in all ages, for any cause, and for no cause, for Sansculottism, for Bonapartism, thinks that, on the whole, the Reformation was an error and failure. Pity that Providence (as King Alphonso wished in the Astronomical case) had not created its man three centuries sooner, and taken a little counsel from him! On the other hand, 'Voltaire's Reformation' was successful; and here, for once, Providence was right. Will Mr. Taylor mention what it was that Voltaire *reformed?* Many things he *de*-formed, deservedly and undeservedly; but the thing that he *formed* or *re*-formed is still unknown to the world.

It is perhaps unnecessary to add, that Mr. Taylor's whole Philosophy is sensual; that is, he recognises nothing that cannot be weighed, measured, and, with one or the other organ, eaten and digested. Logic is his only lamp of life; where this fails, the region of Creation terminates. For him there is no Invisible, Incomprehensible; whosoever, under any name, believes in an Invisible, he treats, with leniency and the loftiest tolerance, as a mystic and lunatic; and if the unhappy crackbrain has any handicraft, literary or other, allows him to go at large, and work at it. Withal he is a great-hearted, strong-minded, and, in many points, interesting man. There is a majestic composure in the attitude he has assumed; massive, immovable, uncomplaining, he sits in a world of Delirium; and for his Future looks with sure faith, — only in the direction of the Past. We take him to be a man of sociable turn, not without kindness; at all events of the most perfect courtesy. He despises the entire Universe, yet speaks respectfully of Translators from the German, and always says that they 'english beautifully.' A certain mild Dogmatism sits well on him; peaceable, incontrovertible, uttering the palpably absurd as if it were a mere truism. On the other hand, there are touches of a grave, scientific obscenity, which are questionable. This word Obscenity we use with reference to our readers, and might also add Profanity, but not with reference to Mr. Taylor; he, as we said, is scientific merely; and where there is no *cœnum* and no *fanum*, there can be no obscenity and no profanity.

To a German we might have compressed all this long description into a single word: Mr. Taylor is simply what they call a *Philister;* every fibre of him is Philistine. With us such men usually take into Politics, and become Codemakers and Utilitarians: it was only in Germany that they ever meddled much with Literature; and there worthy Nicolai has long since terminated his Jesuit-hunt; no Adelung now writes books, *Ueber die Nützlichkeit der Empfindung* (On the Utility of Feeling). Singular enough, now, when that old species had been quite extinct for almost half a century in their own land, appears a natural-born English Philistine, made in all points as they were. With wondering welcome we hail the Strongboned; almost as we might a resuscitated Mammoth. Let no David choose smooth stones from the brook to sling at him: is he not our own Goliath, whose limbs were made in England, whose thews and sinews any soil might be proud of? Is he not, as we said, a man that can stand on his own legs without collapsing when left by himself? In these days, one of the greatest rarities, almost prodigies.

We cheerfully acquitted Mr. Taylor of Religion; but must expect less gratitude when we farther deny him any feeling for true Poetry, as indeed the feelings for Religion and for Poetry of this sort are one and the same. Of Poetry Mr. Taylor knows well what will make a grand, especially a large, *picture* in the imagination : he has even a creative gift of this kind himself, as his style will often testify; but much more he does not know. How indeed should he? Nicolai, too, 'judged of Poetry as he did of Brunswick Mum, simply by *tasting* it.' Mr. Taylor assumes, as a fact known to all thinking creatures, that Poetry is neither more nor less than 'a stimulant.' Perhaps above five hundred times in the *Historic Survey* we see this doctrine expressly acted on. Whether the piece to be judged of is a Poetical Whole, and has what the critics have named a genial life, and what that life is, he inquires not; but, at best, whether it is a Logical Whole, and for most part, simply, whether it is stimulant. The praise is, that it has fine situations, striking scenes, agonising scenes, harrows his feelings, and the like. Schiller's *Robbers* he finds to be stimulant; his *Maid of Orleans* is not stimulant, but 'among the weakest of his tragedies, and composed apparently in ill health.' The author of *Pizarro* is supremely stimulant; he of *Torquato Tasso* is 'too quotidian to be stimulant.' We had understood that alcohol was stimulant in all its shapes; opium also, tobacco, and indeed the whole class of narcotics; but heretofore found Poetry in none of the Pharmacopœias. Nevertheless, it is edifying to observe with what fearless consistency Mr. Taylor, who is no half-man, carries through this theory of stimulation. It lies privily in the heart of many a reader and reviewer; nay Schiller, at one time, said that 'Molière's old 'woman seemed to have become sole Editress of all Re- 'views;' but seldom, in the history of Literature, has she had the honesty to unveil, and ride triumphant, as in these Volumes. Mr. Taylor discovers that the only Poet to be classed with Homer is Tasso; that Shakspeare's Tragedies are cousins-german to those of Otway; that poor moaning, monotonous Macpherson is an epic poet. Lastly, he runs a laboured parallel between Schiller, Goethe and Kotzebue; one is more this, the other more that; one strives hither, the other thither, through the whole string of critical predicables; almost as if we should compare scientifically Milton's *Paradise Lost*, the *Prophecies of Isaiah* and Mat Lewis's *Tales of Terror*.

Such is Mr. Taylor; a strong-hearted oak, but in an unkindly soil, and beat upon from infancy by Trinitarian and Tory Southwesters: such is the result which native vigour, wind-storms and thirsty mould have made out among them; grim boughs dishevelled in multangular complexity, and of the stiffness of brass; a tree crooked every way, unwedgeable and gnarled. What bandages or cordages of ours, or of man's, could straighten it, now that it has grown there for half a century? We simply point out that there is excellent tough *knee-timber* in it, and of straight timber little or none.

In fact, taking Mr. Taylor as he is and must be, and keeping a perpetual account and protest with him on these peculiarities of his, we find that on various parts of his subject he has profitable things to say. The Göttingen group of Poets, 'Bürger and his set,' such as they were, are pleasantly delineated. The like may be said of the somewhat earlier Swiss brotherhood, whereof Bodmer and Breitinger are the central figures; though worthy wonderful Lavater, the wandering Physiognomist and Evangelist, and Protestant Pope, should not have been first forgotten, and then crammed into an insignificant paragraph. Lessing, again, is but poorly managed; his main performance, as was natural, reckoned to be the writing of *Nathan the Wise:* we have no original portrait here, but a pantagraphical reduced copy of some foreign sketches or scratches; quite unworthy of such a man, in such a historical position, standing on the confines of Light and Darkness, like Day on the misty mountain tops. Of Herder also there is much omitted; the *Geschichte der Menschheit* scarcely alluded to; yet some features are given, accurately and even beautifully. A slow-rolling grandiloquence is in Mr. Taylor's best passages, of which this is one: if no poetic light, he has occasionally a glow of true rhetorical heat. Wieland is lovingly painted, yet on the whole faithfully, as he looked some fifty years ago, if not as he now looks: this is the longest article in the *Historic Survey*, and much too long; those Paganising *Dialogues* in particular had never much worth, and at present have scarcely any.

Perhaps the best of all these Essays is that on Klopstock. The sphere of Klopstock's genius does not transcend Mr. Taylor's scale of poetic altitudes; though it perhaps reaches the highest grade there; the 'stimulant' theory recedes into the background; indeed there is a rhetorical amplitude and brilliancy in the *Messias*, which elicits in our critic an instinct truer than his philosophy is. He has honestly studied the *Messias*, and presents a clear outline of it; neither has the still purer spirit of Klopstock's *Odes* escaped him. We have English Biographies of Klopstock, and a miserable Version of his great Work; but perhaps there is no writing in our language that offers so correct an emblem of him as this analysis. Of the *Odes* we shall here present one, in Mr. Taylor's translation, which, though in prose, the reader will not fail to approve of. It is, perhaps, the finest passage in this whole *Historic Survey*.

'THE TWO MUSES.

'I saw — tell me, was I beholding what now happens, or was I beholding futurity? — I saw with the Muse of Britain the Muse of Germany engaged in competitory race, — flying warm to the goal of coronation.

'Two goals, where the prospect terminates, bordered the career: Oaks of the forest shaded the one; near to the other waved Palms in the evening shadow.

'Accustomed to contest, stepped she from Albion proudly into the arena; as she stepped, when, with the Grecian Muse and with her from the Capitol, she entered the lists.

'She beheld the young trembling rival, who trembled yet with dignity; glowing roses worthy of victory streamed flaming over her cheek, and her golden hair flew abroad.

'Already she retained with pain in her tumultuous bosom the contracted breath; already she hung bending forward towards the goal; already the herald was lifting the trumpet, and her eyes swam with intoxicating joy.

'Proud of her courageous rival, prouder of herself, the lofty Britoness measured, but with noble glance, thee, Tuiskone: "Yes, by the bards, I grew up with thee in the grove of oaks:

'"But a tale had reached me that thou wast no more. Pardon, O Muse, if thou beest immortal, pardon that I but now learn it. Yonder at the goal alone will I learn it.

'"There it stands. But dost thou see the still further one, and its crowns also? This represt courage, this proud silence, this look which sinks fiery upon the ground, I know:

'"Yet weigh once again, ere the herald sound a note dangerous to thee. Am I not she who have measured myself with her from Thermopylæ, and with the stately one of the Seven Hills?"

'She spake: the earnest decisive moment drew nearer with the herald. "I love thee," answered quick with looks of flame Teutona, "Britoness, I love thee to enthusiasm;

'"But not warmer than immortality and those Palms. Touch, if so wills thy genius, touch them before me; yet will I, when thou seizest it, seize also the crown.

'"And, O how I tremble! O ye Immortals, perhaps I may reach first the high goal: then, O then, may thy breath attain my loose-streaming hair!"

'The herald shrilled. They flew with eagle-speed. The wide career smoked up clouds of dust. I looked. Beyond the Oak billowed yet thicker the dust, and I lost them.'

'This beautiful allegory,' adds Mr. Taylor, 'requires no 'illustration; but it constitutes one of the reasons for suspect-'ing that the younger may eventually be the victorious 'Muse.' We hope not; but that the generous race may yet last through long centuries. Tuiskone has shot through a mighty space, since this Poet saw her: what if she were now slackening her speed, and the Britoness quickening hers?

If the Essay on Klopstock is the best, that on Kotzebue is undoubtedly the worst, in this Book, or perhaps in any book written by a man of ability in our day. It is one of those acts which, in the spirit of philanthropy, we could wish Mr.

Taylor to conceal in profoundest secrecy; were it not that hereby the 'stimulant' theory, a heresy which still lurks here and there even in our better criticism, is in some sort brought to a crisis, and may the sooner depart from this world, or at least from the high places of it, into others more suitable. Kotzebue, whom all nations and kindreds and tongues and peoples, his own people the foremost, after playing with him for some foolish hour, have swept out of doors as a lifeless bundle of dyed rags, is here scientifically examined, measured, pulse-felt, and pronounced to be living, and a divinity. He has such prolific 'invention;' abounds so in 'fine situations,' in passionate scenes; is so soul-harrowing, so stimulant. The *Proceedings at Bow-Street* are stimulant enough; neither are prolific invention, interesting situations, or soul-harrowing passion wanting among the *authors* (true creators) who promulgate their *works* there; least of all if we follow them to Newgate and the gallows: but when did the *Morning Herald* think of inserting its *Police Reports* among our Anthologies? Mr. Taylor is at the pains to analyse very many of Kotzebue's productions, and translates copiously from two or three: how the Siberian Governor took on when his daughter was about to run away with one Benjowsky, who however was enabled to surrender his prize, there on the beach, with sails hoisted, by 'looking at his wife's picture:' how the people 'lift young Burgundy from the Tun,' not indeed to drink him, for he is not wine but a Duke: how a certain stout-hearted West Indian, that has made a fortune, proposes marriage to his two sisters; but finding the ladies reluctant, solicits their serving-woman, whose reputation is not only cracked, but visibly quite rent asunder; accepts her nevertheless, with her thriving cherub, and is the happiest of men; — with more of the like sort. On the strength of which we are assured that, 'according to 'my judgment, Kotzebue is the greatest dramatic genius that 'Europe has evolved since Shakspeare.' Such is the table which Mr. Taylor has spread for pilgrims in the Prose

Wilderness of Life: thus does he sit like a kind host, ready to carve; and though the viands and beverage are but, as it were, stewed garlic, Yarmouth herrings, and *blue-ruin*, praises them as 'stimulant,' and courteously presses the universe to fall to.

What a purveyor with this palate shall say to Nectar and Ambrosia, may be curious as a question in Natural History, but hardly otherwise. The most of what Mr. Taylor has written on Schiller, on Goethe, and the new Literature of Germany, a reader that loves him, as we honestly do, will consider as unwritten, or written in a state of somnambulism. He who has just quitted Kotzebue's Bear-garden and Fives-court, and pronounces it to be all stimulant and very good, what is there for him to do in the Hall of the Gods? He looks transiently in; asks with mild authority, "Arian or Trinitarian? Quotidian or Stimulant?" and receiving no answer but a hollow echo, which almost sounds like laughter, passes on, muttering that they are dumb idols, or mere Nürnberg waxwork.

It remains to notice Mr. Taylor's Translations. Apart from the choice of subjects, which in probably more than half the cases is unhappy, there is much to be said in favour of these. Compared with the average of British Translations, they may be pronounced of almost ideal excellence; compared with the best Translations extant, for example, the German *Shakspeare*, *Homer*, *Calderon*, they may still be called better than indifferent. One great merit Mr. Taylor has: rigorous adherence to his original; he endeavours at least to copy with all possible fidelity the turn of phrase, the tone, the very metre, whatever stands written for him. With the German language he has now had a long familiarity, and, what is no less essential, and perhaps still rarer among our Translators, has a decided understanding of English. All this of Mr. Taylor's own Translations: in the borrowed pieces, whereof there are several, we seldom, except indeed in those by Shelley and Coleridge, find much worth; sometimes a distinct worthlessness. Mr. Taylor has made no conscience of clearing those unfortunate performances even from their gross blunders. Thus, in that 'excellent version 'by Miss Plumtre,' we find this statement: 'Professor Mül-'ler could not utter a period without introducing the words '*with under*, whether they had business there or not;' which statement, were it only on the ground that Professor Müller was not sent to Bedlam, there to utter periods, we venture to deny. Doubtless his besetting sin was *mitunter*, which indeed means *at the same time*, or the like (etymologically, *with among*), but nowise *with under*. One other instance we shall give, from a much more important subject. Mr. Taylor admits that he does not make much of *Faust:* however, he inserts Shelley's version of the *Mayday Night;* and another scene, evidently rendered by quite a different artist. In this latter, Margaret is in the Cathedral during High-Mass, but her whole thoughts are turned inwards on a secret shame and sorrow: an Evil Spirit is whispering in her ear; the Choir chaunt fragments of the *Dies iræ;* she is like to choke and sink. In the original, this passage is in verse; and, we presume, in the translation also, — founding on the capital letters. The concluding lines are these:

'MARGARET.

I feel imprison'd. The thick pillars gird me.
The vaults low'r o'er me. Air, air, I faint.

EVIL SPIRIT.

Where wilt thou lie concealed? for sin and shame
Remain not hidden — woe is coming *down*.

THE CHOIR.

Quid sum miser tum dicturus?
Quem patronum rogaturus?
Cum vix justus sit securus.

EVIL SPIRIT.

From thee the glorified *avert their view*,
The pure *forbear* to offer thee a hand.

THE CHOIR.

Quid sum miser tum dicturus?

MARGARET.

Neighbour, your ——'

—Your what?—Angels and ministers of grace defend us!—'*Your Drambottle.*' Will Mr. Taylor have us understand, then, that 'the noble German nation,' more especially the fairer half thereof (for the 'Neighbour' is *Nachbarin*, Neighbour*ess*), goes to church with a decanter of brandy in its pocket? Or would he not rather, even forcibly, interpret *Fläschchen* by *vinaigrette*, by *volatile-salts?*—The world has no notice that this passage is a borrowed one, but will, notwithstanding, as the more charitable theory, hope and believe so.

We have now done with Mr. Taylor; and would fain, after all that has come and gone, part with him in good-nature and good-will. He has spoken freely; we have answered freely. Far as we differ from him in regard to German Literature, and to the much more important subjects here connected with it; deeply as we feel convinced that his convictions are wrong and dangerous, are but half true, and, if taken for the whole truth, wholly false and fatal, we have nowise blinded ourselves to his vigorous talent, to his varied learning, his sincerity, his manful independence and self-support. Neither is it for speaking out plainly that we blame him. A man's honest, earnest opinion is the most precious of all he possesses: let him communicate this, if he is to communicate anything. There is, doubtless, a time to speak, and a time to keep silence; yet Fontenelle's celebrated aphorism, *I might have my hand full of truth, and would open only my little finger*, may be practised also to excess, and the little finger itself kept closed. That reserve, and knowing silence, long so universal among us, is less the fruit of active benevolence, of philosophic tolerance, than of indifference and weak conviction. Honest Scepticism, honest Atheism, is better than that withered lifeless Dilettanteism and amateur Eclecticism, which merely toys with all opinions; or than that wicked Machiavelism, which in thought denying everything, except that Power is Power, in words, for its own wise purposes, loudly believes everything: of both which miserable habitudes the day, even in England, is wellnigh over. That Mr. Taylor belongs not, and at no time belonged, to either of these classes, we account a true praise. Of his *Historic Survey* we have endeavoured to point out the faults and the merits: should he reach a second edition, which we hope, perhaps he may profit by some of our hints, and render the work less unworthy of himself and of his subject. In its present state and shape, this English Temple of Fame can content no one. A huge, anomalous, heterogeneous mass, no section of it like another, oriel-window alternating with rabbit-hole, wrought capital on pillar of dried mud; heaped together out of marble, loose earth, rude boulder-stone; hastily roofed-in with shingles: such is the Temple of Fame; uninhabitable either for priest or statue, and which nothing but a continued suspension of the laws of gravity can keep from rushing erelong into a chaos of stone and dust. For the English worshipper, who in the mean while has no other temple, we search out the least dangerous apartments; for the future builder, the materials that will be valuable.

And now, in washing our hands of this all-too sordid but not unnecessary task, one word on a more momentous object. Does not the existence of such a Book, do not many other indications, traceable in France, in Germany, as well as here, betoken that a new era in the spiritual intercourse of Europe is approaching; that instead of isolated, mutually repulsive National Literature, a World Literature may one day be looked for? The better minds of all countries begin to understand each other; and, which follows naturally, to love each other, and help each other; by whom ultimately, all countries in all their proceedings are governed.

Late in man's history, yet clearly at length, it becomes manifest to the dullest, that mind is stronger than matter, that mind is the creator and shaper of matter; that not brute Force, but only Persuasion and Faith is the king of this world. The true Poet, who is but the inspired Thinker, is still an Orpheus whose Lyre tames the savage beasts, and evokes the dead rocks to fashion themselves into palaces and stately inhabited cities. It has been said, and may be repeated, that Literature is fast becoming all in all to us; our Church, our Senate, our whole Social Constitution. The true Pope of Christendom is not that feeble old man in Rome; nor is its Autocrat the Napoleon, the Nicholas, with his half million even of obedient bayonets: such Autocrat is himself but a more cunningly-devised bayonet and military engine in the hands of a mightier than he. The true Autocrat and Pope is that man, the real or seeming Wisest of the past age; crowned after death; who finds his Hierarchy of gifted Authors, his Clergy of assiduous Journalists; whose Decretals, written not on parchment, but on the living souls of men, it were an inversion of the Laws of Nature to *dis*obey. In these times of ours, all Intellect has fused itself into Literature: Literature, Printed Thought, is the molten sea and wonder-bearing chaos, into which mind after mind casts forth its opinion, its feeling, to be molten into the general mass, and to work there; Interest after Interest is engulfed in it, or embarked on it: higher, higher it rises round all the Edifices of Existence; they must all be molten into it, and anew bodied forth from it, or stand unconsumed among its fiery surges. Woe to him whose Edifice is not built of true Asbest, and on the everlasting Rock; but on the false sand, and of the drift-wood of Accident, and the paper and parchment of antiquated Habit! For the power, or powers, exist not on our Earth, that can say to that sea, Roll back, or bid its proud waves be still.

What form so omnipotent an element will assume; how long it will welter to and fro as a wild Democracy, a wild

Anarchy; what Constitution and Organisation it will fashion for itself, and for what depends on it, in the depths of Time, is a subject for prophetic conjecture, wherein brightest hope is not unmingled with fearful apprehension and awe at the boundless unknown. The more cheering is this one thing which we do see and know: That its tendency is to a universal European Commonweal; that the wisest in all nations will communicate and coöperate; whereby Europe will again have its true Sacred College, and Council of Amphictyons; wars will become rarer, less inhuman, and in the course of centuries such delirious ferocity in nations, as in individuals it already is, may be proscribed, and become obsolete forever.

APPENDIX.

JEAN PAUL FRIEDRICH RICHTER'S REVIEW OF MADAME DE STAEL'S 'ALLEMAGNE.'[1]

[1830.]

*** There are few of our readers but have read and partially admired Madame de Staël's *Germany;* the work, indeed, which, with all its vagueness and manifold shortcomings, must be regarded as the precursor, if not parent, of whatever acquaintance with German Literature exists among us. There are few also but have heard of Jean Paul, here and elsewhere, as of a huge mass of intellect, with the strangest shape and structure, yet with thews and sinews like a real Son of Anak. Students of German Literature will be curious to see such a critic as Madame de Staël adequately criticised, in what fashion the best of the Germans write reviews, and what worth the best of them acknowledge in this their chief eulogist and indicator among foreigners. We translate the Essay from Richter's *Kleine Bücherschau*, as it stands there reprinted from the Heidelberg *Jahrbücher*, in which periodical it first appeared, in 1815. We have done our endeavour to preserve the quaint grotesque style so characteristic of Jean Paul; rendering with literal fidelity whatever stood before us, rugged and unmanageable as it often seemed. This article on Madame de Staël passes, justly enough, for the best of his reviews; which, however, let our readers understand, are no important part of his writings. This is not the lion that we see, but only a claw of the lion, whereby some few may recognise him.

To review a Revieweress of two literary Nations is not easy; for you have, as it were, three things at once to give account of. With regard to France and Germany, however, it is chiefly in reference to the judgment which the intellectual Amazon of these two countries has pronounced on them, and thereby on herself, that they come before us here. To write such a *Literary Gazette* of our whole literary Past, enacting editor and so many contributors in a single person, not

[1] FRASER'S MAGAZINE, Nos. 1 and 4.

to say a female one; above all, summoning and spellbinding the spirits of German philosophy — this, it must be owned, would have been even for a Villers, though Villers can now retranslate himself from German into French, no unheroic undertaking. Meanwhile, Madame de Staël had this advantage, that she writes especially for Frenchmen; who, knowing about German art and the German language simply nothing, still gain somewhat, when they learn never so little. On this subject you can scarcely tell them other truths than new ones, whether pleasant or not. They even know more of the English, — as these do of them, — than of the Germans. Our invisibility among the French proceeds, it may be hoped, like that of Mercury, from our proximity to the Sun-god; but in regard to other countries, we should consider, that the constellation of our New Literature having risen only half a century ago, the rays of it are still on the road thither.

Greatly in favour of our Authoress, in this her picture of Germany, was her residence among us; and the title-page might be translated 'Letters *from* Germany' (*de l'Allemagne*), as well as *on* Germany. We Germans are in the habit of limning Paris and London from the distance; which capitals do sit to us, truly, — but only on the bookstall of their works. For the deeper knowledge of a national poetry, not only the poems are necessary, but the poets, at least their country and countrymen: the living multitude are *notæ variorum* to the poem. A German himself could write his best work on French poetry nowhere but in Paris. Now our Authoress, in her acquaintance with the greatest German poets, had, as it were, a living translation of their poems; and Weimar, the focus of German poesy, might be to her what Paris were to the German reviewer of the Parisian.

But what chiefly exalts her to be our critic, and a poetess herself, is the feeling she manifests: with a taste sufficiently French, her heart is German and poetic. When she says,[1]

> 'Toutes les fois que de nos jours on a pu faire entrer un peu de sève étrangère, les Français y ont applaudi avec transport. J. J. Rousseau, Bernardin de Saint-Pierre, Chateaubriand, &c. &c., dans quelques-uns de leurs ouvrages, sont tous, même à leur insçu, de l'école germanique, c'est à dire, qu'ils ne puisent leur talent que dans le fond de leur âme;'

she might have classed her own works first on the list. Everywhere she breathes the æther of higher sentiments than the marsh-miasma of *Salons* and French Materialism could support. The chapters, in Volume Sixth, on philosophy, depict what is Germanism of head badly enough, indeed; but the more warmly and justly what is Germanism of heart, with a pure clearness not unworthy of a Herder.

[1] Tom. ii. p. 6.

For the French, stript bare by encyclopedists, and revolutionists, and conscripts, and struggling under heart-ossification, and contraction of the breast, such German news of a separation and independence between Virtue and Self-Interest, Beauty and Utility, &c. will not come too late: a lively people, for whom pleasure or pain, as daylight or cloudy weather, often hide the upper starry heaven, can at least use star-catalogues, and some planisphere thereof. Many are the jewel-gleams with which she illuminates the depths of the soul against the Gallic lownesses. Of this sort are, for instance, the passages where [1] she refuses to have the Madonna of Beauty made a housemaid of Utility; where she asks, Why Nature has clothed, not the nutritive plants, but only the useless flowers with charms?

> 'D'où vient, cependant, que pour parer l'autel de la Divinité, on chercherait plutôt les inutiles fleurs que les productions nécessaires? D'où vient que ce qui sert au maintien de votre vie aie moins de dignité que les fleurs sans but? C'est que le beau nous rappelle une existence immortelle et divine, dont le souvenir et le regret vivent à la fois dans notre cœur.'

Also [2] the passages where, in contradiction to the principle that places the essence of Art in imitation of Reality, she puts the question:

> 'Le premier des arts, la musique, qu'imite-t-il? De tous les dons de la Divinité, cependant, c'est le plus magnifique, car il semble, pour ainsi dire, superflu. Le soleil nous éclaire, nous respirons l'air du ciel serein, toutes les beautés de la nature servent en quelque façon à l'homme; la musique seule est d'une noble inutilité, et c'est pour cela qu'elle nous émeut si profondement; plus elle est loin de tout but, plus elle se rapproche de cette source intime de nos pensées que l'application à un objet quelconque réserre dans son cours.'

So, likewise, is she the protecting goddess of the higher feelings in love; and the whole Sixth Volume is an altar of religion, which the Gallic pantheon will not be the worse for. Though professing herself a proselyte of the new poetic school, she is a mild judge of sentimentality; [3] and in no case can immoral freedom in the thing represented excuse itself in her eyes, as perhaps it might in those of this same new school, by the art displayed in representing it. Hence comes her too narrow ill-will against Goethe's *Faust* and *Ottilie*. Thus, also, she extends her *just* anger against a faithlessly luxuriating love, in Goethe's *Stella*, to *unjust* anger against Jacobi's *Woldemar;* mistaking in this latter the hero's struggle after a free

[1] Tom. v. p. 100. [2] Tom. v. p. 101. [3] Tom. v. ch. 18.

disencumbered friendship, for the heart-luxury of weakness. Yet the accompanying passage[1] is a fine and true one:

> 'On ne doit pas se mettre par son choix dans une situation où la morale et la sensibilité ne sont pas d'accord; car ce qui est involontaire est si beau, qu'il est affreux d'être condamné à se commander toutes ses actions, et à vivre avec soi-même comme avec sa victime.'

She dwells so much in the heart, as the bee in the flower-cup, that, like this honey-maker, she sometimes lets the tulip-leaves overshadow her and shut her in. Thus she not only declares against the learning (that is, the harmonics and inharmonics) in our German music, but also against our German parallelism between tone and word, — our German individuation of tones and words. Instrumental music of itself is too much for her; mere reflection, letter and science: she wants only voices, not words.[2] But the sort of souls which take-in the pure impression of tones without knowledge of speech, dwell in the inferior animals. Do we not always furnish the tones we hear with secret texts of our own, nay with secret scenery, that their echo within us may be stronger than their voice without? And can our heart feel by other means than being spoken to and answering? Thus pictures, during music, are seen into more deeply and warmly by spectators; nay many masters have, in creating them, acknowledged help from music. All beauties serve each other without jealousy; for to conquer man's heart is the common purpose of all.

As it was for France that our Authoress wrote and shaped her *Germany*, one does not at first see how, with her depth of feeling, she could expect to prosper much there. But Reviewer[3] answereth: The female half she will please at once and immediately; the male, again, by the twofold mediation of art and mockery. First, by art. Indifferent as the Parisian is to religion and deep feeling on the firm ground of the household floor, he likes mightily to see them bedded on the soft fluctuating clouds of art; as court-people like peasants on

[1] Tom. v. p. 180.

[2] Tom. iv. pp. 123–125.

[3] The imperial 'we' is unknown in German reviewing: the '*Recensent*' must there speak in his own poor third person singular; nay stingy printers are in the habit of curtailing him into mere '*Rez.*,' and without any article: '*Rez.* thinks,' '*Rez.* says,' as if the unhappy man were uttering *affidavits*, in a tremulous half-guilty attitude not criticisms *ex cathedrâ*, and oftentimes *inflatis buccis!* The German reviewer, too, is expected, in many cases, to understand something of his subject; and, at all events, to have read his book. Happy England! Were there a bridge built hither, not only all the women in the world, as a wit has said, but faster than they, all the reviewers in the world, would hasten over to us, to exchange their toilsome mud-shovels for light kingly sceptres; and English Literature were one boundless, self-devouring *Review*, and (as in London routs) you had to *do* nothing, but only to *see* others do nothing. — T.

the stage, Dutch dairies in pictures, and Swiss scenes on the plate at dinner; nay they want gods more than they do God, whom, indeed, it is art that first raises to the rank of the gods. High sentiments and deep emotions, which the court at supper must scruple to express as real, can speak out loud and frankly on the court-theatre a little while before. Besides, what is not to be slighted, by a moderated indifference and aversion to true feelings, there is opened the freer room and variety for the representation and show thereof; as we may say, the Emperor Constantine first abolished the punishment of the cross, but on all hands loaded churches and statues with the figure of it.

Here too is another advantage, which whoever likes can reckon in: That certain higher and purer emotions do service to the true earthly ones in the way of foil; as haply, — if a similitude much fitter for a satire than for a review may be permitted, — the thick ham by its tender flowers, or the boar's-head by the citrons in its snout, rather gains than loses.

And though all this went for nothing, still must the religious enthusiasm of our Authoress affect the Parisian and man of the world with a second charm; namely, with the genuine material which lies therein, as well as in any tragedy, for conversational parody. Indeed, those same religious, oldfashioned, sentimental dispositions must, as the *persiflage* thereof has already grown somewhat threadbare and meritless, — they must, if jesting on them is to betoken spirit, be from time to time warmed up anew by some writer, or, still better, by some writeress, of genius.

With the charm of sensibility our gifted eulogist combines, as hinted above, another advantage which may well gain the Parisians for her; namely, the advantage of a true French, — not German, — taste in poetry.

She must, the Reviewer hopes, have satisfied the impartial Parisian by this general sentence, were there nothing more.[1]

'Le grand avantage qu'on peut tirer de l'étude de la littérature allemande, c'est le mouvement d'émulation qu'elle donne; il faut y chercher des forces pour composer soi-même plutôt que des ouvrages tout fait, qu'on puisse transporter ailleurs.'

This thought, which[2] she has more briefly expressed:

'Ce sera presque toujours un chef-d'œuvre qu'une invention étrangère arrangée par un Français,' —

she demonstrates[3] by the words:

'On ne sait pas faire un livre en Allemagne; rarement on y met l'ordre

[1] Tom. iv. p. 86. [2] Page 45. [3] Page 11.

et la méthode qui classent les idées dans la tête du lecteur; et ce n'est point parceque les Français sont impatiens, mais parcequ'ils ont l'esprit juste, qu'ils se fatiguent de ce défaut: les fictions ne sont pas dessinées dans les poésies allemandes avec ces contours fermes et précis qui en assurent l'effet; et le vague de l'imagination correspond à l'obscurité de la pensée.'

In short, our Muses'-hill, as also the other Muses'-hills, the English, the Greek, the Roman, the Spanish, are simply, — what no Frenchman can question, — so many mountain-stairs and terraces, fashioned on various slopes, whereby the Gallic Olympus-Parnassus may, from this side and that, be conveniently reached. As to us Germans in particular, she might express herself so: German works of art can be employed as colour-sheds, and German poets as colour-grinders, by the French pictorial school; as, indeed, from of old our learned lights have been by the French, not adored like light-stars, but stuck into like light-chafers, as people carry those of Surinam, spitted through, for lighting of roads. Frankly will the Frenchman forgive our Authoress her German or British heart, when he finds, in the chapters on the 'classical' and 'romantic' art of poetry, how little this has corrupted or cooled her taste, to the prejudice of the Gallic art of writing. After simply saying,[1]

'La nation française, la plus cultivée des nations latines, penche vers la poésie imitée des Grecs et des Romains,'

she expresses this[2] much better and more distinctly in these words:

'La poésie française étant la plus classique de toutes les poésies modernes, elle est la seule qui ne soit pas répandue parmi le peuple.'

Now Tasso, Calderon, Camoens, Shakspeare, Goethe, continues she, are sung by their respective peoples, even by the lowest classes; whereas it is to be lamented that, indeed,

'Nos poètes français sont admirés par tout ce qu'il y a d'esprits cultivés chez nous et dans le RESTE de l'Europe; mais ils sont tout-à-fait inconnus aux gens de peuple, et aux bourgeois même des villes, parceque les arts en France ne sont pas, comme ailleurs, natifs du pays même où leurs beautés se développent.'

And there is no Frenchman but will readily subscribe this confession. The Reviewer too, though a German, allows the French a similarity to the Greek and Latin classics; nay a greater than any existing people can exhibit; and recognises them willingly as the newest Ancients. He even goes so far, that he equals their Literature, using a quite peculiar and inverse principle of precedency among the classi-

[1] Tom. ii. p. 60. [2] Page 63.

cal ages, to the best age of Greek and Latin Literature, namely, to the *iron*. For as the figurative names, 'golden,' 'iron age,' of themselves signify, considering that gold, a very ductile rather than a useful metal, is found everywhere, and on the surface, even in rivers, and without labour; whereas the firm iron, serviceable not as a symbol and for its splendour, is rare in gold-countries, and gained only in depths and with toil, and seldom in a metallic state: so likewise, among literary ages, an iron one designates the practical utility and laborious nature of the work done, as well as the cunning workmanship bestowed on it; whereby it is clear, that not till the golden and silver ages are done, can the iron one come to maturity. Always one age produces and fashions the next: on the golden stands the silver; this forms the brass; and on the shoulders of all stands the iron. Thus too, our Authoress[1] testifies that the elder French, Montaigne and the rest, were so very like the present Germans,[2] while the younger had not yet grown actually classical; as it were, the end-flourishes and cadences of the past. On which grounds the French classics cannot, without injustice, be paralleled to any earlier Greek classics than to those of the Alexandrian school. Among the Latin classics their best prototypes may be such as Ovid, Pliny the younger, Martial, the two Senecas, Lucan, — though he, more by date than spirit, has been reckoned under our earlier periods; inasmuch as these Romans do, as it were by anticipation, arm and adorn themselves with the brass and iron, not yet come into universal use. A Rousseau would sound in Latin as silvery as a Seneca; Seneca would sound in French as golden as a Rousseau.

Nevertheless, it is an almost universal error in persons who speak of French critics, to imagine that a Géoffroy, or a Laharpe, in equalling his countrymen to the ancient classics, means the classics of the so-called golden age. But what real French classic would take it as praise if you told him that he wrote quite like Homer, like Æschylus, like Aristophanes, like Plato, like Cicero? Without vanity, he might give you to understand, that some small difference would surely be found between those same golden classics and him, which, indeed, was to be referred rather to the higher culture of the time than to his own; whereby he might hope that in regard to various *longueurs*, instances of tastelessness, coarseness, he had less to answer for than many an Ancient. A French tragedy-writer might say, for example, that he flattered himself, if he could not altogether equal the so-named tragic Seven Stars of Alexandria, he still differed a little from the *Seven* of Æschylus. Indeed, Voltaire and others, in their letters, tell us plain-

1 Tom. iv. p. 80.

2 The same thing Jean Paul had long ago remarked in his *Vorschule*, book iii. sec. 779, of the Second Edition.

ly enough, that the writers of the ancient golden age are nowise like them, or specially to their mind.

The genuine French taste of our Authoress displays itself also in detached manifestations; for example, in the armed neutrality which, in common with the French and people of the world, she maintains towards the middle ranks. Peasants and Swiss, indeed, make their appearance, idyl-wise, in French Literature; and a shepherd is as good as a shepherdess. Artists too are admitted by these people: partly as the sort of undefined comets that gyrate equally through suns, earths and satellites; partly as the individual servants of their luxury; and an actress in person is often as dear to them as the part she plays. But as to the middle rank, — excepting perhaps the clergyman, who in the pulpit belongs to the artist guild, and in Catholic countries, without rank of his own, traverses all ranks, — not only are handicraftsmen incapable of poetic garniture, but the entire class of men of business, your Commerce-*Raths*, Legation, Justice, and other *Raths*, and two-thirds of the whole Address-calendar. In short, French human nature produces and sets forth, in its works of art, nothing worse than princes, heroes and nobility: no ground-work and side-work of people; as the trees about Naples shade you, when sitting under them, simply with blossoms, not with leaves, because they have none. This air of pedigree, without which the French Parnassus receiveth no one, Madame de Staël also appears to require, and, by her unfavourable sentence, to feel the want of in Voss's *Luise*, in his *Idyls*, in Goethe's *Dorothea*, in *Meister* and *Faust*. There is too little gentility in them. Tieck's *Sternbald* finds favour, perhaps not less for its treating of *artists*, than by reason of its unpoetical yet pleasing generalities; for the book is rather a *wish* of art, than a *work* of art.

The theatre is, as it were, the *ichnography* (ground-plan) of a people; the prompter's hole (*souffleur*) is the speaking-trumpet of its peculiarities. Our Authoress, in exalting the Gallic *coulisses*, and stage-curtains, and candle-snuffers, and *souffleurs* of their tragic and comic ware, above all foreign theatres, gives the French another and gratifying proof of her taste being similar to theirs.

After so many preliminaries, the reader will doubtless expect the conclusion that our Authoress does prove the wished-for mediatrix between us and France, and in the end procures us a literary general pardon from the latter; nay, that the French are even a little obliged to her for this approximation. But quite the contrary is the Reviewer's opinion.

On the whole, he cannot help sympathising with the French, whom such diluted, filtered extracts and versions from the German must delude into belief of a certain regularity in us, whereof there is no trace extant. Thus, for example, our Authoress begins *Faust* with this passage:

'C'est à nous de nous plonger dans le tumulte de l'activité, dans ces vagues éternelles de la vie, que la naissance et la mort élèvent et précipitent, repoussent et ramènent: nous sommes faits pour travailler à l'œuvre que Dieu nous recommande, et dont le tems accomplit la trâme. Mais toi, qui ne peux concevoir que toi-même, toi, qui trembles en approfondissant ta destinée, et que mon souffle fait tressaillir, laisse-moi, ne me rappelle plus.'

How shall a Frenchman, persuaded perhaps by such smooth samples to study German, guess, that before this passage could become arable, the following tangle grew on it:

'DER GEIST.

In Lebensfluthen, im Thatensturm
Wall' ich auf und ab,
Wehe hin und her!
Geburt und Grab
Ein ewiges Meer,
Ein wechselnd Weben,
Ein glühend Leben,
So schaff' ich am sausenden Webstuhl der Zeit,
Und wirke der Gottheit lebendiges Kleid.

FAUST.

Der du die weite Welt umschweifst,
Geschäftiger Geist, wie nah' fühl'ich mich dir!

DER GEIST.

Du gleichst dem Geist, den du begreifst,
Nicht mir!'[1]

[1] Here is an English version, as literal as we can make it:

'THE SPIRIT.

In Existence' floods, in Action's storm,
I walk and work, above, beneath,
Work and weave, in endless motion!
Birth and death,
An infinite ocean,
A seizing and giving
The fire of living:
'Tis thus at the roaring Loom of Time I ply,
And weave for God the Garment thou seest him by.

So, indeed, is the whole *Faust* of Madame de Staël; all fire-colour bleached out of it; giant masses and groups, for example the *Walpurgisnacht* (Mayday Night), altogether cut away.

The following passage (*Siebenkäs*,[1] book i. sec. 7) occurs in 'the Speech of the dead Christ from the Universe' (*Songe*, she more briefly translates the title of it), where Christ, after saying that there is no God, thus continues:

> 'I travelled through the worlds, I mounted into the suns, and flew with the galaxies through wastes of heaven; but there is no God. I descended as far as being casts its shadow, and looked into the Abyss and cried: Father, where art thou? but I heard only the eternal storm, which no one guides; and the gleaming Rainbow from the west, without a Sun that made it, stood over the Abyss, and trickled down. And when I looked up towards the immeasurable world for the Divine *eye*, it glared down on me with an empty, black, bottomless *eye-socket;* and Eternity lay upon Chaos, eating it, and re-eating it. Cry on, ye discords! cry away the shadows, for He is not!'

These barbaresque sentences have, like all the rest, grown into the following cultivated ones:

> 'J'ai parcouru les mondes, je me suis élevé au-dessus de soleils, et là aussi il n'est point de Dieu; je suis descendu jusqu'aux dernières limites de l'univers, j'ai regardé dans l'abîme, et je me suis écrié: Père, où es-tu? mais je n'ai entendu que la pluie qui tombait goutte à goutte dans l'abîme, et l'éternelle tempête, que nul ordre ne régit, m'a seule répondu. Relevant ensuite mes regards vers la voûte des cieux, je n'y ai trouvé qu'une ORBITE VIDE, noire, et sans fond. L'éternité reposait sur le chaos, et le rongeait, et se dévorait lentement elle-même: redoublez vos plaintes amères et déchirantes; que des cris aigus dispersent les ombres, car c'en est fait.'

He that loves the French must lament that people should decoy them over to us with beauties which are merely painted on with rouge; and should hide not only our fungous excrescences, but our whole adiposity in wide Gallic court-clothes. For, as Goethe's *Faust* actually stands, every good Frenchman, outdoing our Authoress, who wishes no second, must wish the first — at Mephistopheles; and look upon this written hell-journey as an acted Empedocles one into the cra-

FAUST.

Thou who the wide world round outflowest,
Unresting Spirit, how I resemble thee!

THE SPIRIT.

Thou canst resemble spirits whom thou knowest,
Not me!' — T.

[1] By Jean Paul himself. — T.

ter of the German Muse-volcano. To our Authoress he might even say: "Madame, you had too much sense to lend your Germans any of those *traits, pointes, sentences*, that *esprit*, wherewith our writers have so long enchanted us and Europe. *You* showed us, in the German works, their brightest side, their *sensibilité*, the depth of their feelings. You have quite allured us with it. All that offended your taste, you have softened or suppressed, and given us yourself instead of the poem: *tant mieux!* But who will give us *you*, when we read these German works in the original? Jean Jacques says, Let science come, and not the deceiving doctor. We invert it, and say, Let the healing doctoress come, and not the sick poem, till she have healed it."

The Reviewer observes here, that in the foregoing apostrophe there is as cramp a eulogy as that[1] with which Madame de Staël concludes hers on Schiller:

'Peu de tems après la première représentation de Guillaume Tell, le trait mortel atteignit aussi le digne auteur de ce bel ouvrage. Gesler périt au moment où les desseins les plus cruels l'occupaient: Schiller n'avait dans son âme que de généreuses pensées. Ces deux volontés si contraires, la mort, ennemie de tous les projets de l'homme, les a de même brisées.'

This comparison of the shot Gesler with the deceased Schiller, wherein the similarity of the two men turns on their resembling other men in dying, and thereby having their plans interrupted, seems a delicate imitation of Captain Fluellen, who (in *Henry V.*) struggles to prove that Alexander of Macedon and Henry Monmouth are in more than one point like each other.

But to return. Were this castrated edition of the German Hercules, or Poetic God, which Madame de Staël has edited of us, desirable, and of real use for any reader, it would be for German courts, and courtiers themselves: who knows but such a thing might prove the light little flame[2] to indicate the heavy treasure of their native country; which treasure, as they, unlike the French, have all learned German first, they could find no difficulty in digging out. But with such shows of possible union between two altogether different churches, or temples of taste, never let the good, too-credulous French be lured and balked!

Nay, the cunning among them may hit our Authoress with her own hand; for she has written:[3]

[1] Tom. iii. p. 97.

[2] The 'little blue flame,' the '*Springwurzel*' (start-root), &c. &c., are well-known phenomena in miners' magic. —T.

[3] Tom. iv. p. 80.

'Les auteurs français de l'ancien tems ont en général plus de rapports avec les Allemands que les écrivains du siècle de Louis XIV.; car c'est depuis ce tems-là que la littérature française a pris une direction classique.'

And shall we now, he may say, again grow to similarity in culture with those whom we resembled when we had a less degree of it? A German may, indeed, prefer the elder French poetry to the newer French verse; but no Frenchman can leave his holy temple for an antiquated tabernacle of testimony, much less for a mere modern synagogue. The clear water of their poetry will ever exclude, as buoyant and unmixable, the dark fire-holding oil of ours. Or to take it otherwise: as with them the eye is everywhere the ruling organ, and with us the ear; so they, hard of hearing, will retain their poet-peacock, with his glittering tail-mirrors[1] and tail-eyes, drawn back fan-like to the wings, his poor tones and feet notwithstanding; and we, short of sight, will think our unshowy poet-larks and nightingales, with their songs in the clouds and the blossoms, the preferable blessing. Perhaps in the whole of Goethe there are not to be found so many antitheses and witty reflexes as in one moving act of Voltaire; and in all, even the finest cantos of the *Messias*, the Frenchman seeks in vain for such *pointes* as in the *Henriade* exalt every canto, every page, into a perfect holly-bush.

And now, the Reviewer begs to know of any impartial man, What joy shall a Frenchman have in literatures and arts of poetry which advance on him as naked as unfallen Eves or Graces, — he, who is just come from a poet-*assemblée*, where every one has his communion-coat, his mourning-coat, nay, his winding-sheet, trimmed with tassels and tags, and properly perfumed? What will a Fabre d'Olivet[2] say to such eulogising of a foreign literature? he who has so pointedly and distinctly declared:

'Oui, messieurs, ce que l'Indostan fut pour l'Asie, la France le doit être pour l'Europe. La langue française, comme la Sanscrite, doit tendre à l'universalité, elle doit s'enrichir de toutes les connaissances acquises dans les siècles passés, afin de les transmettre aux siècles futurs; destinée à surnoyer sur les débris de cent IDIOMES diverses, elle doit pouvoir sauver du naufrage des temps toutes leurs beautés, et toutes leurs productions remarquables.'

When even a De Staël, with all her knowledge of our language

[1] In French poetry, you must always, like the Christian, consider the latter end, or the last verse; and there, as in life, according to the maxim of the Greek sage, you cannot before the end be called happy.

[2] His *Les Vers Dorés du Pythagore expliqués, &c., précédés d'un Discours sur l'Essence de Poésie*, 1814.

and authors, and with a heart inclined to us, continues nevertheless Gallic in tongue and taste, what blossom-crop are we to look for from the dry timber? For, on the whole, the taste of a people is altogether to be discriminated from the taste of a period: the latter, not the former, easily changes. The taste of a people, rooted down, through centuries, in the nature of the country, in its history, in the whole soul of the body politic, withstands, though under new forms of resistance, all alterations and attacks from without. For this taste is, in its highest sense, nothing other than the outcome and utterance of the inward combination of the man, revealing itself most readily by act and judgment in art, as in that which speaks with all the faculties of man, and to all the faculties of man. Thus poetical taste belongs to the heart: the understanding possesses only the small domain of *rhetorical* taste, which can be learned and proved, and gives its verdict on correctness, language, congruity of images, and the like.

For the rest, if a foreign literature is really to be made a saline manure and fertilising compost for the withered French literature, some altogether different path must be fallen upon than this ridiculous circuit of clipping the Germans into Frenchmen, that these may take pattern by them; of first fashioning us down to the French, that they may fashion themselves up to us. Place, and plant down, and encamp, the Germans with all their stout limbs and full arteries, like dying gladiators, fairly before them; — let them then study these figures as an academy, or refuse to do it. Even to the Gallic speech, in this transference, let utmost boldness be recommended. How else, if not in a similar way, have we Germans worked our former national taste into a free taste; so that by our skill in languages, or our translations, we have welcomed a Homer, Shakspeare, Dante, Calderon, Tasso, with all their peculiarities, repugnant enough to ours, and introduced them undisarmed into the midst of us? Our national taste meanwhile was not lost in this process: in the German, with all its pliability, there is still something indeclinable for other nations; Goethe, and Herder, and Klopstock, and Lessing, can be enjoyed to perfection in no tongue but the German; and not only our æsthetic cosmopolitism (universal friendship), but also our popular individuality, distinguishes us from all other peoples.

If, one day, we are to be presented to foreign countries, — and every German, proud as he may be, will desire it, if he is a bookseller, — the Reviewer could wish much for an Author like our Authoress, to transport us, in such a Cleopatra's ship as her's, into England. Schiller, Goethe, Klinger, Hippel, Lichtenberg, Haller, Kleist, might, simply as they were, in their *naturalibus* and *pontifical-*

ibus, disembark in that Island, without danger of becoming hermits, except in so far as hermits may be worshipped there.

On the *romantic* [1] side, however, we could not wish the Briton to cast his first glance at us: for the Briton, — to whom nothing is so poetical as the commonweal, — requires (being used to the weight of gold), even for a golden age of poetry, the thick golden wing-covers of his epithet-poets; not the transparent gossamer wings of the Romanticists; no many-coloured butterfly-dust; but, at lowest, flower-dust that will grow to something.

But though this gifted Inspectress of Germany has done us little furtherance with the French, nay perhaps hindrance, inasmuch as she has spoken forth our praise needlessly in mere comparisons with the French, instead of speaking it without offensive allusions, — the better service can she do us with another people, namely, with the Germans themselves.

In this respect, not only in the first place may the critic, but also in the second place the patriot, return her his thanks. It is not the outward man, but the inward, that needs mirrors. We cannot wholly see ourselves, except in the eye of a foreign seer. The Reviewer would be happy to see and enter a mirror-gallery, or rather picture-gallery, in which our faces, limned by quite different nations, by Portuguese, by Scotchmen, by Russians, Corsicans, were hanging up, and where we might learn how differently we looked to eyes that were different. By comparison with foreign peculiarity, our own peculiarity discerns and ennobles itself. Thus, for example, our Authoress, profitably for us. holds up and reflects our German *longueurs* (interminabilities), our dull jesting, our fanaticism, and our German indifference to the file.

Against the last error, — against the rule-of-thumb *style* of these days, — reviewers collectively ought really to fire and slash with an especial fury. There was a time, in Germany, when a Lessing, a Winkelmann, filed their periods like Plato or Cicero, and Klopstock and Schiller their verses like Virgil or Horace; when, as Tacitus, we thought more of disleafing than of covering with leaves; in short, of a disleafing, which, as in the vine, ripens and incites the grapes. There was such a time, but the present has *had* it; and we now write, and paint, and patch straightforward, as it comes to hand, and study readers and writers not much, but appear in print. Corrections, at present, seem as costly to us, as if, like Count Alfieri, we had them to make on printing-paper, at the charges of our printer and purse. The public book-market is to be our bleach-green; and

[1] *Romantisch*, 'romantic,' it will be observed, is here used in a scientific sense, and has no concern with the writing or reading (or acting) of 'romances.' — T.

the public, instead of us, is to correct; and then, in the second edition, we can pare off somewhat, and clap on somewhat.

But it is precisely this late correction, when the former author, with his former mood and love, is no longer forthcoming, that works with dubious issue. Thus Schiller justly left his *Robbers* unaltered. On the other hand, the same sun-warmth of creation can, in a second hour, return as a sun-warmth of ripening. Writers who mean to pay the world only in *plated* coins can offer no shadow of reason for preferring first thoughts; since the very thought they write down must, in their heads, during that minute's space, have already gone through several improved editions.

Still deeper thanks than those of the critic to our Authoress, let the patriot give her. Through the whole work there runs a veiled sorrow that Germany should be found kneeling, and, like the camel, raise itself still bent and heavy-laden. Hence her complaints [1] that the present Germans have only a philosophical and no political character; — farther, that the German,[2] even through his moderate climate, in which he has not the extremes of heat and cold to encounter, but without acquirement of hardiness easily secures himself against evils of an equable nature, should be softening into unwarlike effeminacy; — farther, those other complaints,[3] about our division of ranks, our deficiency in diplomatic craft and lying; about the German great, who, to the tedium of the French themselves, still take an interest in Louis Fourteenth's mistresses and anecdotes.[4] Thus she says,[5]

'Les Allemands ont besoin de dédaigner pour devenir les plus forts;'

and two lines lower,

'Ce sont les seuls hommes, peut-être, auxquels on pouvait conseiller l'orgueil comme un moyen de devenir meilleurs.'

She is almost right. Not as if, one towards another, and in words, we did not set ourselves forward, and take airs enough, on printed paper; — each stands beside the others with a ready-plaited garland for him in his hand; — but in actions, and towards foreigners and persons in authority, it is still to be lamented that we possess but two cheeks for the receiving of cuffs, in place of four, like the Janus-head; although, in this cheek-deficiency, we do mend matters a little, when we — turn round, and get the remainder. During the French war, and in the peace before it, there were many statesmen, if not states also, that considered themselves mere *half-stuff*, as rags

[1] Tom. v. ch. 11. [2] Tom. i. p. 20. [3] Tom. i. ch. 2.
[4] Tom. i. ch. 9. [5] Tom. v. p. 200.

in the paper-mill are called, when they are not cut small enough, — till once they were ennobled into *whole-stuff*, when the *devil* (so, in miller-speech, let Napoleon's sceptre be named) had altogether hacked them into finest shreds.

In vol. v. p. 123, is a long harsh passage, where the German subserviency is rated worse than the Italian; because our physiognomies and manners and philosophical systems promise nothing but heart and courage — and yet produce it not. Here, and in other passages regarding Prussia, where[1] she says,

> 'La capitale de la Prusse ressemble à la Prusse elle-même: les édifices et les institutions ont âge d'homme, et rien de plus, parcequ'un seul homme en est l'auteur,'—

one willingly forgives her the exaggeration of her complaints; not only because time has confuted them, and defended us and re-exalted us to our ancient princedoms, but also because her tears of anger over us are only warmer tears of love, with which she sees, in the Germans, falling angels at war with fallen.

The Preface gives a letter from Police-minister and General Savary to Madame, wherein, with much sense, he asserts that the work is not of a French spirit, and that she did well to leave out the name of the *Empereur*, seeing there was no worthy place for him. '*Il n'y pouvait trouver de place qui fût digne de lui*,' says the General; meaning, that among so many great poets and philosophers, of various ages and countries, the Elbese would not have cut the best figure, or looked *digne* (worshipful) enough. The gallant Police-minister deserves here to be discriminated from the vulgar class of lickspittles, who so nimbly pick up and praise whatever falls from princes, especially whatever good, without imitating it; but rather to be ranked among the second and higher class (so to speak), who lick up any rabid saliva of their superior, and thereby run off as mad and fiery as himself. Only thus, and not otherwise, could the General, from those detached portions which the censor had cut out, have divined, as from outpost victories, that the entire field was to be attacked and taken. Accordingly, the whole printed Edition was laid hold of, and, as it were, under a second paper-mill devil, hacked anew into beautiful pulp. Nor is that delicate feeling of the whilom censors and clippers to be contemned, whereby these men, by the faintest allusion, smell out the crown-debts of their crown-robber (usurper), and thereby proclaim them. The Sphinx in Elba, who, unlike the ancient one, spared only him that could not rede his riddle, — (a riddle consisting in this, to make Europe like the *Turkish* grammar, wherein there is but one *conjugation*, one *declension*, no gen-

[1] Tom. i. p. 108.

der, and no exception), — could not but reckon a description of the Germans, making themselves a power within a power, to be ticklish matter. And does not the issue itself testify the sound sense of these upper and under censors? Forasmuch as they had to do with a most deep and polished enemy, whom they could nowise have had understanding enough to see through, were it not that, in such cases, suspicion sees farther than your half-understanding. She may often (might they say), under that patient nun-veil of hers, be as diplomatically mischievous as any nun-prioress.

But, not to forget the Work itself, in speaking of its fortunes, the Reviewer now proceeds to some particular observations on certain chapters; first, however, making a general one or two. No foreigner has yet, with so wide a glance and so wide a heart, apprehended and represented our German style of poetry, as this foreign *lady*. She sees French poetry, — which is a computable glittering crystal, compared with the immeasurable organisation of the German, — really in its true form, though with preference to that form, when she describes it as a *poésie de société*. In the *Vorschule der Aesthetik*,[1] it was, years ago, described even so, though with less affection; and in general terms, still earlier, by Herder. The Germans, again, our Authoress has meted and painted chiefly on the side of their comparability and dissimilarity to the French; and hereby our own self-subsistence and peculiar life has much less clearly disclosed itself to her. In a comparison of Nations, one may skip gaily along, among perfect truths, as along radii, and skip over the centre too, and miss it.

Concerning the chapters in the First Volume, one might say of our Authoress in her absence almost the same thing as before her face. For generalities, such as nations, countries, cities, are seized and judged of by her wide traveller-glance, better than specialities and poets, by her Gallic, narrow, female taste; as, indeed, in general, large masses, by the free scope they yield for allusions, are, in the hands of a gifted writer, the most productive. However, it is chiefly polite Germany, and most of all literary Germany, that has sat to her on this occasion; and of the middle class, nothing but the literary heights have come into view. Moreover, she attributes to climate what she should have looked for in history: thus[2] she finds the temperate regions more favourable to sociality than to poetry, '*ce sont les* '*délices du midi ou les rigueurs du nord qui ébranlent fortement l'imagina-* '*tion;*' therefore, South Germany, that is, Franconia, Swabia, Bavaria and Austria. Now, to say nothing of the circumstance that, in the first three of these countries, the alternation between the flower-splendour of spring and the cloudy cold of winter raises both the temperate warmth and the temperate coldness to the poetical degree,

[1] B. iii. k. 2.

[2] Tom. i. c. 5.

thereby giving them *two* chances, the opinion of our Authoress stands contradicted by mild Saxony, mild Brandenburg, England, Greece, on the one hand, and by warm Naples and cold Russia on the other. Nay, rather extreme frost and extreme heat may be said to oppress and exhaust the poet; and the Castalian fountain either evaporates or freezes. On the other hand, regions lying intermediate between these temperatures are those where mind and poetry are met with unshackled.

In chap. ii., *de l'esprit de conversation,* she describes very justly the art of talking (different from the art of speaking):[1]

'Le genre de bien-être que fait éprouver une conversation animée ne consiste précisément dans le sujet de conversation; les idées ni les connaissances qu'on peut y développer n'en sont pas le principal intérêt; c'est une certaine manière d'agir les uns sur les autres, de se faire plaisir réciproquement et avec rapidité, de parler aussitôt qu'on pense, de jouir à l'instant de soi-même, d'être applaudi (applaudie) sans travail, de manifester son esprit dans toutes les nuances par l'accent, le geste, le regard, enfin de produire à volonté comme une sorte d'électricité, que fait jaillir des étincelles.'

The passage[2] where she counsels the Germans to acquire social culture and resignation in respect of social refinement, merits German attention. It is true, she should not, before denying us and prescribing us the French art of talking, have said:[3]

'L' esprit de conversation a quelquefois *l'inconvénient* d'altérer la sincérité du caractère; ce n'est pas une tromperie combinée, mais improvisée, si l'on peut s'exprimer ainsi:'

which, in plain language, signifies, in this art there is one unpleasant circumstance, that sometimes your honesty of heart suffers thereby; and you play the real, literal knave, though only on the spur of the moment, and without special preparation. For the rest, it must be such passages as this, where she denies us these moral and æsthetic Gallicisms, allowing us, for compensation, nothing but learning, depth of heart and thought; such passages it must be by light of which the *Journal de Paris,* finding us denied not only the *tromperie combinée,* but now even the *improvisée,* has discovered that our Authoress is a secret enemy of the Germans; who will surely (hopes the Journal) get into anger with her, though, as always, not till late. For sharply as she attacks the French, she does it only on the moral side, which these forgive the more easily and feel the more faintly, the more she is in the right; but we again are assaulted in graver wise, and with other consequence, namely on the side of our understanding, which, as com-

[1] Page 68. [2] Page 81. [3] Page 70.

pared with the Gallic, in regard to business, to knowledge of the world, nay to combining and arranging works of art, she everywhere pronounces inferior.

'Les Allemands mettent très-rarement en scène dans leurs comédies des ridicules tirés de leur propre pays; ils n'observent pas les autres; encore moins sont-ils capables de l'examiner eux-mêmes sous les rapports extérieurs, ils croiraient presque manquer à la loyauté qu'ils se doivent.'

To form the plan, to order the whole scenes towards one focus of impression (*effet*), this, says she, is the part of Frenchmen; but the German, out of sheer honesty, cannot do it. Nevertheless, our Lessing vowed that he could remodel every tragedy of Corneille into more cunning and more regular shape; and his criticisms, as well as his *Emilia Galotti*, to say nothing of Schiller and all the better German critics, are answer enough to Madame de Staël's reproach.

Three times, and in as many ways, she accounts for our deficiency in the art of witty speech. First, from our language: but had she forgotten her German when she wrote concerning it, '*La construction ne permet pas toujours de terminer une phrase par l'expression la plus piquante?*'[1] For does not directly, on the contrary, our language, alone among all the modern ones, reserve any word it pleases, any part of speech without exception — nay sometimes a half-word,[2] — naturally and without constraint, for a dessert-wine of conclusion? Madame de Staël should also, to inform herself, have read at least a few dozen volumes of our epigram-anthologies with their thousand end-stings. What do Lessing's dialogues want, or our translations from the French, in regard to pliancy of language? But, on the whole, we always, — this is her second theory of our conversational maladroitness, — wish too much to say something or other, and not, like the French, nothing: a German wishes to express not only himself, but also something else; and under this something we frequently include sentiment, principle, truth, instruction. A sort of disgust comes over us to see a man stand speaking on, and quite coolly determined to show us nothing but himself: for even the narrator of a story is expected to propose rather our enjoyment in it than his own selfish praise for telling it.

In the third place, we are too destitute, complains our Authoress, of wit, consequently of *bon-mots*, and so forth. Reviewer complains, on the other hand, that the French are too destitute thereof. A Hippel, a Lichtenberg, like a Young or Pope, has more and better wit

[1] Tom. i. p. 84.

[2] Paul has made this very sentence an example of his doctrine; one half of the word 'reserve' (*heben*) occurring at the commencement, the other half (*auf*) not till the end. — T.

than a whole French decade will produce. French wit, reflection-wit (Reviewer here perfectly coincides with Jean Paul in his divisions of wit), surprises with one light resemblance, and with its prompt visibility, like a French garden, only once: British and German wit treats us with the comparison of resemblances reflecting one another, and with the continuous enjoyment of an English garden. For the reperusal of Lichtenberg, Reviewer commonly waits a year; for the reperusal of Voltaire ten years; for the reperusal of French Journalists sixty years; for that of Hamann as many minutes. The German of spirit is almost ashamed to be so light-witted as a Frenchman; and must make an effort not to make an effort. If he do not grudge the labour, he can heap up, like Weisse in his *Satires*, more antitheses in a page than a Frenchman in a book. Men of the world, who in German are merely smooth and correct, glitter in French with witty turns; it is will, therefore, that chooses here, not inability. One may say, not this and that Frenchman, but the whole French people, has wit: but so common a wit can, even for that reason, be no deep one.

What farther was to be said against our want of French skill in talking, Reviewer leaves to the English, Spaniards, Italians, who all share it with us.

The following passage[1] may reconcile the French with our Authoress: '*En France la plupart des lecteurs ne veulent jamais être émus, 'ni même s'amuser aux dépens de leur conscience littéraire; le scrupule s'est 'réfugié là.*' In p. 13, she makes Hans Sachs compose *before* the Reformation; and in p. 14, Luther translate the Psalms *and* the Bible. This to a Frenchman, who would show literary, may be detrimental, if he repeats it. In p. 17, she finds a likeness between Wieland's prose and Voltaire's. Give her or give him Voltaire's wit, conciseness, lightness, pliancy, there can be nothing liker. Reviewer has a comfort in having Wieland called at once, by this class of admirers, the German Voltaire, and by that other, the German Greek: he needs not, in that case, reflect and confute, but simply leaves the speakers to their reciprocal annihilation. For the rest, the whole of this chapter, as well as the twelfth, lends and robs the good Wieland so lavishly, that we rather beg to omit it altogether. His Comic Tales are, in her view,[2] *imitées du Grec;* so that most of the French painters, their subjects being mythological, must also be imitators of the Greeks. In p. 62, she must either have misunderstood some Germans, or these must have misunderstood the Greeks, when she says of Fate, in contradistinction to Providence, '*Le sort* (the Greek Fate) *ne compte pour rien les sentimens des hommes.*' Sophocles *seven times* says no to this; and as often Æschylus. Nay, so inexorably

1 Tom. ii. p. 2.

2 Page 67.

does Fate pursue every immorality, especially audacious immorality, that (unlike Providence) it inflicts the punishment, even *under* repentance and reform. In p. 90, she calls Klopstock's Ode to his Future Love a *sujet maniéré :*

> 'Klopstock est moins heureux quand il écrit sur l'amour: il a, comme Dorat, adressé des vers à sa maîtresse future, et ce sujet maniéré n'a pas bien inspiré sa muse: il faut n'avoir pas souffert, pour se jouer avec le sentiment; et quand une personne sérieuse essaie un semblable jeu, toujours une contrainte secrète l'empêche de s'y montrer naturelle.'

How could her soul, that elsewhere responds to all pure-toned chords of love, mistake the yet unloved longing, wherewith the unloved and yet loving youth looks into his future heart, as with a coming home-sickness? Does even the prosaic young man paint him an ideal, why shall not the poetical incorporate and draw nearer to him the dear form that is glancing for him, though as yet unseen? It is true, this holds only of the first love; for a poem on a second, third and future love, would doubtless merit the blame, which, indeed, she probably so meant.

The long passage from Voss's *Louise*[1] seems introduced to bring even the German reader, by the bald translation, into a state of yawning; and the happier French one into snoring and even snorting. Quite as unexpectedly has she extracted from *Maria Stuart,* instead of bright lyric altar-fire, the long farewell of Maria, too long even for German readers, and only for the epos not too short; and rendered it moreover in prose.

To Goethe she does justice where she admires him, but less where she estimates him. His poems she judges more justly than she does his plays. Everywhere, indeed, her taste borders more on the German when applied to short pieces than to long ones; above all, than to theatrical ones; for here the French curtain shrouds up every foreign one. With her opinion of Goethe as a literary *man,* the Germans, since the appearance of his Autobiography, may readily enough dispense.

Of ch. 15, *de l'art dramatique,* Reviewer could undertake to say nothing, except something ill, did time permit.

Shakspeare, in whose child-like and poetic serene soul (as it were, a poetic Christ-child) she celebrates an *ironie presque Machiavellique* in delineating character, she ought to praise less on hearsay, since neither hearsay nor her own feeling can teach her how to praise Goethe's *Faust.* It is probable she knows only the French (un-souled and un-hearted) Shakspeare, and so values the man; but for Goethe's *Faust* too, she should have waited for a French version and perver-

[1] Tom. ii. p. 82.

sion, to give him somewhat better commendation than that she sends him to France with.

If a translation is always but an inverted, pale, secondary rainbow of the original splendour, Madame de Staël's, as in general any French translation of *Faust*, is but a gray, cold, mock-sun to Goethe's real flaming Sun in Leo. At times, in place of a pallid translation, she gives a quite new speech; for example,[1] she makes the Devil say of Faust, '*Cet homme ne sera jamais qu'à demi pervers, et c'est en* '*vain qu'il se flatte de parvenir à l'être entièrement.*' In the original appears no word of this, but merely the long, good, quite different passage, '*Verachte nur Vernunft und Wissenschaft,*' *&c.* That weighty omissions have prevented light translations in her work, is happy for the work of Goethe. This (like Dante's *Divine Comedy*) Diabolic Tragedy, in which whole spiritual universes act and fall, she has contracted and extracted into a love-tale. Of this sole and last zodiacal light which the set sun of Shakspeare has cast up over Germany, our lady Authoress wishes heartily[2] that another such, or more such, may not be written. Reviewer ventures to give her hope of fulfilment herein, and pledges himself for all Frenchmen. Consider only:[3]

> 'Il ne faut y chercher ni le goût, ni le mesure, ni l'art qui choisit et qui termine; mais si l'imagination pouvait se figurer un chaos intellectuel tel qu'on a souvent décrit le chaos matériel, le *Faust* de Goethe devrait avoir été composé à cette époque.'

Readeresses, why will every one of you insist on thinking herself a reader?

Her hard judgment on *Faust*, Madame had beforehand softened[4] by the praise she bestowed on *Götz von Berlichingen*: '*il y a des traits de génie ça et là*,' not only *here* but *there* also, '*dans son drame.*' Less warmly[5] does she praise the *Natural Daughter;* because the personages therein, like shades in Odin's Palace, lead only an imaged life; inasmuch as they bear no real Christian Directory-names, but are merely designated as King, Father, Daughter, &c. As for this last defect, Reviewer fancies he could remedy it, were he but to turn up his French history and pick out at random the words Louis, Orleans, &c. and therewith christen the general titles, father, daughter; for, in the structure of the work, Madame de Staël will confess there are as firm, determinate, beheading machines, arsenic-hats, poison-pills, steel-traps, *oubliettes*, spring-guns, introduced, as could be required of any court, whither the scene of the piece might be transferred.

There is one censure from our Authoress, however, which Re-

[1] Tom. iii. p. 137. [2] Page 160. [3] Page 127.
[4] Tom. iii. p. 402. [5] Page 125.

viewer himself must countersign, though it touches the sweet orange-flower garland, Goethe's *Tasso*. Reviewer had been pleased to notice, in this piece, which cannot be acted in any larger space than within the chambers of thè brain, no downcome, save the outcome, or end; where the moral knot, which can only be loosed in Tasso's heart, is, by cutting of the material knot, by banishment from court, left unloosed to accompany him in exile; and can at any hour raise up a second fifth-act. This want, indeed, is not felt *in* reading the work so much as *after* reading it. Our Authoress, however, points out[1] another want, which, in the piece itself, has a cooling, at least a shadowing influence: that, namely, in the first place, Princess Leonora is drawn not according to the warm climate, but rather as a German maiden; and so thinks and ponders about her love, instead of either sacrificing herself to it or it to herself; and that, secondly, the Poet Tasso acts not like an Italian accustomed to outward movement and business, but like a solitary German, and unskilfully entangles himself in the perplexities of life.

For the rest, her whole praise of Goethe will, in the sour head of a Frenchman, run to sheer censure; and her censure again will remain censure, and get a little sourer, moreover.

Perhaps the kindliest and justest of all her portraitures is that of Schiller. Not only is she, in her poetry, many times a sister of Schiller; but he also, in his intellectual pomp and reflex splendour, is now and then a distant though beatified relation of Corneille and Crebillon. Hence his half-fortune with the French: for, in consideration of a certain likeness to themselves, some unlikeness and greatness will be pardoned. If Gallic tragedy is often a centaur, begotten by an Ixion with a cloud, Schiller also, at times, has confounded a sun-horse and thunder-horse with the horse of the Muses, and mounted and driven the one instead of the other.

The *Donau-Nymphe* (Nymph of the Danube) obtains[2] the honour of an extract, and the praise,

> 'Le sujet de cette pièce semble plus ingénieux que populaire; mais les scènes merveilleuses y sont mêlées et variées avec tant d'art, qu'elle amuse également tous les spectateurs.'

Reviewer has heard Herder, more in earnest than in jest, call the *Zauberflöte* the only good opera the Germans had.

After sufficiently misunderstanding and faint-praising Goethe's *Meister* and *Ottilie*,[3] she ventures, though a lady, and a French one,

[1] Tom. iii. p. 122.

[2] Tom. iv. p. 36.

[3] She finds *Ottilie* not moving enough; — the Reviewer again finds that *Ottilie* not only moves the heart, but crushes it. This more than female Werter excites deeper interest for her love than the male one; and, in an earlier time, would have intoxi-

to let fall this and the other remark about *humeur;* and, as it were, to utter a judgment (here Reviewer founds on the printed words) concerning Swift and Sterne. Sterne's humour, in *Tristram,* she imputes to phraseology;[1] nay, to phrases, not to ideas; and infers that Sterne is not translatable, and Swift is. Nevertheless, both of them have found very pretty lodgings in this country with Bode and Waser. Thereafter, in the same chapter on Romances, she makes Asmus, who has written no romance, the drawbridge for a sally against Jean Paul.

Her shallow sentence, as one more passed on him, may, among so many, — some friendlier, some more hostile, — pass on with the rest; till the right one appear, which shall exaggerate neither praise nor blame; for hitherto, as well the various pricking-girdles (cilices) in which he was to do penance, have been so wide for his body that they slipped to his feet, as in like wise the laurel-wreaths so large for his head that they fell upon his shoulders. Our Authoress dexterously unites both; and every period consists, in front, of a pleasant commendation, and behind of a fatal *mais;* and the left hand of the conclusion never knows what the right hand of the premises doeth. Reviewer can figure this jester comically enough, when he thinks how his face must, above fifteen times, have cheerfully thawed at the first clauses, and then suddenly frozen again at the latter. Those *mais* are his bitterest enemies. Our Authoress blames him for overdoing the pathetic; which blame she herself unduly shares with him in her *Corinne*, as Reviewer, in his long-past critique thereof, in these very *Jahrbücher*, hopes to have proved; and, it may be, had that review of *Corinne* met her eye, she would rather have left various things against J. P. unsaid. In p. 79, she writes, that he knows the human heart only from little German towns, and (hence) '*Il y a souvent dans la peinture de ces mœurs quelque chose de trop* INNOCENT *pour notre siècle.*' Now, it is a question whether J. P. could not, if not altogether disprove, yet uncommonly weaken, this charge of innocence, — by stating that many of his works were written in Leipzig, Weimar, Berlin, &c.; and that, consequently, his alleged innocence was not his blame, but that of those cities. He might also set forth how, in *Titan,* he has collected so much polished court-corruption, recklessness, and refined sin of all sorts, that it is a hardship for him, — saying nothing of those capital cities, — to be implicated in any such guilt as that of innocence.

However, to excuse her half and quarter judgment, let it not be concealed that scarcely have two of his works (*Hesperus* and *Sieben-*

cated all hearts with tears. But what always obstructs a heroine with the female reading world, is the circumstance that she is not the hero.

[1] Tom. iv. p. 79.

kūs) been gone through by her; nay one of them, *Hesperus*, has not so much as been fairly gone into; for, after introducing a not very important scene from *Hesperus*, the couching of a father's eyes by a son, properly a thing which every century does to the other, she tables some shreds of a second incident in this same *Hesperus*, but with a statement that it is from a *different* romance. Of the *Rede des todten Christus* (Speech of the dead Christ), she has indeed omitted the superfluous commencement, but also more than half of the unsuperfluous conclusion, which closes those wounds. Reviewer willingly excuses her, since this author, a comet of moderate nucleus, carries so excessive a comet-train of volumes along with him, that even up to the minute when he writes this, such train has not yet got altogether above the horizon.

On the whole, she usually passes long judgments only on few-volumed writers, — for instance, Tieck, Werner; and short on many-volumed, — for instance, the rich Herder, whom she accommodates in a pretty bowerlet of four sides, or pages. The New Poetic School, at least August Schlegel, whom she saw act in Werner's *Twenty-fourth of February*, might have helped her out a little with instructions and opinions about Herder (nay, even about Jean Paul) as well as about Tieck; the more, as she seems so open to such communications that they often come back from her as mere echoes: for, strictly considered, it is the New, much more than the Old School, that really stands in opposition to the French.

The thirty-second chapter (*des Beaux Arts en Allemagne*) does not require seventeen pages, as *Faust* did, to receive sentence; but only seven, to describe German painting, statuary and music, — not so much compressedly as compressingly. Nevertheless, Reviewer willingly gives up even these seven pages for the sake of the following beautiful remark:[1]

> 'La musique des Allemands est plus variée que celle des Italiens, et c'est en cela peut-être qu'elle est moins bonne: l'esprit est condamné à la variété, — c'est sa misère qui en est la cause; mais les arts, comme le sentiment, ont une admirable monotonie, celle dont on voudrait faire un moment éternel.'

The Fifth Volume treats of Philosophies — the French, the English, the old and new and newest German, and what else from ancient Greece has to do with philosophies. Concerning this volume, a German reviewer can offer his German readers nothing new, except perhaps whimsicalities. While men, — for example, Jacobi, — after long studying and re-studying of great philosophers, so often fall into anxiety lest they may not have understood them, finding the con-

[1] Tom. iv. p. 125.

futation look so easy, women of talent and breeding, simply from their gift of saying No, infer at once that they have seen through them. Reviewer is acquainted with intellectual ladies, who, in the hardest philosophical works, — for instance, Fichte's, — have found nothing but light and ease. Not what is thought, only what is learned, can women fancy as beyond their horizon. From Love they have acquired a boldness, foreign to us, of passing sentence on great men. Besides, they can always, instead of the conception, the idea, substitute a feeling. In p. 78, Madame de Staël says quite naïvely, she does not see why philosophers have striven so much to reduce all things to one principle, be it matter or spirit; one or a pair, it makes little difference, and explains the all no better. In p. 55, she imparts to the Parisians several categories of Kant's, with an *et-cætera ;* as it were an Alphabet, with an *and-so-forth.* If jesting is admissible in a review, the following passage on Schelling[1] may properly stand here :

> 'L'idéal et le réel tiennent, dans son langage, la place de l'intelligence et de la matière, de L'IMAGINATION et de l'expérience; et c'est dans la réunion de ces deux puissances en une harmonie complète, que consiste, selon lui, le principe unique et absolu de l'univers organisé. Cette harmonie, dont les deux POLES et le centre sont l'image, et qui est renfermé dans le nombre de trois, de tout temps si mystérieux, fournit à Schelling des APPLICATIONS *les plus ingénieuses.*'

But we return to earnest. Consider, now, what degree of spirit these three philosophic spirits can be expected to retain, when they have been passed off, and in, and carried through, three heads, as if by distillation ascending, distillation middle and distillation descending : for the three heads are, namely, — the head of the Authoress, who does not half understand the philosophers ; the head of the Parisian, who again half understands our Authoress ; and finally, the head of the Parisianess, who again half understands the Parisian. Through such a series of intermediate glasses the light in the last may readily refract itself into darkness.

Meanwhile, let the former praise remain to her unimpaired, that she still seizes in our philosophy the sunny side, which holds of the heart, to exhibit and illuminate the mossy north side of the French philosophy. Striking expressions of noblest sentiments and views are uncovered, like pearl-muscles, in this philosophic ebb and flow. Precious also, in itself, is the nineteenth chapter, on Marriage Love ; though for this topic, foreign in philosophy, it were hard to find any right conductor into such a discussion, except, indeed, the philosophers Crates and Socrates furnish one.

[1] Tom. v. p. 83.

As the Sixth and last Volume treats of Religion and Enthusiasm, — a French juxtaposition, — it is almost her heart alone that speaks, and the language of this is always a pure and rich one. The separate pearls, from the philosophic ebb, here collect themselves into a pearl necklace. She speaks nobly on Nature, and Man, and Eternity;[1] so likewise on Enthusiasm.[2] Individual baldnesses it were easy for Reviewer to extract, — for they are short; but individual splendours difficult, — for they are too long.

To one who loves not only Germany but mankind, or rather both in each other, her praise and high preference of the German religious temper, in this volume, almost grows to pain: for, as we Germans ourselves complain of our coldness, she could have found a temperate climate here only by contrast with the French ice-field of irreligion from which she comes. Truly, she is in the right. The French, in these very days, have accepted their Sunday as crabbedly as the Germans parted with their Second Sundays, or Holidays, when forced to do it. Thus does the poisonous meadow-saffron of the Revolution, after its autumn-flowers have been left solitary and withered, still keep under ground its narcotic bulb for the awakened spring; almost as if the spirit of Freedom in this Revolution, like the spirit of Christianity, should construct and remodel every foreign people — only not the Jewish, where were the Nativity and Crucifixion.

The bitterness of the Parisian journal-corps, who have charged against this Work of the Baroness more fiercely than against all her Romances, shows us that it is something else than difference of taste that they strike and fire at: their hearts have been doubly provoked by this comparison, and trebly by this discordance in their own most inward feeling, which loves not to expose itself as an outward one. In romances, they took all manner of religion as it came; they could charge it on the characters, and absolve the poetess: but here she herself, — not with foreign lips, but with her own, — has spoken out for religion, and against the country where religion is yet no *rêmigrée*.

A special Pamphlet, published in Paris, on this Work, enlists the method of question and answer in the service of delusion, to exhibit bold beauties, by distorting them from their accompaniments, in the character of bombast. It is but seldom that our Authoress sins, and, in German fashion, against German taste, as where she says,[3]

'Tous les moutons du même troupeau viennent donner, les uns après les autres, leurs coups-de-tête aux idées, qui n'en restent moins ce qu'elles sont.'

[1] Tom. vi. pp. 78-86. [2] Chap. x. [3] Tom. vi. p. 11.

In presence of a descriptive power that delights foreign nations, one might hope the existing French would modestly sink mute — they whose eulogistic manner, in the *Moniteur*, in the senate and everywhere, towards the throne, has at all times been as strained, windy and faded as its object; and in whom, as in men dying the wrong way (while, in common cases, in the cooling of the outward limbs, the heart continues to give heat), nothing remains warm but the members from which the frozen heart lies farthest.

It is difficult, amid so many bright passages, which, like polished gold, not only glitter, but image and exhibit, to select the best. For example, the description of the Alps by night, and of the whole festival of Interlaken;[1] — the remark[2] that both the excess of heat in the east, and of cold in the north, incline the mind to idealism and visuality; — or this, '*Ce qui manque en France, en tout genre, c'est le* '*sentiment et l'habitude du respect.*'[3]

Still more than we admire the Work, is the Authoress, considering also her sex and her nation, to be admired. Probably she is the only woman in Europe, and still more probably the only French person in France, that could have written such a book on Germany. Had Germany been her cradle and school, she might have written a still better work, namely, on France. And so we shall wish this spiritual Amazon strength and heart for new campaigns and victories; and then, should she again prove the revieweress of a reviewer, let no one undertake that matrimonial relation but FRIP.[4]

1 Tom. i. ch. xx. 2 Tom. v. p. 87.

3 Tom. v. p. 27. So likewise, tom. v. pp. 11, 97, 109, 125, 207.

4 *Frip* is the anagram of J. P. F. R., and his common signature in such cases — T.

SUMMARY OF CONTENTS.

VOLTAIRE.

Self-interest; Force of Public Opinion. Novalis, on the worthlessness and worth of French Philosophy. The death-stab of modern Superstition. The burning of a little straw may hide the Stars; but they are still there, and will again be seen. (65).

NOVALIS.

No good Book, or good thing of any sort, shows its best face at first: Improvisators, and their literary soap-bubbles. Men of genius: The wise man's errors more instructive than the truisms of a fool. What is called 'reviewing;' showing how a small Reviewer may triumph over a great Author, and what his triumph is worth. The writings of Novalis of too much importance to be lightly passed by. (p. 79). — Novalis's birth and parentage: Religious and secluded Childhood: Schooling. Applies himself honestly to business. Death of his first love: Communings with Eternity. Influence on his character of this wreck of his first passionate wish: Doctrine of 'Renunciation.' Peace and cheerfulness of his life: Interest in the physical sciences. Acquaintance and literary coöperation with Schlegel and Tieck. Alarming illness: Hopeful literary projects: Gradual bodily decline, and peaceful death. Manners, and personal aspect. (87). — Wonderful depth and originality of his writings: His philosophic mysticism. Idealism not confined to Germany. The Kantean view of the material Universe: Its intellectual and moral bearing on the practical interests of men. Influence on the deep, religious spirit of Novalis: Nature no longer dead, hostile Matter; but the veil and mysterious Garment of the Unseen: The Beauty of Goodness, the only real, final possession. (99). — Extracts from the *Lehrlinge zu Sais, &c.;* Manifold significance of all natural phenomena to the true observer; Beauty and omnipotence of childlike intuition; How the chastened understanding may be brought into harmony with the deepest intuitions, and the most rigid facts: Nature, as viewed by the superstitious fanatic, the utilitarian inquirer, the sceptical idealist, and the regenerate Soul of man: The mechanics and dynamics of Thought; Eclectic Philosophers: Philosophic Fragments. (108). — Novalis as a Poet: Extracts from *Hymns to the Night,* and *Heinrich von Ofterdingen.* His writings an unfathomed mine, where the keenest intellect may find occupation enough: His power of intense abstraction: His chief fault a certain undue passiveness. Likeness to Dante and Pascal. Intelligent, well-informed minds should endeavour to understand even Mysticism. Mechanical Superciliousness *versus* living Belief in God; the victory not doubtful. (122).

SIGNS OF THE TIMES.

Our grand business, not to *see* what lies dimly in the distance; but to *do* what lies clearly at hand: Prophetic folly, and spiritual contagion.

The Present always an important time. The Age of Machinery, in every outward and inward sense: Cases in point, — from hatching Chickens, to developing the young Idea; from 'Interrogating Nature,' up to delivering one's soul from Purgatory. (p. 135). — No Philosophy of Mind to be found out of Germany. Mathematics all gone to mechanism. Locke's Essay, a singular emblem of the spirit of the times: Scotch and French mental-mechanism. The Machine of Society: Social mechanism more prized than individual worth. All wise inventions or discoveries, all great movements whatsoever spring inevitably from the individual souls of men. Mechanical and Dynamical provinces of human activity: Men have lost their belief in the Invisible: and believe, and hope, and work only in the Visible. Intellectual dapperlings, and their 'closet-logic' rushlights: *One* wise man stronger than *all* men foolish. (142). — Religion no longer a thousand-voiced Psalm, from the heart of Man to his invisible Father; but a wise, prudential feeling, grounded on mere calculation. The working Church of England at this moment in the Editors of Newspapers. Even Poetry has no eye for the Invisible: Not a matin or vesper hymn to the Spirit of Beauty; but a fierce clashing of cymbals, as children pass through the fire to Moloch. Our 'superior morality' properly an 'inferior criminality:' Truth and Virtue no longer loved, as they ought and must be loved: Beyond money and money's worth, our only blessedness is Popularity. (155). — Bright lights, as well as gloomy shadows. The wisdom and heroic worth of our forefathers we may yet recover. The darkest hour is nearest the dawn. (159).

JEAN PAUL FRIEDRICH RICHTER AGAIN.

The best celebrity does not always spread the fastest. Richter's slow, but sure reception in England. His life, like most literary lives, somewhat barren of outward incidents; yet containing a deeper worth than any such interest could impart. Difficulty and value of real Biography. Insufficiency of Otto's Life of Richter. (p. 162). — Richter's birth, parentage and pedigree: His Father, a poor, hard-working Clergyman, loved and venerated by his flock. Not by money, or money's worth, that Man lives and has his being: To a rich spirit, Life cannot be poor. Young Paul's Idyl-Kingdom and little Pastoral World, sketched by himself: O God! I thank thee for my Father! (170). — Early education: Latin vocables; dreary reading; child-glimpses into the infinity of Nature, and his own Soul. In his thirteenth year the family removed to a better church-living at Schwarzenbach. He now got access to books, and better teaching. Early theological speculations, 'inclining strongly to the heterodox side.' Loses his Father: Pecuniary troubles. Aversion for History and Geography. A school-disputation: Paul triumphant over Orthodoxy and dull Authority: 'Silence, Sirrah!' (176). — At Leipzig University: Obtains little furtherance from established teachers; and endeavours to work out an intellectual basis of his own. Poverty, not in the shape of Parsimony, but in the far sterner one of actual Want. His Mother, quite unable to help herself, could afford him no assistance. A high, cheerful Stoicism grew up in him: Wise maxims for so young a man. His first productions: No demand for them. Magazine writing. He lived, like the young ravens, how he could: He had looked Desperation in the face, and found that for him she was not desperate. Blessings of early poverty. (180). — Richter's gallant self-dependence: His free and easy style of dress: Horror of his more courtly neighbours: Seven-years' costume controversy; and final magnanimous compliance with the wishes of all Christian persons. (189). — His singular literary establishment at Hof. Of all literary phenomena, that of a literary man daring to believe that he is *poor*, may be regarded as the rarest. No 'Men of Letters' now; only 'Literary Gentlemen,' and a degree of rickety Debility unexampled in the history of Literature. Richter survives his exclusion from the little 'West-end' of Hof. His sudden and decisive triumph, after a valiant struggle of ten years. His poor Mother is released from her troubles: The Hof household broken up. His reception by the high and titled of his country: His marriage. (194). — Removes to Weimar: Illustrious companionship: Literary activity. Receives a pension from the Prince Primate Dalberg: Settles in Baireuth: Public honour, and domestic happiness: Unwearied diligence in his vocation. Loss of his only son: Sickness, and almost total blindness: Death. (204). — Richter's intellectual and literary character. Extracts; Miniature sketches of Herder, Jacobi, Goethe, Luther, Klopstock, Schiller; A fair-weather scene; A bridegroom and bride; On Daughter-full Houses. Richter's vastness of Imagination: Rapt, deep, Old-Hebrew spirit of his *Dreams:* His Dream of Atheism. A true Poet, and among the highest of his time, though he wrote no verses. (208).

ON HISTORY.

History, man's earliest and simplest expression of Thought: As we *do* nothing but enact History, so likewise we *say* little but recite it. Ancient and modern historians. Vanity of all would-be 'Philosophies of History:' Before Philosophy can teach by Experience, Philosophy must first know how to do it; and above all, have the Experience intelligibly recorded. Infinite complexity of the simplest facts constituting the Experience of Life. The living, actual History of Humanity consists of far other and more fruitful activities than those recorded in history-books. (p. 228). — Worth and worthlessness of historic testimonies; the Seer, and mere Onlookers. Inevitable discrepancy between a mere linear Narrative of 'successive events;' and the actual, infinitely-related Aggregate of Activities, the daily record of which could alone constitute a complete History. Better were it that mere earthly historians should lower their pretensions to Philosophy; and aim only at some faithful picture of the things acted. (232). — The historical Artist, and the historical Artisan.

Growing feeling of the infinite nature of History. Division of labour: The Political and the Ecclesiastic historian: Church History, could it speak wisely, would have momentous secrets to teach. Histories of a less ambitious character. Old healthy identity of Priest and Philosopher. Historic Ideals: Necessity for honest insight. (235).

LUTHER'S PSALM.

The great Reformer's love of music and poetry, one of the most significant features in his character. His poetic feeling not so much expressed in fit Words, as in fit Actions. And yet it is the same Luther, whether acting, speaking or writing. His Psalm, *Eine feste Burg ist unser Gott.* (p. 241).

SCHILLER.

Correspondence between Schiller and Goethe. Natural curiosity respecting great men: Value of the scantiest memorials that will help to make them intelligible. It can be no true greatness, that a close inspection would abate a worthy admiration of. The Letters of Schiller and Goethe: Their entire sincerity of style: Turn mostly on compositions, publications, philosophies. An instructive record of the mental progress of their respective writers. (p. 245). — Schiller's mode of thought and utterance more European than national: His ready and general acceptance with foreigners. High struggle, and prophetic burden of every true Poet. Schiller's personal history. His life emphatically a literary one: Something Priestlike, almost monastic in its character. His parentage and youth: Schooling: Hardships and oppressions from the Duke of Würtemberg: Not in Law, or Medicine; nor in any marketable occupation, can his soul find content and a home. His restless struggling to get free. Publication of the *Robbers*. Escape from the harsh tyranny of the Duke. Henceforth a Literary Man; and need appear in no other character. (251). — His mild, honest character everywhere gains him friends. His connexion with Goethe the most important event of his literary life: Their mutual esteem, and zealous coöperation. Schiller's quiet, unconquered heroism through fifteen years of unremitted pain. The foolish Happiness-controversy: The whole argument, like every other, lies in the confusion of language: True Welfare, and mere sensuous Enjoyment: Mind *versus* Matter. (265). — Schiller's character as a man. In his life the social affections played no deeply absorbing part: It was toward the Ideal, not the Actual, that his faith and hope were chiefly directed: His habits were solitary; his chief business and pleasure lay in silent meditation. Some account of his ordinary mode of life. He mingles little in the controversies of his time; and alludes to them only from afar. His high conception of the mission of the true Poet. His genius reflective rather than creative; philosophical and oratorical rather than essentially poetic.

For the most part, the Common is to him still the Common. Closely connected with this imperfection, both as cause and consequence, is his singular want of Humour. Yet there is a tone in some of his later pieces, breathing of the very highest region of Art. (273). — Schiller's dramatic success. Illustrations of his mental progress; turbid ferocities of the *Robbers*, contrasted with the placidly victorious strength of his maturer works. The like progress visible in his smaller Poems: His *Alpenlied.* Schiller's Philosophic talent: Interest in Kant's System. His *Æsthetic Letters.* Schiller and Goethe. (283).

THE NIBELUNGEN LIED.

About the year 1757, a certain antiquarian tendency in literature, a fonder, more earnest looking back into the Past, began to manifest itself in all nations. Growth and fruit of this tendency in Germany. The *Nibelungen*, a kind of rude German Epos: It belongs specially to us English Teutones, as well as to the German. Northern Archæology, a chaos of immeasurable shadows: The *Heldenbuch*, the most important of these subsidiary Fictions; and throwing some little light on the *Nibelungen:* Outline of the Story. Early adventures of the brave Siegfried, whose history lies at the heart of the whole Northern Traditions: His Invulnerability, wonderful Sword Balmung, and Cloak of Darkness: His subsequent history belongs to the Song of the Nibelungen. (p. 296). — Singular poetic excellence of that old Epic Song: Simplicity, and clear decisive ring of its language: Deeds of high temper, harsh self-denial, daring and death, stand embodied in soft, quick-flowing, joyfully-modulated verse: Wonderful skill in the construction of the story; and the healthy subordination of the marvellous to the actual. Abstract of the Poem, — How Siegfried wooed and won the beautiful Chriemhild; and how marvellously he vanquished the Amazonian Brunhild for king Gunther: Heyday of peace and gladdest sunshine. Jealousy of queen Brunhild: How the two queens rated one another; and how Chriemhild extinguished Brunhild. Brunhild in black revenge gets Siegfried murdered: Unhappy Chriemhild, her husband's grave is all that remains to her: Her terrible doomsday vengeance. (314). — Antiquarian researches into the origin of the *Nibelungen Lied:* Historical coincidences. The oldest Tradition, and the oldest Poem of Modern Europe. Who the gifted Singer may have been, remains altogether dark: The whole spirit of Chivalry, of Love and heroic Valour, must have lived in him and inspired him: A true old Singer, taught of Nature herself! (345).

GERMAN LITERATURE OF THE FOURTEENTH AND FIFTEENTH CENTURIES.

Historical literary significance of *Reynard the Fox.* The Troubadour Period in general Literature, to which the Swabian Era in Germany answers. General decay of Poetry: Futile attempts to account for such decay: The world seems to have rhymed itself out; and stern business, not sportfully, but with harsh endeavour, was now to be done. Italy, for a time, a splendid exception in Dante and Petrarch. The change not a fall from a higher spiritual state to a lower; but rather, a passing from youth into manhood. (p. 355). — Literature now became more and more Didactic, consisting of wise Apologues, Fables, Satires, Moralities: This Didactic Spirit reached its acme at the era of the Reformation. Its gradual rise: The *Striker*, and others. Some account of Hugo von Trimberg: A cheerful, clear-sighted, gentle-hearted man, with a quiet, sly humour in him: His *Renner*, a singular old book; his own simple, honest, mildly decided character everywhere visible in it. (364). — Boner, and his *Edelstein*, a collection of Fables done into German rhyme from Latin originals: Not so much a Translator as a free Imitator; he tells his story in his own way, and freely appends his own moral. Fable, the earliest and simplest product of Didactic Poetry: The Fourteenth Century an age of Fable in a wider sense: Narratives and Mysteries. A serious warning to Critics! Adventures of *Tyll Eulenspiegel.* (376). — In the religious Cloisters, also were not wanting men striving with purer enthusiasm after the highest problem of manhood, a life of spiritual Truth: Johann Tauler, and Thomas à Kempis. On all hands an aspect of full progress: Robber Barons, and Merchant Princes. The spirit of Inquiry, of Invention, conspicuously busy: Gunpowder, Printing, Paper. In Literature, the Didactic, especially the Æsopic spirit became abundantly manifest. (389). — *Reynard the Fox*, the best of all Apologues; for some centuries a universal household possession, and secular Bible: Antiquarian researches into its origin and history: Not the work of any single author, but a growth and contribution of many generations and countries. A rude, wild Parody of Human Life, full of meaning and high moral purpose: Its dramatic consistency: Occasional coarseness, and other imperfections. Philological interest of the old Low-German original: The language of our old Saxon Fatherland, still curiously like our own. The Age of Apologue, like that of Chivalry and Love-singing, now gone. Where are now our People's-Books? (400).

TAYLOR'S HISTORIC SURVEY OF GERMAN POETRY.

Upwards of half a century since German Literature began to make its way in England. Hannah More's trumpet-blast against these modern 'Huns and Vandals.' Our knowledge now becoming better, if only because more general. Claims of Mr. Taylor's Book to a respectful examination: Its value and shortcomings. (p. 415). — What would be implied by a Complete History of German Poetry: The History of a nation's Poetry the essence of its History, political, economic, scientific, religious. Such a History of the Germans would not be wanting in peculiar human interest: Their poetical Infancy and Boyhood; Enthusiastic Youth; Free Manhood; Spiritual Vastation, and New Birth. (423). — Mr. Taylor's 'Historic Survey,' a mere aggregate of fragmentary Notices, held together by the Bookbinder's packthread: Its incredible misstatements of facts, and general incorrectness and insufficiency. He goes through Germany, scenting out Infidelity with the nose of an ancient Heresy-hunter; though for opposite purposes. Mr. Taylor's whole Philosophy sensual; he recognises nothing that cannot be weighed and measured, eaten and digested: Every fibre of him Philistine. (429.) — The best Essay in the book, that on Klopstock: Beautiful allegory of *The Two Muses.* Foolish admiration for Kotzebue and his like. His scepticism at least honest and worthy of respect. Literature fast becoming all in all to us, our Church, our Senate, our whole Social Constitution. Its tendency to a general European Commonweal; whereby the wisest in all nations may communicate and coöperate. (445).

APPENDIX.

RICHTER'S REVIEW OF MADAME DE STAEL'S 'ALLEMAGNE.'

To review a Revieweress of two literary Nations no easy task. Madame de Staël's peculiar advantages and fitness, in everything but a comprehension of her subject: Her French intellect, and German heart. Parisian refinement: Classical indifference to the 'household-stuff' of Religion, and to mere Work-people. How she bleaches and clear-starches the Rainbow; and even makes a polished gentleman of the German Hercules. German dingy impracticability, notwithstanding: Mere Nightingales, compared with Peacocks. Poor naked, unfallen Eves and Graces; How shall they be presented at our Parisian Court! (p. 455). — Value, and deep human interest of national peculiarities. We cannot wholly see ourselves, except in the eye of a foreign seer. Use and abuse of the literary file. German political subserviency; and French Imperial sycophancy. German conversational maladroitness: Awkward tendency to try and say *something truly;* rather than, like the polished Frenchman, to say *nothing elegantly.* German wit, and French witticisms. Shallow estimate of Goethe: Better insight into Schiller: Jean Paul's literary delinquencies. Intellectual ladies, and their easy solution of metaphysical insolvabilities. Madame de Staël's high and earnest character: The language of her heart always a noble, pure and rich one. (466).

END OF VOL. II.